THE
INFERNO
OF
DANTE

THE
INFERNO
OF
DANTE

A NEW VERSE TRANSLATION BY

ROBERT PINSKY

ILLUSTRATED BY

MICHAEL MAZUR

WITH NOTES BY NICOLE PINSKY

FOREWORD BY JOHN FRECCERO

FARRAR, STRAUS AND GIROUX

NEW YORK

Grateful acknowledgment is made to Arnaldo Mondadori Editore
for the permission to reprint the Inferno *from the Meridiani edition.*

Library of Congress Cataloging-in-Publication Data
Dante Alighieri, 1265–1321.
[Inferno. English & Italian]
The Inferno of Dante : a new verse translation / Robert Pinsky ;
illustrated by Michael Mazur. — 1st ed.
p.   cm.
"A bilingual edition"—CIP front matter.
1. Hell—Poetry.   I. Pinsky, Robert.   II. Title.
PQ4315.2.P47   1994   851'.1—dc20   93-40169 CIP

FRONTISPIECE

"Woe to you, wicked souls! Give up the thought

Of Heaven! I come to ferry you across
Into eternal dark on the opposite side,
Into fire and ice!"

(III, 69–72)

For Frank Bidart

Acknowledgments

I am grateful to the friends and advisers who have given me the benefit of their learning, judgment, and encouragement. I also thank the editors of magazines in which sections of this translation first appeared: *American Poetry Review, The Boston Phoenix, Boston Review, Columbia, The Harvard Review, New England Review, Poetry, The Paris Review, Provincetown Arts, Quarterly West, Raritan, Salmagundi, Salt Hill Journal, Threepenny Review,* and *TriQuarterly.*

R.P.

CONTENTS

FOREWORD

In spite of Dante's reputation as the greatest of Christian poets, there is no sign of Christian forgiveness in the *Inferno*. The dominant theme is not mercy but justice, dispensed with the severity of the ancient law of retribution. The moral system of Hell owes more to ancient philosophy than it does to medieval classifications of virtues and vices, while the landscape of the underworld derives from Virgil more than from the poetically impoverished visions of the Middle Ages. The punishments themselves are reminiscent of ancient mythology, or perhaps even of the Marquis de Sade, but certainly not of the Gospels. Christ is never directly mentioned, we are told that pity should be extinguished here, and perhaps worst of all, the pain and despair of the damned seem to separate them from the rest of humanity and from one another, leaving them radically alone in the midst of an infernal crowd.

A city, according to St. Augustine, is a group of people joined together by their love of the same object. Ultimately, however, there can be only two objects of human love: God or the self. All other loves are masks for these. It follows that there are only two cities: the City of God, where all love Him to the exclusion of self, and the City of Man, where self-interest makes every sinner an enemy to every other. The bonds of charity form a community of the faithful, while sin disperses them and leaves only a crowd. In Dante's poem, Hell is the parody of a city, point zero in the scale of cosmic love. Like Augustine's City of Man, it is meant to represent the social consequences of insatiable desire when it remains earthbound.

The City of God and the City of Man were thought to be spiritual states, the antithetical allegiances of those who actually live together in the real city. At the Last Judgment, sinners and saints would be definitively separated and sent to their respective cities, Heaven or Hell. The earthly city was therefore an encampment in which saints and sinners met and mingled as pilgrims en route to opposite destinations. Once they arrived at their respective goals, however, the damned were forever separated from the blessed.

Dante's *Inferno* is a vision of the City of Man in the afterlife, which is why it contains no glimmer of forgiveness. At the same time, it may also be thought of as a radical representation of the world in which we live, stripped of all temporizing and all hope. Hell is the state of the soul after death, but it is also the state of the world as seen by an exile whose experience has taught him no longer to trust the world's values. The ruined portals and fallen bridges of Hell are emblems of the failure of all bonds among the souls who might once have been members of the human community.

The sense in which Hell stands for the real world has never been lost on Dante's readers. What medieval readers would have referred to as the moral allegory reappears in contemporary interpretations by authors as diverse as Albert Camus (*The Fall*), where the infernal city is Amsterdam, and LeRoi Jones (Amiri Baraka), whose nightmare in the Newark ghetto is entitled *The System of Dante's Hell*.

The principal dramatic contrast in the poem is between the pilgrim and his guide on one hand, who are journeying through Hell, and, on the other, the souls they encounter, who are imprisoned there forever. The progress of the poem is measured by the journey, while the episodic encounters provide the substance of what Dante has to tell us about his life and times. Because of the contrast between the perspective of the pilgrim, who looks forward to his salvation, and the perspective of the damned, who have no future, conversation in Hell is charged with irony. Much of what the sinners have to say about their lives or their actions is undermined by their guilt or self-delusion. Their testimony is self-serving, as one would expect of any prisoner's account of his or her conviction, except that here, as we learn from the inscription on the gates, all have received the same sentence, with no hope of appeal, and none has been framed. Justice in Hell is meant to be objective, measured out by a bureaucratic monster in proportion to the specific gravity of the sin. Such a mechanical administration of punishment leaves no room for judicial error or caprice.

Few of Dante's readers have derived much satisfaction from the triumph of this somewhat anonymous justice. Like Dante's protagonist, we find ourselves moved by the souls in Hell despite the moral system that condemns them so pitilessly. Where divine justice sees only black or white, we find mitigating circumstances. If Francesca is an adulteress, she is also a victim of literary seduction. Brunetto is a sodomite, but he is also a father figure who taught the poet how to make himself eternal. Ulysses is a thief, yet he pronounces an oration on the dignity of man. The irony in these portraits derives from the fact that the prodigious historicity of Dante's characters, their individuality, seems to matter not at all in the way they are classified. In the either/or of the afterlife, distinctions are obliterated and the soul's place in Hell is determined dispassionately, by the flick of a monster's tail.

For a modern interpreter, the easiest way to deal with irony such as this is to ignore it, to assume that the abstract moral system is irrelevant to a discussion of the great figures of the *Inferno*. Such an approach goes back to Coleridge, who proposed that we "suspend disbelief" in order to appreciate the power of Dante's poetry without endorsing the religious conviction that it claims as its inspiration. In this century, Benedetto Croce suggested that since we are no longer concerned in the modern world with medieval theology, we may safely ignore it and consider only the work's lyrical passages. The preference for "feeling" over "meaning" in poetry was later to reappear in the work of Erich Auerbach, who maintained that we should separate Dante's didactic intent from his power of representation. In his masterful reading of Canto X in his book *Mimesis*, he conceded that Dante intended to give his characters an allegorical meaning, but claimed that the power and the historicity of his characterizations were so great as to overwhelm whatever doctrinal meaning they were meant to convey. Over the centuries, according to Auerbach, the sheer force of Dante's verses gradually came to subvert his moralizing intention, transforming a medieval system of punishments and rewards into an autonomous, secular world, much like this one, in which thoroughly human characters no longer *signify* anything, as Dante may have wished, but simply *are* in all of their tragic humanity.

A reading such as this runs the risk of ignoring something essential about the poem. The clash between the humanity of the damned and the implacable judgment to which they are subjected is not simply an accident of history, the abyss that separates medieval standards of morality from our own, but rather reflects a fundamental division in Dante's own consciousness. Irony in the *Inferno* arises from the discrepancy between the perspective of the pilgrim, which is much like ours, and that of the poet, who, by journey's end, claims to share God's view. The distance that separates the traveler's naïveté from the omniscience of the poet is the poem's story: the transformation of the pilgrim into the poet, whose work we read.

By ignoring this irony, Auerbach was able to claim that Dante's realism had created an autonomous world, in which judgment seems no longer relevant. His dismissal of medieval moralizing is understandable. We are moved by the sympathetic portrayal of the damned, but often so repelled by their sadistic punishment that we would prefer to accept the fiction, pretending that God, rather than the author, determined those punishments. It is almost easier to imagine that Dante actually saw Brunetto among the sodomites in Hell—" 'Are you here, Ser Brunetto?' " (*Inf.*, XV, 26)—than to conceive of his using such affectionate and deferential language with someone whose reputation he was about to besmirch forever. Apart from Dante's text, we know nothing whatever of Brunetto's proclivities, so that we must choose between accepting the biting irony and accepting the realistic illusion. No pupil could so gratuitously betray his teacher, we reason; it must be that God put him there.

This tempting but simplistic reading misses the plot, which is about Dante more than it is about his characters. The reason these biting ironies are so important is that they generate the story of the descent into Hell. When Dante sees the glutton Ciacco, for example, he asks about the " 'men of good reason' " whose purpose in life was the good of the city. Ciacco answers, " 'Their souls are among the blackest in Hell' " (*Inf.*, VI, 71, 76). The gap between the pilgrim's perception of the good and the author's could not be more pointed or relevant to the story. Again, the vulnerable and victimized Francesca is the Francesca of the pilgrim, but the adulteress justly punished is the Francesca seen by the narrator. The clash of perspectives on her, as on many of the characters in Hell, thematizes the conversion of a thoroughly human and fallible protagonist into the uncompromising narrator who tells his story. By attributing misapplied sympathy to the pilgrim while leaving condemnation for the most part to the narrator, Dante plots the descent as a penitential autobiography, a narrative of conversion in the tradition of Augustine's *Confessions*.

The exchanges with the damned serve to call into question all of the comfortable conventions that most of the time serve to mask from us our own mortality. Hell is a limit situation, like the prison camp or the cancer ward, where all illusions are stripped away and one has no choice but to acknowledge one's powerlessness. The journey is therefore an allegory of education, like Plato's Myth of the Cave, except that all of Hell must be traversed in order to reach the cave, point zero, from which Plato thought the journey began. This journey begins at a point minus one, an illusory world of inverted values, in which one lives with a false image of one's self. These illusions must be destroyed before any spiritual progress can be made. The descent into Hell is meant to be destructive, its irony corrosive, in order to clear the way for the ascent.

The descent questions and destroys Dante's earlier illusions, represented perhaps by the shadowy world of the prologue scene (*Inf.*, I). Before he was exiled from the city of Florence on a trumped-up charge of political corruption, Dante seemed to be at the summit of his career, "Midway on our life's journey," as he says in the first verse of the poem. He was a prior of the City of Florence—equivalent perhaps to alderman—and the most celebrated love poet of his city. The descent into Hell clearly stands for the torment he must have felt with his exile; before long, however, he must also have come to realize that his suffering was a necessary prelude to his spiritual transformation. This is implied by the poem's symbolic cosmology, which places Purgatory and Heaven to the South, reachable only by traveling down from our hemisphere, through the cone of Hell. Such a trajectory dramatizes Augustine's mystic injunction: "Descend, so that you may ascend."

Unlike Plato's allegories, however, Dante's journey is autobiographical. Several passages are explicitly so and serve to reinforce the sense in which the descent into Hell may be thought of as a descent into Dante's past. There is, for example, a reference to the poet's military service at the battle of Caprona (*Inf.*, XXI, 94), perhaps an allusion to his trip to Rome during the Jubilee Year in Canto XVIII, 28, and, most enigmatically, a reference in Canto XIX to an incident in which Dante says that he smashed one of the holes in the baptismal font in the Baptistery of Florence—a feat clearly impossible to accomplish with one's bare hands—in order to save someone from drowning. Whatever the significance of that incident, if indeed it ever took place, the mystery is compounded by Dante's claim finally to have cleared it up in these verses: "let this be / My seal to clear the matter" (*Inf.*, XIX, 18–19).

The most important part of a poet's biography, however, is his poetry. The great number of autocitations in Dante's text, passages that clearly hark back to his earlier poetry, are at the same time autobiographical allusions. They, too, are subject to ironic interpretation; in a poet such as Dante, for whom style is of a sacred order, autocitation is autocritique. His entire career as poet was a preparation for the *Divine Comedy*, which recapitulates and, at the same time, radically changes all that went before. From the vantage point of the *Comedy*, each of the successive stages of Dante's poetic career was both mistaken and necessary for his development as poet, much as the sins recounted by Augustine seem retrospectively to have been both regrettable and necessary for the structure of the *Confessions*. The paradox was familiar to Christians, who thought of the sin of Adam and Eve precisely as a "fortunate fall" (*felix culpa*), inasmuch as it prepared the way for the coming of Christ.

The subject of Dante's poetry had always been Love—it continued to be Love, profoundly transformed, in the *Divine Comedy*. For Dante, as for many of his contemporaries, love and poetry were inseparable, as is suggested by the imagery of birds in flight that seems to recur each time those two subjects come together in the poem—the Italian word *penne* means both "pens" and "wings," suggesting both poetic inspiration and erotic flight. In the *Inferno*, bird imagery abounds in the canto of Francesca da Rimini (*Inf.*, V), which is perhaps Dante's most famous meditation on sinful love.

When Francesca attributes her weakness to her "gentle heart"—"Love, which in gentle hearts is quickly born" (*Inf.*, V, 89)—her words echo lines from Dante's earlier love poetry, where he claimed that "Love and the gentle heart are one." If Francesca's words are undercut by her damnation, Dante's are as well, so that she stands as a surrogate for Dante's own poetic past. Her account of her seduction by literature might be taken as a veiled confession of a similar susceptibility on Dante's part. St. Augustine confessed to the same weakness when he expressed regret for having wept bitter tears for Dido, who killed herself for love, while shedding none for himself, although he was dying a spiritual death.

By far the most important autobiographical allusion is also the most indirect, for the canto of Ulysses offers no verbal echoes of Dante's work, yet functions as an antitype of Dante's journey, an example of overreaching that is meant as the author's *memento mori*:

> *I sorrowed then, and when I turn my mind*
> *To what I saw next, sorrow again—and force*

My art to make its genius more restrained
Than is my usual bent, lest it should run
Where virtue doesn't . . .

(*Inf.*, XXVI, 20–24)

Several details suggest that the figure of Ulysses is not simply a dramatic episode in Dante's descent but is, rather, an example of what might have become of Dante had he not been rescued in the dark woods. The epic hero is alluded to twice in the *Purgatorio* and explicitly recalled in the song of the Siren (*Purg.*, XIX, 1ff.). He is mentioned for the last time in *Paradiso*, XXVII, 83, when the pilgrim looks down from the constellation of the Gemini at the "mad wake of Ulysses." No other character in the poem has such an afterlife, which suggests that his journey is meant to contrast with Dante's, representing the fate from which the poet was saved by the intervention of Virgil and three blessed ladies.

In the symbolic geography of the poem, Dante and Ulysses travel toward the same objective: the mountain of Purgatory in the southern hemisphere. On any reading, this is the mountain "Mantled in rays of that bright planet that shows / The road to everyone, whatever our journey" (*Inf.*, I, 14–15). Ulysses died a shipwreck en route, "as pleased an Other" (*Inf.*, XXVI, 134), within sight of the mountaintop, while Dante began his voyage through the earth after having survived a metaphoric shipwreck of his own: "As one still panting, ashore from dangerous seas, / Looks back at the deep he has escaped" (*Inf.*, I, 18–19). Survival and shipwreck seem equally fortuitous, or perhaps *gratuitous*, in the etymological sense, but the existence of the story depends upon the difference, "as pleased an Other."

The speech of Ulysses to his men, an oration on the dignity of man (" 'You were not born to live as a mere brute does, / But for the pursuit of knowledge and the good' " (*Inf.*, XXVI, 114–15), expresses principles that do not differ appreciably from those expressed in Dante's *Convivio*, a philosophical work begun around the time of his exile from Florence and left unfinished. There is in the *Convivio* the same philosophical self-confidence that we sense in Ulysses' speech, with its emphasis on a purely human rationality and no mention of the need for spiritual self-discipline or humility. Ulysses' fate constitutes a palinode, a retrospective retraction of the *Convivio*. Both the shipwreck of Ulysses and the metaphoric near shipwreck of the first canto represent the disaster that awaits the proud self-reliance of a philosophy unaided by faith.

Ulysses was a traditional emblem in antiquity of the soul's journey, without a guide, to its celestial home. *Nostos* was the word in Greek that described the circular course of the soul, from its home, through myriad adventures, back to its home. If Dante's Ulysses ends a shipwreck, it was not simply because he did not know Homer's text—in the Middle Ages, every schoolboy knew that Ulysses returned home, even if no one knew the text firsthand—but, rather, because in a Christian context, any such journey, alone, was doomed to failure. The first scene of the poem, with the poet's unsuccessful attempt to scale the mountain, illustrates precisely that point. The Christian journey to the same objective was very different. It is perhaps epitomized by the journey on the back of the monster Geryon, which at the same time functions as the emblem of Dante's poetic enterprise.

The journey on Geryon is flight to the depths, with Virgil as the pilgrim's guide and protector. The imagery accompanying the description of that flight is clearly nautical. Geryon's flight is a navigation, just as Ulysses' navigation is metaphorically a flight—" 'We made wings of our oars, in an insane / Flight' " (*Inf.*, XXVI, 120–21). An additional symmetry is established by the fact that the flight on Geryon produces fear in the pilgrim when he remembers contrary examples—Phaëthon and Icarus—just as the disastrous flight of Ulysses evokes the contrary example of the flight of Elijah's chariot. Geryon is obviously Dante's answer to antiquity's Ulysses.

There is a further detail that distinguishes Geryon from all the metaphoric vehicles of spiritual progress to be found in the philosophical tradition: the feet of the soul, the chariot, the ship, and the soul's wings. Dante's monster embodies a confessional paradox, inasmuch as it is an evil—"fraud's foul emblem" (*Inf.*, XVII, 6)—which nevertheless can be employed for the soul's salvation, provided one trust in Providence and abandon one's self-reliance, represented by the rope girdle that the pilgrim tosses into the abyss. The surliness of the monster before and during the flight, in contrast to its departure when its mission is accomplished, "like an arrow from the string" (*Inf.*, XVII, 127), suggests the deliberate harnessing of evil in order to favor the soul's progress. Geryon seems forced to collaborate in Hell's "command performance" for the pilgrim's visit, only to snap back into place, like the giant later on, when the pilgrim has passed. This, we have suggested, is the mechanism that characterizes Christian confession.

After the final vision of the *Paradiso*, the pilgrim becomes the poet who has been with us from the beginning. In one sense, then, the story of the poem is how the pilgrim got there, that is, how the story came to be written. Throughout the poem, references to the progress of the journey, particularly when there are images of flight or navigation, refer equally well to the progress of the poem. So it is with the monster Geryon, which is an emblem not only of the confessional theme but also of Dante's poetry. Dante's arch address to the reader, "I vow / By my *Commedia*'s lines," suggests that he takes great pride in this poetic tour de force, whose fictionality he scarcely bothers to conceal.

The flight on the back of the monster is different from other metaphoric flights to the absolute because of the presence of a guide—the ancient Neoplatonist Plotinus had specified that on the mind's journey to the One, no guide was necessary. In the first canto of the *Inferno*, the abortive attempt to scale the mountain seems very much an attempt to reach enlightenment—the sun shining on the mountaintop—in a way that the Neoplatonists thought was possible: without a guide. If this were all there were to the journey to God, the climb would have succeeded and the poem could have ended with that upward glance (I, 12). For Christians, however, intellectual enlightenment is not the same as virtue. Virtue requires an act of the *will*, so that one may *do* what the reason tells us is the good. The three beasts that block the way are the beasts within us, dispositions toward sin that we cannot exorcise without supernatural help. The descent into Hell under Virgil's guidance is directed toward surmounting those obstacles, and the *Purgatorio* tells the story of the successful climb.

The guidance of Virgil is the guidance of his text. The encounter with the Roman shade stands for an encounter with the *Aeneid*. Readers sometimes wonder why, if Aristotle is referred to in Limbo as "Master of those who know" (*Inf.*, IV, 116), Dante should have chosen Virgil as his guide rather than the Greek philosopher. For one thing, Virgil was the poet of Empire, of that universal monarchy for which Dante felt such great nostalgia. In order to celebrate the Empire, Virgil had his hero Aeneas descend into the underworld in order to find his father and to receive from him prophecies regarding Rome's future glories. Dante borrowed several details from Aeneas' descent and suggested in the *Inferno* that Virgil had been to Hell before.

Another reason for choosing Virgil was that he had written the *Fourth Eclogue* to celebrate the birth of a child to a Roman official. The eclogue had an enormous success and was universally believed in the Middle Ages to have been Messianic, predicting the coming of Christ. Perhaps most important of all, however, was the sense in which Dante believed he could supplant Roman tragedy with his "Comedy" and transform Virgilian pathos into Christian joy.

Triumphalist translations of the *Aeneid* into English have obscured for us the extent to which Virgil is the poet of loss, a poet for whom death seemed stronger than Aeneas' love for Dido, stronger than the eternity of Rome, stronger even than poetry, as revealed by the death of Orpheus. According to some of the early Church fathers, Christ was a new Orpheus, descending and this time succeeding in bringing back his beloved, the human soul, from the Underworld. Dante may well have thought of himself, if not as a new Orpheus, then as a new Virgil, returning for his love and finding her beyond death in the Earthly Paradise. The search for Beatrice and her return are the story of the *Purgatorio* and the *Paradiso*, where Virgil cannot discern clearly, or at all. For the moment, which is to say for the *Inferno*, Virgil remains expert on the much more familiar terrain that the pilgrim must traverse.

Finally, a word should be said about the style in which the poem is written. Dante called it the "Comedy" (the adjective "divine" was added in the sixteenth century), by which he meant not only that it had a happy ending, but also that it was written in a humble and everyday style. In antiquity, it was important to adopt the appropriate style for different subject matter: the "high," or tragic, style for the most weighty subjects, the "low," or comic, for everyday or vulgar subjects. The Gospels were said to have changed all of this, by using humble speech—the parables, say, or the exchange between Christ and the Samaritan woman at the well—for the weightiest matter of all: our Redemption. One could say that the tragic realism with which we are familiar in our own literature, where the profoundest matters can be conveyed in dialectical and vulgar speech, was made possible by the revolution in rhetoric brought about by Christianity, which could represent salvation itself by a glass of water.

Dante wrote precisely in the humble speech of Scripture, a language he hoped everyone would understand. He was among the first in the Middle Ages to do so, writing this most serious of poems not in Latin, as one might have expected, but in the everyday speech of his city. Ultimately, this is the justification for another contemporary translation, apart from its power and extraordinary accuracy. The poem is written in a language that we speak *now*, no matter which language we speak. Robert Pinsky renews for us a Dante for our own time and does so with admirable clarity and grace.

John Freccero

TRANSLATOR'S NOTE

I have tried to make an *Inferno* in English that stays true to the nature of English, and that conveys the meaning of the Italian as accurately as possible, in lines of *terza rima* that will suggest some of the force and suppleness of Dante's form. Above all, I have tried to translate a poem: in passages where my English is not literal, I hope that it is faithful to the spirit.

Dante invented *terza rima* (the interlocking rhyme pattern *aba, bcb, cdc,* etc.) for the *Commedia*, and its effect—combining onward movement with a feeling of conclusiveness in each step—seems integral to the poem, something well worth trying to approximate.

It may be helpful to say a few words about rhyme:

Italian is rich in rhyme, while English—despite having a far greater number of words—is relatively poor in rhyme. Therefore, the triple rhymes of the original can put tremendous strain on an English translation. One response to this strain, one way of dealing with the torturous demands of *terza rima* in English, has been to force the large English lexicon to supply rhymes: squeezing unlikely synonyms to the ends of lines, and bending idiom ruthlessly to get them there.

This translation rejects that solution and instead makes a more flexible definition of rhyme, or of the kind and degree of like sound that constitute rhyme.

But on the other hand, I have not accepted just any similar sounds as rhyming: the translation is based on a fairly systematic rhyming norm that defines rhyme as the same consonant-sounds—however much vowels may differ—at the ends of words. For example, the opening tercets of Canto I include the triads "tell/feel/well," "sleep/stop/up," and "night/thought/it."

This system of like sounds happens to correspond to some preference of my own ear, a personal taste: for me such rhymes as, say, "swans/stones" or "gibe/club" or "south/both" often sound more beautiful and interesting than such hard-rhyme combinations as "bones/stones," "rub/club," or "south/mouth." This idea of harmony seems even more clear with disyllabic or "feminine" endings: "faces/houses" is more appealing than "faces/places"; "flavor/quiver" has more interest than "flavor/savor" or "giver/quiver."

The reader who recognizes these examples I have taken from poems by Yeats, who is a master of such consonantal rhyming, might speculate that such sounds are *similar for English*: roughly as "like," perhaps, in the context of English and its great sprawling matrix of sounds, as are *"terra/guerra"* or *"belle/stelle"* in the tighter Italian fabric.

But such speculation aside, and regardless of my own predilections, consonantal or "Yeatsian" rhyme can supply an audible scaffold of English *terza rima*, a scaffold that does not distort the English sentence, or draw excessively on the reaches of the English lexicon. In this scaffolding, mere vowel rhymes—even as close as "claim/feign" or "state/raid"—have been arbitrarily excluded, as taking away some of the backbone or stringency of effect. The goal is to make enough of a formal demand to support the English sentence, but not so monstrous a demand as to buckle it, or to mangle the particularly delicate gestures English syntax and idiom make as they accomplish work another language might perform with inflected endings.

(It remains to add that by extension words which end in vowels can be rhymed by a consistent system in which round vowels rhyme with one another—"now/throw," or "clue/saw"; as can closed vowels—"be/why" or "stay/cloy"; and, that disyllabic rhyme so sticks out in English that it can acceptably be made a step more approximate, as in "bitter/enter/blunder"—perhaps it *must* be made more approximate, in order to avoid the comic feeling of limerick, or of W. S. Gilbert.)

This is a brief outline of the general principles behind a work which in practice, as the reader will see, does not apply them without occasional compromises and slidings. As to hard rhymes, there are many, but as I worked I often found myself revising them out, or striving to make them the first and third members of a triad, rather than adjacent, to keep them from leaping out of a pattern I have labored to make expressive in its variations.

Though we call it a form, verse is physical, and in this sense the sounds of a poem are its body. By devising *terza rima* as the body for a poem about the fates of souls and bodies, Dante added an expressive element as well as a kind of movement. His variations in tone and idiom—from direct to elaborately rhetorical, for example, or from high to low—have an emotional truth that moves in counterpoint with the current of interlocking rhymes.

In Canto XII, when Virgil and Dante come down a rocky slope and approach the chief centaur Chiron, wise teacher of heroes, Chiron makes an interesting observation to his followers:

> As we came close,
> Chiron drew an arrow's notch back through the tangle

> Of beard along his jaw to clear a space
> For his large mouth, and to the others he said:
> "Have you observed how that one's steps displace

> Objects his body touches? Feet of the dead
>   Are not accustomed to behave like that."

Dante displaces the physical stones of the infernal world, though shades like Virgil who dwell there do not. And yet, in an apparent contradiction, Virgil sometimes carries the body of Dante about, as in Canto XXIII:

> My leader took me up at once, and did
>   As would a mother awakened by a noise
>   Who sees the flames around her, and takes her child,

> Concerned for him more than herself, and flies
>   Not staying even to put on a shift:
>   Supine he gave himself to the rocky place

> Where the hard bank slopes downward to the cleft,
>   Forming one side of the adjacent pouch.
>   No water coursing a sluice was ever as swift

> To turn a landmill's wheel on its approach
>   Toward the vanes, as my master when he passed
>   On down that bank that slanted to the ditch,

> Hurtling along with me upon his breast
>   Not like his mere companion, but like his child.

I suggest that this is not simply an inconsistency, but another indication that the relation between the two poets, living and dead, Christian and pagan, one of them still embarked on his venture, the other having completed his, is a relation between worlds: a point of intersection within a dense web of moral and physical realities.

Embodiment, in some such sense, is the *Inferno*'s action, and its meaning, and its method. The prosodic embodiment Dante invented for his poem is characterized by tremendous forward movement, a movement that, in English, the prose translations have sometimes rendered more effectively than those in verse. To catch some of that quality, at once propulsive and epigrammatic, I have allowed myself the liberty of enjambment, at times letting the sentence run over the rhymed line ending more aggressively than in the original, and also crossing freely from tercet to tercet. This translation is not line-for-line, nor tercet-for-tercet. In order to represent Dante's succinct, compressed quality along with the flow of *terza rima*, I have often found it necessary to write fewer lines in English than he uses in Italian. The Italian line and sentence not being the same as the English line and sentence, I have hoped to imitate some of Dante's formal energy, in the body of an English equivalent. This equivalent form, rising from the flow and arrest of the enjambed English sentences, seemed to require stanza breaks between the tercets of the translation—partly because the white space is a visual register of the consonantal *terza rima*.

To the image of Virgil skidding downhill on his back, while clasping Dante to his chest, Dante adds the simile of water coursing through a sluice to turn the regularly spaced vanes of a millwheel. This simile can serve as an image of the relation of lines and stanzas, like regular vanes, to the surging fluid of the sentence. At the same time, the motion of the embracing poets represents a related dynamism of spirit, word, and matter. This translation's arrangement of rhyme, sentence, line, and stanza attempts hopefully, sometimes perhaps desperately, to find a commensurate relation of elements—improvised and imperfect at every point but pushing on: trying to turn the wheel surely enough to accomplish what work it can.

A PLAN OF DANTE'S
JOURNEY THROUGH HELL

CANTO	LOCALE	DEMONS, ETC.
I	Dark Woods	Three Beasts
II	Entrance	
III	Fore-Hell	Charon

Across Acheron to Limbo (1st Circle) & the Incontinent Sins (Circles 2–5)

IV	1st Circle (Limbo)	
V	2nd Circle	Minos
VI	3rd Circle	Cerberus
VII	4th Circle	Plutus
VIII	5th Circle	Phlegyas

Across Styx to the City of Dis (6th Circle)

IX–XI	6th Circle (Dis)	Furies

Across Phlegethon to the Plain of Fire (7th Circle): The Violent Sins

XII	7th Circle, Ring 1	Minotaur
XIII	7th Circle, Ring 2	Harpies
XIV	7th Circle, Ring 3	
XV–XVI	7th Circle, Ring 3	
XVII	7th Circle, Ring 3	

Carried by Geryon to Malebolge (8th Circle): Sins of Fraud

XVIII	Pouch 1	The Malebranche
"	Pouch 2	"
XIX	Pouch 3	"
XX	Pouch 4	"
XXI–XXII	Pouch 5	"
XXIII	Pouch 6	"
XXIV–XXV	Pouch 7	"
XXVI–XXVII	Pouch 8	"
XXVIII	Pouch 9	"
XXIX–XXX	Pouch 10	"

Lowered by Antaeus to the Pit (9th Circle): Sins of Betrayal

XXXI–XXXIV	The Pit of Hell:	Giants
	Caina	Lucifer
	Antenora	"
	Ptolomea	"
	Judecca	"

A map and "aerial view" of Hell is provided in the illustration for Canto XI.

THE INFERNO OF DANTE

I

> . . . *when I came to stop*
> *Below a hill that marked one end of the valley*
> *That had pierced my heart with terror, I looked up*
>
> *Toward the crest and saw its shoulders already*
> *Mantled in rays of that bright planet that shows*
> *The road to everyone, whatever our journey.*

(10–15)

Nel mezzo del cammin di nostra vita
  mi ritrovai per una selva oscura,
  che la diritta via era smarrita.
Ahi quanto a dir qual era è cosa dura
  esta selva selvaggia e aspra e forte
  che nel pensier rinova la paura!
Tant' è amara che poco è più morte;
  ma per trattar del ben ch'i' vi trovai,
  dirò de l'altre cose ch'i' v'ho scorte.
10 Io non so ben ridir com' i' v'intrai,
  tant' era pien di sonno a quel punto
  che la verace via abbandonai.
Ma poi ch'i' fui al piè d'un colle giunto,
  là dove terminava quella valle
  che m'avea di paura il cor compunto,
guardai in alto e vidi le sue spalle
  vestite già de' raggi del pianeta
  che mena dritto altrui per ogne calle.
Allor fu la paura un poco queta,
20 che nel lago del cor m'era durata
  la notte ch'i' passai con tanta pieta.
E come quei che con lena affannata,
  uscito fuor del pelago a la riva,
  si volge a l'acqua perigliosa e guata,
così l'animo mio, ch'ancor fuggiva,
  si volse a retro a rimirar lo passo
  che non lasciò già mai persona viva.
Poi ch'èi posato un poco il corpo lasso,
  ripresi via per la piaggia diserta,
30 sì che 'l piè fermo sempre era 'l più basso.
Ed ecco, quasi al cominciar de l'erta,
  una lonza leggera e presta molto,
  che di pel macolato era coverta;
e non mi si partia dinanzi al volto,
  anzi 'mpediva tanto il mio cammino,
  ch'i' fui per ritornar più volte vòlto.
Temp' era dal principio del mattino,
  e 'l sol montava 'n sù con quelle stelle
  ch'eran con lui quando l'amor divino

CANTO I

Midway on our life's journey, I found myself
   In dark woods, the right road lost. To tell
   About those woods is hard—so tangled and rough

And savage that thinking of it now, I feel
   The old fear stirring: death is hardly more bitter.
   And yet, to treat the good I found there as well

I'll tell what I saw, though how I came to enter
   I cannot well say, being so full of sleep
   Whatever moment it was I began to blunder

Off the true path. But when I came to stop
   Below a hill that marked one end of the valley
   That had pierced my heart with terror, I looked up

Toward the crest and saw its shoulders already
   Mantled in rays of that bright planet that shows
   The road to everyone, whatever our journey.

Then I could feel the terror begin to ease
   That churned in my heart's lake all through the night.
   As one still panting, ashore from dangerous seas,

Looks back at the deep he has escaped, my thought
   Returned, still fleeing, to regard that grim defile
   That never left any alive who stayed in it.

After I had rested my weary body awhile
   I started again across the wilderness,
   My left foot always lower on the hill,

And suddenly—a leopard, near the place
   The way grew steep: lithe, spotted, quick of foot.
   Blocking the path, she stayed before my face

And more than once she made me turn about
   To go back down. It was early morning still,
   The fair sun rising with the stars attending it

₄₀ *mosse di prima quelle cose belle;*
sì ch'a bene sperar m'era cagione
di quella fiera a la gaetta pelle
l'ora del tempo e la dolce stagione;
ma non sì che paura non mi desse
la vista che m'apparve d'un leone.
Questi parea che contra me venisse
con la test' alta e con rabbiosa fame,
sì che parea che l'aere ne tremesse.
Ed una lupa, che di tutte brame
₅₀ *sembiava carca ne la sua magrezza,*
e molte genti fé già viver grame,
questa mi porse tanto di gravezza
con la paura ch'uscia di sua vista,
ch'io perdei la speranza de l'altezza.
E qual è quei che volontieri acquista,
e giugne 'l tempo che perder lo face,
che 'n tutti suoi pensier piange e s'attrista;
tal mi fece la bestia sanza pace,
che, venendomi 'ncontro, a poco a poco
₆₀ *mi ripigneva là dove 'l sol tace.*
Mentre ch'i' rovinava in basso loco,
dinanzi a li occhi mi si fu offerto
chi per lungo silenzio parea fioco.
Quando vidi costui nel gran diserto,
«Miserere di me», gridai a lui,
«qual che tu sii, od ombra od omo certo!».
Rispuosemi: «Non omo, omo già fui,
e li parenti miei furon lombardi,
mantoani per patrïa ambedui.
₇₀ *Nacqui sub Iulio, ancor che fosse tardi,*
e vissi a Roma sotto 'l buono Augusto
nel tempo de li dèi falsi e bugiardi.
Poeta fui, e cantai di quel giusto
figliuol d'Anchise che venne di Troia,
poi che 'l superbo Ilïón fu combusto.
Ma tu perché ritorni a tanta noia?
perché non sali il dilettoso monte
ch'è principio e cagion di tutta gioia?».
«Or se' tu quel Virgilio e quella fonte
₈₀ *che spandi di parlar sì largo fiume?»,*
rispuos' io lui con vergognosa fronte.

As when Divine Love set those beautiful
  Lights into motion at creation's dawn,
  And the time of day and season combined to fill

My heart with hope of that beast with festive skin—
  But not so much that the next sight wasn't fearful:
  A lion came at me, his head high as he ran,

Roaring with hunger so the air appeared to tremble.
  Then, a grim she-wolf—whose leanness seemed to compress
  All the world's cravings, that had made miserable

Such multitudes; she put such heaviness
  Into my spirit, I lost hope of the crest.
  Like someone eager to win, who tested by loss

Surrenders to gloom and weeps, so did that beast
  Make me feel, as harrying toward me at a lope
  She forced me back toward where the sun is lost.

While I was ruining myself back down to the deep,
  Someone appeared—one who seemed nearly to fade
  As though from long silence. I cried to his human shape

In that great wasteland: "Living man or shade,
  Have pity and help me, whichever you may be!"
  "No living man, though once I was," he replied.

"My parents both were Mantuans from Lombardy,
  And I was born *sub Julio*, the latter end.
  I lived in good Augustus's Rome, in the day

Of the false gods who lied. A poet, I hymned
  Anchises' noble son, who came from Troy
  When superb Ilium in its pride was burned.

But you—why go back down to such misery?
  Why not ascend the delightful mountain, source
  And principle that causes every joy?"

"Then are you Virgil? Are you the font that pours
  So overwhelming a river of human speech?"
  I answered, shamefaced. "The glory and light are yours,

«O de li altri poeti onore e lume,
  vagliami 'l lungo studio e 'l grande amore
  che m'ha fatto cercar lo tuo volume.
Tu se' lo mio maestro e 'l mio autore,
  tu se' solo colui da cu' io tolsi
  lo bello stilo che m'ha fatto onore.
Vedi la bestia per cu' io mi volsi;
  aiutami da lei, famoso saggio,
90 ch'ella mi fa tremar le vene e i polsi».
«A te convien tenere altro vïaggio»,
  rispuose, poi che lagrimar mi vide,
  «se vuo' campar d'esto loco selvaggio;
ché questa bestia, per la qual tu gride,
  non lascia altrui passar per la sua via,
  ma tanto lo 'mpedisce che l'uccide;
e ha natura sì malvagia e ria,
  che mai non empie la bramosa voglia,
  e dopo 'l pasto ha più fame che pria.
100 Molti son li animali a cui s'ammoglia,
  e più saranno ancora, infin che 'l veltro
  verrà, che la farà morir con doglia.
Questi non ciberà terra né peltro,
  ma sapïenza, amore e virtute,
  e sua nazion sarà tra feltro e feltro.
Di quella umile Italia fia salute
  per cui morì la vergine Cammilla,
  Eurialo e Turno e Niso di ferute.
Questi la caccerà per ogne villa,
110 fin che l'avrà rimessa ne lo 'nferno,
  là onde 'nvidia prima dipartilla.
Ond' io per lo tuo me' penso e discerno
  che tu mi segui, e io sarò tua guida,
  e trarrotti di qui per loco etterno;
ove udirai le disperate strida,
  vedrai li antichi spiriti dolenti,
  che la seconda morte ciascun grida;
e vederai color che son contenti
  nel foco, perché speran di venire
120 quando che sia a le beate genti.

That poets follow—may the love that made me search
    Your book in patient study avail me, Master!
    You are my guide and author, whose verses teach

The graceful style whose model has done me honor.
    See this beast driving me backward—help me resist,
    For she makes all my veins and pulses shudder."

70 "A different path from this one would be best
    For you to find your way from this feral place,"
    He answered, seeing how I wept. "This beast,

The cause of your complaint, lets no one pass
    Her way—but harries all to death. Her nature
    Is so malign and vicious she cannot appease

Her voracity, for feeding makes her hungrier.
    Many are the beasts she mates: there will be more,
    Until the Hound comes who will give this creature

A painful death. Not nourished by earthly fare,
80   He will be fed by wisdom, goodness and love.
    Born between Feltro and Feltro, he shall restore

Low Italy, as Nisus fought to achieve.
    And Turnus, Euryalus, Camilla the maiden—
    All dead from wounds in war. He will remove

This lean wolf, hunting her through every region
    Till he has thrust her back to Hell's abyss
    Where Envy first dispatched her on her mission.

Therefore I judge it best that you should choose
    To follow me, and I will be your guide
90   Away from here and through an eternal place:

To hear the cries of despair, and to behold
    Ancient tormented spirits as they lament
    In chorus the second death they must abide.

Then you shall see those souls who are content
    To dwell in fire because they hope some day
    To join the blessed: toward whom, if your ascent

A le quai poi se tu vorrai salire,
    anima fia a ciò più di me degna:
    con lei ti lascerò nel mio partire;
ché quello imperador che là sù regna,
    perch' i' fu' ribellante a la sua legge,
    non vuol che 'n sua città per me si vegna.
In tutte parti impera e quivi regge;
    quivi è la sua città e l'alto seggio:
    oh felice colui cu' ivi elegge!».
130 E io a lui: «Poeta, io ti richeggio
    per quello Dio che tu non conoscesti,
    acciò ch'io fugga questo male e peggio,
che tu mi meni là dov'or dicesti,
    sì ch'io veggia la porta di san Pietro
    e color cui tu fai cotanto mesti».
Allor si mosse, e io li tenni dietro.

Continues, your guide will be one worthier than I—
  When I must leave you, you will be with her.
  For the Emperor who governs from on high

00 Wills I not enter His city, where none may appear
  Who lived like me in rebellion to His law.
  His empire is everything and everywhere,

But that is His kingdom, His city, His seat of awe.
  Happy is the soul He chooses for that place!"
  I: "Poet, please—by the God you did not know—

Help me escape this evil that I face,
  And worse. Lead me to witness what you have said,
  Saint Peter's gate, and the multitude of woes—"

Then he set out, and I followed where he led.

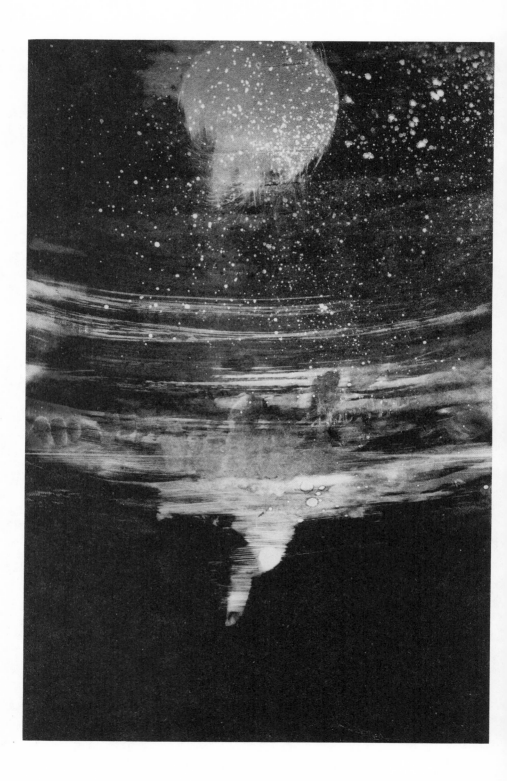

II

Day was departing, and the darkening air
   Called all earth's creatures to their evening quiet
   While I alone was preparing as though for war

To struggle with my journey . . .

(1–4)

CANTO II

Lo giorno se n'andava, e l'aere bruno
   togliea li animai che sono in terra
   da le fatiche loro; e io sol uno
m'apparecchiava a sostener la guerra
   sì del cammino e sì de la pietate,
   che ritrarrà la mente che non erra.
O muse, o alto ingegno, or m'aiutate;
   o mente che scrivesti ciò ch'io vidi,
   qui si parrà la tua nobilitate.
10 Io cominciai: «Poeta che mi guidi,
   guarda la mia virtù s'ell' è possente,
   prima ch'a l'alto passo tu mi fidi.
Tu dici che di Silvïo il parente,
   corruttibile ancora, ad immortale
   secolo andò, e fu sensibilmente.
Però, se l'avversario d'ogne male
   cortese i fu, pensando l'alto effetto
   ch'uscir dovea di lui, e 'l chi e 'l quale,
non pare indegno ad omo d'intelletto;
20 ch'e' fu de l'alma Roma e di suo impero
   ne l'empireo ciel per padre eletto:
la quale e 'l quale, a voler dir lo vero,
   fu stabilita per lo loco santo
   u' siede il successor del maggior Piero.
Per quest' andata onde li dai tu vanto,
   intese cose che furon cagione
   di sua vittoria e del papale ammanto.
Andovvi poi lo Vas d'elezïone,
   per recarne conforto a quella fede
30 ch'è principio a la via di salvazione.
Ma io, perché venirvi? o chi 'l concede?
   Io non Enëa, io non Paulo sono;
   me degno a ciò né io né altri 'l crede.
Per che, se del venire io m'abbandono,
   temo che la venuta non sia folle.
   Se' savio; intendi me' ch'i' non ragiono».

CANTO II

Day was departing, and the darkening air
   Called all earth's creatures to their evening quiet
   While I alone was preparing as though for war

To struggle with my journey and with the spirit
   Of pity, which flawless memory will redraw:
   O Muses, O genius of art, O memory whose merit

Has inscribed inwardly those things I saw—
   Help me fulfill the perfection of your nature.
   I commenced: "Poet, take my measure now:

10 Appraise my powers before you trust me to venture
   Through that deep passage where you would be my guide.
   You write of the journey Silvius's father

Made to immortal realms although he stayed
   A mortal witness, in his corruptible body.
   That the Opponent of all evil bestowed

Such favor on him befits him, chosen for glory
   By highest heaven to be the father of Rome
   And of Rome's empire—later established Holy,

Seat of great Peter's heir. You say he came
20 To that immortal world, and things he learned
   There led to the papal mantle—and triumph for him.

Later, the Chosen Vessel too went and returned,
   Carrying confirmation of that faith
   Which opens the way with salvation at its end.

But I—what cause, whose favor, could send me forth
   On such a voyage? I am no Aeneas or Paul:
   Not I nor others think me of such worth,

And therefore I have my fears of playing the fool
   To embark on such a venture. You are wise:
30 You know my meaning better than I can tell."

E qual è quei che disvuol ciò che volle
      e per novi pensier cangia proposta,
      sì che dal cominciar tutto si tolle,
40 tal mi fec' ïo 'n quella oscura costa,
      perché, pensando, consumai la 'mpresa
      che fu nel cominciar cotanto tosta.
      «S'i' ho ben la parola tua intesa»,
      rispuose del magnanimo quell' ombra,
      «l'anima tua è da viltade offesa;
      la qual molte fïate l'omo ingombra
      sì che d'onrata impresa lo rivolve,
      come falso veder bestia quand' ombra.
      Da questa tema acciò che tu ti solve,
50 dirotti perch' io venni e quel ch'io 'ntesi
      nel primo punto che di te mi dolve.
      Io era tra color che son sospesi,
      e donna mi chiamò beata e bella,
      tal che di comandare io la richiesi.
      Lucevan li occhi suoi più che la stella;
      e cominciommi a dir soave e piana,
      con angelica voce, in sua favella:
      "O anima cortese mantoana,
      di cui la fama ancor nel mondo dura,
60 e durerà quanto 'l mondo lontana,
      l'amico mio, e non de la ventura,
      ne la diserta piaggia è impedito
      sì nel cammin, che vòlt' è per paura;
      e temo che non sia già sì smarrito,
      ch'io mi sia tardi al soccorso levata,
      per quel ch'i' ho di lui nel cielo udito.
      Or movi, e con la tua parola ornata
      e con ciò c'ha mestieri al suo campare,
      l'aiuta sì ch'i' ne sia consolata.
70 I' son Beatrice che ti faccio andare;
      vegno del loco ove tornar disio;
      amor mi mosse, che mi fa parlare.
      Quando sarò dinanzi al segnor mio,
      di te mi loderò sovente a lui".
      Tacette allora, e poi comincia' io:
      "O donna di virtù, sola per cui
      l'umana spezie eccede ogne contento
      di quel ciel c'ha minor li cerchi sui,

And then, like one who unchooses his own choice
    And thinking again undoes what he has started,
    So I became: a nullifying unease

Overcame my soul on that dark slope and voided
    The undertaking I had so quickly embraced.
    "If I understand," the generous shade retorted,

"Cowardice grips your spirit—which can twist
    A man away from the noblest enterprise
    As a trick of vision startles a shying beast.

40 To ease your burden of fear, I will disclose
    Why I came here, and what I heard that compelled
    Me first to feel compassion for you: it was

A lady's voice that called me where I dwelled
    In Limbo—a lady so blessed and fairly featured
    I prayed her to command me. Her eyes out-jeweled

The stars in splendor. 'O generous Mantuan spirit,'
    She began in a soft voice of angelic sound,
    'Whose fame lives still, that the world will still inherit

As long as the world itself shall live: my friend—
50   No friend of Fortune—has found his way impeded
    On the barren slope, and fear has turned him round.

I fear he may be already lost, unaided:
    So far astray, I've come from Heaven too late.
    Go now, with your fair speech and what is needed

To save him; offer the help you have to give
    Before he is lost, and I will be consoled.
    I am Beatrice, come from where I crave

To be again, who ask this. As love has willed,
    So have I spoken. And when I return
60   Before my Lord, He will hear your praises told.'

Then she was silent; and I in turn began,
    'O Lady of goodness, through whom alone mankind
    Exceeds what the sky's least circle can contain

Canto II / 17

tanto m'aggrada il tuo comandamento,
80 che l'ubidir, se già fosse, m'è tardi;
    più non t'è uo' ch'aprirmi il tuo talento.
Ma dimmi la cagion che non ti guardi
    de lo scender qua giuso in questo centro
    de l'ampio loco ove tornar tu ardi".
"Da che tu vuo' saver cotanto a dentro,
    dirotti brievemente", mi rispuose,
    "perch' i' non temo di venir qua entro.
Temer si dee di sole quelle cose
    c'hanno potenza di fare altrui male;
90 de l'altre no, ché non son paurose.
I' son fatta da Dio, sua mercé, tale,
    che la vostra miseria non mi tange,
    né fiamma d'esto 'ncendio non m'assale.
Donna è gentil nel ciel che si compiange
    di questo 'mpedimento ov' io ti mando,
    sì che duro giudicio là sù frange.
Questa chiese Lucia in suo dimando
    e disse:—Or ha bisogno il tuo fedele
    di te, e io a te lo raccomando—.
100 Lucia, nimica di ciascun crudele,
    si mosse, e venne al loco dov' i' era,
    che mi sedea con l'antica Rachele.
Disse:—Beatrice, loda di Dio vera,
    ché non soccorri quei che t'amò tanto,
    ch'uscì per te de la volgare schiera?
Non odi tu la pieta del suo pianto,
    non vedi tu la morte che 'l combatte
    su la fiumana ove 'l mar non ha vanto?—.
Al mondo non fur mai persone ratte
110 a far lor pro o a fuggir lor danno,
    com' io, dopo cotai parole fatte,
venni qua giù del mio beato scanno,
    fidandomi del tuo parlare onesto,
    ch'onora te e quei ch'udito l'hanno".
Poscia che m'ebbe ragionato questo,
    li occhi lucenti lagrimando volse,
    per che mi fece del venir più presto.
E venni a te così com' ella volse:
    d'inanzi a quella fiera ti levai
120 che del bel monte il corto andar ti tolse.

Within its compass: so sweet is your command
    Had I already obeyed, it would feel too late.
    But tell me how you so fearlessly descend

To such a center—from that encompassing state
    You long to see again?' 'You yearn for the answer
    Deeply,' she said, 'so I will tell in short

70 How I can come to Limbo, yet feel no terror:
    Fear befits things with power for injury,
    Not things that lack such power. God the Creator

Has by His mercy made me such that I
    Cannot feel what you suffer: none of this fire
    Assails me. In Heaven a Lady feels such pity

For this impediment where I send you, severe
    Judgment is broken by her grace on high.
    To Lucy she said: "Your faithful follower

Needs you: I commend him to you." Lucy, the foe
80   Of every cruelty, found me where I sat
    With Rachel of old, and urged me: "Beatrice, true

Glory of God, can you not come to the aid
    Of one who had such love for you he rose
    Above the common crowd? Do you not heed

The pity of his cries? And do your eyes
    Not see death near him, in a flood the ocean
    Itself can boast no power to surpass?"

Never on earth was anyone spurred to motion
    So quickly, to seize advantage or fly from danger,
90   As at these words I hurried here from Heaven—

Trusting your eloquence, whose gift brings honor
    Both to yourself and to all those who listen.'
    Having said this, she turned toward me the splendor

Of her eyes lucent with tears—which made me hasten
    To save you, even more eagerly than before:
    And so I rescued you on the fair mountain

Dunque: che è? perché, perché restai,
   perché tanta viltà nel core allette,
   perché ardire e franchezza non hai,
poscia che tai tre donne benedette
   curan di te ne la corte del cielo,
   e 'l mio parlar tanto ben ti promette?».
Quali fioretti dal notturno gelo
   chinati e chiusi, poi che 'l sol li 'mbianca,
   si drizzan tutti aperti in loro stelo,
130 tal mi fec' io di mia virtude stanca,
   e tanto buono ardire al cor mi corse,
   ch'i' cominciai come persona franca:
«Oh pietosa colei che mi soccorse!
   e te cortese ch'ubidisti tosto
   a le vere parole che ti porse!
Tu m'hai con disiderio il cor disposto
   sì al venir con le parole tue,
   ch'i' son tornato nel primo proposto.
Or va, ch'un sol volere è d'ambedue:
140 tu duca, tu segnore e tu maestro».
   Così li dissi; e poi che mosso fue,
intrai per lo cammino alto e silvestro.

Where the beast blocked the short way up. Therefore,
What is this? Why, why should you hold back?
Why be a coward rather than bolder, freer—

Since in the court of Heaven for your sake
    Three blessed ladies watch, and words of mine
    Have promised a good as great as you might seek?"

As flowers bent and shrunken by night at dawn
    Unfold and straighten on their stems, to wake
    Brightened by sunlight, so I grew strong again—

Good courage coursing through my heart, I spoke
    Like one set free: "How full of true compassion
    Was she who helped me, how courteous and quick

Were you to follow her bidding—and your narration
    Has restored my spirit. Now, on: for I feel eager
    To go with you, and cleave to my first intention.

From now, we two will share one will together:
    You are my teacher, my master, and my guide."
    So I spoke, and when he moved I followed after

And entered on that deep and savage road.

III

. . . so *Adam's evil seed*
Swoop from the bank when each is called, as sure

As a trained falcon, to cross to the other side
Of the dark water; and before one throng can land
On the far shore, on this side new souls crowd.

(95–99)

CANTO III

'Per me si va ne la città dolente,
  per me si va ne l'etterno dolore,
  per me si va tra la perduta gente.
Giustizia mosse il mio alto fattore;
  fecemi la divina podestate,
  la somma sapïenza e 'l primo amore.
Dinanzi a me non fuor cose create
  se non etterne, e io etterna duro.
  Lasciate ogne speranza, voi ch'intrate'.
10 Queste parole di colore oscuro
  vid' ïo scritte al sommo d'una porta;
  per ch'io: «Maestro, il senso lor m'è duro».
Ed elli a me, come persona accorta:
  «Qui si convien lasciare ogne sospetto;
  ogne viltà convien che qui sia morta.
Noi siam venuti al loco ov' i' t'ho detto
  che tu vedrai le genti dolorose
  c'hanno perduto il ben de l'intelletto».
E poi che la sua mano a la mia puose
20 con lieto volto, ond' io mi confortai,
  mi mise dentro a le segrete cose.
Quivi sospiri, pianti e alti guai
  risonavan per l'aere sanza stelle,
  per ch'io al cominciar ne lagrimai.
Diverse lingue, orribili favelle,
  parole di dolore, accenti d'ira,
  voci alte e fioche, e suon di man con elle
facevano un tumulto, il qual s'aggira
  sempre in quell' aura sanza tempo tinta,
30 come la rena quando turbo spira.
E io ch'avea d'orror la testa cinta,
  dissi: «Maestro, che è quel ch'i' odo?
  e che gent' è che par nel duol sì vinta?».

CANTO III

THROUGH ME YOU ENTER INTO THE CITY OF WOES,
  THROUGH ME YOU ENTER INTO ETERNAL PAIN,
  THROUGH ME YOU ENTER THE POPULATION OF LOSS.

JUSTICE MOVED MY HIGH MAKER, IN POWER DIVINE,
  WISDOM SUPREME, LOVE PRIMAL. NO THINGS WERE
  BEFORE ME NOT ETERNAL; ETERNAL I REMAIN.

ABANDON ALL HOPE, YOU WHO ENTER HERE.
  These words I saw inscribed in some dark color
  Over a portal. "Master," I said, "make clear

Their meaning, which I find too hard to gather."
  Then he, as one who understands: "All fear
  Must be left here, and cowardice die. Together,

We have arrived where I have told you: here
  You will behold the wretched souls who've lost
  The good of intellect." Then, with good cheer

In his expression to encourage me, he placed
  His hand on mine: so, trusting to my guide,
  I followed him among things undisclosed.

The sighs, groans and laments at first were so loud,
  Resounding through starless air, I began to weep:
  Strange languages, horrible screams, words imbued

With rage or despair, cries as of troubled sleep
  Or of a tortured shrillness—they rose in a coil
  Of tumult, along with noises like the slap

Of beating hands, all fused in a ceaseless flail
  That churns and frenzies that dark and timeless air
  Like sand in a whirlwind. And I, my head in a swirl

Of error, cried: "Master, what is this I hear?
  What people are these, whom pain has overcome?"
  He: "This is the sorrowful state of souls unsure,

Ed elli a me: «Questo misero modo
   tegnon l'anime triste di coloro
   che visser sanza 'nfamia e sanza lodo.
Mischiate sono a quel cattivo coro
   de li angeli che non furon ribelli
   né fur fedeli a Dio, ma per sé fuoro.
40 Caccianli i ciel per non esser men belli,
   né lo profondo inferno li riceve,
   ch'alcuna gloria i rei avrebber d'elli».
E io: «Maestro, che è tanto greve
   a lor che lamentar li fa sì forte?».
   Rispuose: «Dicerolti molto breve.
Questi non hanno speranza di morte,
   e la lor cieca vita è tanto bassa,
   che 'nvidïosi son d'ogne altra sorte.
Fama di loro il mondo esser non lassa;
50   misericordia e giustizia li sdegna:
   non ragioniam di lor, ma guarda e passa».
E io, che riguardai, vidi una 'nsegna
   che girando correva tanto ratta,
   che d'ogne posa mi parea indegna;
e dietro le venìa sì lunga tratta
   di gente, ch'i' non averei creduto
   che morte tanta n'avesse disfatta.
Poscia ch'io v'ebbi alcun riconosciuto,
   vidi e conobbi l'ombra di colui
60   che fece per viltade il gran rifiuto.
Incontanente intesi e certo fui
   che questa era la setta d'i cattivi,
   a Dio spiacenti e a' nemici sui.
Questi sciaurati, che mai non fur vivi,
   erano ignudi e stimolati molto
   da mosconi e da vespe ch'eran ivi.
Elle rigavan lor di sangue il volto,
   che, mischiato di lagrime, a' lor piedi
   da fastidiosi vermi era ricolto.
70 E poi ch'a riguardar oltre mi diedi,
   vidi genti a la riva d'un gran fiume;
   per ch'io dissi: «Maestro, or mi concedi
ch'i' sappia quali sono, e qual costume
   le fa di trapassar parer sì pronte,
   com' i' discerno per lo fioco lume».

Whose lives earned neither honor nor bad fame.
And they are mingled with angels of that base sort
Who, neither rebellious to God nor faithful to Him,

Chose neither side, but kept themselves apart—
Now Heaven expels them, not to mar its splendor,
And Hell rejects them, lest the wicked of heart

Take glory over them." And then I: "Master,
What agony is it, that makes them keen their grief
With so much force?" He: "I will make brief answer:

40 They have no hope of death, but a blind life
So abject, they envy any other fate.
To all memory of them, the world is deaf.

Mercy and justice disdain them. Let us not
Speak of them: look and pass on." I looked again:
A whirling banner sped at such a rate

It seemed it might never stop; behind it a train
Of souls, so long that I would not have thought
Death had undone so many. When more than one

I recognized had passed, I beheld the shade
50 Of him who made the Great Refusal, impelled
By cowardice: so at once I understood

Beyond all doubt that this was the dreary guild
Repellent both to God and His enemies—
Hapless ones never alive, their bare skin galled

By wasps and flies, blood trickling down the face,
Mingling with tears for harvest underfoot
By writhing maggots. Then, when I turned my eyes

Farther along our course, I could make out
People upon the shore of some great river.
60 "Master," I said, "it seems by this dim light

That all of these are eager to cross over—
Can you tell me by what law, and who they are?"
He answered, "Those are things you will discover

Canto III / 27

Ed elli a me: «Le cose ti fier conte
quando noi fermerem li nostri passi
su la trista riviera d'Acheronte».
Allor con li occhi vergognosi e bassi,
80 temendo no 'l mio dir li fosse grave,
infino al fiume del parlar mi trassi.
Ed ecco verso noi venir per nave
un vecchio, bianco per antico pelo,
gridando: «Guai a voi, anime prave!
Non isperate mai veder lo cielo:
i' vegno per menarvi a l'altra riva
ne le tenebre etterne, in caldo e 'n gelo.
E tu che se' costì, anima viva,
pàrtiti da cotesti che son morti».
90 Ma poi che vide ch'io non mi partiva,
disse: «Per altra via, per altri porti
verrai a piaggia, non qui, per passare:
più lieve legno convien che ti porti».
E 'l duca lui: «Caron, non ti crucciare:
vuolsi così colà dove si puote
ciò che si vuole, e più non dimandare».
Quinci fuor quete le lanose gote
al nocchier de la livida palude,
che 'ntorno a li occhi avea di fiamme rote.
100 Ma quell' anime, ch'eran lasse e nude,
cangiar colore e dibattero i denti,
ratto che 'nteser le parole crude.
Bestemmiavano Dio e lor parenti,
l'umana spezie e 'l loco e 'l tempo e 'l seme
di lor semenza e di lor nascimenti.
Poi si ritrasser tutte quante insieme,
forte piangendo, a la riva malvagia
ch'attende ciascun uom che Dio non teme.
Caron dimonio, con occhi di bragia,
110 loro accennando, tutte le raccoglie;
batte col remo qualunque s'adagia.
Come d'autunno si levan le foglie
l'una appresso de l'altra, fin che 'l ramo
vede a la terra tutte le sue spoglie,
similemente il mal seme d'Adamo
gittansi di quel lito ad una ad una,
per cenni come augel per suo richiamo.

When we have paused at Acheron's dismal shore."
   I walked on with my head down after that,
   Fearful I had displeased him, and spoke no more.

Then, at the river—an old man in a boat:
   White-haired, as he drew closer shouting at us,
   "Woe to you, wicked souls! Give up the thought

70 Of Heaven! I come to ferry you across
   Into eternal dark on the opposite side,
   Into fire and ice! And you there—leave this place,

You living soul, stand clear of these who are dead!"
   And then, when he saw that I did not obey:
   "By other ports, in a lighter boat," he said,

"You will be brought to shore by another way."
   My master spoke then, "Charon, do not rage:
   Thus is it willed where everything may be

Simply if it is willed. Therefore, oblige,
80   And ask no more." That silenced the grizzled jaws
   Of the gray ferryman of the livid marsh,

Who had red wheels of flame about his eyes.
   But at his words the forlorn and naked souls
   Were changing color, cursing the human race,

God and their parents. Teeth chattering in their skulls,
   They called curses on the seed, the place, the hour
   Of their own begetting and their birth. With wails

And tears they gathered on the evil shore
   That waits for all who don't fear God. There demon
90   Charon beckons them, with his eyes of fire;

Crowded in a herd, they obey if he should summon,
   And he strikes at any laggards with his oar.
   As leaves in quick succession sail down in autumn

Until the bough beholds its entire store
   Fallen to the earth, so Adam's evil seed
   Swoop from the bank when each is called, as sure

Così sen vanno su per l'onda bruna,
    e avanti che sien di là discese,
120   anche di qua nuova schiera s'auna.
«Figliuol mio», disse 'l maestro cortese,
    «quelli che muoion ne l'ira di Dio
    tutti convegnon qui d'ogne paese;
e pronti sono a trapassar lo rio,
    ché la divina giustizia li sprona,
    sì che la tema si volve in disio.
Quinci non passa mai anima buona;
    e però, se Caron di te si lagna,
    ben puoi sapere omai che 'l suo dir suona».
130 Finito questo, la buia campagna
    tremò sì forte, che de lo spavento
    la mente di sudore ancor mi bagna.
La terra lagrimosa diede vento,
    che balenò una luce vermiglia
    la qual mi vinse ciascun sentimento;
e caddi come l'uom cui sonno piglia.

As a trained falcon, to cross to the other side
  Of the dark water; and before one throng can land
  On the far shore, on this side new souls crowd.

"My son," said the gentle master, "here are joined
  The souls of all who die in the wrath of God,
  From every country, all of them eager to find

Their way across the water—for the goad
  Of Divine Justice spurs them so, their fear
  Is transmuted to desire. Souls who are good

Never pass this way; therefore, if you hear
  Charon complaining at your presence, consider
  What that means." Then, the earth of that grim shore

Began to shake: so violently, I shudder
  And sweat recalling it now. A wind burst up
  From the tear-soaked ground to erupt red light and batter

My senses—and so I fell, as though seized by sleep.

IV

"We are lost, afflicted only this one way:
  That having no hope, we live in longing." I heard
  These words with heartfelt grief that seized on me

Knowing how many worthy souls endured
  Suspension in that Limbo.

(31–35)

CANTO IV

Ruppemi l'alto sonno ne la testa
un greve truono, sì ch'io mi riscossi
come persona ch'è per forza desta;
e l'occhio riposato intorno mossi,
dritto levato, e fiso riguardai
per conoscer lo loco dov' io fossi.
Vero è che 'n su la proda mi trovai
de la valle d'abisso dolorosa
che 'ntrono accoglie d'infiniti guai.
10   Oscura e profonda era e nebulosa
tanto che, per ficcar lo viso a fondo,
io non vi discernea alcuna cosa.
«Or discendiam qua giù nel cieco mondo»,
cominciò il poeta tutto smorto.
«Io sarò primo, e tu sarai secondo».
E io, che del color mi fui accorto,
dissi: «Come verrò, se tu paventi
che suoli al mio dubbiare esser conforto?».
Ed elli a me: «L'angoscia de le genti
20   che son qua giù, nel viso mi dipigne
quella pietà che tu per tema senti.
Andiam, ché la via lunga ne sospigne».
Così si mise e così mi fé intrare
nel primo cerchio che l'abisso cigne.
Quivi, secondo che per ascoltare,
non avea pianto mai che di sospiri
che l'aura etterna facevan tremare;
ciò avvenia di duol sanza martìri,
ch'avean le turbe, ch'eran molte e grandi,
30   d'infanti e di femmine e di viri.
Lo buon maestro a me: «Tu non dimandi
che spiriti son questi che tu vedi?
Or vo' che sappi, innanzi che più andi,
ch'ei non peccaro; e s'elli hanno mercedi,
non basta, perché non ebber battesmo,
ch'è porta de la fede che tu credi;
e s'e' furon dinanzi al cristianesmo,
non adorar debitamente a Dio:
e di questi cotai son io medesmo.

CANTO IV

Breaking the deep sleep that filled my head,
   A heavy clap of thunder startled me up
   As though by force; with rested eyes I stood

Peering to find where I was—in truth, the lip
   Above the chasm of pain, which holds the din
   Of infinite grief: a gulf so dark and deep

And murky that though I gazed intently down
   Into the canyon, I could see nothing below.
   "Now we descend into the sightless zone,"

10   The poet began, dead pale now: "I will go
   Ahead, you second." I answered, seeing his pallor,
   "How can I venture here if even you,

Who have encouraged me every time I falter,
   Turn white with fear?" And he: "It is the pain
   People here suffer that paints my face this color

Of pity, which you mistake for fear. Now on:
   Our long road urges us forward." And he entered
   The abyss's first engirdling circle, and down

He had me enter it too. Here we encountered
20   No laments that we could hear—except for sighs
   That trembled the timeless air: they emanated

From the shadowy sadnesses, not agonies,
   Of multitudes of children and women and men.
   He said, "And don't you ask, what spirits are these?

Before you go on, I tell you: they did not sin;
   If they have merit, it can't suffice without
   Baptism, portal to the faith you maintain.

Some lived before the Christian faith, so that
   They did not worship God aright—and I
30   Am one of these. Through this, no other fault,

40 *Per tai difetti, non per altro rio,*
    semo perduti, e sol di tanto offesi
    che sanza speme vivemo in disio».
    Gran duol mi prese al cor quando lo 'ntesi,
    però che gente di molto valore
    conobbi che 'n quel limbo eran sospesi.
    «Dimmi, maestro mio, dimmi, segnore»,
    comincia' io per volere esser certo
    di quella fede che vince ogne errore:
    «uscicci mai alcuno, o per suo merto
50 *o per altrui, che poi fosse beato?».*
    E quei che 'ntese il mio parlar coverto,
    rispuose: «Io era nuovo in questo stato,
    quando ci vidi venire un possente,
    con segno di vittoria coronato.
    Trasseci l'ombra del primo parente,
    d'Abèl suo figlio e quella di Noè,
    di Moïsè legista e ubidente;
    Abraàm patrïarca e Davìd re,
    Israèl con lo padre e co' suoi nati
60 *e con Rachele, per cui tanto fé,*
    e altri molti, e feceli beati.
    E vo' che sappi che, dinanzi ad essi,
    spiriti umani non eran salvati».
    Non lasciavam l'andar perch' ei dicessi,
    ma passavam la selva tuttavia,
    la selva, dico, di spiriti spessi.
    Non era lunga ancor la nostra via
    di qua dal sonno, quand' io vidi un foco
    ch'emisperio di tenebre vincia.
70 *Di lungi n'eravamo ancora un poco,*
    ma non sì ch'io non discernessi in parte
    ch'orrevol gente possedea quel loco.
    «O tu ch'onori scïenzïa e arte,
    questi chi son c'hanno cotanta onranza,
    che dal modo de li altri li diparte?».

We are lost, afflicted only this one way:
    That having no hope, we live in longing." I heard
    These words with heartfelt grief that seized on me

Knowing how many worthy souls endured
    Suspension in that Limbo. "Dear sir, my master,"
    I began, wanting to be reassured

In the faith that conquers every error, "Did ever
    Anyone go forth from here—by his own good
    Or perhaps another's—to join the blessed, after?"

40 He understood my covert meaning, and said,
    "I was new to this condition, when I beheld
    A Mighty One who descended here, arrayed

With a crown of victory. And He re-called
    Back from this place the shade of our first parent,
    And his son Abel, and other shades who dwelled

In Limbo. Noah, and Moses the obedient
    Giver of laws, went with Him, and Abraham
    The patriarch. King David and Israel went,

And Israel's sire and children, and Rachel for whom
50   He labored so long, and many others—and His
    Coming here made them blessed, and rescued them.

Know this: no human soul was saved, till these."
    We did not stop our traveling while he spoke,
    But kept on passing through the woods—not trees,

But a wood of thronging spirits; nor did we make
    Much distance from the place where I had slept,
    When I saw a fire that overcame a bleak

Hemisphere of darkness. Well before we stopped
    To address them, I could see people there and sense
60   They were honorable folk. "O Master apt

In science and art, who honor both, what wins
    These shades distinction? Who are they who command
    A place so separate from the other ones?"

E quelli a me: «L'onrata nominanza
che di lor suona sù ne la tua vita,
grazïa acquista in ciel che sì li avanza».
Intanto voce fu per me udita:
«Onorate l'altissimo poeta;
l'ombra sua torna, ch'era dipartita».
Poi che la voce fu restata e queta,
vidi quattro grand' ombre a noi venire:
sembianz' avevan né trista né lieta.
Lo buon maestro cominciò a dire:
«Mira colui con quella spada in mano,
che vien dinanzi ai tre sì come sire:
quelli è Omero poeta sovrano;
l'altro è Orazio satiro che vene;
Ovidio è 'l terzo, e l'ultimo Lucano.
Però che ciascun meco si convene
nel nome che sonò la voce sola,
fannomi onore, e di ciò fanno bene».
Così vid' i' adunar la bella scola
di quel segnor de l'altissimo canto
che sovra li altri com' aquila vola.
Da ch'ebber ragionato insieme alquanto,
volsersi a me con salutevol cenno,
e 'l mio maestro sorrise di tanto;
e più d'onore ancora assai mi fenno,
ch'e' sì mi fecer de la loro schiera,
sì ch'io fui sesto tra cotanto senno.
Così andammo infino a la lumera,
parlando cose che 'l tacere è bello,
sì com' era 'l parlar colà dov' era.
Venimmo al piè d'un nobile castello,
sette volte cerchiato d'alte mura,
difeso intorno d'un bel fiumicello.
Questo passammo come terra dura;
per sette porte intrai con questi savi:
giugnemmo in prato di fresca verdura.

And he: "Their honored names, which still resound
  In your life above, have earned them Heaven's grace,
  Advancing them here." Meanwhile a voice intoned:

"Hail the great Poet, whose shade had left this place
  And now returns!" After the voice fell still,
  I saw four great shades making their way to us,

70 Their aspect neither sad nor joyful. "Note well,"
  My master began, "the one who carries a sword
  And strides before the others, as fits his role

Among these giants: he is Homer, their lord
  The sovereign poet; the satirist follows him—
  Horace, with Lucan last, and Ovid third:

That lone voice just now hailed me by a name
  Each of them shares with me; in such accord
  They honor me well." And so I saw, all come

Together there, the splendid school of the lord
80   Of highest song who like an eagle soars high
  Above the others. After they had shared a word

Among themselves, they turned and greeted me
  With cordial gestures, at which my master smiled;
  And far more honor: that fair company

Then made me one among them—so as we traveled
  Onward toward the light I made a sixth
  Amid such store of wisdom. Thus we strolled,

Speaking of matters I will not give breath,
  Silence as fitting now as speech was there.
90   At length, a noble castle blocked our path,

Encircled seven times by a barrier
  Of lofty walls, and defended round about
  By a handsome stream we strode across: it bore

Our weight like solid ground; and after that
  I passed through seven gateways with the sages.
  We came to a fresh green meadow, where we met

Genti v'eran con occhi tardi e gravi,
    di grande autorità ne' lor sembianti:
    parlavan rado, con voci soavi.
Traemmoci così da l'un de' canti,
    in loco aperto, luminoso e alto,
    sì che veder si potien tutti quanti.
Colà diritto, sovra 'l verde smalto,
    mi fuor mostrati li spiriti magni,
120   che del vedere in me stesso m'essalto.
I' vidi Eletra con molti compagni,
    tra' quai conobbi Ettor ed Enea,
    Cesare armato con li occhi grifagni.
Vidi Cammilla e la Pantasilea;
    da l'altra parte vidi 'l re Latino
    che con Lavina sua figlia sedea.
Vidi quel Bruto che cacciò Tarquino,
    Lucrezia, Iulia, Marzìa e Corniglia;
    e solo, in parte, vidi 'l Saladino.
130   Poi ch'innalzai un poco più le ciglia,
    vidi 'l maestro di color che sanno
    seder tra filosofica famiglia.
Tutti lo miran, tutti onor li fanno:
    quivi vid' ïo Socrate e Platone,
    che 'nnanzi a li altri più presso li stanno;
Democrito che 'l mondo a caso pone,
    Dïogenès, Anassagora e Tale,
    Empedoclès, Eraclito e Zenone;
e vidi il buono accoglitor del quale,
140   Dïascoride dico; e vidi Orfeo,
    Tulïo e Lino e Seneca morale;
Euclide geomètra e Tolomeo,
    Ipocràte, Avicenna e Galïeno,
    Averoìs che 'l gran comento feo.

A group of people. With grave, deliberate gazes
    And manners of great authority, they spoke
    Sparingly and in gentle, courtly voices.

100 We drew aside to a place where we could look
    From a spacious well-lit height and view them all:
    On that enameled green I saw—and take

Glory within me for having seen them, still—
    The spirits of the great: I saw Electra
    With many companions, among whom I knew well

Which shades were those of Aeneas and of Hector,
    And Caesar—who wore his armor, falcon-eyed.
    I saw Camilla, and Penthesilea beside her;

I saw King Latinus on the other side,
110   And sitting by him his daughter Lavinia.
    I saw that Brutus from whom Tarquin fled,

I saw Lucretia, Julia, Marcia, Cornelia;
    And sitting at a distance separately
    I saw lone Saladin of Arabia.

I raised my eyes a little, and there was he
    Who is acknowledged Master of those who know,
    Sitting in a philosophic family

Who look to him and do him honor. I saw
    Nearest him, in front, Plato and Socrates.
120   I saw Democritus, who strove to show

That the world is chance; Zeno, Empedocles,
    Anaxagoras, Thales, Heraclitus,
    Diogenes. The collector of qualities

Of things, Dioscorides. And Orpheus,
    Cicero, Linus, Seneca the moralist,
    Euclid the geometer, Ptolemy, Hippocrates,

Galen, Avicenna, Averroës who discussed
    The Philosopher in his great commentary—
    I saw so many I cannot tally the list;

Io non posso ritrar di tutti a pieno,
 però che sì mi caccia il lungo tema,
 che molte volte al fatto il dir vien meno.
La sesta compagnia in due si scema:
 per altra via mi mena il savio duca,
 fuor de la queta, ne l'aura che trema.
E vegno in parte ove non è che luca.

130 For my demanding theme so pulls my story,
  To multiply the telling would be too little
  For the multitude of fact that filled my journey.

The company of six divide and dwindle
  To two; my wise guide leads me from that quiet
  Another way—again I see air tremble,

And come to a part that has no light inside it.

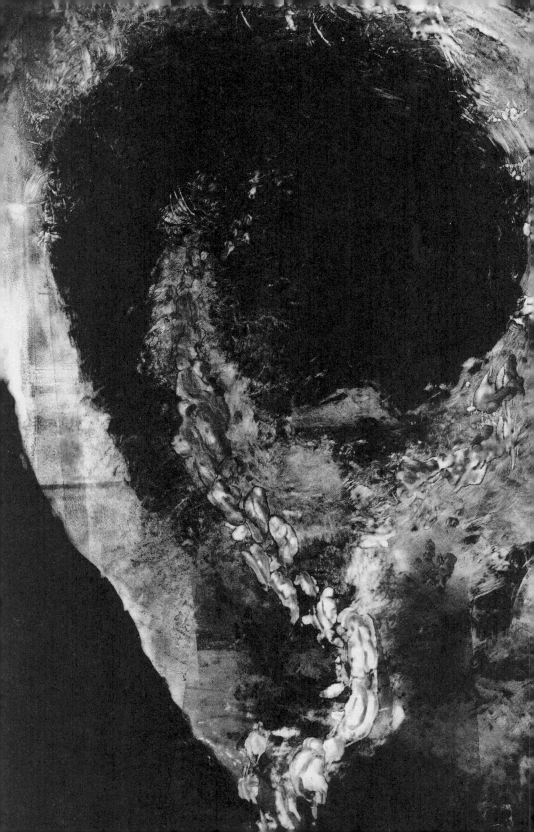

V

. . . *All light is mute, with a bellowing like the ocean*
Turbulent in a storm of warring winds,
The hurricane of Hell in perpetual motion

Sweeping the ravaged spirits . . .

(28–31)

CANTO V

Così discesi del cerchio primaio
  giù nel secondo, che men loco cinghia
  e tanto più dolor, che punge a guaio.
Stavvi Minòs orribilmente, e ringhia:
  essamina le colpe ne l'intrata;
  giudica e manda secondo ch'avvinghia.
Dico che quando l'anima mal nata
  li vien dinanzi, tutta si confessa;
  e quel conoscitor de le peccata
10 vede qual loco d'inferno è da essa;
  cignesi con la coda tante volte
  quantunque gradi vuol che giù sia messa.
Sempre dinanzi a lui ne stanno molte:
  vanno a vicenda ciascuna al giudizio,
  dicono e odono e poi son giù volte.
«O tu che vieni al doloroso ospizio»,
  disse Minòs a me quando mi vide,
  lasciando l'atto di cotanto offizio,
«guarda com' entri e di cui tu ti fide;
20 non t'inganni l'ampiezza de l'intrare!».
  E 'l duca mio a lui: «Perché pur gride?
Non impedir lo suo fatale andare:
  vuolsi così colà dove si puote
  ciò che si vuole, e più non dimandare».
Or incomincian le dolenti note
  a farmisi sentire; or son venuto
  là dove molto pianto mi percuote.
Io venni in loco d'ogne luce muto,
  che mugghia come fa mar per tempesta,
30 se da contrari venti è combattuto.

CANTO V

So I descended from first to second circle—
  Which girdles a smaller space and greater pain,
  Which spurs more lamentation. Minos the dreadful

Snarls at the gate. He examines each one's sin,
  Judging and disposing as he curls his tail:
  That is, when an ill-begotten soul comes down,

It comes before him, and confesses all;
  Minos, great connoisseur of sin, discerns
  For every spirit its proper place in Hell,

10 And wraps himself in his tail with as many turns
  As levels down that shade will have to dwell.
  A crowd is always waiting: here each one learns

His judgment and is assigned a place in Hell.
  They tell; they hear—and down they all are cast.
  "You, who have come to sorrow's hospice, think well,"

Said Minos, who at the sight of me had paused
  To interrupt his solemn task mid-deed:
  "Beware how you come in and whom you trust,

Don't be deceived because the gate is wide."
20   My leader answered, "Must you too scold this way?
  His destined path is not for you to impede:

Thus is it willed where every thing may be
  Because it has been willed. So ask no more."
  And now I can hear the notes of agony

In sad crescendo beginning to reach my ear;
  Now I am where the noise of lamentation
  Comes at me in blasts of sorrow. I am where

All light is mute, with a bellowing like the ocean
  Turbulent in a storm of warring winds,
30   The hurricane of Hell in perpetual motion

La bufera infernal, che mai non resta,
   mena li spirti con la sua rapina;
   voltando e percotendo li molesta.
Quando giungon davanti a la ruina,
   quivi le strida, il compianto, il lamento;
   bestemmian quivi la virtù divina.
Intesi ch'a così fatto tormento
   enno dannati i peccator carnali,
   che la ragion sommettono al talento.
40 E come li stornei ne portan l'ali
   nel freddo tempo, a schiera larga e piena,
   così quel fiato li spiriti mali
di qua, di là, di giù, di sù li mena;
   nulla speranza li conforta mai,
   non che di posa, ma di minor pena.
E come i gru van cantando lor lai,
   faccendo in aere di sé lunga riga,
   così vid' io venir, traendo guai,
ombre portate da la detta briga;
50   per ch'i' dissi: «Maestro, chi son quelle
   genti che l'aura nera sì gastiga?».
«La prima di color di cui novelle
   tu vuo' saper», mi disse quelli allotta,
   «fu imperadrice di molte favelle.
A vizio di lussuria fu sì rotta,
   che libito fé licito in sua legge,
   per tòrre il biasmo in che era condotta.
Ell' è Semiramìs, di cui si legge
   che succedette a Nino e fu sua sposa:
60   tenne la terra che 'l Soldan corregge.
L'altra è colei che s'ancise amorosa,
   e ruppe fede al cener di Sicheo;
   poi è Cleopatràs lussurïosa.
Elena vedi, per cui tanto reo
   tempo si volse, e vedi 'l grande Achille,
   che con amore al fine combatteo.
Vedi Parìs, Tristano»; e più di mille
   ombre mostrommi e nominommi a dito,
   ch'amor di nostra vita dipartille.
70 Poscia ch'io ebbi 'l mio dottore udito
   nomar le donne antiche e ' cavalieri,
   pietà mi giunse, e fui quasi smarrito.

Sweeping the ravaged spirits as it rends,
    Twists, and torments them. Driven as if to land,
    They reach the ruin: groaning, tears, laments,

And cursing of the power of Heaven. I learned
    They suffer here who sinned in carnal things—
    Their reason mastered by desire, suborned.

As winter starlings riding on their wings
    Form crowded flocks, so spirits dip and veer
    Foundering in the wind's rough buffetings,

40 Upward or downward, driven here and there
    With never ease from pain nor hope of rest.
    As chanting cranes will form a line in air,

So I saw souls come uttering cries—wind-tossed,
    And lofted by the storm. "Master," I cried,
    "Who are these people, by black air oppressed?"

"First among these you wish to know," he said,
    "Was empress of many tongues—she so embraced
    Lechery that she decreed it justified

Legally, to evade the scandal of her lust:
50   She is that Semiramis of whom we read,
    Successor and wife of Ninus, she possessed

The lands the Sultan rules. Next, she who died
    By her own hand for love, and broke her vow
    To Sychaeus's ashes. After her comes lewd

And wanton Cleopatra. See Helen, too,
    Who caused a cycle of many evil years;
    And great Achilles, the hero whom love slew

In his last battle. Paris and Tristan are here—"
    He pointed out by name a thousand souls
60   Whom love had parted from our life, or more.

When I had heard my teacher tell the rolls
    Of knights and ladies of antiquity,
    Pity overwhelmed me. Half-lost in its coils,

I' cominciai: «Poeta, volontieri
 parlerei a quei due che 'nsieme vanno,
 e paion sì al vento esser leggieri».
Ed elli a me: «Vedrai quando saranno
 più presso a noi; e tu allor li priega
 per quello amor che i mena, ed ei verranno».
Sì tosto come il vento a noi li piega,
80 mossi la voce: «O anime affannate,
 venite a noi parlar, s'altri nol niega!».
Quali colombe dal disio chiamate
 con l'ali alzate e ferme al dolce nido
 vegnon per l'aere, dal voler portate;
cotali uscir de la schiera ov' è Dido,
 a noi venendo per l'aere maligno,
 sì forte fu l'affettüoso grido.
«O animal grazïoso e benigno
 che visitando vai per l'aere perso
90 noi che tignemmo il mondo di sanguigno,
se fosse amico il re de l'universo,
 noi pregheremmo lui de la tua pace,
 poi c'hai pietà del nostro mal perverso.
Di quel che udire e che parlar vi piace,
 noi udiremo e parleremo a voi,
 mentre che 'l vento, come fa, ci tace.
Siede la terra dove nata fui
 su la marina dove 'l Po discende
 per aver pace co' seguaci sui.
100 Amor, ch'al cor gentil ratto s'apprende,
 prese costui de la bella persona
 che mi fu tolta; e 'l modo ancor m'offende.
Amor, ch'a nullo amato amar perdona,
 mi prese del costui piacer sì forte,
 che, come vedi, ancor non m'abbandona.
Amor condusse noi ad una morte.
 Caina attende chi a vita ci spense».
 Queste parole da lor ci fuor porte.

"Poet," I told him, "I would willingly
  Speak with those two who move along together,
  And seem so light upon the wind." And he:

"When they drift closer—then entreat them hither,
  In the name of love that leads them: they will respond."
  Soon their course shifted, and the merciless weather

70 Battered them toward us. I called against the wind,
  "O wearied souls! If Another does not forbid,
  Come speak with us." As doves whom desire has summoned,

With raised wings steady against the current, glide
  Guided by will to the sweetness of their nest,
  So leaving the flock where Dido was, the two sped

Through the malignant air till they had crossed
  To where we stood—so strong was the compulsion
  Of my loving call. They spoke across the blast:

"O living soul, who with courtesy and compassion
80 Voyage through black air visiting us who stained
  The world with blood: if heaven's King bore affection

For such as we are, suffering in this wind,
  Then we would pray to Him to grant you peace
  For pitying us in this, our evil end.

Now we will speak and hear as you may please
  To speak and hear, while the wind, for our discourse,
  Is still. My birthplace is a city that lies

Where the Po finds peace with all its followers.
  Love, which in gentle hearts is quickly born,
90 Seized him for my fair body—which, in a fierce

Manner that still torments my soul, was torn
  Untimely away from me. Love, which absolves
  None who are loved from loving, made my heart burn

With joy so strong that as you see it cleaves
  Still to him, here. Love gave us both one death.
  Caina awaits the one who took our lives."

Quand' io intesi quell' anime offense,
china' il viso, e tanto il tenni basso,
fin che 'l poeta mi disse: «Che pense?».

Quando rispuosi, cominciai: «Oh lasso,
quanti dolci pensier, quanto disio
menò costoro al doloroso passo!».

Poi mi rivolsi a loro e parla' io,
e cominciai: «Francesca, i tuoi martìri
a lagrimar mi fanno tristo e pio.

Ma dimmi: al tempo d'i dolci sospiri,
a che e come concedette amore
che conosceste i dubbiosi disiri?».

E quella a me: «Nessun maggior dolore
che ricordarsi del tempo felice
ne la miseria; e ciò sa 'l tuo dottore.

Ma s'a conoscer la prima radice
del nostro amor tu hai cotanto affetto,
dirò come colui che piange e dice.

Noi leggiavamo un giorno per diletto
di Lancialotto come amor lo strinse;
soli eravamo e sanza alcun sospetto.

Per più fïate li occhi ci sospinse
quella lettura, e scolorocci il viso;
ma solo un punto fu quel che ci vinse.

Quando leggemmo il disïato riso
esser basciato da cotanto amante,
questi, che mai da me non fia diviso,

la bocca mi basciò tutto tremante.
Galeotto fu 'l libro e chi lo scrisse:
quel giorno più non vi leggemmo avante».

Mentre che l'uno spirto questo disse,
l'altro piangëa; sì che di pietade
io venni men così com' io morisse.

E caddi come corpo morto cade.

These words were borne across from them to us.
　　When I had heard those afflicted souls, I lowered
　　My head, and held it so till I heard the voice

100　Of the poet ask, "What are you thinking?" I answered,
　　"Alas—that sweet conceptions and passion so deep
　　Should bring them here!" Then, looking up toward

The lovers: "Francesca, your suffering makes me weep
　　For sorrow and pity—but tell me, in the hours
　　Of sweetest sighing, how and in what shape

Or manner did Love first show you those desires
　　So hemmed by doubt?" And she to me: "No sadness
　　Is greater than in misery to rehearse

Memories of joy, as your teacher well can witness.
110　But if you have so great a craving to measure
　　Our love's first root, I'll tell it, with the fitness

Of one who weeps and tells. One day, for pleasure,
　　We read of Lancelot, by love constrained:
　　Alone, suspecting nothing, at our leisure.

Sometimes at what we read our glances joined,
　　Looking from the book each to the other's eyes,
　　And then the color in our faces drained.

But one particular moment alone it was
　　Defeated us: *the longed-for smile*, it said,
120　*Was kissed by that most noble lover*: at this,

This one, who now will never leave my side,
　　Kissed my mouth, trembling. A Galeotto, that book!
　　And so was he who wrote it; that day we read

No further." All the while the one shade spoke,
　　The other at her side was weeping; my pity
　　Overwhelmed me and I felt myself go slack:

Swooning as in death, I fell like a dying body.

V I

Three-headed Cerberus, monstrous and cruel,

Barks doglike at the souls immersed here, louder
  For his triple throat.

(12–14)

Al tornar de la mente, che si chiuse
  dinanzi a la pietà d'i due cognati,
  che di trestizia tutto mi confuse,
novi tormenti e novi tormentati
  mi veggio intorno, come ch'io mi mova
  e ch'io mi volga, e come che io guati.
Io sono al terzo cerchio, de la piova
  etterna, maladetta, fredda e greve;
  regola e qualità mai non l'è nova.
10 Grandine grossa, acqua tinta e neve
  per l'aere tenebroso si riversa;
  pute la terra che questo riceve.
Cerbero, fiera crudele e diversa,
  con tre gole caninamente latra
  sovra la gente che quivi è sommersa.
Li occhi ha vermigli, la barba unta e atra,
  e 'l ventre largo, e unghiate le mani;
  graffia li spirti ed iscoia ed isquatra.
Urlar li fa la pioggia come cani;
20 de l'un de' lati fanno a l'altro schermo;
  volgonsi spesso i miseri profani.
Quando ci scorse Cerbero, il gran vermo,
  le bocche aperse e mostrocci le sanne;
  non avea membro che tenesse fermo.
E 'l duca mio distese le sue spanne,
  prese la terra, e con piene le pugna
  la gittò dentro a le bramose canne.
Qual è quel cane ch'abbaiando agogna,
  e si racqueta poi che 'l pasto morde,
30 ché solo a divorarlo intende e pugna,
cotai si fecer quelle facce lorde
  de lo demonio Cerbero, che 'ntrona
  l'anime sì, ch'esser vorrebber sorde.

CANTO VI

Upon my mind's return from swooning shut
   At hearing the piteous tale of those two kin,
   Which confounded me with sadness at their plight,

I see new torments and tormented ones again
   Wherever I step or look. I am in the third
   Circle, a realm of cold and heavy rain—

A dark, accursed torrent eternally poured
   With changeless measure and nature. Enormous hail
   And tainted water mixed with snow are showered

10 Steadily through the shadowy air of Hell;
   The soil they drench gives off a putrid odor.
   Three-headed Cerberus, monstrous and cruel,

Barks doglike at the souls immersed here, louder
   For his triple throat. His eyes are red, his beard
   Grease-black, he has the belly of a meat-feeder

And talons on his hands: he claws the horde
   Of spirits, he flays and quarters them in the rain.
   The wretches, howling like dogs where they are mired

And pelted, squirm about again and again,
20   Turning to make each side a shield for the other.
   Seeing us, Cerberus made his three mouths yawn

To show the fangs—his reptile body aquiver
   In all its members. My leader, reaching out
   To fill both fists with as much as he could gather,

Threw gobbets of earth down each voracious throat.
   Just as a barking dog grows suddenly still
   The moment he begins to gnaw his meat,

Struggling and straining to devour it all,
   So the foul faces of Cerberus became—
30   Who thundered so loudly at the souls in Hell

Noi passavam su per l'ombre che adona
    la greve pioggia, e ponavam le piante
    sovra lor vanità che par persona.
Elle giacean per terra tutte quante,
    fuor d'una ch'a seder si levò, ratto
    ch'ella ci vide passarsi davante.
40 «O tu che se' per questo 'nferno tratto»,
    mi disse, «riconoscimi, se sai:
    tu fosti, prima ch'io disfatto, fatto».
E io a lui: «L'angoscia che tu hai
    forse ti tira fuor de la mia mente,
    sì che non par ch'i' ti vedessi mai.
Ma dimmi chi tu se' che 'n sì dolente
    loco se' messo, e hai sì fatta pena,
    che, s'altra è maggio, nulla è sì spiacente».
Ed elli a me: «La tua città, ch'è piena
50 d'invidia sì che già trabocca il sacco,
    seco mi tenne in la vita serena.
Voi cittadini mi chiamaste Ciacco:
    per la dannosa colpa de la gola,
    come tu vedi, a la pioggia mi fiacco.
E io anima trista non son sola,
    ché tutte queste a simil pena stanno
    per simil colpa». E più non fé parola.
Io li rispuosi: «Ciacco, il tuo affanno
    mi pesa sì, ch'a lagrimar mi 'nvita;
60 ma dimmi, se tu sai, a che verranno
li cittadin de la città partita;
    s'alcun v'è giusto; e dimmi la cagione
    per che l'ha tanta discordia assalita».
E quelli a me: «Dopo lunga tencione
    verranno al sangue, e la parte selvaggia
    caccerà l'altra con molta offensione.
Poi appresso convien che questa caggia
    infra tre soli, e che l'altra sormonti
    con la forza di tal che testé piaggia.

They wished that they were deaf. We two had come
    Over the shades subdued by the heavy rain—
    Treading upon their emptinesses, which seem

Like real bodies. All lay on the ground but one,
    Who sat up, seeing us pass. "You who are led
    Through this Hell—recognize me if you can:

You who were made before I was unmade."
    And I to him: "The anguish you endure
    Perhaps effaces whatever memory I had,

40 Making it seem I have not seen you before;
    But tell me who you are, assigned so sad
    A station as punishment—if any is more

Agony, none is so repellent." He said:
    "Your city, so full of envy that the sack
    Spills over, held me once when I enjoyed

The bright life up above. The name I took
    Among you citizens was Ciacco; the sin
    Of gluttony brought me here. You see me soak

To ruin in battering rain—but not alone,
50   For all of these around me share the same
    Penalty for the same transgression as mine."

Then he fell silent, but I answered him,
    "Ciacco, I feel your misery; its weight
    Bids me to weep. But what of things to come?—

Tell if you can the divided city's fate,
    And of the citizens: is any one just?
    And tell me why such schism threatens it."

He answered, "After long argument they must
    Descend to bloodshed, and the rustic bloc
60   With much offense will expel the other first.

Then, through the power of one who while we speak
    Is temporizing, that party too will fall
    Within three years, the ousted coming back

Canto VI / *59*

70 *Alte terrà lungo tempo le fronti,*
   tenendo l'altra sotto gravi pesi,
   come che di ciò pianga o che n'aonti.
Giusti son due, e non vi sono intesi;
   superbia, invidia e avarizia sono
   le tre faville c'hanno i cuori accesi».
Qui puose fine al lagrimabil suono.
   E io a lui: «Ancor vo' che mi 'nsegni
   e che di più parlar mi facci dono.
Farinata e 'l Tegghiaio, che fuor sì degni,
80   *Iacopo Rusticucci, Arrigo e 'l Mosca*
   e li altri ch'a ben far puoser li 'ngegni,
dimmi ove sono e fa ch'io li conosca;
   ché gran disio mi stringe di savere
   se 'l ciel li addolcia o lo 'nferno li attosca».
E quelli: «Ei son tra l'anime più nere;
   diverse colpe giù li grava al fondo:
   se tanto scendi, là i potrai vedere.
Ma quando tu sarai nel dolce mondo,
   priegoti ch'a la mente altrui mi rechi:
90   *più non ti dico e più non ti rispondo».*
Li diritti occhi torse allora in biechi;
   guardommi un poco e poi chinò la testa:
   cadde con essa a par de li altri ciechi.
E 'l duca disse a me: «Più non si desta
   di qua dal suon de l'angelica tromba,
   quando verrà la nimica podesta:
ciascun rivederà la trista tomba,
   ripiglierà sua carne e sua figura,
   udirà quel ch'in etterno rimbomba».
100 *Sì trapassammo per sozza mistura*
   de l'ombre e de la pioggia, a passi lenti,
   toccando un poco la vita futura;
per ch'io dissi: «Maestro, esti tormenti
   crescerann' ei dopo la gran sentenza,
   o fier minori, o saran sì cocenti?».

With head held high; and long will they prevail
    Despite the others' cries of shame and despair
    Under their burdens. Only two men of all

Are truly just—whose words the rest ignore,
    For the triple sparks of envy, greed, and pride
    Ignite their hearts." "I'd have you tell me more,"

70 I pleaded, once his grievous words were said,
    "Farinata, Mosca, Tegghiaio, men of good reason,
    Jacopo Rusticucci, Arrigo: the good

Was their hearts' purpose in life, so tell what portion
    Their souls inherit now. I long to know
    If they feel Heaven's sweetness, or Infernal poison."

He said, "Their souls are among the blackest in Hell,
    With different faults that weigh them to the pit.
    If you descend that far you may see them all—

But pray you: when you return to earth's sweet light,
80   Recall my memory there to the human world.
    Now, I respond and speak no more." With that,

His eyes went crooked and squinted, his head rolled;
    He regarded me a moment, then bent his head
    And fell back down with the others, blind and quelled.

"He will not wake again," my master said,
    "Until the angel's conclusive trumpet sounds
    And the hostile Power comes—and the waiting dead

Wake to go searching for their unhappy tombs:
    And resume again the form and flesh they had,
90   And hear that which eternally resounds."

So with slow steps we traversed that place of mud
    Through rain and shades commingled, once or twice
    Speaking of the future life: and so I said,

"Master, these torments—tell me, will they increase
    After the Judgment, or lessen, or merely endure,
    Burning as much as now?" He said, "In this,

Ed elli a me: «Ritorna a tua scïenza,
   che vuol, quanto la cosa è più perfetta,
   più senta il bene, e così la doglienza.
Tutto che questa gente maladetta
110   in vera perfezion già mai non vada,
   di là più che di qua essere aspetta».
Noi aggirammo a tondo quella strada,
   parlando più assai ch'i' non ridico;
   venimmo al punto dove si digrada:
quivi trovammo Pluto, il gran nemico.

Go back to your science, which teaches that the more
   A creature is perfect, the more it perceives the good—
   And likewise, pain. The accursèd people here

100 Can never come to true perfection; instead,
   They can expect to come closer then than now."
   Traveling the course of the encircling road,

And speaking more than I repeat, we two
   Continued our way, until the circuit came
   To where the path descends—and there we saw

Plutus, the great Enemy, and confronted him.

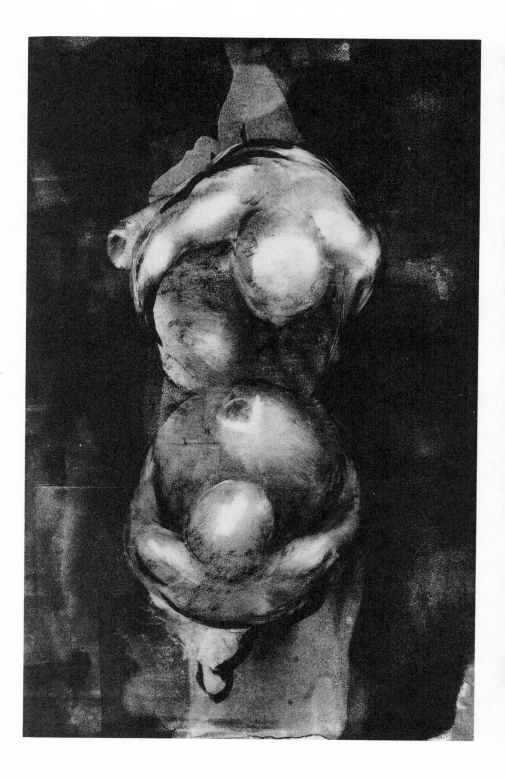

VII

Each pushes a weight against his chest, and howls
  At his opponent each time that they clash:
  "Why do you squander?" and "Why do you hoard?" Each wheels

To roll his weight back round again: they rush
  Toward the circle's opposite point, collide
  Painfully once more, and curse each other afresh . . .

(25–30)

«Pape Satàn, pape Satàn aleppe!»,
    cominciò Pluto con la voce chioccia;
    e quel savio gentil, che tutto seppe,
disse per confortarmi: «Non ti noccia
    la tua paura; ché, poder ch'elli abbia,
    non ci torrà lo scender questa roccia».
Poi si rivolse a quella 'nfiata labbia,
    e disse: «Taci, maladetto lupo!
    consuma dentro te con la tua rabbia.
10 *Non è sanza cagion l'andare al cupo:*
    vuolsi ne l'alto, là dove Michele
    fé la vendetta del superbo strupo».
Quali dal vento le gonfiate vele
    caggiono avvolte, poi che l'alber fiacca,
    tal cadde a terra la fiera crudele.
Così scendemmo ne la quarta lacca,
    pigliando più de la dolente ripa
    che 'l mal de l'universo tutto insacca.
Ahi giustizia di Dio! tante chi stipa
20 *nove travaglie e pene quant' io viddi?*
    e perché nostra colpa sì ne scipa?
Come fa l'onda là sovra Cariddi,
    che si frange con quella in cui s'intoppa,
    così convien che qui la gente riddi.
Qui vid' i' gente più ch'altrove troppa,
    e d'una parte e d'altra, con grand' urli,
    voltando pesi per forza di poppa.
Percotëansi 'ncontro; e poscia pur lì
    si rivolgea ciascun, voltando a retro,
30 *gridando: «Perché tieni?» e «Perché burli?».*
Così tornavan per lo cerchio tetro
    da ogne mano a l'opposito punto,
    gridandosi anche loro ontoso metro;

"Pape Satàn, pape Satàn, aleppe!"
 Plutus began in a guttural, clucking voice.
 The courteous sage who knew all reassured me:

"Don't let fear harm you; whatever power he has
 Cannot prevent us climbing down this rock."
 Then, turning back toward that swollen face,

He answered—"Silence, accursèd wolf! Attack
 Your own insides with your devouring rage:
 Bound for the pit, this is no causeless trek.

10 It is willed above, where Michael wreaked revenge
 On pride's rebellion." Just as sails swollen with wind
 As soon as the mast is snapped collapse and plunge,

That savage beast fell shrinking to the ground.
 So we descended to the fourth defile
 To experience more of that despondent land

That sacks up all the universe's ill.
 Justice of God! Who is it that heaps together
 So much peculiar torture and travail?

How is it that we choose to sin and wither?
20 Like waves above Charybdis, each crashing apart
 Against the one it rushes to meet, here gather

People who hurry forward till they must meet
 And dance their round. Here I saw more souls
 Than elsewhere, spreading far to the left and right:

Each pushes a weight against his chest, and howls
 At his opponent each time that they clash:
 "Why do you squander?" and "Why do you hoard?" Each wheels

To roll his weight back round again: they rush
 Toward the circle's opposite point, collide
30 Painfully once more, and curse each other afresh;

poi si volgea ciascun, quand' era giunto,
  per lo suo mezzo cerchio a l'altra giostra.
E io, ch'avea lo cor quasi compunto,
dissi: «Maestro mio, or mi dimostra
  che gente è questa, e se tutti fuor cherci
  questi chercuti a la sinistra nostra».
40 Ed elli a me: «Tutti quanti fuor guerci
  sì de la mente in la vita primaia,
  che con misura nullo spendio ferci.
Assai la voce lor chiaro l'abbaia,
  quando vegnono a' due punti del cerchio
  dove colpa contraria li dispaia.
Questi fuor cherci, che non han coperchio
  piloso al capo, e papi e cardinali,
  in cui usa avarizia il suo soperchio».
E io: «Maestro, tra questi cotali
50 dovre' io ben riconoscere alcuni
  che furo immondi di cotesti mali».
Ed elli a me: «Vano pensiero aduni:
  la sconoscente vita che i fé sozzi,
  ad ogne conoscenza or li fa bruni.
In etterno verranno a li due cozzi:
  questi resurgeranno del sepulcro
  col pugno chiuso, e questi coi crin mozzi.
Mal dare e mal tener lo mondo pulcro
  ha tolto loro, e posti a questa zuffa:
60 qual ella sia, parole non ci appulcro.
Or puoi, figliuol, veder la corta buffa
  d'i ben che son commessi a la fortuna,
  per che l'umana gente si rabuffa;
ché tutto l'oro ch'è sotto la luna
  e che già fu, di quest' anime stanche
  non poterebbe farne posare una».
«Maestro mio», diss' io, «or mi dì anche:
  questa fortuna di che tu mi tocche,
  che è, che i ben del mondo ha sì tra branche?».
70 E quelli a me: «Oh creature sciocche,
  quanta ignoranza è quella che v'offende!
  Or vo' che tu mia sentenza ne 'mbocche.

And after that refrain each one must head
　　Through his half-circle again, to his next joust.
　　My own heart pained by those collisions, I said:

"Who are these, Master?—and are the shades who contest
　　Here on our left all clergy, with tonsured head?"
　　He answered: "Every one of the shades here massed

In the first life had a mind so squinty-eyed
　　That in his spending he heeded no proportion—
　　A fact they bark out plainly when they collide

40　At the circle's facing points, that mark division
　　Between opposite faults. Those bare of head
　　Were clerics, cardinals, popes, in whom the passion

Of avarice has wrought excess." I said,
　　"Among these, Master, I'm sure I'll recognize
　　Some who were thus polluted." He replied,

"The thought you hold is vain: just as the ways
　　That made these souls so foul were undiscerning,
　　So they are dim to discernment in this place.

Here they will keep eternally returning
50　To the two butting places: from the grave
　　These will arise fists closed; and those, pates shining.

Wrongness in how to give and how to have
　　Took the fair world from them and brought them this,
　　Their ugly brawl, which words need not retrieve.

Now you can see, my son, how ludicrous
　　And brief are all the goods in Fortune's ken,
　　Which humankind contend for: you see from this

How all the gold there is beneath the moon,
　　Or that there ever was, could not relieve
60　One of these weary souls." I: "Master, say then

What is this Fortune you mention, that it should have
　　The world's goods in its grip?" He: "Foolish creatures,
　　How great an ignorance plagues you. May you receive

Colui lo cui saver tutto trascende,
fece li cieli e diè lor chi conduce
sì, ch'ogne parte ad ogne parte splende,
distribuendo igualmente la luce.
Similemente a li splendor mondani
ordinò general ministra e duce
che permutasse a tempo li ben vani
80 di gente in gente e d'uno in altro sangue,
oltre la difension d'i senni umani;
per ch'una gente impera e l'altra langue,
seguendo lo giudicio di costei,
che è occulto come in erba l'angue.
Vostro saver non ha contasto a lei:
questa provede, giudica, e persegue
suo regno come il loro li altri dèi.
Le sue permutazion non hanno triegue:
necessità la fa esser veloce;
90 sì spesso vien chi vicenda consegue.
Quest' è colei ch'è tanto posta in croce
pur da color che le dovrien dar lode,
dandole biasmo a torto e mala voce;
ma ella s'è beata e ciò non ode:
con l'altre prime creature lieta
volve sua spera e beata si gode.
Or discendiamo omai a maggior pieta;
già ogne stella cade che saliva
quand' io mi mossi, e 'l troppo star si vieta».
100 Noi ricidemmo il cerchio a l'altra riva
sovr' una fonte che bolle e riversa
per un fossato che da lei deriva.
L'acqua era buia assai più che persa;
e noi, in compagnia de l'onde bige,
intrammo giù per una via diversa.
In la palude va c'ha nome Stige
questo tristo ruscel, quand' è disceso
al piè de le maligne piagge grige.

My teaching: He who made all of Heaven's features
  In His transcendent wisdom gave them guides
  So each part shines on all the others, all nature's

Illumination apportioned. So too, for goods
  Of worldly splendor He assigned a guide
  And minister—she, when time seems proper, spreads

70 Those vanities from race to race, this blood
  Then that, beyond prevention of human wit.
  Thus one clan languishes for another's good

According to how her judgment may dictate—
  Which is invisible, like a snake in grass.
  Your wisdom cannot resist her; in her might

Fortune, like any other god, foresees,
  Judges, and rules her appointed realm. No truces
  Can stop her turning. Necessity decrees

That she be swift, and so men change their places
80 In rapid permutation. She is cursed
  Too often by those who ought to sing her praises,

Wrongfully blamed and defamed. But she is blest,
  And does not hear it; happy among the choir
  Of other primal creatures, she too is placed

In bliss, rejoicing as she turns her sphere.
  Now we descend to greater wretchedness:
  Already every star that was rising higher

When I set out is sinking, and long delays
  Have been forbidden us." We traveled across
90 To the circle's farther edge, above the place

Where a foaming spring spills over into a fosse.
  The water was purple-black; we followed its current
  Down a strange passage. This dismal watercourse

Descends the grayish slopes until its torrent
  Discharges into the marsh whose name is Styx.
  Gazing intently, I saw there were people warrened

Canto VII / 71

E io, che di mirare stava inteso,
110   vidi genti fangose in quel pantano,
      ignude tutte, con sembiante offeso.
  Queste si percotean non pur con mano,
    ma con la testa e col petto e coi piedi,
      troncandosi co' denti a brano a brano.
  Lo buon maestro disse: «Figlio, or vedi
    l'anime di color cui vinse l'ira;
      e anche vo' che tu per certo credi
che sotto l'acqua è gente che sospira,
    e fanno pullular quest' acqua al summo,
120   come l'occhio ti dice, u' che s'aggira.
  Fitti nel limo dicon: "Tristi fummo
    ne l'aere dolce che dal sol s'allegra,
      portando dentro accidïoso fummo:
or ci attristiam ne la belletta negra".
  Quest' inno si gorgoglian ne la strozza,
    ché dir nol posson con parola integra».
  Così girammo de la lorda pozza
    grand' arco, tra la ripa secca e 'l mézzo,
      con li occhi vòlti a chi del fango ingozza.
130 Venimmo al piè d'una torre al da sezzo.

Within that bog, all naked and muddy—with looks
    Of fury, striking each other: with a hand
    But also with their heads, chests, feet, and backs,

100 Teeth tearing piecemeal. My kindly master explained:
    "These are the souls whom anger overcame,
    My son; know also, that under the water are found

Others, whose sighing makes these bubbles come
    That pock the surface everywhere you look.
    Lodged in the slime they say: 'Once we were grim

And sullen in the sweet air above, that took
    A further gladness from the play of sun;
    Inside us, we bore acedia's dismal smoke.

We have this black mire now to be sullen in.'
110   This canticle they gargle from the craw,
    Unable to speak whole words." We traveled on

Through a great arc of swamp between that slough
    And the dry bank—all the while with eyes
    Turned toward those who swallow the muck below;

And then at length we came to a tower's base.

VIII

     . . . *for some time*
   Before we reached the lofty tower's base
   Our eyes were following two points of flame

 Visible at the top; and answering these
   Another returned the signal, so far away
   The eye could barely catch it.

       (1–6)

Io dico, seguitando, ch'assai prima
  che noi fossimo al piè de l'alta torre,
  li occhi nostri n'andar suso a la cima
per due fiammette che i vedemmo porre,
  e un'altra da lungi render cenno,
  tanto ch'a pena il potea l'occhio tòrre.
E io mi volsi al mar di tutto 'l senno;
  dissi: «Questo che dice? e che risponde
  quell' altro foco? e chi son quei che 'l fenno?».
10 Ed elli a me: «Su per le sucide onde
  già scorgere puoi quello che s'aspetta,
  se 'l fummo del pantan nol ti nasconde».
Corda non pinse mai da sé saetta
  che sì corresse via per l'aere snella,
  com' io vidi una nave piccioletta
venir per l'acqua verso noi in quella,
  sotto 'l governo d'un sol galeoto,
  che gridava: «Or se' giunta, anima fella!».
«Flegïàs, Flegïàs, tu gridi a vòto»,
20 disse lo mio segnore, «a questa volta:
  più non ci avrai che sol passando il loto».
Qual è colui che grande inganno ascolta
  che li sia fatto, e poi se ne rammarca,
  fecesi Flegïàs ne l'ira accolta.
Lo duca mio discese ne la barca,
  e poi mi fece intrare appresso lui;
  e sol quand' io fui dentro parve carca.
Tosto che 'l duca e io nel legno fui,
  segando se ne va l'antica prora
30 de l'acqua più che non suol con altrui.
Mentre noi corravam la morta gora,
  dinanzi mi si fece un pien di fango,
  e disse: «Chi se' tu che vieni anzi ora?».

CANTO VIII

Continuing, I tell how for some time
    Before we reached the lofty tower's base
    Our eyes were following two points of flame

Visible at the top; and answering these
    Another returned the signal, so far away
    The eye could barely catch it. I turned to face

My sea of knowledge and said, "O Master, say:
    What does this beacon mean? And the other fire—
    What answer does it signal? And who are they

10 Who set it there?" He said: "It should be clear:
    Over these fetid waves, you can perceive
    What is expected—if this atmosphere

Of marsh fumes doesn't hide it." Bow never drove
    Arrow through air so quickly as then came
    Skimming across the water a little skiff

Guided by a single boatman at the helm:
    "Now, evil soul," he cried out, "you are caught!"
    "Phlegyas, Phlegyas—you roar in vain this time,"

My lord responded. "You'll have us in your boat
20   Only as long as it takes to cross the fen."
    Like one convinced that he has been the butt

Of gross deception, and bursting to complain,
    Phlegyas held his wrath. We boarded the boat,
    My leader first—it bobbed without a sign

Of being laden until it carried my weight.
    As soon as we embarked, the ancient prow
    Turned swiftly from shore; it made a deeper cut

Into the water than it was wont to do
    With others. In the dead channel one rose abeam
30   Coated with mud, and addressed me: "Who are you,

Canto VIII / 77

E io a lui: «S'i' vegno, non rimango;
　　ma tu chi se', che sì se' fatto brutto?».
　　Rispuose: «Vedi che son un che piango».

E io a lui: «Con piangere e con lutto,
　　spirito maladetto, ti rimani;
　　ch'i' ti conosco, ancor sie lordo tutto».

40　Allor distese al legno ambo le mani;
　　per che 'l maestro accorto lo sospinse,
　　dicendo: «Via costà con li altri cani!».

Lo collo poi con le braccia mi cinse;
　　basciommi 'l volto e disse: «Alma sdegnosa,
　　benedetta colei che 'n te s'incinse!

Quei fu al mondo persona orgogliosa;
　　bontà non è che sua memoria fregi:
　　così s'è l'ombra sua qui furïosa.

Quanti si tegnon or là sù gran regi
50　che qui staranno come porci in brago,
　　di sé lasciando orribili dispregi!».

E io: «Maestro, molto sarei vago
　　di vederlo attuffare in questa broda
　　prima che noi uscissimo del lago».

Ed elli a me: «Avante che la proda
　　ti si lasci veder, tu sarai sazio:
　　di tal disïo convien che tu goda».

Dopo ciò poco vid' io quello strazio
　　far di costui a le fangose genti,
60　che Dio ancor ne lodo e ne ringrazio.

Tutti gridavano: «A Filippo Argenti!»;
　　e 'l fiorentino spirito bizzarro
　　in sé medesmo si volvea co' denti.

Quivi il lasciammo, che più non ne narro;
　　ma ne l'orecchie mi percosse un duolo,
　　per ch'io avante l'occhio intento sbarro.

To come here before your time?" And I to him:
  "Although I come, I do not come to remain—"
  Then added, "Who are you, who have become

So brutally foul?" "You see me: I am one
  Who weeps," he answered. And I to him, "In weeping
  And sorrow remain, cursed soul—for I have seen

Through all that filth: I know you!" He started gripping
  With both hands at the boat. My master stood
  And thrust him back off, saying, "Back to safekeeping

40 Among the other dogs." And then my guide
  Embraced my neck and kissed me on the face
  And said, "Indignant soul, blessed indeed

Is she who bore you. Arrogant in his vice
  Was that one when he lived. No goodness whatever
  Adorning his memory, his shade is furious.

In the world above, how many a self-deceiver
  Now counting himself a mighty king will sprawl
  Swinelike amid the mire when life is over,

Leaving behind a name that men revile."
50 And I said, "Master, truly I should like
  To see that spirit pickled in this swill,

Before we've made our way across the lake."
  And he to me: "Before we see the shore,
  You will be satisfied, for what you seek

Is fitting." After a little, I saw him endure
  Fierce mangling by the people of the mud—
  A sight I give God thanks and praises for:

"Come get Filippo Argenti!" they all cried,
  And crazed with rage the Florentine spirit bit
60 At his own body. Let no more be said

Of him, but that we left him still beset;
  New cries of lamentation reached my ear,
  And I leaned forward to peer intently out.

Lo buon maestro disse: «Omai, figliuolo,
s'appressa la città c'ha nome Dite,
coi gravi cittadin, col grande stuolo».

70 E io: «Maestro, già le sue meschite
là entro certe ne la valle cerno,
vermiglie come se di foco uscite

fossero». Ed ei mi disse: «Il foco etterno
ch'entro l'affoca le dimostra rosse,
come tu vedi in questo basso inferno».

Noi pur giugnemmo dentro a l'alte fosse
che vallan quella terra sconsolata:
le mura mi parean che ferro fosse.

Non sanza prima far grande aggirata,
80 venimmo in parte dove il nocchier forte
«Usciteci», gridò: «qui è l'intrata».

Io vidi più di mille in su le porte
da ciel piovuti, che stizzosamente
dicean: «Chi è costui che sanza morte

va per lo regno de la morta gente?».
E 'l savio mio maestro fece segno
di voler lor parlar segretamente.

Allor chiusero un poco il gran disdegno
e disser: «Vien tu solo, e quei sen vada
90 che sì ardito introò per questo regno.

Sol si ritorni per la folle strada:
pruovi, se sa; ché tu qui rimarrai,
che li ha' iscorta sì buia contrada».

Pensa, lettor, se io mi sconfortai
nel suon de le parole maladette,
ché non credetti ritornarci mai.

«O caro duca mio, che più di sette
volte m'hai sicurtà renduta e tratto
d'alto periglio che 'ncontra mi stette,

100 non mi lasciar», diss' io, «così disfatto;
e se 'l passar più oltre ci è negato,
ritroviam l'orme nostre insieme ratto».

My kindly master said, "A city draws near
    Whose name is Dis, of solemn citizenry
    And mighty garrison." I: "Already clear

Are mosques—I see them there within the valley,
    Baked red as though just taken from the fire."
    And he, "It is fire blazing eternally

70 Inside of them that makes them so appear
    Within this nether Hell." We had progressed
    Into the deep-dug moats that circle near

The walls of that bleak city, which seemed cast
    Of solid iron; we journeyed on, to complete
    An immense circuit before we reached at last

A place where the boatman shouted, "Now get out!
    Here is the entrance." Above the gates I saw
    More than a thousand of those whom Heaven had spat

Like rain, all raging: "Who is this, who'd go
80 Without death through the kingdom of the dead?"
    And my wise master made a sign, to show

That he desired to speak with them aside.
    And then they tempered their great disdain a bit,
    Answering: "You, by yourself, may come inside;

But let that other depart, who dares set foot
    Within this kingdom. Let him retrace alone
    His foolish way—try if he can!—and let

You remain here, who have guided such a one
    Over terrain so dark." You judge, O reader,
90 If I did not lose heart, or believe then,

Hearing that cursèd voice, that I would never
    Return from there. "O my dear guide," I said,
    "Who has restored my confidence seven times over,

And drawn me out of peril—stay at my side,
    Do not desert me now like this, undone.
    If we can go no farther, let us instead

E quel segnor che lì m'avea menato,
 mi disse: «Non temer; ché 'l nostro passo
 non ci può tòrre alcun: da tal n'è dato.
Ma qui m'attendi, e lo spirito lasso
 conforta e ciba di speranza buona,
 ch'i' non ti lascerò nel mondo basso».
Così sen va, e quivi m'abbandona
110 lo dolce padre, e io rimagno in forse,
 che sì e no nel capo mi tenciona.
Udir non potti quello ch'a lor porse;
 ma ei non stette là con essi guari,
 che ciascun dentro a pruova si ricorse.
Chiuser le porte que' nostri avversari
 nel petto al mio segnor, che fuor rimase
 e rivolsesi a me con passi rari.
Li occhi a la terra e le ciglia avea rase
 d'ogne baldanza, e dicea ne' sospiri:
120 «Chi m'ha negate le dolenti case!».
E a me disse: «Tu, perch' io m'adiri,
 non sbigottir, ch'io vincerò la prova,
 qual ch'a la difension dentro s'aggiri.
Questa lor tracotanza non è nova;
 ché già l'usaro a men segreta porta,
 la qual sanza serrame ancor si trova.
Sovr' essa vedestù la scritta morta:
 e già di qua da lei discende l'erta,
 passando per li cerchi sanza scorta,
130 tal che per lui ne fia la terra aperta».

Retrace our steps together." That nobleman
   Who led me there then told me, "Do not fear:
   None can deprive us of the passage One

100 Has willed for us to have. Wait for me here
   And feed your spirit hope and comfort: remember,
   I won't abandon you in this nether sphere."

So he goes away and leaves me, the gentle father,
   While I remain in doubt, with yes and no
   Vying in my head. What they discussed together

Or what my guide proposed, I do not know,
   For they were out of hearing. Before much time,
   The demons scrambled back, where we would go—

And then I saw our adversaries slam
110 The portals of the entrance in the face
   Of my master, who remained outside and came

Back to me walking slowly, with downcast eyes.
   His brow devoid of confidence, he said,
   "Who has denied me this abode of sighs?"

And then he said to me, "Don't be dismayed
   By my vexation: I will conquer this crew,
   However they contrive to block our road.

This insolence of theirs is nothing new;
   At a less secret gate they've shown it before,
120 One still unbolted and open, as you know:

You read the deadly inscription that it bore.
   Already on this side of it—down the steep pass,
   Passing the circles without an escort—be sure

Someone is coming to open the city to us."

IX

. . . *we in our turn*
Stepped forward toward the city and through the gate . . .

(94–95)

Quel color che viltà di fuor mi pinse
   veggendo il duca mio tornare in volta,
   più tosto dentro il suo novo ristrinse.
Attento si fermò com' uom ch'ascolta;
   ché l'occhio nol potea menare a lunga
   per l'aere nero e per la nebbia folta.
«Pur a noi converrà vincer la punga»,
   cominciò el, «se non . . . Tal ne s'offerse.
   Oh quanto tarda a me ch'altri qui giunga!».
10 I' vidi ben sì com' ei ricoperse
   lo cominciar con l'altro che poi venne,
   che fur parole a le prime diverse;
ma nondimen paura il suo dir dienne,
   perch' io traeva la parola tronca
   forse a peggior sentenzia che non tenne.
«In questo fondo de la trista conca
   discende mai alcun del primo grado,
   che sol per pena ha la speranza cionca?».
Questa question fec' io; e quei «Di rado
20 incontra», mi rispuose, «che di noi
   faccia il cammino alcun per qual io vado.
Ver è ch'altra fïata qua giù fui,
   congiurato da quella Eritòn cruda
   che richiamava l'ombre a' corpi sui.
Di poco era di me la carne nuda,
   ch'ella mi fece intrar dentr' a quel muro,
   per trarne un spirto del cerchio di Giuda.
Quell' è 'l più basso loco e 'l più oscuro,
   e 'l più lontan dal ciel che tutto gira:
30 ben so 'l cammin; però ti fa sicuro.

The outward color cowardice painted me
  When I beheld my leader turning back
  Repressed his own new pallor more hurriedly.

He paused with an attentive air, but like
  One listening, not watching—for the eye
  Saw little in air so dark and fog so thick.

"We have to win this battle," he started to say,
  "Or else . . . and she, who offered so much aid—
  Late though it seems to be, and still on the way."

10 I could see plainly how he strove to hide
  His sentence's beginning with its close,
  In different words from those he would have said—

Scaring me none the less, each broken phrase
  Leading me to a meaning perhaps much worse
  Than any it held. "Does anyone whose place

Is the first circle, where the only curse
  Is having no hope, ever come down so far
  As this grim hollow?" I asked him. "Such a course,"

He said, "is rare among us, though once before
20 I have been down here—beckoned as a shade
  By wicked Erichtho, the conjuror

Who used to summon spirits of the dead
  Back to their bodies. My own flesh was but still
  A little while denuded of my shade,

The time she made me enter within this wall
  To draw a spirit from the circle of Judas—
  Which is the lowest and darkest place of all,

And farthest from the heaven whose dome encloses
  Everything in creation. I know the way:
30 Be sure of that. This quagmire which produces

Questa palude che 'l gran puzzo spira
cigne dintorno la città dolente,
u' non potemo intrare omai sanz' ira».
E altro disse, ma non l'ho a mente;
però che l'occhio m'avea tutto tratto
ver' l'alta torre a la cima rovente,
dove in un punto furon dritte ratto
tre furïe infernal di sangue tinte,
che membra feminine avieno e atto,
e con idre verdissime eran cinte;
serpentelli e ceraste avien per crine,
onde le fiere tempie erano avvinte.
E quei, che ben conobbe le meschine
de la regina de l'etterno pianto,
«Guarda», mi disse, «le feroci Erine.
Quest' è Megera dal sinistro canto;
quella che piange dal destro è Aletto;
Tesifón è nel mezzo»; e tacque a tanto.
Con l'unghie si fendea ciascuna il petto;
battiensi a palme e gridavan sì alto,
ch'i' mi strinsi al poeta per sospetto.
«Vegna Medusa: sì 'l farem di smalto»,
dicevan tutte riguardando in giuso;
«mal non vengiammo in Tesëo l'assalto».
«Volgiti 'n dietro e tien lo viso chiuso;
ché se 'l Gorgón si mostra e tu 'l vedessi,
nulla sarebbe di tornar mai suso».
Così disse 'l maestro; ed elli stessi
mi volse, e non si tenne a le mie mani,
che con le sue ancor non mi chiudessi.
O voi ch'avete li 'ntelletti sani,
mirate la dottrina che s'asconde
sotto 'l velame de li versi strani.
E già venìa su per le torbide onde
un fracasso d'un suon, pien di spavento,
per cui tremavano amendue le sponde,
non altrimenti fatto che d'un vento
impetüoso per li avversi ardori,
che fier la selva e sanz' alcun rattento
li rami schianta, abbatte e porta fori;
dinanzi polveroso va superbo,
e fa fuggir le fiere e li pastori.

40

50

60

70

So strong a stench surrounds the city of woe
    We cannot enter now except with wrath."
    And he said more that I don't remember now—

My eyes were on the tower we stood beneath,
    For at its glowing top three hellish Furies
    Suddenly appeared: like women, but with a wreath

Of bright green hydras girdled about their bodies,
    Bloodstained, with squirming vipers in a crown
    Fringing their savage temples. "The fierce Erinyes,"

40 He said, who knew those handmaids of the queen
    Of eternal sorrows: "Megaera on the left;
    Alecto howls on the right; and in between,

Tisiphone." Each one was clawing her breast,
    And each was beating herself—and screamed so loud
    I pressed against him, flinching at the blast.

"O let Medusa come," the Furies bayed
    As they looked down, "to make him stone! We grieve
    Not avenging the assault of Theseus!" He said,

"Turn your back; close your eyes: should Gorgon arrive
50 And show herself, then if you looked at her—
    There would be no returning back above."

He turned me around himself, and to make sure,
    Not trusting mine alone he covered my face
    With his hands too. O you whose mind is clear:

Understand well the lesson that underlies
    The veil of these strange verses I have written.
    Across the turbid waves now came the noise

Of a fearsome crash, by which both shores were shaken:
    A sound like that of a wind that gathers force
60 From waves of heat in violent collision

And batters the forest, and on its unchecked course
    Shatters the branches and tears them to the ground
    And sweeps them off in dustclouds, with scornful roars,

Li occhi mi sciolse e disse: «Or drizza il nerbo
del viso su per quella schiuma antica
per indi ove quel fummo è più acerbo».
Come le rane innanzi a la nimica
biscia per l'acqua si dileguan tutte,
fin ch'a la terra ciascuna s'abbica,
vid' io più di mille anime distrutte
80   fuggir così dinanzi ad un ch'al passo
passava Stige con le piante asciutte.
Dal volto rimovea quell' aere grasso,
menando la sinistra innanzi spesso;
e sol di quell' angoscia parea lasso.
Ben m'accorsi ch'elli era da ciel messo,
e volsimi al maestro; e quei fé segno
ch'i' stessi queto ed inchinassi ad esso.
Ahi quanto mi parea pien di disdegno!
Venne a la porta e con una verghetta
90   l'aperse, che non v'ebbe alcun ritegno.
«O cacciati del ciel, gente dispetta»,
cominciò elli in su l'orribil soglia,
«ond' esta oltracotanza in voi s'alletta?
Perché recalcitrate a quella voglia
a cui non puote il fin mai esser mozzo,
e che più volte v'ha cresciuta doglia?
Che giova ne le fata dar di cozzo?
Cerbero vostro, se ben vi ricorda,
ne porta ancor pelato il mento e 'l gozzo».
100   Poi si rivolse per la strada lorda,
e non fé motto a noi, ma fé sembiante
d'omo cui altra cura stringa e morda
che quella di colui che li è davante;
e noi movemmo i piedi inver' la terra,
sicuri appresso le parole sante.
Dentro li 'ntrammo sanz' alcuna guerra;
e io, ch'avea di riguardar disio
la condizion che tal fortezza serra,

And the wild beasts and shepherds flee at the sound.
　　Taking his hands from my eyes, he said, "Now look:
　　There where the very harshest fumes abound,

Across the ancient scum." As frogs are quick
　　To vanish through water and hunch on bottom sand
　　As soon as they see their enemy the snake,

70　So I saw more than a thousand souls of the ruined
　　Flee before one who strode across the Styx
　　Dry-shod as though on land. With his left hand

He cleared the polluted air before his face
　　And only in that annoyance did he seem tired.
　　I knew assuredly he was sent to us

From Heaven, and I turned my head to regard
　　The master—who signaled that I should be mute
　　And bow before him. Ah, to me he appeared

So full of high disdain! He went to the gate
80　And opened it by means of a little wand,
　　And there was no resistance. "O race cast out

From Heaven, exiles despised there," he intoned
　　From that grim threshold, "Why this insolence?
　　Why do you kick against that Will whose end

Cannot be thwarted, and whose punishments
　　Many times over have increased your pain?
　　What use to butt at what the fates dispense?

Remember, your Cerberus's throat and chin,
　　For just this reason, still are stripped of fur."
90　Then he turned back on the filthy path again,

Not speaking a word to us, but with the air
　　Of one whom other matters must concern
　　Than those who stand before him. And so, secure

After those holy words, we in our turn
　　Stepped forward toward the city and through the gate,
　　Entering without dispute. Anxious to learn

Canto IX / 91

com' io fui dentro, l'occhio intorno invio:
110   e veggio ad ogne man grande campagna,
        piena di duolo e di tormento rio.
Sì come ad Arli, ove Rodano stagna,
        sì com' a Pola, presso del Carnaro
        ch'Italia chiude e suoi termini bagna,
fanno i sepulcri tutt' il loco varo,
        così facevan quivi d'ogne parte,
        salvo che 'l modo v'era più amaro;
ché tra li avelli fiamme erano sparte,
        per le quali eran sì del tutto accesi,
120   che ferro più non chiede verun' arte.
Tutti li lor coperchi eran sospesi,
        e fuor n'uscivan sì duri lamenti,
        che ben parean di miseri e d'offesi.
E io: «Maestro, quai son quelle genti   ·
        che, seppellite dentro da quell' arche,
        si fan sentir coi sospiri dolenti?».
E quelli a me: «Qui son li eresïarche
        con lor seguaci, d'ogne setta, e molto
        più che non credi son le tombe carche.
130   Simile qui con simile è sepolto,
        e i monimenti son più e men caldi».
        E poi ch'a la man destra si fu vòlto,
passammo tra i martìri e li alti spaldi.

What their condition was who populate
    A fortress so guarded, I cast my eye around
    As soon as I was in—and saw a great

100   Plain filled with woe and torment. As on the land
    At Arles where the river Rhône grows more subdued,
    Or at Pola where the Quarnero sets a bound

For Italy, bathing her borders, on every side
    The ground is made uneven by the tombs—
    So it was here: but these were of a mode

More bitter, for among the graves were flames
    That made the sepulchers glow with fiercer heat
    Than a smith could need. Among these catacombs

The lids were raised, with sounds of woe so great
110   Those within surely suffered horrible pain.
    "Master," I said, "who are these people that are shut

Ensepulchered within these coffers of stone,
    Making their sounds of anguish from inside?"
    He answered, "Here, arch-heretics lie—and groan

Along with all the converts that they made,
    The followers of every sect, with like
    Entombed with like. A greater multitude

Crowds into these graves than you may think they take.
    Some sepulchers grow hotter, and some less."
120   He turned to the right, and we continued to walk

Between the anguish and the high parapets.

X

"What are you doing?" he said. "Go back again!
And see where Farinata has sat up straight . . ."

(28–29)

CANTO X

Ora sen va per un secreto calle,
  tra 'l muro de la terra e li martìri,
  lo mio maestro, e io dopo le spalle.
«O virtù somma, che per li empi giri
  mi volvi», cominciai, «com' a te piace,
  parlami, e sodisfammi a' miei disiri.
La gente che per li sepolcri giace
  potrebbesi veder? già son levati
  tutt' i coperchi, e nessun guardia face».
10 E quelli a me: «Tutti saran serrati
  quando di Iosafàt qui torneranno
  coi corpi che là sù hanno lasciati.
Suo cimitero da questa parte hanno
  con Epicuro tutti suoi seguaci,
  che l'anima col corpo morta fanno.
Però a la dimanda che mi faci
  quinc' entro satisfatto sarà tosto,
  e al disio ancor che tu mi taci».
E io: «Buon duca, non tegno riposto
20 a te mio cuor se non per dicer poco,
  e tu m'hai non pur mo a ciò disposto».
«O Tosco che per la città del foco
  vivo ten vai così parlando onesto,
  piacciati di restare in questo loco.
La tua loquela ti fa manifesto
  di quella nobil patrïa natio,
  a la qual forse fui troppo molesto».
Subitamente questo suono uscìo
  d'una de l'arche; però m'accostai,
30 temendo, un poco più al duca mio.
Ed el mi disse: «Volgiti! Che fai?
  Vedi là Farinata che s'è dritto:
  da la cintola in sù tutto 'l vedrai».

And now, along the narrow pathway that ran
  Between those tortures and the city wall,
  I followed my master. "O matchless power," I began,

"Who lead me through evil's circles at your will,
  Speak to me with the answers that I crave
  About these souls and the sepulchers they fill:

Might they be seen? The cover of each grave
  Is lifted open, and no one is on guard."
  "When they return from Jehoshaphat above,"

10 He answered, "bearing the bodies that they had,
  All shall be closed. Here Epicurus lies
  With all his followers, who call the soul dead

When the flesh dies. The question that you raise
  Will soon be answered now that we are inside—
  And so will the secret wish you don't express."

I said, "Dear guide, believe me: I do not hide
  My heart from you, except through my intention
  To speak but little, the way that you have said

Earlier I ought to be disposed." "O Tuscan!—
20 Who travel alive through this, the city of fire,
  While speaking in so courteous a fashion—

If it should please you, stop a moment here.
  Your way of speaking shows that you were born
  In the same noble fatherland: there where

I possibly have wrought excessive harm."
  This sound erupted from a coffer of stone—
  I drew back toward my guide in my alarm.

"What are you doing?" he said. "Go back again!
  And see where Farinata has sat up straight;
30 From the waist up, you may behold the man."

Io avea già il mio viso nel suo fitto;
    ed el s'ergea col petto e con la fronte
    com' avesse l'inferno a gran dispitto.
E l'animose man del duca e pronte
    mi pinser tra le sepulture a lui,
    dicendo: «Le parole tue sien conte».
40 Com' io al piè de la sua tomba fui,
    guardommi un poco, e poi, quasi sdegnoso,
    mi dimandò: «Chi fuor li maggior tui?».
Io ch'era d'ubidir disideroso,
    non gliel celai, ma tutto gliel' apersi;
    ond' ei levò le ciglia un poco in suso;
poi disse: «Fieramente furo avversi
    a me e a miei primi e a mia parte,
    sì che per due fïate li dispersi».
«S'ei fur cacciati, ei tornar d'ogne parte»,
50   rispuos' io lui, «l'una e l'altra fïata;
    ma i vostri non appreser ben quell'arte».
Allor surse a la vista scoperchiata
    un'ombra, lungo questa, infino al mento:
    credo che s'era in ginocchie levata.
Dintorno mi guardò, come talento
    avesse di veder s'altri era meco;
    e poi che 'l sospecciar fu tutto spento,
piangendo disse: «Se per questo cieco
    carcere vai per altezza d'ingegno,
60   mio figlio ov' è? e perché non è teco?».
E io a lui: «Da me stesso non vegno:
    colui ch'attende là, per qui mi mena
    forse cui Guido vostro ebbe a disdegno».
Le sue parole e 'l modo de la pena
    m'avean di costui già letto il nome;
    però fu la risposta così piena.
Di sùbito drizzato gridò: «Come
    dicesti? elli ebbe? non viv' elli ancora?
    non fiere li occhi suoi lo dolce lume?».

Already my eyes were on his: he sat upright,
  And seemed by how he bore his chest and brow
  To have great scorn for Hell. My leader set

Firm hands upon me at once, and made me go
  Forward between the rows of sepulchers,
  Saying: "Choose fitting words," as we wended through.

At his tomb's foot, I felt his proud gaze pierce
  Mine for a moment; and then as if in disdain
  He spoke and asked me, "Who were your ancestors?"

40 Eager to comply with that, I made all plain,
  Concealing nothing: whereupon he raised
  His brows a little. Then he said, "These men

Were enemies to me; they fiercely opposed
  Me and my forebears and my party—so, twice,
  I scattered them." "If ousted and abused,"

I answered, "they returned to claim their place
  From every quarter: yours have not learned that art
  Of return so well." Then suddenly the face

Of a shade appeared beside him, showing the part
50 From the chin up—I think through having risen
  Erect on his knees: his gaze began to dart

Anxiously round me, as though in expectation
  Of someone with me. But when that hope was gone
  He wept: "If you can journey through this blind prison

By virtue of high genius—where is my son,
  And why is he not with you?" And my rejoinder:
  "My own strength has not brought me, but that of one

Who guides me through here, and is waiting yonder—
  Toward one your Guido perhaps had scorned." I well
60 Deduced his name from his words and from his manner

Of punishment, and thus could answer in full.
  Suddenly straightening up, the shade cried out,
  "What?—did I hear you say he 'had'? Oh tell:

70   Quando s'accorse d'alcuna dimora
        ch'io facëa dinanzi a la risposta,
        supin ricadde e più non parve fora.
      Ma quell' altro magnanimo, a cui posta
        restato m'era, non mutò aspetto,
        né mosse collo, né piegò sua costa;
      e sé continüando al primo detto,
        «S'elli han quell' arte», disse, «male appresa,
        ciò mi tormenta più che questo letto.
      Ma non cinquanta volte fia raccesa
80   la faccia de la donna che qui regge,
        che tu saprai quanto quell' arte pesa.
      E se tu mai nel dolce mondo regge,
        dimmi: perché quel popolo è sì empio
        incontr' a' miei in ciascuna sua legge?».
      Ond' io a lui: «Lo strazio e 'l grande scempio
        che fece l'Arbia colorata in rosso,
        tal orazion fa far nel nostro tempio».
      Poi ch'ebbe sospirando il capo mosso,
        «A ciò non fu' io sol», disse, «né certo
90   sanza cagion con li altri sarei mosso.
      Ma fu' io solo, là dove sofferto
        fu per ciascun di tòrre via Fiorenza,
        colui che la difesi a viso aperto».
      «Deh, se riposi mai vostra semenza»,
        prega' io lui, «solvetemi quel nodo
        che qui ha 'nviluppata mia sentenza.
      El par che voi veggiate, se ben odo,
        dinanzi quel che 'l tempo seco adduce,
        e nel presente tenete altro modo».
100   «Noi veggiam, come quei c'ha mala luce,
        le cose», disse, «che ne son lontano;
        cotanto ancor ne splende il sommo duce.
      Quando s'appressano o son, tutto è vano
        nostro intelletto; e s'altri non ci apporta,
        nulla sapem di vostro stato umano.

Is he not still alive? Does the sweet light
   Not strike his eyes?" Perceiving my delay
   In giving any answer, he fell back flat,

Face upward, appearing no more. But not so he,
   The great soul at whose beckoning I had paused;
   He did not change his features in any way,

70 Nor bend his neck or waist. "The point you raised—"
   He resumed where interrupted: "My kin not good
   At learning that art—I feel more agonized

By that accursèd fact than by this bed.
   But when the Lady's face who rules this place
   Has kindled fewer than fifty times," he said,

"Then you will know how heavy that art weighs.
   Now tell me (may you regain the sweet world's vantage),
   Why is that people so fierce in its decrees

Toward my kin?" I answered, "It was the carnage
80   And devastation that dyed the Arbia red
   Which made the prayers in our temple savage."

Shaking his head, "I was not alone," he sighed.
   "And surely I would not have chosen to join
   The others without some cause, but where all agreed

To level Florence—there, I was alone:
   One, who defended her before them all."
   "Ah, pray you (so may your seed find peace again)

Unravel a knot that makes my reason fail,"
   I said. "If I hear rightly, you seem to foresee
90   What time will bring, and yet you seem to deal

Differently with the present." He answered me:
   "Like someone with faulty vision, we can behold
   Remote things well, for so much light does He

Who rules supreme still grant us; but we are foiled
   When things draw near us, and our intelligence
   Is useless when they are present. So of your world

Però comprender puoi che tutta morta
fia nostra conoscenza da quel punto
che del futuro fia chiusa la porta».
Allor, come di mia colpa compunto,
110 dissi: «Or direte dunque a quel caduto
che 'l suo nato è co' vivi ancor congiunto;
e s'i' fui, dianzi, a la risposta muto,
fate i saper che 'l fei perché pensava
già ne l'error che m'avete soluto».
E già 'l maestro mio mi richiamava;
per ch'i' pregai lo spirto più avaccio
che mi dicesse chi con lu' istava.
Dissemi: «Qui con più di mille giaccio:
qua dentro è 'l secondo Federico
120 e 'l Cardinale; e de li altri mi taccio».
Indi s'ascose; e io inver' l'antico
poeta volsi i passi, ripensando
a quel parlar che mi parea nemico.
Elli si mosse; e poi, così andando,
mi disse: «Perché se' tu sì smarrito?».
E io li sodisfeci al suo dimando.
«La mente tua conservi quel ch'udito
hai contra te», mi comandò quel saggio;
«e ora attendi qui», e drizzò 'l dito:
130 «quando sarai dinanzi al dolce raggio
di quella il cui bell' occhio tutto vede,
da lei saprai di tua vita il vïaggio».
Appresso mosse a man sinistra il piede:
lasciammo il muro e gimmo inver' lo mezzo
per un sentier ch'a una valle fiede,
che 'nfin là sù facea spiacer suo lezzo.

In its present state, we have no evidence
   Or knowledge, except if others bring us word:
   Thus you can understand that with no sense

100 Left to us, all our knowledge will be dead
   From that Moment when the future's door is shut."
   Then, moved by compunction for my fault, I said:

"Will you now tell the one who fell back flat
   His son is truly still among the living?
   Tell him what caused my silence: that my thought

Had wandered into that error which your resolving
   Just wiped away." And now I heard my guide
   Calling me back; so, hurriedly contriving

To learn, I begged the shade to say if he could
110   Who lay there with him, and I heard him answer:
   "I lie with over a thousand of the dead;

The second Frederick is among the number,
   And the Cardinal; of others I will not speak."
   With that he hid himself. I walked back over

To the ancient poet, with my thoughts at work
   Mulling the words that bore such menace to me.
   My guide set out, and as we walked he spoke:

"Why is it you're disturbed?" I told him why;
   "Preserve in memory what you have heard
120   Against yourself," the sage advised. "And I pray

You, listen"—he raised a finger at the word.
   "When you confront her radiance, whose eyes can see
   Everything in their fair clarity, be assured

Then you shall learn what your life's journey will be."
   He turned to the left; and leaving the city wall
   Behind our backs we continued on our way

Toward the center which was now our goal,
   Following a path that strikes the valley floor:
   And from that valley rose an odor so foul

130 The stench repelled us even high up there.

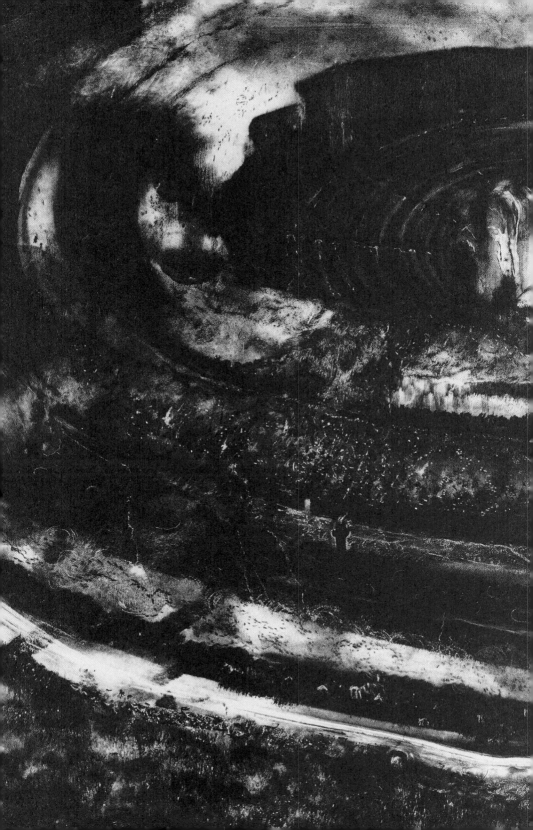

XI

"My son,
Within these rocks three lesser circles fall,

Each one below another, like those you have seen,
And all of them are packed with accursèd souls;
In order that hereafter the sight alone

May be sufficient, you will hear what rules
Determine how and why they are constrained."

(14–20)

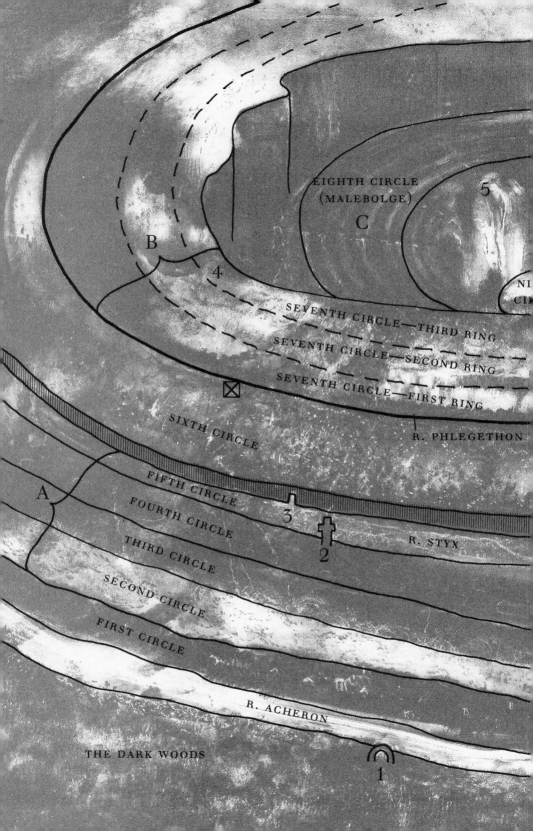

EIGHTH CIRCLE
(MALEBOLGE)

5

C

B

4

NI
CI

SEVENTH CIRCLE—THIRD RING

SEVENTH CIRCLE—SECOND RING

SEVENTH CIRCLE—FIRST RING

SIXTH CIRCLE

R. PHLEGETHON

FIFTH CIRCLE

FOURTH CIRCLE

A

3

THIRD CIRCLE

2

R. STYX

SECOND CIRCLE

FIRST CIRCLE

R. ACHERON

THE DARK WOODS

1

KEY

⊠   *Dante and Virgil in Canto XI*

1   *Entrance*

2   *Tower*

3   *Gates of Dis*

4   *Encounter with Geryon*

5   *Giants*

A   *Sins of Incontinence*

B   *Sins of Violence*

C   *Sins of Fraud*

D   *Sins of Betrayal*

In su l'estremità d'un'alta ripa
  che facevan gran pietre rotte in cerchio,
  venimmo sopra più crudele stipa;
e quivi, per l'orribile soperchio
  del puzzo che 'l profondo abisso gitta,
  ci raccostammo, in dietro, ad un coperchio
d'un grand' avello, ov' io vidi una scritta
  che dicea: 'Anastasio papa guardo,
  lo qual trasse Fotin de la via dritta'.
10 «Lo nostro scender conviene esser tardo,
  sì che s'ausi un poco in prima il senso
  al tristo fiato; e poi no i fia riguardo».
Così 'l maestro; e io «Alcun compenso»,
  dissi lui, «trova che 'l tempo non passi
  perduto». Ed elli: «Vedi ch'a ciò penso».
«Figliuol mio, dentro da cotesti sassi»,
  cominciò poi a dir, «son tre cerchietti
  di grado in grado, come que' che lassi.
Tutti son pien di spirti maladetti;
20 ma perché poi ti basti pur la vista,
  intendi come e perché son costretti.
D'ogne malizia, ch'odio in cielo acquista,
  ingiuria è 'l fine, ed ogne fin cotale
  o con forza o con frode altrui contrista.
Ma perché frode è de l'uom proprio male,
  più spiace a Dio; e però stan di sotto
  li frodolenti, e più dolor li assale.
Di vïolenti il primo cerchio è tutto;
  ma perché si fa forza a tre persone,
30 in tre gironi è distinto e costrutto.

Up on the topmost rim of a deep-cut bank
　　Formed by a circle of massive, fissured rock,
　　We stood above a pen more cruel. The stink

Thrown up from the abyss had grown so thick
　　Its excess drove us to shelter in the space
　　Behind a great tomb's lid. It bore a plaque

Inscribed: "I hold Pope Anastasius,
　　Drawn by Photinus from the proper path."
　　"We must put off descending farther than this,"

10　My master said, "until this rotten breath
　　Has become familiar to our sense of smell."
　　"Discover some matter to fill the lost time with,

Pray you," I answered, "so we may use it well."
　　"I am so minded," he said, and then: "My son,
　　Within these rocks three lesser circles fall,

Each one below another, like those you have seen,
　　And all of them are packed with accursèd souls;
　　In order that hereafter the sight alone

May be sufficient, you will hear what rules
20　Determine how and why they are constrained.
　　The end of every wickedness that feels

Heaven's hatred is injustice—and each end
　　Of this kind, whether by force or fraud, afflicts
　　Some other person. But since fraud is found

In humankind as its peculiar vice,
　　It angers God more: so the fraudulent
　　Are lower, and suffer more unhappiness.

The whole first circle is for the violent;
　　But, because violence involves a deed
30　Against three persons, its apportionment

A Dio, a sé, al prossimo si pòne
  far forza, dico in loro e in lor cose,
  come udirai con aperta ragione.
Morte per forza e ferute dogliose
  nel prossimo si danno, e nel suo avere
  ruine, incendi e tollette dannose;
onde omicide e ciascun che mal fiere,
  guastatori e predon, tutti tormenta
  lo giron primo per diverse schiere.
40 Puote omo avere in sé man vïolenta
  e ne' suoi beni; e però nel secondo
  giron convien che sanza pro si penta
qualunque priva sé del vostro mondo,
  biscazza e fonde la sua facultade,
  e piange là dov' esser de' giocondo.
Puossi far forza ne la deïtade,
  col cor negando e bestemmiando quella,
  e spregiando natura e sua bontade;
e però lo minor giron suggella
50 del segno suo e Soddoma e Caorsa
  e chi, spregiando Dio col cor, favella.
La frode, ond' ogne cosc̈ïenza è morsa,
  può l'omo usare in colui che 'n lui fida
  e in quel che fidanza non imborsa.
Questo modo di retro par ch'incida
  pur lo vinco d'amor che fa natura;
  onde nel cerchio secondo s'annida
ipocresia, lusinghe e chi affattura,
  falsità, ladroneccio e simonia,
60 ruffian, baratti e simile lordura.
Per l'altro modo quell' amor s'oblia
  che fa natura, e quel ch'è poi aggiunto,
  di che la fede spezïal si cria;
onde nel cerchio minore, ov' è 'l punto
  de l'universo in su che Dite siede,
  qualunque trade in etterno è consunto».

And fabrication are in three rings: to God,
    To one's self, or one's neighbor, all violence
    Is done—to them, or to their things instead,

As I'll explain. By violence, death and wounds
    Of grievous kinds are inflicted on one's neighbor;
    And on his property—arson, ruinous offense,

Extortion. So the first ring is the harbor
    Of torment for the homicides and those
    Who strike out wrongfully: despoiler, robber,

40 And plunderer, in various companies.
    One may lay violent hands on his own being,
    Or what belongs to himself, and all of these

Repent in vain within the second ring:
    He who deprives himself of your world sins thus;
    Or gambles; or dissipates whatever thing

He has of worth; or weeps when he should rejoice.
    Violence against the Deity, too, exists:
    To deny and blaspheme Him in the heart does this,

As does despising Nature and her gifts;
50   Therefore the smallest ring imprints its mark
    On Sodom and Cahors and him who speaks

Contemptuously of God with all his heart.
    Fraud, which bites every conscience, a man may play
    Either on one who trusts him, or one who does not.

The latter of the two is seen to destroy
    Only those bonds of love that nature makes:
    So in the second circle hypocrisy,

Flatterers, sorcery, larceny, simoniacs,
    With pimps, barrators, and such filth have their nest.
60   But the other kind of fraud not only forsakes

The love that nature makes, but the special trust
    That further, added love creates: therefore
    At the universe's core, inside the least

E io: «Maestro, assai chiara procede
la tua ragione, e assai ben distingue
questo baràtro e 'l popol ch'e' possiede.

70 Ma dimmi: quei de la palude pingue,
che mena il vento, e che batte la pioggia,
e che s'incontran con sì aspre lingue,

perché non dentro da la città roggia
sono ei puniti, se Dio li ha in ira?
e se non li ha, perché sono a tal foggia?».

Ed elli a me «Perché tanto delira»,
disse, «lo 'ngegno tuo da quel che sòle?
o ver la mente dove altrove mira?

Non ti rimembra di quelle parole
80 con le quai la tua Etica pertratta
le tre disposizion che 'l ciel non vole,

incontenenza, malizia e la matta
bestialitade? e come incontenenza
men Dio offende e men biasimo accatta?

Se tu riguardi ben questa sentenza,
e rechiti a la mente chi son quelli
che sù di fuor sostegnon penitenza,

tu vedrai ben perché da questi felli
sien dipartiti, e perché men crucciata
90 la divina vendetta li martelli».

«O sol che sani ogne vista turbata,
tu mi contenti sì quando tu solvi,
che, non men che saver, dubbiar m'aggrata.

Ancora in dietro un poco ti rivolvi»,
diss'io, «là dove di' ch'usura offende
la divina bontade, e 'l groppo solvi».

«Filosofia», mi disse, «a chi la 'ntende,
nota, non pure in una sola parte,
come natura lo suo corso prende

Circle, the seat of Dis, every betrayer
     Eternally is consumed." "Master, you state
     All of this lucidly, and you make clear

Just what it is that distinguishes this pit
     And those it holds. But what of those condemned
     To languish in the thick marsh, that other set

70   Beaten by rain, those driven by the wind,
     And those who collide and clash with angry tongues:
     How is it that all these are not confined

In the red city to suffer, if their wrongs
     Have brought God's anger on them? And if not,
     Then why are they in such a plight?" "What brings

Your thoughts to wander so from the proper route?
     Where has your mind been gazing? Don't you recall
     A passage in your *Ethics*, the words that treat

Three dispositions counter to Heaven's will:
80   Incontinence, malice, insane brutality?
     And how incontinence is less distasteful

To God, and earns less blame? Think carefully
     About this doctrine, consider who they are
     Whose punishment is above, outside: you'll see

Clearly why they are apart from the wicked here,
     And why His vengeance smites them with less wrath."
     "O sun, that makes all troubled vision clear,

You give solutions I am so contented with
     That asking, no less than knowing, pleases me.
90   But please," I said, "could we retrace our path

Back to the place where you said usury
     Offends celestial Goodness, and solve that knot?"
     He said, "For the comprehending, philosophy

Serves in more places than one to demonstrate
     How Nature takes her own course from the design
     Of the Divine Intelligence, and Its art.

Canto XI / 113

100 dal divino 'ntelletto e da sua arte;
        e se tu ben la tua Fisica note,
        tu troverai, non dopo molte carte,
     che l'arte vostra quella, quanto pote,
        segue, come 'l maestro fa 'l discente;
        sì che vostr' arte a Dio quasi è nepote.
     Da queste due, se tu ti rechi a mente
        lo Genesì dal principio, convene
        prender sua vita e avanzar la gente;
     e perché l'usuriere altra via tene,
110   per sé natura e per la sua seguace
        dispregia, poi ch'in altro pon la spene.
     Ma seguimi oramai che 'l gir mi piace;
        ché i Pesci guizzan su per l'orizzonta,
        e 'l Carro tutto sovra 'l Coro giace,
     e 'l balzo via là oltra si dismonta».

Study your *Physics* well, and you'll be shown
    In not too many pages that your art's good
    Is to follow Nature insofar as it can,

100 As a pupil emulates his master; God
    Has as it were a grandchild in your art.
    By these two, man should thrive and gain his bread—

If you remember Genesis—from the start.
    But since the usurer takes a different way,
    He contemns Nature both in her own sort

And in her follower as well, while he
    Chooses to invest his hope another place.
    But now come follow me: it pleases me

To go now; for above us in the skies
110   The Fish are quivering at the horizon's edge,
    And the whole Wagon lies over Caurus—and this,

Farther ahead, is where we descend the ridge."

XII

"These are the tyrants given to blood and plunder.
  Here they lament the merciless harm they did:

Here's Alexander, and he who held Sicily under
  For many a sad year, fierce Dionysius;
  That black hair there is Azzolino's; and yonder,

That other fairer head is Obizzo of Esti's:
  In the world above, the man his stepson slew."

(98–104)

Era lo loco ov' a scender la riva
venimmo, alpestro e, per quel che v'er' anco,
tal, ch'ogne vista ne sarebbe schiva.
Qual è quella ruina che nel fianco
di qua da Trento l'Adice percosse,
o per tremoto o per sostegno manco,
che da cima del monte, onde si mosse,
al piano è sì la roccia discoscesa,
ch'alcuna via darebbe a chi sù fosse:
10 cotal di quel burrato era la scesa;
e 'n su la punta de la rotta lacca
l'infamïa di Creti era distesa
che fu concetta ne la falsa vacca;
e quando vide noi, sé stesso morse,
sì come quei cui l'ira dentro fiacca.
Lo savio mio inver' lui gridò: «Forse
tu credi che qui sia 'l duca d'Atene,
che sù nel mondo la morte ti porse?
Pàrtiti, bestia, ché questi non vene
20 ammaestrato da la tua sorella,
ma vassi per veder le vostre pene».
Qual è quel toro che si slaccia in quella
c'ha ricevuto già 'l colpo mortale,
che gir non sa, ma qua e là saltella,
vid' io lo Minotauro far cotale;
e quello accorto gridò: «Corri al varco;
mentre ch'e' 'nfuria, è buon che tu ti cale».
Così prendemmo via giù per lo scarco
di quelle pietre, che spesso moviensi
30 sotto i miei piedi per lo novo carco.
Io gia pensando; e quei disse: «Tu pensi
forse a questa ruina, ch'è guardata
da quell' ira bestial ch'i' ora spensi.

CANTO XII

The alp-like place we came for our descent
   Down the steep bank was one no eye would seek,
   Because of what was there. This side of Trent,

There is a place a landslide fell and struck
   The Adige's flank: because of unstable ground
   Or earthquake, rocks once tumbled from the peak

And formed a passage where people can descend.
   Such was the footing we had down that ravine—
   And at the broken chasm's edge we found

10 The infamy of Crete, conceived within
   The false cow's shell. When he saw us come his way
   He bit himself in rage like one insane.

My master called, "Perhaps you think you see
   The Duke of Athens—the one who dealt you death
   Up in the world. Beast, take yourself away:

This is no man your sister taught; in truth,
   He has come here to witness your punishment."
   As a bull breaks loose in the deathblow's aftermath,

And plunges back and forth, but though unspent
20   Cannot go forward, so did the Minotaur act.
   My wary guide cried, "Run to the descent—

Go quickly, while he's raging." So we picked
   Our way down over a rubble of scattered stone
   That shifted under me often as I walked,

With the new weight. While I was climbing down
   I thought to myself; and soon my master said,
   "You may be thinking about this ruined terrain

Or vo' che sappi che l'altra fïata
     ch'i' discesi qua giù nel basso inferno,
     questa roccia non era ancor cascata.
Ma certo poco pria, se ben discerno,
     che venisse colui che la gran preda
     levò a Dite del cerchio superno,
40 da tutte parti l'alta valle feda
     tremò sì, ch'i' pensai che l'universo
     sentisse amor, per lo qual è chi creda
più volte il mondo in caòsso converso;
     e in quel punto questa vecchia roccia,
     qui e altrove, tal fece riverso.
Ma ficca li occhi a valle, ché s'approccia
     la riviera del sangue in la qual bolle
     qual che per vïolenza in altrui noccia».
Oh cieca cupidigia e ira folle,
50 che sì ci sproni ne la vita corta,
     e ne l'etterna poi sì mal c'immolle!
Io vidi un'ampia fossa in arco torta,
     come quella che tutto 'l piano abbraccia,
     secondo ch'avea detto la mia scorta;
e tra 'l piè de la ripa ed essa, in traccia
     corrien centauri, armati di saette,
     come solien nel mondo andare a caccia.
Veggendoci calar, ciascun ristette,
     e de la schiera tre si dipartiro
60 con archi e asticciuole prima elette;
e l'un gridò da lungi: «A qual martiro
     venite voi che scendete la costa?
     Ditel costinci; se non, l'arco tiro».
Lo mio maestro disse: «La risposta
     farem noi a Chirón costà di presso:
     mal fu la voglia tua sempre sì tosta».

Guarded by the feral rage that I defied
      And quelled just now. Know then: that other time
30   I journeyed here, this rock had not yet slid.

It must have been a little before He came
      To Dis, if I have reckoned rightly, to take
      The great spoil of the upper circle with Him—

When the deep, fetid valley began to shake
      Everywhere, so that I thought the universe
      Felt love: the force that has brought chaos back

Many times over, say some philosophers.
      And at that moment this ancient rock, both here
      And elsewhere, tumbled to where it now appears.

40   But keep your eyes below us, for coming near
      Is the river of blood—in which boils everyone
      Whose violence hurt others." O blind desire

Of covetousness, O anger gone insane—
      That goad us on through life, which is so brief,
      To steep in eternal woe when life is done.

I saw a broad moat bending in a curve
      Encircling the plain, just as my guide had said:
      Between the moat and the bottom of the cliff

Centaurs who were armed with bows and arrows sped
50   In file, as on a hunt they might be found
      When they were in the world. When we appeared

They halted, and three came forward from the band
      With bows and shafts they chose, held ready to aim.
      One hailed us from a distance: "You who descend

The hillside, for what torment have you come?
      Tell us from there—if not, I draw my bow!"
      "We will make answer to Chiron," my guide told him,

"Who is beside you; you always brought yourself woe
      Because your will was hasty." He nudged me and said,
60   "That one is Nessus: he who met death through

Poi mi tentò, e disse: «Quelli è Nesso,
    che morì per la bella Deianira,
    e fé di sé la vendetta elli stesso.
70 E quel di mezzo, ch'al petto si mira,
    è il gran Chirón, il qual nodrì Achille;
    quell' altro è Folo, che fu sì pien d'ira.
Dintorno al fosso vanno a mille a mille,
    saettando qual anima si svelle
    del sangue più che sua colpa sortille».
Noi ci appressammo a quelle fiere isnelle:
    Chirón prese uno strale, e con la cocca
    fece la barba in dietro a le mascelle.
Quando s'ebbe scoperta la gran bocca,
80 disse a' compagni: «Siete voi accorti
    che quel di retro move ciò ch'el tocca?
Così non soglion far li piè d'i morti».
    E 'l mio buon duca, che già li er' al petto,
    dove le due nature son consorti,
rispuose: «Ben è vivo, e sì soletto
    mostrar li mi convien la valle buia;
    necessità 'l ci 'nduce, e non diletto.
Tal si partì da cantare alleluia
    che mi commise quest' officio novo:
90 non è ladron, né io anima fuia.
Ma per quella virtù per cu' io movo
    li passi miei per sì selvaggia strada,
    danne un de' tuoi, a cui noi siamo a provo,
e che ne mostri là dove si guada,
    e che porti costui in su la groppa,
    ché non è spirto che per l'aere vada».
Chirón si volse in su la destra poppa,
    e disse a Nesso: «Torna, e sì li guida,
    e fa cansar s'altra schiera v'intoppa».

Fair Deianira, and by himself satisfied
    Vengeance for himself. The middle one whose gaze
    Is directed at his breast, with lowered head,

Is the great Chiron, tutor of Achilles.
    The other is Pholus, full of rage. They circle
    The moat by thousands; if any soul should rise

Out of the blood more than its guilt makes lawful,
    They pierce it with their arrows." As we came close,
    Chiron drew an arrow's notch back through the tangle

70 Of beard along his jaw to clear a space
    For his large mouth, and to the others he said:
    "Have you observed how that one's steps displace

Objects his body touches? Feet of the dead
    Are not accustomed to behave like that."
    And my good leader, who by this time stood

Quite near the Centaur's chest, just opposite
    The place where Chiron's two natures joined, replied:
    "He is indeed alive, and in that state,

Alone; it falls to me to be his guide
80   Through the dark valley. It is necessity,
    And not his pleasure, that puts him on this road.

From singing alleluia one came to me
    To give me this strange mission; he is no thief,
    Nor I a spirit given to larceny.

But by the Power that lets me walk a path
    So savage, give us a member of your pack
    To come along as companion to us both

And show us where the ford is—and on his back
    Carry this one who, not a spirit, cannot
90   Fly through the air." Then Chiron turned and spoke,

Bending his torso toward Nessus on his right,
    "Go back and guide them, then; and turn away
    The challenge of any other troops you meet."

Canto XII / 123

Or ci movemmo con la scorta fida
　　lungo la proda del bollor vermiglio,
　　dove i bolliti facieno alte strida.
Io vidi gente sotto infino al ciglio;
　　e 'l gran centauro disse: «E' son tiranni
　　che dier nel sangue e ne l'aver di piglio.
Quivi si piangon li spietati danni;
　　quivi è Alessandro, e Dïonisio fero
　　che fé Cicilia aver dolorosi anni.
E quella fronte c'ha 'l pel così nero,
110　è Azzolino; e quell' altro ch'è biondo,
　　è Opizzo da Esti, il qual per vero
fu spento dal figliastro sù nel mondo».
　　Allor mi volsi al poeta, e quei disse:
　　«Questi ti sia or primo, e io secondo».
Poco più oltre il centauro s'affisse
　　sovr' una gente che 'nfino a la gola
　　parea che di quel bulicame uscisse.
Mostrocci un'ombra da l'un canto sola,
　　dicendo: «Colui fesse in grembo a Dio
120　lo cor che 'n su Tamisi ancor si cola».
Poi vidi gente che di fuor del rio
　　tenean la testa e ancor tutto 'l casso;
　　e di costoro assai riconobb' io.
Così a più a più si facea basso
　　quel sangue, sì che cocea pur li piedi;
　　e quindi fu del fosso il nostro passo.
«Sì come tu da questa parte vedi
　　lo bulicame che sempre si scema»,
　　disse 'l centauro, «voglio che tu credi
130 che da quest' altra a più a più giù prema
　　lo fondo suo, infin ch'el si raggiunge
　　ove la tirannia convien che gema.
La divina giustizia di qua punge
　　quell' Attila che fu flagello in terra,
　　e Pirro e Sesto; e in etterno munge
le lagrime, che col bollor diserra,
　　a Rinier da Corneto, a Rinier Pazzo,
　　che fecero a le strade tanta guerra».
Poi si rivolse e ripassossi 'l guazzo.

Now with a trusty escort, we made our way
 Along the boiling crimson—those boiled inside
 Shrieking beside us. On some it came so high

It covered their eyebrows. The mighty centaur said,
 "These are the tyrants given to blood and plunder.
 Here they lament the merciless harm they did:

100 Here's Alexander, and he who held Sicily under
 For many a sad year, fierce Dionysius;
 That black hair there is Azzolino's; and yonder,

That other fairer head is Obizzo of Esti's:
 In the world above, the man his stepson slew."
 I turned toward the poet, whose answer was,

"Let him be first guide, I your second, now."
 A little farther on, the centaur stopped
 At a crowd seeming to rise from the boiling flow

Up to the throat. He showed us one who kept
110 Off to one side. "Within the bosom of God
 He stabbed another's heart, and it has dripped

Blood ever since upon the Thames," he said.
 I saw some others whose head and even chest
 Came up above the stream, and in that crowd

Were many I recognized. The blood decreased,
 Sinking by more and more until it cooked
 Only the feet, and that is where we crossed.

"To here, you have seen the boiling stream contract,"
 He said. "From here, its bed grows deeper again
120 Till it completes its circle, to reconnect

With where God's justice makes the tyrants groan:
 It goads Attila, a scourge on earth, and Pyrrhus,
 And Sextus; there also are eternally drawn

The tears, unlocked by boiling, milked from the eyes
 Of Rinier Pazzo and Rinier da Corneto—men
 Who brought such warfare to the public ways."

Then he turned back, and crossed the ford again.

Canto XII / 125

XIII

". . . and through the mournful wood
Our bodies will be hung: with every one
Fixed on the thornbush of its wounding shade."

(100–2)

Non era ancor di là Nesso arrivato,
   quando noi ci mettemmo per un bosco
   che da neun sentiero era segnato.
Non fronda verde, ma di color fosco;
   non rami schietti, ma nodosi e 'nvolti;
   non pomi v'eran, ma stecchi con tòsco.
Non han sì aspri sterpi né sì folti
   quelle fiere selvagge che 'n odio hanno
   tra Cecina e Corneto i luoghi cólti.
10 Quivi le brutte Arpie lor nidi fanno,
   che cacciar de le Strofade i Troiani
   con tristo annunzio di futuro danno.
Ali hanno late, e colli e visi umani,
   piè con artigli, e pennuto 'l gran ventre;
   fanno lamenti in su li alberi strani.
E 'l buon maestro «Prima che più entre,
   sappi che se' nel secondo girone,
   mi cominciò a dire, «e sarai mentre
che tu verrai ne l'orribil sabbione.
20 Però riguarda ben; sì vederai
   cose che torrien fede al mio sermone».
Io sentia d'ogne parte trarre guai
   e non vedea persona che 'l facesse;
   per ch'io tutto smarrito m'arrestai.
Cred' ïo ch'ei credette ch'io credesse
   che tante voci uscisser, tra quei bronchi,
   da gente che per noi si nascondesse.
Però disse 'l maestro: «Se tu tronchi
   qualche fraschetta d'una d'este piante,
30 li pensier c'hai si faran tutti monchi».
Allor porsi la mano un poco avante
   e colsi un ramicel da un gran pruno;
   e 'l tronco suo gridò: «Perché mi schiante?».

Nessus had not yet reached the other side
   When we moved forward into woods unmarked
   By any path. The leaves not green, earth-hued;

The boughs not smooth, knotted and crooked-forked;
   No fruit, but poisoned thorns. Of the wild beasts
   Near Cecina and Corneto, that hate fields worked

By men with plough and harrow, none infests
   Thickets that are as rough or dense as this.
   Here the repellent Harpies make their nests,

10 Who drove the Trojans from the Strophades
   With dire announcements of the coming woe.
   They have broad wings, a human neck and face,

Clawed feet, and swollen, feathered bellies; they caw
   Their lamentations in the eerie trees.
   Here the good master began, "Before you go

Farther, be aware that now you are in this,
   The second ring—and so you shall be until
   The horrible sand. Look well, for here one sees

Things which in words would be incredible."
20 On every side, I heard wailing voices grieve,
   Yet I could not see anyone there to wail,

And so I stopped, bewildered. I believe
   My guide believed that in my belief the voices
   I heard from somewhere in among the grove

Came somehow from people who were in hiding places—
   And therefore the master said, "If you remove
   A little branch from any one of these pieces

Of foliage around us, the thoughts you have
   Will also be broken off." I reached my hand
30 A little in front of me and twisted off

Da che fatto fu poi di sangue bruno,
  ricominciò a dir: «Perché mi scerpi?
  non hai tu spirto di pietade alcuno?
Uomini fummo, e or siam fatti sterpi:
  ben dovrebb' esser la tua man più pia,
  se state fossimo anime di serpi».
40 Come d'un stizzo verde ch'arso sia
  da l'un de' capi, che da l'altro geme
  e cigola per vento che va via,
sì de la scheggia rotta usciva insieme
  parole e sangue; ond' io lasciai la cima
  cadere, e stetti come l'uom che teme.
«S'elli avesse potuto creder prima»,
  rispuose 'l savio mio, «anima lesa,
  ciò c'ha veduto pur con la mia rima,
non averebbe in te la man distesa;
50 ma la cosa incredibile mi fece
  indurlo ad ovra ch'a me stesso pesa.
Ma dilli chi tu fosti, sì che 'n vece
  d'alcun' ammenda tua fama rinfreschi
  nel mondo sù, dove tornar li lece».
E 'l tronco: «Sì col dolce dir m'adeschi,
  ch'i' non posso tacere; e voi non gravi
  perch' ïo un poco a ragionar m'inveschi.
Io son colui che tenni ambo le chiavi
  del cor di Federigo, e che le volsi,
60 serrando e diserrando, sì soavi,
che dal secreto suo quasi ogn' uom tolsi;
  fede portai al glorïoso offizio,
  tanto ch'i' ne perde' li sonni e ' polsi.
La meretrice che mai da l'ospizio
  di Cesare non torse li occhi putti,
  morte comune e de le corti vizio,

One shoot of a mighty thornbush—and it moaned,
  "Why do you break me?" Then after it had grown
  Darker with blood, it began again and mourned,

"Why have you torn me? Have you no pity, then?
  Once we were men, now we are stumps of wood:
  Your hand should show some mercy, though we had been

The souls of serpents." As flames spurt at one side
  Of a green log oozing sap at the other end,
  Hissing with escaping air, so that branch flowed

40 With words and blood together—at which my hand
  Released the tip, and I stood like one in dread.
  "Had he been able to credit or comprehend

Before, O wounded spirit," my sage replied,
  "What he had witnessed only in my verses,
  His hand would never have performed this deed

Against you. But the fact belief refuses
  Compelled me, though it grieves me, thus to prompt him.
  But tell him who you are, so that his praises

May make amends by freshening your fame
50   When he returns again to the world above,
  As he is permitted." And the broken stem:

"Your words have so much sweetness they contrive
  To draw me out of silence: I am enticed
  To talk a little while, may it not prove

Burdensome to you. I am he who possessed
  Both keys to Frederick's heart—and I turned either,
  Unlocking and locking with so soft a twist

I kept his secrets from almost any other.
  To this, my glorious office, I stayed so true
60   I lost both sleep and life. The harlot that never

Takes its whore's eyes from Caesar's retinue—
  The common fatal Vice of courts—inflamed
  All minds against me; and they, inflamed so,

infiammò contra me li animi tutti;
e li 'nfiammati infiammar sì Augusto,
che ' lieti onor tornaro in tristi lutti.

70 L'animo mio, per disdegnoso gusto,
credendo col morir fuggir disdegno,
ingiusto fece me contra me giusto.

Per le nove radici d'esto legno
vi giuro che già mai non ruppi fede
al mio segnor, che fu d'onor sì degno.

E se di voi alcun nel mondo riede,
conforti la memoria mia, che giace
ancor del colpo che 'nvidia le diede».

Un poco attese, e poi «Da ch'el si tace»,
80 disse 'l poeta a me, «non perder l'ora;
ma parla, e chiedi a lui, se più ti piace».

Ond' ïo a lui: «Domandal tu ancora
di quel che credi ch'a me satisfaccia;
ch'i' non potrei, tanta pietà m'accora».

Perciò ricominciò: «Se l'om ti faccia
liberamente ciò che 'l tuo dir priega,
spirito incarcerato, ancor ti piaccia

di dirne come l'anima si lega
in questi nocchi; e dinne, se tu puoi,
90 s'alcuna mai di tai membra si spiega».

Allor soffiò il tronco forte, e poi
si convertì quel vento in cotal voce:
«Brievemente sarà risposto a voi.

Quando si parte l'anima feroce
dal corpo ond' ella stessa s'è disvelta,
Minòs la manda a la settima foce.

Cade in la selva, e non l'è parte scelta;
ma là dove fortuna la balestra,
quivi germoglia come gran di spelta.

100 Surge in vermena e in pianta silvestra:
l'Arpie, pascendo poi de le sue foglie,
fanno dolore, e al dolor fenestra.

So inflamed Augustus that the honors I claimed
   In gladness were converted into pain.
   My mind, in its disdainful temper, assumed

Dying would be a way to escape disdain,
   Making me treat my juster self unjustly.
   And by this tree's strange roots, I swear again:

70 I never betrayed my lord, who was so worthy
   Of honor. If you return to the world above,
   Either of you, please comfort my memory

Still prostrate from the blow that Envy gave."
   The poet waited a moment, then said to me,
   "Since he is silent, don't waste the time you have,

But speak, and ask him what you wish." And I:
   "You question him, and ask what you discern
   Would satisfy me; I cannot because of pity

That fills my heart." Therefore my guide began,
80   "For this man freely to do the thing you say,
   Imprisoned spirit, tell him if you can

And if it pleases you, in just what way
   The soul is bound in knots like these; give word
   Also, if any soul could be set free

From members such as these." It puffed air hard,
   And soon that exhalation became a voice.
   "You shall be answered briefly then," it uttered;

"When the fierce soul has quit the fleshly case
   It tore itself from, Minos sends it down
90   To the seventh depth. It falls to this wooded place—

No chosen spot, but where fortune flings it in—
   And there it sprouts like a grain of spelt, to shoot
   Up as a sapling, then a wild plant: and then

The Harpies, feeding on the foliage, create
   Pain, and an outlet for the pain as well.
   We too shall come like the rest, each one to get

Canto XIII / 133

Come l'altre verrem per nostre spoglie,
  ma non però ch'alcuna sen rivesta,
  ché non è giusto aver ciò ch'om si toglie.
Qui le strascineremo, e per la mesta
  selva saranno i nostri corpi appesi,
  ciascuno al prun de l'ombra sua molesta».
Noi eravamo ancora al tronco attesi,
110 credendo ch'altro ne volesse dire,
  quando noi fummo d'un romor sorpresi,
similemente a colui che venire
  sente 'l porco e la caccia a la sua posta,
  ch'ode le bestie, e le frasche stormire.
Ed ecco due da la sinistra costa,
  nudi e graffiati, fuggendo sì forte,
  che de la selva rompieno ogne rosta.
Quel dinanzi: «Or accorri, accorri, morte!».
  E l'altro, cui pareva tardar troppo,
120 gridava: «Lano, sì non furo accorte
le gambe tue a le giostre dal Toppo!».
  E poi che forse li fallìa la lena,
  di sé e d'un cespuglio fece un groppo.
Di rietro a loro era la selva piena
  di nere cagne, bramose e correnti
  come veltri ch'uscisser di catena.
In quel che s'appiattò miser li denti,
  e quel dilaceraro a brano a brano;
  poi sen portar quelle membra dolenti.
130 Presemi allor la mia scorta per mano,
  e menommi al cespuglio che piangea
  per le rotture sanguinenti in vano.
«O Iacopo», dicea, «da Santo Andrea,
  che t'è giovato di me fare schermo?
  che colpa ho io de la tua vita rea?».
Quando 'l maestro fu sovr' esso fermo,
  disse: «Chi fosti, che per tante punte
  soffi con sangue doloroso sermo?».

His cast-off body—but not for us to dwell
　　Within again, for justice must forbid
　　Having what one has robbed oneself of; still,

100　Here we shall drag them, and through the mournful wood
　　Our bodies will be hung: with every one
　　Fixed on the thornbush of its wounding shade."

We both were still attentive when it was done,
　　Thinking it might have more to say to us—
　　When an uproar surprised us, just as when

A hunter mindful of wild boar and the chase
　　Suddenly hears the beasts and crashing brush.
　　There on our left came two at a desperate pace,

Naked, torn, so hard pressed they seemed to crash
110　Headlong through every tangle the wood contained.
　　The one in front cried, "Come now, come in a rush,

O death!" The other shouted, falling behind,
　　"Your legs were not so nimble when you ran
　　At the jousting of the Toppo, Lano my friend!"

And then, perhaps because his breath began
　　To fail him, he stopped and hunched against a bush
　　As if to make himself and its branches one.

Behind them, eager as greyhounds off the leash,
　　Black bitches filled the woods, avid and quick.
120　They set their teeth on the one who stopped to crouch,

And tore his limbs apart; and then they took
　　The wretched members away. Then my escort
　　Led me by one hand to the bush—which spoke,

Grieving in vain through places where it was hurt
　　And bled: "Jacopo da Santo Andrea," it cried,
　　"What did you gain by shielding in me? What part

Had I in your sinful life?" My master said,
　　When he was standing above it, "And who were you,
　　Who through so many wounds exhale this blood

Ed elli a noi: «O anime che giunte
140   siete a veder lo strazio disonesto
c'ha le mie fronde sì da me disgiunte,
raccoglietele al piè del tristo cesto.
I' fui de la città che nel Batista
mutò 'l primo padrone; ond' ei per questo
sempre con l'arte sua la farà trista;
e se non fosse che 'n sul passo d'Arno
rimane ancor di lui alcuna vista,
que' cittadin che poi la rifondarno
sovra 'l cener che d'Attila rimase,
150   avrebber fatto lavorare indarno.
Io fei gibetto a me de le mie case».

Mixed with sad words?" It answered, "O souls—you two
   Who arrive to see this shameful havoc crush
   My leaves and tear them from me—gather them now,

And bring them to the foot of this wretched bush.
   In life I was of the city that chose to leave
   Mars, her first patron, and take the Baptist: for which

The art of Mars will always make her grieve.
   And if his semblance did not in part remain
   Still at the Arno, she would not survive—

And later, when they pitched the city again
   Over the ashes left by Attila, those
   Striving to refound it would have worked in vain.

And I—I made my own house be my gallows."

XIV

All over the sand
Distended flakes of fire drifted from aloft

Slowly as mountain snow without a wind.

(23–25)

Poi che la carità del natio loco
  mi strinse, raunai le fronde sparte
  e rende'le a colui, ch'era già fioco.
Indi venimmo al fine ove si parte
  lo secondo giron dal terzo, e dove
  si vede di giustizia orribil arte.
A ben manifestar le cose nove,
  dico che arrivammo ad una landa
  che dal suo letto ogne pianta rimove.
10 La dolorosa selva l'è ghirlanda
  intorno, come 'l fosso tristo ad essa;
  quivi fermammo i passi a randa a randa.
Lo spazzo era una rena arida e spessa,
  non d'altra foggia fatta che colei
  che fu da' piè di Caton già soppressa.
O vendetta di Dio, quanto tu dei
  esser temuta da ciascun che legge
  ciò che fu manifesto a li occhi mei!
D'anime nude vidi molte gregge
20 che piangean tutte assai miseramente,
  e parea posta lor diversa legge.
Supin giacea in terra alcuna gente,
  alcuna si sedea tutta raccolta,
  e altra andava continüamente.
Quella che giva 'ntorno era più molta,
  e quella men che giacëa al tormento,
  ma più al duolo avea la lingua sciolta.
Sovra tutto 'l sabbion, d'un cader lento,
  piovean di foco dilatate falde,
30 come di neve in alpe sanza vento.
Quali Alessandro in quelle parti calde
  d'Indïa vide sopra 'l süo stuolo
  fiamme cadere infino a terra salde,
per ch'ei provide a scalpitar lo suolo
  con le sue schiere, acciò che lo vapore
  mei si stingueva mentre ch'era solo:

Compelled by the love I bear my native place,
   I gathered the scattered sprays and gave them again
   To him who was already faint of voice.

From there we proceeded to the boundary line
   At which the third and second rings divide:
   And there a dreadful form of justice is seen.

To make these new things clear: we two now stood
   On a plain whose bed rejects all plants—bare, flat,
   Garlanded all around by the woeful wood

10 Just as the wood is by the sorrowful moat.
   And here we stayed our steps at the very edge.
   The ground was dry deep sand, resembling that

Which Cato trod. O vengeance of God, how much
   Should you be feared by all of those who read
   What my eyes saw! It was a great assemblage

Of naked souls in herds, all of whom mourned
   Most miserably and seemed to be subject
   To different laws. Some lay upon the ground,

Supine; some sat hunched up; while others walked
20   Restlessly about. It seemed that those who moved
   Were the more numerous, those who lay abject

In torment, fewest—but it was they who grieved
   With tongues most loosened by pain. All over the sand
   Distended flakes of fire drifted from aloft

Slowly as mountain snow without a wind.
   As when Alexander in India's hottest region
   Saw flames fall on his army, intact to the ground,

And had his soldiers tramp the accumulation
   To extinguish them before the fire could spread,
30   Eternal fire descended in such profusion

tale scendeva l'etternale ardore;
onde la rena s'accendea, com' esca
sotto focile, a doppiar lo dolore.

40 Sanza riposo mai era la tresca
de le misere mani, or quindi or quinci
escotendo da sé l'arsura fresca.

I' cominciai: «Maestro, tu che vinci
tutte le cose, fuor che ' demon duri
ch'a l'intrar de la porta incontra uscinci,

chi è quel grande che non par che curi
lo 'ncendio e giace dispettoso e torto,
sì che la pioggia non par che 'l maturi?».

E quel medesmo, che si fu accorto
50 ch'io domandava il mio duca di lui,
gridò: «Qual io fui vivo, tal son morto.

Se Giove stanchi 'l suo fabbro da cui
crucciato prese la folgore aguta
onde l'ultimo dì percosso fui;

o s'elli stanchi li altri a muta a muta
in Mongibello a la focina negra,
chiamando "Buon Vulcano, aiuta, aiuta!",

sì com' el fece a la pugna di Flegra,
e me saetti con tutta sua forza:
60 non ne potrebbe aver vendetta allegra».

Allora il duca mio parlò di forza
tanto, ch'i' non l'avea sì forte udito:
«O Capaneo, in ciò che non s'ammorza

la tua superbia, se' tu più punito;
nullo martiro, fuor che la tua rabbia,
sarebbe al tuo furor dolor compito».

Poi si rivolse a me con miglior labbia,
dicendo: «Quei fu l'un d'i sette regi
ch'assiser Tebe; ed ebbe e par ch'elli abbia

70 Dio in disdegno, e poco par che 'l pregi;
ma, com' io dissi lui, li suoi dispetti
sono al suo petto assai debiti fregi.

Or mi vien dietro, e guarda che non metti,
ancor, li piedi ne la rena arsiccia;
ma sempre al bosco tien li piedi stretti».

Tacendo divenimmo là 've spiccia
fuor de la selva un picciol fiumicello,
lo cui rossore ancor mi raccapriccia.

Sand kindled like tinder under flint, and made
  The pain redouble—with their dancing hands
  Not resting even for a moment they pawed

Themselves now here, now there, and beat the brands
  Of fresh fire off. "O Master," I began,
  "Who vanquish all except the stubborn fiends

That opposed us at the gate: who is that one,
  The great one seeming to pay no heed to the fire,
  Who lies disdainful and scowling, so that the rain

40 Seems not to ripen him?" He appeared to hear
  Me ask about him, and shouted, "What I was
  Alive, I am in death! Though Jove may wear

His smith out, from whom anger made him seize
  The sharpened bolt that smote me my last day;
  And though he wears out every smith he has

At Mongibello's black forge; and though he cry,
  'Help, help, good Vulcan!' just the way he did
  Amid the battle of Phlegra, and hurl at me

With all his might—he still will not have had
50 The pleasure of his vengeance." Then my guide
  Spoke with more force than I had heard, and said,

"O Capaneus, that this unquenched pride
  Remains in you just punishes you the more:
  No torment but this raging of yours could goad

With agony enough to match your ire."
  Then gentler, to me: "He was one of seven kings
  Who besieged Thebes, and bore—seems still to bear—

Disdain for God. But as I said, his revilings
  Earn his breast fitting badges. Now follow my steps:
60 Tread, not the scorching sand, but a path that clings

Close to the wood." In silence we reached a place
  Where gushing from the woods a small stream poured
  So red that it still makes me shudder. As issues

Quale del Bulicame esce ruscello
che parton poi tra lor le peccatrici,
tal per la rena giù sen giva quello.
Lo fondo suo e ambo le pendici
fatt' era 'n pietra, e ' margini dallato;
per ch'io m'accorsi che 'l passo era lici.
«Tra tutto l'altro ch'i' t'ho dimostrato,
poscia che noi intrammo per la porta
lo cui sogliare a nessuno è negato,
cosa non fu da li tuoi occhi scorta
notabile com' è 'l presente rio,
che sovra sé tutte fiammelle ammorta».
Queste parole fuor del duca mio;
per ch'io 'l pregai che mi largisse 'l pasto
di cui largito m'avëa il disio.
«In mezzo mar siede un paese guasto»,
diss' elli allora, «che s'appella Creta,
sotto 'l cui rege fu già 'l mondo casto.
Una montagna v'è che già fu lieta
d'acqua e di fronde, che si chiamò Ida;
or è diserta come cosa vieta.
Rëa la scelse già per cuna fida
del suo figliuolo, e per celarlo meglio,
quando piangea, vi facea far le grida.
Dentro dal monte sta dritto un gran veglio,
che tien volte le spalle inver' Dammiata
e Roma guarda come süo speglio.
La sua testa è di fin oro formata,
e puro argento son le braccia e 'l petto,
poi è di rame infino a la forcata;
da indi in giuso è tutto ferro eletto,
salvo che 'l destro piede è terra cotta;
e sta 'n su quel, più che 'n su l'altro, eretto.
Ciascuna parte, fuor che l'oro, è rotta
d'una fessura che lagrime goccia,
le quali, accolte, fóran quella grotta.

That stream from Bulicame that is shared
   Among the prostitutes, so this brook flowed
   Down and across the sand. It was stone-floored;

Stone lined both banks and the margins on each side;
   And I could see that this would be our route.
   "In all that I have shown you," my master said,

70 "Since first we entered through that open gate
   Whose threshold no one ever is denied,
   Nothing your eyes have seen is so worth note

As this present stream which quenches in its flood
   All of the flames above it." So word for word
   My master spoke, and I asked him for the food

To fill the appetite these words inspired.
   He answered, "In the middle of the sea
   Lies a waste land called Crete, a realm whose lord

Governed the world in its age of purity.
80   The mountain Ida is there, which once was glad
   With foliage and waters, and now must lie

Deserted, like some worn thing by time decayed.
   Long ago Rhea chose it for her child
   As his safe cradle; and since they had to hide,

Made all there shout whenever her infant wailed.
   Within the mountain stands an immense Old Man,
   Who turns his back toward Damietta, to hold

His gaze on Rome as on his mirror: of fine
   Gold is his head, pure silver his arms and breast;
90   Down to the fork is brass, and from there down

The choicest iron comprises all the rest
   But the right foot, of clay baked hard as brick:
   On it, more weight than on the left is pressed.

Every part but the gold head bears a crack,
   A fissure dripping tears that collect and force
   Their passage down the cavern from rock to rock

Canto XIV / 145

Lor corso in questa valle si diroccia;
  fanno Acheronte, Stige e Flegetonta;
  poi sen van giù per questa stretta doccia,
infin, là dove più non si dismonta,
  fanno Cocito; e qual sia quello stagno
120   tu lo vedrai, però qui non si conta».
E io a lui: «Se 'l presente rigagno
  si diriva così dal nostro mondo,
  perché ci appar pur a questo vivagno?».
Ed elli a me: «Tu sai che 'l loco è tondo;
  e tutto che tu sie venuto molto,
  pur a sinistra, giù calando al fondo,
non se' ancor per tutto 'l cerchio vòlto;
  per che, se cosa n'apparisce nova,
  non de' addur maraviglia al tuo volto».
130 E io ancor: «Maestro, ove si trova
  Flegetonta e Letè? ché de l'un taci,
  e l'altro di' che si fa d'esta piova».
«In tutte tue question certo mi piaci»,
  rispuose, «ma 'l bollor de l'acqua rossa
  dovea ben solver l'una che tu faci.
Letè vedrai, ma fuor di questa fossa,
  là dove vanno l'anime a lavarsi
  quando la colpa pentuta è rimossa».
Poi disse: «Omai è tempo da scostarsi
140   dal bosco; fa che di retro a me vegne:
  li margini fan via, che non son arsi,
e sopra loro ogne vapor si spegne».

Into this valley's depth, where as a source
    They form the Acheron, Styx, and Phlegethon.
    Then their way down is by this narrow course

100 Until, where all descending has been done,
    They form Cocytus—and about that pool
    I shall say nothing, for you will see it soon."

And I to him: "But if this stream does fall
    Thus from our world, then why does it appear
    At only this border?" And he: "As you know well,

The place is round; although you have come far,
    Toward the pit by left turns always down,
    You haven't completed all the circle: therefore,

If anything new appears that we haven't seen,
110   It should not bring amazement to your face."
    And I said, "Where are Lethe and Phlegethon?

For you are silent regarding one of these,
    And say the rain of tears creates the other."
    He: "All your questions please me; but in one case

The boiling of this red water should give the answer.
    Lethe you shall see, but out of this abyss:
    There where, repented guilt removed, souls gather

To cleanse themselves." Then, "Now it is time for us
    To leave the wood. The margins are not afire,
120   And make a pathway—over them, come close

Behind me: every flame is extinguished here."

XV

"*If any of this flock, O son,*

Stops even for an instant, he must lie still
 A hundred years, not brushing off the fire
 That strikes him. Go, then: I'll follow at your heel . . ."

(33–36)

Ora cen porta l'un de' duri margini;
  e 'l fummo del ruscel di sopra aduggia,
  sì che dal foco salva l'acqua e li argini.
Qual i Fiamminghi tra Guizzante e Bruggia,
  temendo 'l fiotto che 'nver' lor s'avventa,
  fanno lo schermo perché 'l mar si fuggia;
e qual i Padoan lungo la Brenta,
  per difender lor ville e lor castelli,
  anzi che Carentana il caldo senta:
10 a tale imagine eran fatti quelli,
  tutto che né sì alti né sì grossi,
  qual che si fosse, lo maestro félli.
Già eravam da la selva rimossi
  tanto, ch'i' non avrei visto dov' era,
  perch' io in dietro rivolto mi fossi,
quando incontrammo d'anime una schiera
  che venian lungo l'argine, e ciascuna
  ci riguardava come suol da sera
guardare uno altro sotto nuova luna;
20 e sì ver' noi aguzzavan le ciglia
  come 'l vecchio sartor fa ne la cruna.
Così adocchiato da cotal famiglia,
  fui conosciuto da un, che mi prese
  per lo lembo e gridò: «Qual maraviglia!».
E io, quando 'l suo braccio a me distese,
  ficcaï li occhi per lo cotto aspetto,
  sì che 'l viso abbrusciato non difese
la conoscenza süa al mio 'ntelletto;
  e chinando la mano a la sua faccia,
30 rispuosi: «Siete voi qui, ser Brunetto?».
E quelli: «O figliuol mio, non ti dispiaccia
  se Brunetto Latino un poco teco
  ritorna 'n dietro e lascia andar la traccia».

Now the firm margin bears us, under the vapor
   Rising from the stream to form a shade and fend
   The fire off, sheltering both banks and water.

As Flemings between Wissant and Bruges, to defend
   Against the tide that rushes in on them,
   Construct a bulwark to drive the sea from land;

And Paduans on the Brenta do, to stem
   The water and protect their castle and town
   Before Carentana feels the heat—in the same

10 Manner those banks were made, except the one
   Who built them did not make them as high or thick,
   Whoever he was. And I could not have seen

The wood that lay behind us, had I looked back,
   When we encountered another troop of souls
   Who looked at us the way that men will look

At one another at dusk, when daylight fails
   Under a new moon: knitting their brows at us
   The way old tailors do when threading needles.

While I was being examined by them thus,
20   One recognized me, and took me by the hem,
   Crying, "Why what a marvel!" I fixed my eyes

On his scorched face as he reached out his arm,
   And the baked features I saw did not forestall
   My knowing him—I reached back down to him,

My hand toward his face, and answered his call:
   "Are you here, Ser Brunetto?" He replied,
   "My son, may it not displease you, if awhile

Brunetto Latini turns back to walk instead
   With you a little, and lets the train go on."
30   "I beg it of you with all my heart," I said—

I' dissi lui: «Quanto posso, ven preco;
   e se volete che con voi m'asseggia,
   faròl, se piace a costui che vo seco».
«O figliuol», disse, «qual di questa greggia
   s'arresta punto, giace poi cent' anni
   sanz' arrostarsi quando 'l foco il feggia.
40 Però va oltre: i' ti verrò a' panni;
   e poi rigiugnerò la mia masnada,
   che va piangendo i suoi etterni danni».
Io non osava scender de la strada
   per andar par di lui; ma 'l capo chino
   tenea com' uom che reverente vada.
El cominciò: «Qual fortuna o destino
   anzi l'ultimo dì qua giù ti mena?
   e chi è questi che mostra 'l cammino?».
«Là sù di sopra, in la vita serena»,
50 rispuos' io lui, «mi smarri' in una valle,
   avanti che l'età mia fosse piena.
Pur ier mattina le volsi le spalle:
   questi m'apparve, tornand' ïo in quella,
   e reducemi a ca per questo calle».
Ed elli a me: «Se tu segui tua stella,
   non puoi fallire a glorïoso porto,
   se ben m'accorsi ne la vita bella;
e s'io non fossi sì per tempo morto,
   veggendo il cielo a te così benigno,
60 dato t'avrei a l'opera conforto.
Ma quello ingrato popolo maligno
   che discese di Fiesole ab antico,
   e tiene ancor del monte e del macigno,
ti si farà, per tuo ben far, nimico;
   ed è ragion, ché tra li lazzi sorbi
   si disconvien fruttare al dolce fico.
Vecchia fama nel mondo li chiama orbi;
   gent' è avara, invidiosa e superba:
   dai lor costumi fa che tu ti forbi.

"And should you prefer that you and I sit down,
    If it pleases him with whom I go, I will."
    He said, "If any of this flock, O son,

Stops even for an instant, he must lie still
    A hundred years, not brushing off the fire
    That strikes him. Go, then: I'll follow at your heel,

And then rejoin my band who walk in a choir
    Lamenting their eternal woes." Afraid
    To step down to his level from where we were,

40 I bent my head, as in reverence. He said,
    "What destiny or fortune makes you come
    Before your final day; and who is this guide?"

"In the bright life above," I answered him,
    "I came into a valley and lost my way,
    Before my age had reached its ripening time—

I turned my back on the place but yesterday.
    He appeared to me at dawn, when I had turned
    To go back down, and this path is the way

By which he leads me home." Then he returned:
50   "If you keep navigating by your star
    You'll find a glorious port, if I discerned

Well in the fair life. Had my years been more,
    So I could witness how heaven has been kind
    To you, I would have wished your work good cheer.

But that ungrateful, malignant folk who descend
    From those brought down from Fiesole long ago,
    And who still smack of mountains and rocky ground,

Will make themselves, for good things that you do,
    Your enemies—and there is reason in that:
60   Among the bitter sorb-trees, it seems undue

When the sweet fig in season comes to fruit.
    The world's old saying is that they are blind:
    A people greedy, envious, proud—see fit

70 La tua fortuna tanto onor ti serba,
   che l'una parte e l'altra avranno fame
   di te; ma lungi fia dal becco l'erba.
Faccian le bestie fiesolane strame
   di lor medesme, e non tocchin la pianta,
   s'alcuna surge ancora in lor letame,
in cui riviva la sementa santa
   di que' Roman che vi rimaser quando
   fu fatto il nido di malizia tanta».
«Se fosse tutto pieno il mio dimando»,
80   rispuos' io lui, «voi non sareste ancora
   de l'umana natura posto in bando;
ché 'n la mente m'è fitta, e or m'accora,
   la cara e buona imagine paterna
   di voi quando nel mondo ad ora ad ora
m'insegnavate come l'uom s'etterna:
   e quant' io l'abbia in grado, mentr' io vivo
   convien che ne la mia lingua si scerna.
Ciò che narrate di mio corso scrivo,
   e serbolo a chiosar con altro testo
90   a donna che saprà, s'a lei arrivo.
Tanto vogl' io che vi sia manifesto,
   pur che mia coscïenza non mi garra,
   ch'a la Fortuna, come vuol, son presto.
Non è nuova a li orecchi miei tal arra:
   però giri Fortuna la sua rota
   come le piace, e 'l villan la sua marra».
Lo mio maestro allora in su la gota
   destra si volse in dietro e riguardommi;
   poi disse: «Bene ascolta chi la nota».

To cleanse their habits from yourself. You'll find
　　Your fortune holds such honor as will induce
　　One party and the other to contend

In hunger to consume you—then the grass
　　Will be well kept at a distance from the goat.
　　Let the Fiesolan beasts go find their mess

70　By feeding on themselves, and spare the shoot
　　(If any still should grow on their heap of dung)
　　In which the sacred seed is living yet

Of Romans who remained when Florence went wrong,
　　Becoming a nest for the malevolent."
　　"Could I have everything for which I long,

You would not still endure this banishment
　　Away from human nature," I replied.
　　"Your image—dear, fatherly, benevolent—

Being fixed inside my memory, has imbued
80　My heart: when in the fair world, hour by hour
　　You taught me, patiently, it was you who showed

The way man makes himself eternal; therefore,
　　The gratitude I feel toward you makes fit
　　That while I live, I should declare it here.

And what you tell me of my future, I write—
　　And keep it with another text as well,
　　Till both are glossed by a lady of good wit

And knowledge, if I reach her. This much still
　　I say: so long as conscience is not betrayed,
90　I am prepared for Fortune to do her will.

My ears find nothing strange in what you have said:
　　As Fortune pleases let her wheel be turned,
　　And as he must let the peasant turn his spade."

When he heard these words my master's head inclined
　　Toward the right, and looking at me he said,
　　"He who has listened well will understand."

100 *Né per tanto di men parlando vommi*
con ser Brunetto, e dimando chi sono
li suoi compagni più noti e più sommi.
Ed elli a me: «Saper d'alcuno è buono;
de li altri fia laudabile tacerci,
ché 'l tempo saria corto a tanto suono.
In somma sappi che tutti fur cherci
e litterati grandi e di gran fama,
d'un peccato medesmo al mondo lerci.
Priscian sen va con quella turba grama,
110 *e Francesco d'Accorso anche; e vedervi,*
s'avessi avuto di tal tigna brama,
colui potei che dal servo de' servi
fu trasmutato d'Arno in Bacchiglione,
dove lasciò li mal protesi nervi.
Di più direi; ma 'l venire e 'l sermone
più lungo esser non può, però ch'i' veggio
là surger nuovo fummo del sabbione.
Gente vien con la quale esser non deggio.
Sieti raccomandato il mio Tesoro,
120 *nel qual io vivo ancora, e più non cheggio».*
Poi si rivolse, e parve di coloro
che corrono a Verona il drappo verde
per la campagna; e parve di costoro
quelli che vince, non colui che perde.

And none the less I continued as I had
    In speech with Ser Brunetto—would he tell
    Which among his companions had enjoyed

100 Most eminence and fame in life? "It is well,"
    He answered, "for me to say the names of some
    But nothing of the rest. To name them all

Would demand speaking more words than we have time—
    All clerics and men of letters, all renowned,
    And in the world all stained by this one crime.

Priscian trudges in that unhappy band,
    As does Francesco d'Accorso. And if you crave
    To see such scurf, among them you can find

One whom the Servant of Servants asked to leave
110 The Arno for Bacchiglione; and there
    He left his body, distended in its nerve

And muscle. And now, although I would say more,
    My speech and walking with you must be brief:
    On the sand, I see new smoke rise, where appear

New souls, with whom I must not be. I live
    In my *Tesoro*—your judgment being won
    For it, I ask no more." And he went off,

Seeming to me like one of those who run
    Competing for the green cloth in the races
120 Upon Verona's field—and of them, like one

Who gains the victory, not one who loses.

XVI

We stopped; the three

Resumed their old lament—and when they had raced
Up to us, linked their bodies in a wheel.

(15–17)

Già era in loco onde s'udia 'l rimbombo
de l'acqua che cadea ne l'altro giro,
simile a quel che l'arnie fanno rombo,
quando tre ombre insieme si partiro,
correndo, d'una torma che passava
sotto la pioggia de l'aspro martiro.
Venian ver' noi, e ciascuna gridava:
«Sòstati tu ch'a l'abito ne sembri
esser alcun di nostra terra prava».
10 Ahimè, che piaghe vidi ne' lor membri,
ricenti e vecchie, da le fiamme incese!
Ancor men duol pur ch'i' me ne rimembri.
A le lor grida, il mio dottor s'attese;
volse 'l viso ver' me, e «Or aspetta»,
disse, «a costor si vuole esser cortese.
E se non fosse il foco che saetta
la natura del loco, i' dicerei
che meglio stesse a te che a lor la fretta».
Ricominciar, come noi restammo, ei
20 l'antico verso; e quando a noi fuor giunti,
fenno una rota di sé tutti e trei.
Qual sogliono i campion far nudi e unti,
avvisando lor presa e lor vantaggio,
prima che sien tra lor battuti e punti,
così rotando, ciascuno il visaggio
drizzava a me, sì che 'n contraro il collo
faceva ai piè continüo vïaggio.
E «Se miseria d'esto loco sollo
rende in dispetto noi e nostri prieghi»,
30 cominciò l'uno, «e 'l tinto aspetto e brollo,
la fama nostra il tuo animo pieghi
a dirne chi tu se', che i vivi piedi
così sicuro per lo 'nferno freghi.
Questi, l'orme di cui pestar mi vedi,
tutto che nudo e dipelato vada,
fu di grado maggior che tu non credi:

I was already where we heard the noise
   Of water winding downward as it spilled
   To the next circle with a sound like bees,

When three shades bolted from a troop that filed
   Under the rain of torment. Running toward us,
   They cried: "Stop here, O you who are appareled

Like one in our own degenerate city's dress."
   Ah me!—what wounds both old and new I saw
   Where flames had burned their limbs: the same distress

10 Pains me again when I recall it now.
   My teacher heeded their cries, then faced me to say,
   "Now wait a little: to these three, one should show

Courtesy. Were it not for the fire let fly
   By the nature of this place, I'd say such haste
   Befits you more than them." We stopped; the three

Resumed their old lament—and when they had raced
   Up to us, linked their bodies in a wheel.
   As champions, naked and oiled, before the thrust

And parry begin, will eye their grip and circle
20   Seeking advantage, so each directed his face
   Toward me, turning his neck against the pull

Of the ever-moving feet. "If our sandy place
   Of squalor and charred features scorched of hair,"
   One of them said, "lead you to show to us,

And what we ask, contempt—may our fame inspire
   You to inform us who you are who pass
   Through Hell with living footsteps. This man here,

Whose tracks you see me trample, though he goes
   Naked and peeled was of a rank more high
30   Than you suppose: his noble grandmother was

nepote fu de la buona Gualdrada;
   Guido Guerra ebbe nome, e in sua vita
   fece col senno assai e con la spada.
40 L'altro, ch'appresso me la rena trita,
   è Tegghiaio Aldobrandi, la cui voce
   nel mondo sù dovria esser gradita.
E io, che posto son con loro in croce,
   Iacopo Rusticucci fui, e certo
   la fiera moglie più ch'altro mi nuoce».
S'i' fossi stato dal foco coperto,
   gittato mi sarei tra lor di sotto,
   e credo che 'l dottor l'avria sofferto;
ma perch' io mi sarei brusciato e cotto,
50   vinse paura la mia buona voglia
   che di loro abbracciar mi facea ghiotto.
Poi cominciai: «Non dispetto, ma doglia
   la vostra condizion dentro mi fisse,
   tanta che tardi tutta si dispoglia,
tosto che questo mio segnor mi disse
   parole per le quali i' mi pensai
   che qual voi siete, tal gente venisse.
Di vostra terra sono, e sempre mai
   l'ovra di voi e li onorati nomi
60   con affezion ritrassi e ascoltai.
Lascio lo fele e vo per dolci pomi
   promessi a me per lo verace duca;
   ma 'nfino al centro pria convien ch'i' tomi».
«Se lungamente l'anima conduca
   le membra tue», rispuose quelli ancora,
   «e se la fama tua dopo te luca,
cortesia e valor dì se dimora
   ne la nostra città sì come suole,
   o se del tutto se n'è gita fora;
70 ché Guglielmo Borsiere, il qual si duole
   con noi per poco e va là coi compagni,
   assai ne cruccia con le sue parole».

The good Gualdrada; his own name used to be
   Guido Guerra, and in his life he attained
   Much with his counsel and his sword. And he

Who treads the sand behind my feet is named
   Tegghiaio Aldobrandi, a man whose voice
   The world should more have prized. And I, condemned

With them, am Jacopo Rusticucci, whose fierce
   Wife more than anything brought me wretchedness."
   Could I be shielded from the fire, at this

40 I would have thrown myself down into the fosse
   Among them—and so my teacher would permit,
   I think; but knowing how that fiery place

Would burn and bake me, fear drained the appetite
   My good will gave me to embrace them. I said,
   "No: it was not contempt but sorrow I felt

At your condition—inscribed so deep inside
   It will not leave me soon—when this my lord
   Spoke words to me which I knew prophesied

Such men as you were coming. I always heard
50 (Since I am of your city), and have told over
   Lovingly, your names and actions, both revered.

I leave the bitter gall behind, and aspire
   Toward the sweet fruits promised by my guide,
   But first I must go downward to the core."

"As your soul long may guide your limbs," he said,
   "With your fame shining after you: so tell
   If courtesy and valor still abide

Within our city, where they used to dwell.
   Or are they gone from it entirely now—
60 By Guglielmo Borsiere, who came to Hell

Only a short time past, whom you see go
   Among our legion, we have heard things said
   That cause us much affliction." "Newcomers to you,

«La gente nuova e i sùbiti guadagni
  orgoglio e dismisura han generata,
  Fiorenza, in te, sì che tu già ten piagni».
Così gridai con la faccia levata;
  e i tre, che ciò inteser per risposta,
  guardar l'un l'altro com' al ver si guata.
«Se l'altre volte sì poco ti costa»,
80 rispuoser tutti, «il satisfare altrui,
  felice te se sì parli a tua posta!
Però, se campi d'esti luoghi bui
  e torni a riveder le belle stelle,
  quando ti gioverà dicere "I' fui",
fa che di noi a la gente favelle».
  Indi rupper la rota, e a fuggirsi
  ali sembiar le gambe loro isnelle.
Un amen non saria possuto dirsi
  tosto così com' e' fuoro spariti;
90 per ch'al maestro parve di partirsi.
Io lo seguiva, e poco eravam iti,
  che 'l suon de l'acqua n'era sì vicino,
  che per parlar saremmo a pena uditi.
Come quel fiume c'ha proprio cammino
  prima dal Monte Viso 'nver' levante,
  da la sinistra costa d'Apennino,
che si chiama Acquacheta suso, avante
  che si divalli giù nel basso letto,
  e a Forlì di quel nome è vacante,
100 rimbomba là sovra San Benedetto
  de l'Alpe per cadere ad una scesa
  ove dovria per mille esser recetto;
così, giù d'una ripa discoscesa,
  trovammo risonar quell'acqua tinta,
  sì che 'n poc' ora avria l'orecchia offesa.
Io avea una corda intorno cinta,
  e con essa pensai alcuna volta
  prender la lonza a la pelle dipinta.
Poscia ch'io l'ebbi tutta da me sciolta,
110 sì come 'l duca m'avea comandato,
  porsila a lui aggroppata e ravvolta.

O Florence, and sudden profits, have led to pride
   And excess that you already mourn!" I spoke
   With face uplifted; the three, who understood,

Then looked at one another with the look
   Of men who hear the truth. "If times occur,"
   They all replied, "when it again will take

70   So little effort to answer another's desire,
   Count yourself happy speaking as you wish.
   Therefore, if you escape from this dark sphere

To see the beauty of the stars, and relish
   The pleasure then of saying, 'I was there'—
   Speak word of us to others." Then in a rush

They broke their wheel, and as they fled, the blur
   Of legs resembled wings; it took less time
   Than saying "Amen" for them to disappear.

And then my master left, I after him;
80   And we had traveled but a little distance
   Before the sound of falling water came

From so near we could scarcely hear our voices.
   As the river which is first to carve its course
   East down the Apennines from Viso's sources—

Called Acquacheta up high, before it pours
   To its low bed at Forlì—clears the spine
   Above San Benedetto dell'Alpe and roars

In a single cataract that might have been
   A thousand; just so, down a precipitous bank,
90   Dark water drummed so loudly it would pain

Our ears before much longer. I had a hank
   Of cord wrapped round me—with it I had planned
   To take the leopard with the painted flank;

I loosed it from me at my master's command
   And passed it to him, knotted and coiled up.
   Turning to the right he flung it from his hand

Ond' ei si volse inver' lo destro lato,
    e alquanto di lunge da la sponda
    la gittò giuso in quell'alto burrato.
'E' pur convien che novità risponda',
    dicea fra me medesmo, 'al novo cenno
    che 'l maestro con l'occhio sì seconda'.
Ahi quanto cauti li uomini esser dienno
    presso a color che non veggion pur l'ovra,
120   ma per entro i pensier miran col senno!
El disse a me: «Tosto verrà di sovra
    ciò ch'io attendo e che il tuo pensier sogna;
    tosto convien ch'al tuo viso si scovra».
Sempre a quel ver c'ha faccia di menzogna
    de' l'uom chiuder le labbra fin ch'el puote,
    però che sanza colpa fa vergogna;
ma qui tacer nol posso; e per le note
    di questa comedìa, lettor, ti giuro,
    s'elle non sien di lunga grazia vòte.
130   ch'i' vidi per quell' aere grosso e scuro
    venir notando una figura in suso,
    maravigliosa ad ogne cor sicuro,
sì come torna colui che va giuso
    talora a solver l'àncora ch'aggrappa
    o scoglio o altro che nel mare è chiuso,
che 'n sù si stende e da piè si rattrappa.

Some distance off the edge and down the slope,
  Into the depth of the abyss. I thought,
  "Some strangeness surely will answer from the deep

100 The strange signal the master just set out,
  And follows so attentively with his eye"—
  One must take care with those who have the wit

Not only to observe the action, but see
  The thought as well! For, "Soon now will arise
  The thing I look for: soon," he said to me,

"What your mind dreams will be before your eyes."
  A man should close his lips, if he's able to,
  When faced by truth that has the face of lies,

But here I cannot be silent; reader, I vow
110 By my *Commedia*'s lines—so may they not fail
  Of lasting favor—that as I was peering through

That murky air, a shape swam up to instill
  Amazement in the firmest heart: a thing
  Rising the way a man who dives to pull

His anchor free from shoals it is caught among,
  Or something else hidden in the sea, with feet
  Drawn in beneath him, surges—surfacing

Back from the deep with both arms held up straight.

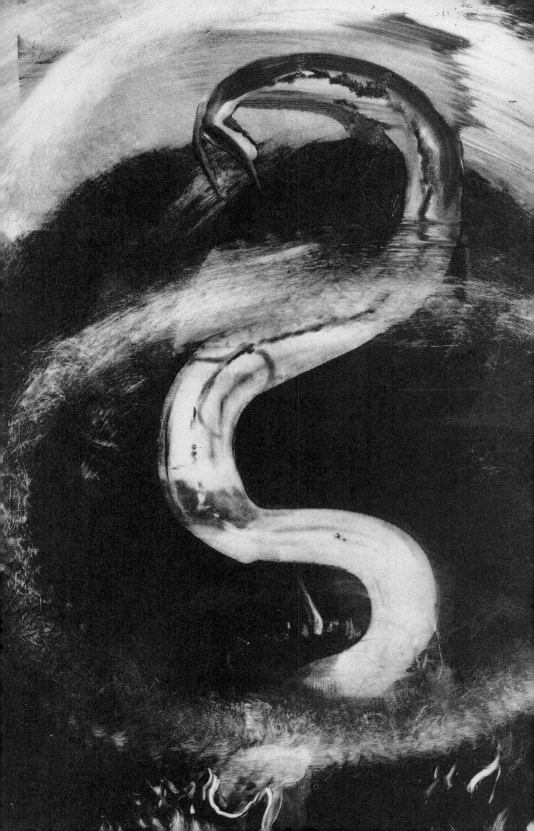

XVII

>   . . . *I saw*
> *Nothing at all around me but the beast.*
> *Onward he swam with motion more and more slow*
>
> *As he wheeled round descending; but that I guessed*
> *Only by feeling the wind against my face . . .*

(103–7)

«Ecco la fiera con la coda aguzza,
  che passa i monti e rompe i muri e l'armi!
  Ecco colei che tutto 'l mondo appuzza!».
Sì cominciò lo mio duca a parlarmi;
  e accennolle che venisse a proda,
  vicino al fin d'i passeggiati marmi.
E quella sozza imagine di froda
  sen venne, e arrivò la testa e 'l busto,
  ma 'n su la riva non trasse la coda.
10 La faccia sua era faccia d'uom giusto,
  tanto benigna avea di fuor la pelle,
  e d'un serpente tutto l'altro fusto;
due branche avea pilose insin l'ascelle;
  lo dosso e 'l petto e ambedue le coste
  dipinti avea di nodi e di rotelle.
Con più color, sommesse e sovraposte
  non fer mai drappi Tartari né Turchi,
  né fuor tai tele per Aragne imposte.
Come talvolta stanno a riva i burchi,
20 che parte sono in acqua e parte in terra,
  e come là tra li Tedeschi lurchi
lo bivero s'assetta a far sua guerra,
  così la fiera pessima si stava
  su l'orlo che di pietra il sabbion serra.
Nel vano tutta sua coda guizzava,
  torcendo in sù la venenosa forca
  ch'a guisa di scorpion la punta armava.
Lo duca disse: «Or convien che si torca
  la nostra via un poco insino a quella
30 bestia malvagia che colà si corca».
Però scendemmo a la destra mammella,
  e diece passi femmo in su lo stremo,
  per ben cessar la rena e la fiammella.
E quando noi a lei venuti semo,
  poco più oltre veggio in su la rena
  gente seder propinqua al loco scemo.

"Behold the beast that has the pointed tail,
   That crosses mountains, leaves walls and weapons broken,
   And makes the stench of which the world is full!"

So did my leader address me, then paused to beckon
   Him ashore near where the causeway came to an end.
   And fraud's foul emblem came closer, till he had taken

His head and chest from the deep to rest on land
   Before us, not drawing his tail up onto the bank.
   His face was a just man's face, outwardly kind,

10 And he was like a serpent all down his trunk.
   He had two paws, both hairy to the armpits;
   His back and breast and both sides down to the shank

Were painted with designs of knots and circlets.
   No Tartar or Turk has ever woven a cloth
   More colored in field and figure, nor were the nets

Arachne loomed. The way beached boats are both
   On land and partly in water, or the way
   The beaver squats to battle fish to the death

In the deep-drinking Germans' land—so lay
20   That worst of beasts upon the edge of stone
   That bounds the sand. His tail was quivery

And restless in the void where it hung down
   Squirming its venomed fork with an upward twist,
   Armed like a scorpion. "Now we must incline

Our path a little—as far as the evil beast
   That crouches over there," my master said.
   So we descended on the right, and paced

Ten steps along the edge to keep well wide
   Of sand and flames. Coming to where he was,
30   I saw on the sand just on from where we stood

Quivi 'l maestro «Acciò che tutta piena
esperïenza d'esto giron porti»,
mi disse, «va, e vedi la lor mena.

40 Li tuoi ragionamenti sian là corti;
mentre che torni, parlerò con questa,
che ne conceda i suoi omeri forti».

Così ancor su per la strema testa
di quel settimo cerchio tutto solo
andai, dove sedea la gente mesta.

Per li occhi fora scoppiava lor duolo;
di qua, di là soccorrien con le mani
quando a' vapori, e quando al caldo suolo:

non altrimenti fan di state i cani
50 or col ceffo or col piè, quando son morsi
o da pulci o da mosche o da tafani.

Poi che nel viso a certi li occhi porsi,
ne' quali 'l doloroso foco casca,
non ne conobbi alcun; ma io m'accorsi

che dal collo a ciascun pendea una tasca
ch'avea certo colore e certo segno,
e quindi par che 'l loro occhio si pasca.

E com' io riguardando tra lor vegno,
in una borsa gialla vidi azzurro
60 che d'un leone avea faccia e contegno.

Poi, procedendo di mio sguardo il curro,
vidine un'altra come sangue rossa,
mostrando un'oca bianca più che burro.

E un che d'una scrofa azzurra e grossa
segnato avea lo suo sacchetto bianco,
mi disse: «Che fai tu in questa fossa?

Or te ne va; e perché se' vivo anco,
sappi che 'l mio vicin Vitalïano
sederà qui dal mio sinistro fianco.

70 Con questi Fiorentin son padoano:
spesse fïate mi 'ntronan li orecchi
gridando: "Vegna 'l cavalier sovrano,

Some people sitting near the open space.
    The master said, "To experience this ring
    Fully, go forward: learn what their state is,

But let your conversation not be long.
    Till you return, I'll parley with this beast,
    So we may borrow his shoulders." I went along

The seventh circle's margin alone, and passed
    To where those doleful people sat. Their woes
    Burst from their eyes, their hands were doing their best

40 To shield them from the torments, shifting place
    From here to there—one moment from falling flames,
    The next, the burning ground: just like the ways

Of dogs in summer when they scratch, sometimes
    With paw and others with muzzle, they behaved
    As though fleas or flies or gadflies bit their limbs.

When I grew closer to the people grieved
    By the flames falling on them, I did not find
    Any I recognized, but I perceived

Each had a purse hung round his neck—adorned
50   With certain colors and a certain device,
    Which each of them with hungry eyes consumed.

Looking among them, I saw a yellow purse
    That bore a lion in azure. Looking farther,
    I saw another, blood-red, that showed a goose

Depicted in a color whiter than butter.
    Then one of them—whose wallet, which was white,
    Displayed a pregnant sow portrayed in azure—

Said to me: "What are you doing in this pit?
    Be off with you! And since you are living, know
60   My neighbor Vitaliano will come to sit

Here on my left. These Florentines din me so
    Because I am a Paduan; often they cry,
    'Bring on the sovereign knight whose sack will show

che recherà la tasca con tre becchi!"'».
   Qui distorse la bocca e di fuor trasse
   la lingua, come bue che 'l naso lecchi.
  E io, temendo no 'l più star crucciasse
   lui che di poco star m'avea 'mmonito,
   torna'mi in dietro da l'anime lasse.
  Trova' il duca mio ch'era salito
80   già su la groppa del fiero animale,
   e disse a me: «Or sie forte e ardito.
  Omai si scende per sì fatte scale;
   monta dinanzi, ch'i' voglio esser mezzo,
   sì che la coda non possa far male».
  Qual è colui che sì presso ha 'l riprezzo
   de la quartana, c'ha già l'unghie smorte,
   e triema tutto pur guardando 'l rezzo,
  tal divenn' io a le parole porte;
   ma vergogna mi fé le sue minacce,
90   che innanzi a buon segnor fa servo forte.
  I' m'assettai in su quelle spallacce;
   sì volli dir, ma la voce non venne
   com' io credetti: «Fa che tu m'abbracce».
  Ma esso, ch'altra volta mi sovvenne
   ad altro forse, tosto ch'i' montai
   con le braccia m'avvinse e mi sostenne;
  e disse: «Gerïon, moviti omai:
   le rote larghe, e lo scender sia poco;
100   pensa la nova soma che tu hai».
  Come la navicella esce di loco
   in dietro in dietro, sì quindi si tolse;
   e poi ch'al tutto si sentì a gioco,
  là 'v' era 'l petto, la coda rivolse,
   e quella tesa, come anguilla, mosse,
   e con le branche l'aere a sé raccolse.

Three goats!' " With that, he twisted his mouth awry
   In a perverse grimace, and like an ox
   Licking its nose, thrust out his tongue at me.

Then, fearing that a longer stay might vex
   Him who had cautioned that the time I spent
   With them be brief, I left those worn-out souls—

70 And found my leader already on our mount,
   Seated upon that savage creature's back.
   He said, "Be bold and strong; for now the descent

Must be by such a stairway. The place you take
   Should be in front, so I can come between
   To protect you from the tail." Like those who shake,

Feeling the quartan fever coming on—
   Their nails already blue, so that they shiver
   At the mere sight of shade—such I was then;

But shame rebuked me, which makes a servant braver
80   In a good master's presence. I took my seat
   Upon those ugly shoulders. I did endeavor

(But my voice would not come the way I thought)
   To say, "Be sure you hold me tight!" But he,
   Who'd rescued me from other dangers, put

His two strong arms around me to steady me
   As soon as I had mounted up, commanding,
   "Geryon, move ahead—but carefully:

Keep your arcs wide; go slowly when descending;
   Be mindful of this new burden that you bear."
90   As a boat moves back and back, to leave its landing,

So slowly did Geryon withdraw from shore.
   Then when he felt himself quite free, he turned
   And brought his tail to where his foreparts were,

And stretching it out he moved it so it churned
   The way a swimming eel does; and his paws
   Gathered the air toward him. When Phaëthon spurned

Canto XVII / 175

Maggior paura non credo che fosse
quando Fetonte abbandonò li freni,
per che 'l ciel, come pare ancor, si cosse;
né quando Icaro misero le reni
110   sentì spennar per la scaldata cera,
gridando il padre a lui «Mala via tieni!»,
che fu la mia, quando vidi ch'i' era
ne l'aere d'ogne parte, e vidi spenta
ogne veduta fuor che de la fera.
Ella sen va notando lenta lenta;
rota e discende, ma non me n'accorgo
se non che al viso e di sotto mi venta.
Io sentia già da la man destra il gorgo
far sotto noi un orribile scroscio,
120   per che con li occhi 'n giù la testa sporgo.
Allor fu' io più timido a lo stoscio,
però ch'i' vidi fuochi e senti' pianti;
ond' io tremando tutto mi raccoscio.
E vidi poi, chè nol vedea davanti,
lo scendere e 'l girar per li gran mali
che s'appressavan da diversi canti.
Come 'l falcon ch'è stato assai su l'ali,
che sanza veder logoro o uccello
fa dire al falconiere «Omè, tu cali!»,
130   discende lasso onde si move isnello,
per cento rote, e da lunge si pone
dal suo maestro, disdegnoso e fello;
così ne puose al fondo Gerïone
al piè al piè de la stagliata rocca,
e, discarcate le nostre persone,
si dileguò come da corda cocca.

The reins, so that the sky as one still sees
    Was scorched, I doubt that there was greater fear
    (Nor when pathetic Icarus felt his thighs

100 Unfeathering from the melting wax, to hear
    His father crying, "You are falling now!")
    Than mine, perceiving I was in sheer air—

Surrounded by it, and realizing I saw
    Nothing at all around me but the beast.
    Onward he swam with motion more and more slow

As he wheeled round descending; but that I guessed
    Only by feeling the wind against my face
    And from below. On our right the sound increased

From the whirlpool roaring horribly under us.
110   I stretched my head out forward, looking down—
    Growing more frightened even than I was,

Because as we descended I heard the din
    Of lamentations and I could see the fire.
    And so I shook, the more tightly holding on.

And I saw then—I had not seen it before—
    That he was wheeling and making his descent,
    For the great torments now were drawing near

On every side. As a falcon being sent
    Stays on the wing seeing no lure or bird
120   A long while, making the falconer lament,

"Ah me, you are sinking now!"—and comes down tired,
    With many wheelings, where it swiftly set out,
    And alights peeved and sullen, far from its lord:

So Geryon circled and landed at the foot
    Of the jagged rock; and once unburdening
    His shoulders of our bodies, he did not wait,

But vanished like an arrow from the string.

XVIII

   . . . *I saw deep down in the fosse*
  People immersed in filth that seemed to drain

From human privies. Searching it with my eyes
 I saw one there whose head was so befouled
 With shit, you couldn't tell which one he was—

Layman or cleric.

     (104–9)

Luogo è in inferno detto Malebolge,
   tutto di pietra di color ferrigno,
   come la cerchia che dintorno il volge.
Nel dritto mezzo del campo maligno
   vaneggia un pozzo assai largo e profondo,
   di cui suo loco dicerò l'ordigno.
Quel cinghio che rimane adunque è tondo
   tra 'l pozzo e 'l piè de l'alta ripa dura,
   e ha distinto in dieci valli il fondo.
10 Quale, dove per guardia de le mura
   più e più fossi cingon li castelli,
   la parte dove son rende figura,
tale imagine quivi facean quelli;
   e come a tai fortezze da' lor sogli
   a la ripa di fuor son ponticelli,
così da imo de la roccia scogli
   movien che ricidien li argini e ' fossi
   infino al pozzo che i tronca e raccogli.
In questo luogo, de la schiena scossi
20   di Gerïon, trovammoci; e 'l poeta
   tenne a sinistra, e io dietro mi mossi.
A la man destra vidi nova pieta,
   novo tormento e novi frustatori,
   di che la prima bolgia era repleta.
Nel fondo erano ignudi i peccatori;
   dal mezzo in qua ci venien verso 'l volto,
   di là con noi, ma con passi maggiori,
come i Roman per l'essercito molto,
   l'anno del giubileo, su per lo ponte
30   hanno a passar la gente modo colto,
che da l'un lato tutti hanno la fronte
   verso 'l castello e vanno a Santo Pietro,
   da l'altra sponda vanno verso 'l monte.

There is a place called Malebolge in Hell,
   Constructed wholly of iron-colored stones,
   Including the circumferential wall.

Right in the center of this malign field yawns
   A wide deep pit: concerning its design
   I shall say more in time. A belt remains

Between the base of that high wall of stone
   And the central pit, a circular band divided
   In ten concentric valleys, as in a plan

10 Where guardian moats successively are graded
   Around a castle's walls. In such a place
   A series of small bridges would be provided,

Out from the fortress threshold and across
   To the last bank: just so from the rock wall's foot
   Ran spokewise ridges, crossing over each fosse

And its embankment, extending to the pit
   That gathers them and cuts them off. This place
   Was where we found ourselves when we alit

From Geryon's back; the poet, leading us,
20 Held to the left, and I came on behind.
   To my right side I saw new tortures, new woes,

And new tormentors, with whom the first ditch teemed.
   Down at its bottom were naked sinners. The crowd
   Massed on our side of the center paced the ground

Headed toward us, while those on the other side
   Walked facing as we did, but with a greater pace:
   As when the Romans, because of the multitude

Gathered for the Jubilee, had pilgrims cross
   The bridge with one side kept for all those bound
30 Toward St. Peter's, facing the Castle, while those

Di qua, di là, su per lo sasso tetro
vidi demon cornuti con gran ferze,
che li battien crudelmente di retro.
Ahi come facean lor levar le berze
a le prime percosse! già nessuno
le seconde aspettava né le terze.
40 Mentr' io andava, li occhi miei in uno
furo scontrati; e io sì tosto dissi:
«Già di veder costui non son digiuno».
Per ch'ïo a figurarlo i piedi affissi;
e 'l dolce duca meco si ristette,
e assentio ch'alquanto in dietro gissi.
E quel frustato celar si credette
bassando 'l viso; ma poco li valse,
ch'io dissi: «O tu che l'occhio a terra gette,
se le fazion che porti non son false,
50 Venedico se' tu Caccianemico.
Ma che ti mena a sì pungenti salse?».
Ed elli a me: «Mal volontier lo dico;
ma sforzami la tua chiara favella,
che mi fa sovvenir del mondo antico.
I' fui colui che la Ghisolabella
condussi a far la voglia del marchese,
come che suoni la sconcia novella.
E non pur io qui piango bolognese;
anzi n'è questo loco tanto pieno,
60 che tante lingue non son ora apprese
a dicer 'sipa' tra Sàvena e Reno;
e se di ciò vuoi fede o testimonio,
rècati a mente il nostro avaro seno».
Così parlando il percosse un demonio
de la sua scurïada, e disse: «Via,
ruffian! qui non son femmine da conio».

Headed toward the Mount were all assigned
   The other side. Along the dismal rock
   In both directions, I saw demons—horned

And carrying large scourges; and they struck
   Savagely from behind. Ah, at the first blow
   How terribly they forced them to be quick

Lifting their heels! None waited to undergo
   The second or the third. As I walked on,
   One of the wretches looking from below

40 Met my eyes: instantly I said, "I have seen
   This fellow before," and paused to make him out;
   And my kind leader gave me leave to turn

A short way back. That tortured spirit thought
   To hide himself by lowering his face,
   But that did little good, and I cried out:

"You, looking at the ground there—surely if those
   Features you wear are not false, you are named
   Venedico Caccianemico. Say what it is

That brings you sauces of such a pungent kind."
50   And he to me: "I tell it unwillingly;
   But your plain speech compels me, bringing to mind

Memories of the former world. It was I
   Who brought Ghisolabella to do the will
   Of the Marchese, however it may be

That the obscene history is told. But still,
   I am not the only Bolognese here,
   Crying in torment—in truth, the place is so full

That there are fewer tongues alive up there
   Between Savena and Reno, being taught
60   How to say *sipa*; and if what you desire

Is evidence to confirm it—just give some thought
   To our avaricious nature." And as he spoke,
   A demon came and lashed him, crying out,

I' mi raggiunsi con la scorta mia;
   poscia con pochi passi divenimmo
   là 'v' uno scoglio de la ripa uscìa.
70 Assai leggeramente quel salimmo;
   e vòlti a destra su per la sua scheggia,
   da quelle cerchie etterne ci partimmo.
Quando noi fummo là dov' el vaneggia
   di sotto per dar passo a li sferzati,
   lo duca disse: «Attienti, e fa che feggia
lo viso in te di quest' altri mal nati,
   ai quali ancor non vedesti la faccia
   però che son con noi insieme andati».
Del vecchio ponte guardavam la traccia
80 che venìa verso noi da l'altra banda,
   e che la ferza similmente scaccia.
E 'l buon maestro, sanza mia dimanda,
   mi disse: «Guarda quel grande che vene,
   e per dolor non par lagrime spanda:
quanto aspetto reale ancor ritene!
   Quelli è Iasón, che per cuore e per senno
   li Colchi del monton privati féne.
Ello passò per l'isola di Lenno
   poi che l'ardite femmine spietate
90 tutti li maschi loro a morte dienno.
Ivi con segni e con parole ornate
   Isifile ingannò, la giovinetta
   che prima avea tutte l'altre ingannate.
Lasciolla quivi, gravida, soletta;
   tal colpa a tal martiro lui condanna;
   e anche di Medea si fa vendetta.
Con lui sen va chi da tal parte inganna;
   e questo basti de la prima valle
   sapere e di color che 'n sé assanna».
100 Già eravam là 've lo stretto calle
   con l'argine secondo s'incrocicchia,
   e fa di quello ad un altr' arco spalle.
Quindi sentimmo gente che si nicchia
   ne l'altra bolgia e che col muso scuffa,
   e sé medesma con le palme picchia.

"Get moving, pimp! This is no place to look
   For women to sell!" Rejoining my escort,
   I came with him to where a ridge of rock

Jutted from the bank; we climbed it without much effort,
   And turning right along its craggy bridge
   Left that eternal circling. We reached the part

70 Where a space yawning underneath the ridge
   Gives passage to the scourged, and there he said,
   "Stop: let the sight of this other great assemblage

Of ill-begotten souls impress you; they strode
   The way we did, so you could not see their faces."
   From the old bridge we looked down at the crowd

Filing toward us, also driven by lashes.
   The kind guide said, without my questioning,
   "See where that great one sheds, as he advances,

No tears for pain—how much the look of a king
80 He still keeps! He is Jason, who took the ram
   Of Colchis by courage and canny reckoning.

He passed the isle of Lemnos after the time
   When its bold, pitiless women killed every male;
   His deceitful gifts and fair words overcame

The young Hypsipyle there, who'd had the skill
   To deceive the rest. He left her great with child,
   Forlorn; and such guilt brings him torment in Hell,

Avenging Medea as well. With him are sealed
   All those who cheat such ways: let this suffice
90 For the first valley, and knowledge of those held

Between its jaws." We had now reached the place
   At which the narrow pathway cuts across
   The second bank, the shoulder of which supplies

The abutment for another arch's base.
   Now we could hear the sounds of people's screams
   From the next fosse's pocket, and the noise

Le ripe eran grommate d'una muffa,
per l'alito di giù che vi s'appasta,
che con li occhi e col naso facea zuffa.

Lo fondo è cupo sì, che non ci basta
110 loco a veder sanza montare al dosso
de l'arco, ove lo scoglio più sovrasta.

Quivi venimmo; e quindi giù nel fosso
vidi gente attuffata in uno sterco
che da li uman privadi parea mosso.

E mentre ch'io là giù con l'occhio cerco,
vidi un col capo sì di merda lordo,
che non parëa s'era laico o cherco.

Quei mi sgridò: «Perché se' tu sì gordo
di riguardar più me che li altri brutti?».

120 E io a lui: «Perché, se ben ricordo,
già t'ho veduto coi capelli asciutti,
e se' Alessio Interminei da Lucca:
però t'adocchio più che li altri tutti».

Ed elli allor, battendosi la zucca:
«Qua giù m'hanno sommerso le lusinghe
ond'io non ebbi mai la lingua stucca».

Appresso ciò lo duca «Fa che pinghe»,
mi disse, «il viso un poco più avante,
sì che la faccia ben con l'occhio attinghe

130 di quella sozza e scapigliata fante
che là si graffia con l'unghie merdose,
e or s'accoscia e ora è in piedi stante.

Taïde è, la puttana che rispuose
al drudo suo quando disse "Ho io grazie
grandi apo te?": "Anzi maravigliose!".

E quinci sian le nostre viste sazie».

Made by their puffing snouts and by their palms
    As they struck themselves. The banks were caked with mold
    That clings there, formed by an exhalation that steams

100 From down below, offensive to behold
    And to inhale. The bottom is so far down
    That we could nowhere see it until we scaled

The ridge's high point at the arch's crown.
    When we had reached it, I saw deep down in the fosse
    People immersed in filth that seemed to drain

From human privies. Searching it with my eyes
    I saw one there whose head was so befouled
    With shit, you couldn't tell which one he was—

Layman or cleric. Looking at me, he howled,
110   "And why are you so greedy to look at me
    When all of these are just as filthy?" I called:

"Because, if memory serves me properly,
    I saw you once when your hair was dry, before—
    I know you are Alessio Interminei

Of Lucca, which is why I eye you more
    Than all the rest." And he then, beating his head:
    "Down here is where my flatteries, that store

With which my tongue seemed never to be cloyed,
    Have sunk me." Then my leader gave me advice:
120   "Extend your gaze a little farther ahead,

So that your eyes may fully observe the face
    Of that disheveled strumpet who in the mire
    Scratches her body, as she stands or squats,

With shit-rimmed fingers—she is Thaïs, the whore
    Who, asked, *'And is my favor with you great?'*
    Replied, *'Enormous,'* to her paramour—

And let our sight be satisfied with that."

XIX

"*Beneath my head are souls who preceded me
In simony, mashed flat and squeezed . . .*"

(68–69)

O Simon mago, o miseri seguaci
   che le cose di Dio, che di bontate
   deon essere spose, e voi rapaci
per oro e per argento avolterate,
   or convien che per voi suoni la tromba,
   però che ne la terza bolgia state.
Già eravamo, a la seguente tomba,
   montati de lo scoglio in quella parte
   ch'a punto sovra mezzo 'l fosso piomba.
10 O somma sapïenza, quanta è l'arte
   che mostri in cielo, in terra e nel mal mondo,
   e quanto giusto tua virtù comparte!
Io vidi per le coste e per lo fondo
   piena la pietra livida di fóri,
   d'un largo tutti e ciascun era tondo.
Non mi parean men ampi né maggiori
   che que' che son nel mio bel San Giovanni,
   fatti per loco d'i battezzatori;
l'un de li quali, ancor non è molt' anni,
20 rupp' io per un che dentro v'annegava:
   e questo sia suggel ch' ogn'omo sganni.
Fuor de la bocca a ciascun soperchiava
   d'un peccator li piedi e de le gambe
   infino al grosso, e l'altro dentro stava.
Le piante erano a tutti accese intrambe;
   per che sì forte guizzavan le giunte,
   che spezzate averien ritorte e strambe.
Qual suole il fiammeggiar de le cose unte
   muoversi pur su per la strema buccia,
30 tal era lì dai calcagni a le punte.
«Chi è colui, maestro, che si cruccia
   guizzando più che li altri suoi consorti»,
   diss' io, «e cui più roggia fiamma succia?».
Ed elli a me: «Se tu vuo' ch'i' ti porti
   là giù per quella ripa che più giace,
   da lui saprai di sé e de' suoi torti».

CANTO XIX

O Simon Magus, and O you wretched crowd
   Of those who follow him and prostitute
   In your rapacity the things of God

Which should be brides of righteousness, to get
   Silver and gold—it is time the trumpet sounded
   For you: the third pouch is where you are put.

Now we were at the next tomb, having ascended
   To where the ridge hangs over the fosse's middle.
   O Supreme Wisdom, your mighty art is extended

10 Through Heaven, on earth, and in the world of evil,
   And with what justice is your Power assigned!
   I saw that the livid stone which lined the channel,

Both walls and floor, was full of holes, all round
   And of an equal size. They seemed to me
   Not any wider or smaller than those designed

For the baptizings in my fair San Giovanni—
   One of which many years ago I broke,
   To save one drowning there: and let this be

My seal to clear the matter. From each hole stuck
20   A sinner's feet and legs: the rest of him,
   From the calf up, inside. They twitched and shook

Because the soles of both feet were aflame—
   So violently, it seemed their joints could burst
   Rope or snap withes. As flames on oil will skim

Across the surface, so here the quick fire coursed
   From heel to toe. "Master," I asked, "tell me,
   Who is that one who seems to squirm the worst

And to be sucked by the reddest flames?" And he:
   "If you desire for me to carry you there,
30   By that bank sloping down more gradually,

E io: «Tanto m'è bel, quanto a te piace:
   tu se' segnore, e sai ch'i' non mi parto
   dal tuo volere, e sai quel che si tace».
40 Allor venimmo in su l'argine quarto;
   volgemmo e discendemmo a mano stanca
   là giù nel fondo foracchiato e arto.
Lo buon maestro ancor de la sua anca
   non mi dipuose, sì mi giunse al rotto
   di quel che sì piangeva con la zanca.
«O qual che se' che 'l di sù tien di sotto,
   anima trista come pal commessa»,
   comincia' io a dir, «se puoi, fa motto».
Io stava come 'l frate che confessa
50   lo perfido assessin, che, poi ch'è fitto,
   richiama lui per che la morte cessa.
Ed el gridò: «Se' tu già costì ritto,
   se' tu già costì ritto, Bonifazio?
   Di parecchi anni mi mentì lo scritto.
Se' tu sì tosto di quell' aver sazio
   per lo qual non temesti tòrre a 'nganno
   la bella donna, e poi di farne strazio?».
Tal mi fec' io, quai son color che stanno,
   per non intender ciò ch'è lor risposto,
60   quasi scornati, e risponder non sanno.
Allor Virgilio disse: «Dilli tosto:
   "Non son colui, non son colui che credi"»;
   e io rispuosi come a me fu imposto.
Per che lo spirto tutti storse i piedi;
   poi, sospirando e con voce di pianto,
   mi disse: «Dunque che a me richiedi?
Se di saper ch'i' sia ti cal cotanto,
   che tu abbi però la ripa corsa,
   sappi ch'i' fui vestito del gran manto;

Then you can speak with him directly and hear
From him about himself and his misdeeds."
And I: "I like what pleases you. You are

My lord, you know I follow where your will leads—
You also know the things I leave unsaid."
Then we came onto the fourth dike; where its sides

Slope down we descended to our left, and stood
Upon its narrow, perforated floor,
My master not releasing me from his side

40 Until he reached the hole of that sufferer
Whose legs thrashed out such sorrow. I began,
"O miserable soul, whoever you are,

Planted here like a fence post upside down:
Speak, if you can." I stood as does the friar
Who has confessed a vile assassin—head down,

And tied in place—who calls him back to defer
Death for a little while; and then he cried,
"Boniface, are you already standing there—

Already standing there? The writing lied
50 By several years! Are you so soon replete
With all that getting, for which you weren't afraid

To take the beautiful Lady by deceit,
And then to do her outrage?" I became
Like those who, feeling laughed at, hesitate,

Not comprehending what's been said to them
And helpless to reply. Then Virgil said,
"Answer him quickly: say you are not him,

Not who he thinks." I spoke as I was bid,
At which the shade squirmed hard with both his feet;
60 Then, sighing and in a mournful voice, replied,

"What do you ask me, then? If you were brought
Down from the bank to discover who I am,
Then know that I was vested with the great

70 e veramente fui figliuol de l'orsa,
cupido sì per avanzar li orsatti,
che sù l'avere e qui me misi in borsa.
Di sotto al capo mio son li altri tratti
che precedetter me simoneggiando,
per le fessure de la pietra piatti.
Là giù cascherò io altresì quando
verrà colui ch'i' credea che tu fossi,
allor ch'i' feci 'l sùbito dimando.
Ma più è 'l tempo già che i piè mi cossi
80 e ch'i' son stato così sottosopra,
ch'el non starà piantato coi piè rossi:
ché dopo lui verrà di più laida opra,
di ver' ponente, un pastor sanza legge,
tal che convien che lui e me ricuopra.
Nuovo Iasón sarà, di cui si legge
ne' Maccabei; e come a quel fu molle
suo re, così fia lui chi Francia regge».
Io non so s'i' mi fui qui troppo folle,
ch'i' pur rispuosi lui a questo metro:
90 «Deh, or mi dì: quanto tesoro volle
Nostro Segnore in prima da san Pietro
ch'ei ponesse le chiavi in sua balìa?
Certo non chiese se non "Viemmi retro".
Né Pier né li altri tolsero a Matia
oro od argento, quando fu sortito
al loco che perdé l'anima ria.
Però ti sta, ché tu se' ben punito;
e guarda ben la mal tolta moneta
ch'esser ti fece contra Carlo ardito.
100 E se non fosse ch'ancor lo mi vieta
la reverenza de le somme chiavi
che tu tenesti ne la vita lieta,

Mantle of power; a son who truly came
    Out of the she-bear, I longèd so much to advance
    The cubs that filling my purse was my great aim—

And here I have pursed myself, to my expense.
    Beneath my head are souls who preceded me
    In simony, mashed flat and squeezed through dense

70 Layers of fissured rock. I too shall lie
    Pushed down in turn when that other one has come:
    My abrupt question assumed that you were he.

But already longer is the span of time
    I have been cooking my feet while planted reversed
    Than he, feet scarlet, will be planted the same:

For then a lawless shepherd of the west
    Will follow him, of uglier deeds, well chosen
    For covering him and me when both are pressed

Under his skull. He'll be a second Jason,
80   And as the first, so Maccabees recounts,
    Was treated softly by his monarch, this one

Will get soft treatment from the King of France."
    In my reply, I don't know if I erred
    With too much boldness in my vehemence:

"Pray tell me: how much treasure did our Lord
    Ask of Saint Peter before He put the keys
    Into his keeping? Surely He required

Nothing but 'Follow me.' Neither did those
    With Peter, or Peter himself, take silver or gold
90   From Matthias, who was chosen for that place

Lost by the guilty soul. Stay where you're held,
    For these are your deservèd punishments—
    Guard well the ill-earned gains that made you bold

In opposing Charles. Except that reverence
    For the great keys you held in the happy life
    Forbids, my speech would be still more intense:

Canto XIX / *195*

io userei parole ancor più gravi;
   ché la vostra avarizia il mondo attrista,
   calcando i buoni e sollevando i pravi.
Di voi pastor s'accorse il Vangelista,
   quando colei che siede sopra l'acque
   puttaneggiar coi regi a lui fu vista;
quella che con le sette teste nacque,
110   e da le diece corna ebbe argomento,
   fin che virtute al suo marito piacque.
Fatto v'avete dio d'oro e d'argento;
   e che altro è da voi a l'idolatre,
   se non ch'elli uno, e voi ne orate cento?
Ahi, Costantin, di quanto mal fu matre,
   non la tua conversion, ma quella dote
   che da te prese il primo ricco patre!».
E mentr' io li cantava cotai note,
   o ira o coscïenza che 'l mordesse,
120   forte spingava con ambo le piote.
I' credo ben ch'al mio duca piacesse,
   con sì contenta labbia sempre attese
   lo suon de le parole vere espresse.
Però con ambo le braccia mi prese;
   e poi che tutto su mi s'ebbe al petto,
   rimontò per la via onde discese.
Né si stancò d'avermi a sé distretto,
   sì men portò sovra 'l colmo de l'arco
   che dal quarto al quinto argine è tragetto.
130 Quivi soavemente spuose il carco,
   soave per lo scoglio sconcio ed erto
   che sarebbe a le capre duro varco.
Indi un altro vallon mi fu scoperto.

For avarice like yours distributes grief,
    Afflicting the world by trampling on the good
    And raising the wicked. Shepherds like yourself

100   The Evangelist intended, when he said
    That she who sits upon the waters was seen
    By him in fornication with kings. She had

Seven heads from birth, and from ten horns had drawn
    Her strength—so long as virtue pleased her spouse.
    You made a god of gold and silver: wherein

Is it you differ from the idolatrous—
    Save that you worship a hundred, they but one?
    Ah Constantine! What measure of wickedness

Stems from that mother—not your conversion, I mean:
110   Rather the dowry that the first rich Father
    Accepted from you!" And while I sang this strain,

Whether he felt the bite of conscience, or anger,
    He kicked out hard with both his feet; indeed,
    I think my guide approved, with a look of pleasure

Listening to the sound of true words said.
    And then he lifted me in his arms again,
    My weight full on his chest; and when he had,

He climbed the same path he had taken down;
    Nor did he tire while holding me embraced
120   But carried me to the summit of the span

From the fourth dike to the fifth, then gently released
    His burden—gently because the passage was hard,
    So steep and rocky that goats might be hard pressed;

And there before me another valley appeared.

XX

But as my sight
Moved down their bodies, I sensed a strange distortion
That made the angle of chin and chest not right—

The head was twisted backwards: some cruel torsion
Forced face toward kidneys, and the people strode
Backwards, because deprived of forward vision.

(10–15)

CANTO XX

Di nova pena mi conven far versi
  e dar matera al ventesimo canto
  de la prima canzon, ch'è d'i sommersi.
Io era già disposto tutto quanto
  a riguardar ne lo scoperto fondo,
  che si bagnava d'angoscioso pianto;
e vidi gente per lo vallon tondo
  venir, tacendo e lagrimando, al passo
  che fanno le letane in questo mondo.
10 Come 'l viso mi scese in lor più basso,
  mirabilmente apparve esser travolto
  ciascun tra 'l mento e 'l principio del casso,
ché da le reni era tornato 'l volto,
  e in dietro venir li convenia,
  perché 'l veder dinanzi era lor tolto.
Forse per forza già di parlasia
  si travolse così alcun del tutto;
  ma io nol vidi, né credo che sia.
Se Dio ti lasci, lettor, prender frutto
20 di tua lezione, or pensa per te stesso
  com' io potea tener lo viso asciutto,
quando la nostra imagine di presso
  vidi sì torta, che 'l pianto de li occhi
  le natiche bagnava per lo fesso.
Certo io piangea, poggiato a un de' rocchi
  del duro scoglio, sì che la mia scorta
  mi disse: «Ancor se' tu de li altri sciocchi?
Qui vive la pietà quand' è ben morta;
  chi è più scellerato che colui
30 che al giudicio divin passion comporta?

CANTO XX

The new pains of Hell that I saw next demand
   New lines for this Canto XX of the first Canzon,
   Which is of those submerged in the underground.

Readying myself at the cliff's brink, I looked down
   Into the canyon my master had revealed
   And saw that it was watered by tears of pain:

All through the circular valley I beheld
   A host of people coming, weeping but mute.
   They walked at a solemn pace that would be called

10 Liturgical here above. But as my sight
   Moved down their bodies, I sensed a strange distortion
   That made the angle of chin and chest not right—

The head was twisted backwards: some cruel torsion
   Forced face toward kidneys, and the people strode
   Backwards, because deprived of forward vision.

Perhaps some time a palsy has wrung the head
   Of a man straight back like these, or a terrible stroke—
   But I've never seen one do so, and doubt it could.

Reader (God grant you benefit of this book)
20   Try to imagine, yourself, how I could have kept
   Tears of my own from falling for the sake

Of our human image so grotesquely reshaped,
   Contorted so the eyes' tears fell to wet
   The buttocks at the cleft. Truly I wept,

Leaning on an outcrop of that rocky site,
   And my master spoke to me: "Do you suppose
   You are above with the other fools even yet?

Here, pity lives when it is dead to these.
   Who could be more impious than one who'd dare
30   To sorrow at the judgment God decrees?

Drizza la testa, drizza, e vedi a cui
 s'aperse a li occhi d'i Teban la terra;
 per ch'ei gridavan tutti: "Dove rui,
Anfïarao? perché lasci la guerra?".
 E non restò di ruinare a valle
 fino a Minòs che ciascheduno afferra.
Mira c'ha fatto petto de le spalle;
 perché volse veder troppo davante,
 di retro guarda e fa retroso calle.
40 Vedi Tiresia, che mutò sembiante
 quando di maschio femmina divenne,
 cangiandosi le membra tutte quante;
e prima, poi, ribatter li convenne
 li duo serpenti avvolti, con la verga,
 che rïavesse le maschili penne.
Aronta è quel ch'al ventre li s'atterga,
 che ne' monti di Luni, dove ronca
 lo Carrarese che di sotto alberga,
ebbe tra ' bianchi marmi la spelonca
50 per sua dimora; onde a guardar le stelle
 e 'l mar non li era la veduta tronca.
E quella che ricuopre le mammelle,
 che tu non vedi, con le trecce sciolte,
 e ha di là ogne pilosa pelle,
Manto fu, che cercò per terre molte;
 poscia si puose là dove nacqu' io;
 onde un poco mi piace che m'ascolte.
Poscia che 'l padre suo di vita uscìo
 e venne serva la città di Baco,
60 questa gran tempo per lo mondo gio.
Suso in Italia bella giace un laco,
 a piè de l'Alpe che serra Lamagna
 sovra Tiralli, c'ha nome Benaco.
Per mille fonti, credo, e più si bagna
 tra Garda e Val Camonica e Pennino
 de l'acqua che nel detto laco stagna.
Loco è nel mezzo là dove 'l trentino
 pastore e quel di Brescia e 'l veronese
 segnar poria, s'e' fesse quel cammino.
70 Siede Peschiera, bello e forte arnese
 da fronteggiar Bresciani e Bergamaschi,
 ove la riva 'ntorno più discese.

Raise your head—raise it and see one walking near
    For whom the earth split open before the eyes
    Of all the Thebans. 'Why are you leaving the war,

Amphiaraus,' the others shouted, 'what place
    Are you rushing to?' as he plunged down the crevice
    To Minos, who seizes all. See Amphiaraus

Making his shoulders his breast; because his purpose
    Was seeing too far ahead, he looks behind
    And stumbles backwards. And here is Tiresias—

40 The seer who changed from male to female, unmanned
    Through all his body until the day he struck
    A second time with his staff at serpents entwined

And resumed his manly plumage. He with his back
    Shoved nose to the other's front is called Aruns.
    Living on the slopes the Carrarese work

From villages below, he had clear vistas:
    From his cave among white marble he could scan
    The stars, or gaze at waves below in the distance.

And she, whose loose hair covers her breasts unseen
50 On the side away from you, where other hair grows,
    Was Manto—who searched through many lands, and then

Settled in the place where I was born. Of this,
    Hear me awhile: her father dead, and Bacchus's
    City enslaved, she for a long time chose

To roam the world. Where a wall of mountains rises
    To form fair Italy's border above Tirolo
    Lies Lake Benaco, fed by a thousand sources:

Garda and Val Camonica and Pennino
    Are watered by streams that settle in that lake.
60 The island amid it the pastors of Trentino,

Brescia, or Verona might bless, if they should take
    A way that leads there. At the shore's low place,
    Peschiera's splendid fortress towers make

Ivi convien che tutto quanto caschi
ciò che 'n grembo a Benaco star non può,
e fassi fiume giù per verdi paschi.
Tosto che l'acqua a correr mette co,
non più Benaco, ma Mencio si chiama
fino a Governol, dove cade in Po.
Non molto ha corso, ch'el trova una lama,
ne la qual si distende e la 'mpaluda;
e suol di state talor esser grama.
Quindi passando la vergine cruda
vide terra, nel mezzo del pantano,
sanza coltura e d'abitanti nuda.
Lì, per fuggire ogne consorzio umano,
ristette coi suoi servi a far sue arti,
e visse, e vi lasciò suo corpo vano.
Li uomini poi che 'ntorno erano sparti
s'accolsero a quel loco, ch'era forte
per lo pantan ch'avea da tutte parti.
Fer la città sovra quell'ossa morte;
e per colei che 'l loco prima elesse,
Mantüa l'appellar sanz' altra sorte.
Già fuor le genti sue dentro più spesse,
prima che la mattia da Casalodi
da Pinamonte inganno ricevesse.
Però t'assenno che, se tu mai odi
originar la mia terra altrimenti,
la verità nulla menzogna frodi».
E io: «Maestro, i tuoi ragionamenti
mi son sì certi e prendon sì mia fede,
che li altri mi sarien carboni spenti.
Ma dimmi, de la gente che procede,
se tu ne vedi alcun degno di nota;
ché solo a ciò la mia mente rifiede».
Allor mi disse: «Quel che da la gota
porge la barba in su le spalle brune.
fu—quando Grecia fu di maschi vòta,
sì ch'a pena rimaser per le cune—
augure, e diede 'l punto con Calcanta
in Aulide a tagliar la prima fune.
Euripilo ebbe nome, e così 'l canta
l'alta mia tragedìa in alcun loco:
ben lo sai tu che la sai tutta quanta.

80

90

100

110

Their challenge to the Brescians and Bergamese.
    There, all the cascades Benaco cannot contain
    Within its bosom join in one river that flows

Through rich green pasture. As soon as it starts to run,
    The water, Benaco no more, is Mincio instead,
    And joining the Po at Govèrnolo, it soon

70 Spreads to a marsh—in summer, sometimes fetid.
    There Manto the savage virgin saw in mid-fen
    A stretch of dry land, untilled, uninhabited:

And there she stayed and lived, where she could shun
    All humans to ply her arts in a place she shared
    Only with servants. And when her life was gone

And her soul descended, there its shell was interred.
    Afterward, families scattered about that country
    Gathered where marsh on all sides made a ward

Against attackers. And when they built their city
80   Over her bones, with no lots or divination
    They named it Mantua. Before fool Casalodi

Was deceived by Pinamonte, its population
    Was larger. So let no other history,
    I charge you, belie my city's true inception."

I: "Master, your speech inspires such certainty
    And confidence that any contradiction
    Of what you say would be dead coals to me.

But speak again of these souls in sad procession:
    Are any passing below us worthy of note?
90   For my mind keeps turning back in that direction."

Then he: "That one, whose beard has spread in a mat
    That covers his brown shoulders, was augur when Greece
    Was short of males. He divined the time to cut

The first ship's cable at Aulis, along with Calchas.
    His name, as my tragedy sings—you who know it
    Entirely know the passage—is Eurypylus.

Quell'altro che ne' fianchi è così poco,
  Michele Scotto fu, che veramente
  de le magiche frode seppe 'l gioco.
Vedi Guido Bonatti; vedi Asdente,
  ch'avere inteso al cuoio e a lo spago
120 ora vorrebbe, ma tardi si pente.
Vedi le triste che lasciaron l'ago,
  la spuola e 'l fuso, e fecersi 'ndivine;
  fecer malie con erbe e con imago.
Ma vienne omai, ché già tiene 'l confine
  d'amendue li emisperi e tocca l'onda
  sotto Sobilia Caino e le spine;
e già iernotte fu la luna tonda:
  ben ten de' ricordar, ché non ti nocque
  alcuna volta per la selva fonda».
130 Sì mi parlava, e andavamo introcque.

That other with skinny flanks is Michael Scot,
    Who truly knew the game of magic fraud.
    See Guido Bonatti; and Asdente—too late,

He wishes he'd stuck to leather and cobbler's thread,
    Repenting here his celebrated predictions.
    And this wretched crowd of women all chose to trade

Loom, spindle and thimble for the telling of fortunes,
    Potions, wax images, incantation and charm.
    But come: already, Cain-in-the-moon positions

Both hemispheres with his pale blue thorns, his term
    Closes in the waves below Seville—the round moon
    That, deep in the wood last night, brought you no harm."

Even while he spoke the words, we were moving on.

XXI

"*You're not out in the Serchio for a swim!*
If you don't want to feel our hooks—like this!—

Then stay beneath the pitch."

(50–52)

Così di ponte in ponte, altro parlando
che la mia comedìa cantar non cura,
venimmo; e tenavamo 'l colmo, quando
restammo per veder l'altra fessura
di Malebolge e li altri pianti vani;
e vidila mirabilmente oscura.
Quale ne l'arzanà de' Viniziani
bolle l'inverno la tenace pece
a rimpalmare i legni lor non sani,
10 ché navicar non ponno—in quella vece
chi fa suo legno novo e chi ristoppa
le coste a quel che più vïaggi fece;
chi ribatte da proda e chi da poppa;
altri fa remi e altri volge sarte;
chi terzeruolo e artimon rintoppa—:
tal, non per foco ma per divin' arte,
bollia là giuso una pegola spessa,
che 'nviscava la ripa d'ogne parte.
I' vedea lei, ma non vedëa in essa
20 mai che le bolle che 'l bollor levava,
e gonfiar tutta, e riseder compressa.
Mentr' io là giù fisamente mirava,
lo duca mio, dicendo «Guarda, guarda!»
mi trasse a sé del loco dov' io stava.
Allor mi volsi come l'uom cui tarda
di veder quel che li convien fuggire
e cui paura sùbita sgagliarda,
che, per veder, non indugia 'l partire:
e vidi dietro a noi un diavol nero
30 correndo su per lo scoglio venire.
Ahi quant' elli era ne l'aspetto fero!
e quanto mi parea ne l'atto acerbo,
con l'ali aperte e sovra i piè leggero!

And so we went from bridge to bridge, and spoke
   Of things which my *Commedia* does not mean
   To sing. We reached the summit, stopping to look

At the next fissure of Malebolge, the vain
   Lamenting that was next—and what I beheld
   Was an astounding darkness. As is done

In winter, when the sticky pitch is boiled
   In the Venetian Arsenal to caulk
   Their unsound vessels while no ship can be sailed,

10 And so instead one uses the time to make
   His ship anew, another one repairs
   Much-voyaged ribs, and some with hammers strike

The prow, and some the stern; and this one makes oars
   While that one might twist rope, another patch
   The jib and mainsail—so, not by any fires

But by some art of Heaven, a heavy pitch
   Was boiling there below, which overglued
   The banks on every side. I saw that much,

But could see nothing in it but the flood
20 Of bubbles the boiling raised, and the whole mass
   Swelling and settling. While I stared down, my guide,

Crying, "Watch out!—watch out!" pulled me across
   Toward him from where I stood. I turned my head
   Like someone eager to find out what it is

He must avoid, who finding himself dismayed
   By sudden fear, while he is turning back
   Does not delay his flight: what I beheld

Hurrying from behind us up the rock
   Was a black demon. Ah, in his looks a brute,
30 How fierce he seemed in action—running the track

L'omero suo, ch'era aguto e superbo,
carcava un peccator con ambo l'anche,
e quei tenea de' piè ghermito 'l nerbo.
Del nostro ponte disse: «O Malebranche,
ecco un de li anzïan di Santa Zita!
Mettetel sotto, ch'i' torno per anche
40   a quella terra, che n'è ben fornita:
ogn' uom v'è barattier, fuor che Bonturo:
del no, per li denar, vi si fa ita».
Là giù 'l buttò, e per lo scoglio duro
si volse; e mai non fu mastino sciolto
con tanta fretta a seguitar lo furo.
Quel s'attuffò, e tornò sù convolto;
ma i demon che del ponte avean coperchio,
gridar: «Qui non ha loco il Santo Volto!
qui si nuota altrimenti che nel Serchio!
50   Però, se tu non vuo' di nostri graffi,
non far sopra la pegola soverchio».
Poi l'addentar con più di cento raffi,
disser: «Coverto convien che qui balli,
sì che, se puoi, nascosamente accaffi».
Non altrimenti i cuoci a' lor vassalli
fanno attuffare in mezzo la caldaia
la carne con li uncin, perché non galli.
Lo buon maestro «Acciò che non si paia
che tu ci sia», mi disse, «giù t'acquatta
60   dopo uno scheggio, ch'alcun schermo t'aia;
e per nulla offension che mi sia fatta,
non temer tu, ch'i' ho le cose conte,
perch' altra volta fui a tal baratta».

With his wings held outspread, and light of foot:
  Over one high sharp shoulder he had thrown
  A sinner, carrying both haunches' weight

On the one side, with one hand holding on
  To both the ankles. Reaching our bridge, he spoke:
  "O Malebranche, here is another one

Of Santa Zita's elders! While I go back
  To bring more from his homeland, thrust him below.
  His city gives us an abundant stock:

40 Every citizen there except Bonturo
  Practices barratry; and given cash
  They can contrive a *yes* from any *no*."

He hurled the sinner down, then turned to rush
  Back down the rocky crag; and no mastiff
  Was ever more impatient to shake the leash

And run his fastest after a fleeing thief.
  The sinner sank below, only to rise
  Rump up—but demons under the bridge's shelf

Cried, "Here's no place to show your Sacred Face!
50 You're not out in the Serchio for a swim!
  If you don't want to feel our hooks—like this!—

Then stay beneath the pitch." They struck at him
  With over a hundred hooks, and said, "You'll need
  To dance in secret here—so grab what scam

You're able to, in darkness." Then they did
  Just as cooks have their scullions do to steep
  The meat well into the cauldron—with a prod

From their forks keeping it from floating up.
  My good guide said, "So it will not be seen
60 That you are here, find some jagged outcrop

And crouch behind it to give yourself a screen.
  No matter what offenses they offer me,
  Do not be frightened: I know how things are done

Poscia passò di là dal co del ponte;
  e com' el giunse in su la ripa sesta,
  mestier li fu d'aver sicura fronte.
Con quel furore e con quella tempesta
  ch'escono i cani a dosso al poverello
  che di sùbito chiede ove s'arresta,
70 usciron quei di sotto al ponticello,
  e volser contra lui tutt' i runcigli;
  ma el gridò: «Nessun di voi sia fello!
Innanzi che l'uncin vostro mi pigli,
  traggasi avante l'un di voi che m'oda,
  e poi d'arruncigliarmi si consigli».
Tutti gridaron: «Vada Malacoda!»;
  per ch'un si mosse—e li altri stetter fermi—
  e venne a lui dicendo: «Che li approda?».
«Credi tu, Malacoda, qui vedermi
80 esser venuto», disse 'l mio maestro,
  «sicuro già da tutti vostri schermi,
sanza voler divino e fato destro?
  Lascian' andar, ché nel cielo è voluto
  ch'i' mostri altrui questo cammin silvestro».
Allor li fu l'orgoglio sì caduto,
  ch'e' si lasciò cascar l'uncino a' piedi,
  e disse a li altri: «Omai non sia feruto».
E 'l duca mio a me: «O tu che siedi
  tra li scheggion del ponte quatto quatto,
90 sicuramente omai a me ti riedi».
Per ch'io mi mossi e a lui venni ratto;
  e i diavoli si fecer tutti avanti,
  sì ch'io temetti ch'ei tenesser patto;
così vid' ïo già temer li fanti
  ch'uscivan patteggiati di Caprona,
  veggendo sé tra nemici cotanti.

Here—once before I was in such a fray."
    And then he passed beyond the bridge's head,
    And coming to the sixth bank suddenly

He needed to keep a steady front. They bayed
    And rushed at him with all the rage and uproar
    Of dogs that charge some wretched vagabond

70 Who suddenly is forced to plead; they tore
    From under the bridge and raised their forks at him;
    But he cried, "Not so savage!—before you dare

To touch me with your forks, choose one to come
    Forward to hear me out, and then decide
    Whether to hook me." They all cried out one name:

"Let Malacoda go!" So the others stood
    While one strode forward to him, sneering, "What
    Good will it do him?" So my master said,

"Do you, O Malacoda, think I could get
80   Through all of your defenses safely as this
    Except by Heaven's will and happy fate?

Now let us pass—for Heaven also decrees
    That I should show another this savage road."
    The demon's pride fell so much he let loose

His hook, which fell down at his feet, and said:
    "Now no one strike him." To me, my leader called,
    "Now you may come back safely to my side,

You who crouch squatting behind the splintered shield
    Of stone, upon the bridge." At this I stirred
90 And quickly joined him—and the devils milled

Toward us, pressing forward, so that I feared
    They might not keep the pact. So I once saw
    The soldiers frightened when they removed their guard

Out of Caprona by treaty—as they withdrew
    Passing among so many enemies.
    I kept as close by my guide as I could go,

I' m'accostai con tutta la persona
lungo 'l mio duca, e non torceva li occhi
da la sembianza lor ch'era non buona.

100 Ei chinavan li raffi e «Vuo' che 'l tocchi»,
diceva l'un con l'altro, «in sul groppone?».
E rispondien: «Sì, fa che gliel' accocchi».

Ma quel demonio che tenea sermone
col duca mio, si volse tutto presto
e disse: «Posa, posa, Scarmiglione!».

Poi disse a noi: «Più oltre andar per questo
iscoglio non si può, però che giace
tutto spezzato al fondo l'arco sesto.

E se l'andare avante pur vi piace,
110 andatevene su per questa grotta;
presso è un altro scoglio che via face.

Ier, più oltre cinqu' ore che quest' otta,
mille dugento con sessanta sei
anni compié che qui la via fu rotta.

Io mando verso là di questi miei
a riguardar s'alcun se ne sciorina;
gite con lor, che non saranno rei».

«Tra'ti avante, Alichino, e Calcabrina»,
cominciò elli a dire, «e tu, Cagnazzo;
120 e Barbariccia guidi la decina.

Libicocco vegn' oltre e Draghignazzo,
Cirïatto sannuto e Graffiacane
e Farfarello e Rubicante pazzo.

Cercate 'ntorno le boglienti pane;
costor sian salvi infino a l'altro scheggio
che tutto intero va sovra le tane».

«Omè, maestro, che è quel ch'i' veggio?»,
diss' io, «deh, sanza scorta andianci soli,
se tu sa' ir; ch'i' per me non la cheggio.

And all the while I did not take my eyes
　　Away from their expressions . . . which were not good!
　　They lowered their hooks, but I heard one give voice:

100　"Should I just touch him on the rump?" Replied
　　The others, "Yes—go on and give him a cut."
　　But the demon who was talking with my guide

Turned around instantly on hearing that,
　　Saying, "Hold—hold, Scarmiglione!" To us
　　He said, "You can't go farther by this route,

Because along this ridge the sixth arch lies
　　All shattered at the bottom. But if you still
　　Wish to go forward, a ridge not far from this

Does have a place where you can cross at will.
110　It was yesterday, five hours later than now,
　　That the twelve hundred and sixty-sixth year fell

Since the road here was ruined. I'm sending a crew
　　Out of my company in that direction
　　To see if sinners are taking the air. You go

With them, for they'll not harm you in any fashion.
　　Come, Alichino and Calcabrina," he cried,
　　"And you, Cagnazzo; and to be the captain

Of all ten, Barbariccia. And in the squad,
　　Take Libicocco and Draghignazzo too,
120　And Ciriatto with his tusky head,

And also Graffiacane and Farfarello,
　　And crazy Rubicante. Search all around
　　The pools of boiling tar. And see these two

Get safely over to where the dens are spanned
　　By the next ridge, whose arc is undestroyed."
　　"O me! O master, what do I see," I groaned;

"We need no escort if you know the road—
　　And as for me, I want none. If you are cautious,
　　As is your custom, then how can you avoid

Canto XXI / 217

130 *Se tu se' sì accorto come suoli,*
  non vedi tu ch'e' digrignan li denti
  e con le ciglia ne minaccian duoli?».
Ed elli a me: «Non vo' che tu paventi;
  lasciali digrignar pur a lor senno,
  ch'e' fanno ciò per li lessi dolenti».
Per l'argine sinistro volta dienno;
  ma prima avea ciascun la lingua stretta
  coi denti, verso lor duca, per cenno;
ed elli avea del cul fatto trombetta.

Seeing them grind their teeth and with ferocious
　　Brows threaten to do us harm?" And he returned,
　　"I tell you, have no fear: it is the wretches

Who boil here that they menace—so let them grind
　　As fiercely as they like, and scowl their worst."
　　And then the company of devils turned,

Wheeling along the left-hand bank. But first
　　Each signaled their leader with the same grimace:
　　Baring their teeth, through which the tongue was pressed;

And the leader made a trumpet of his ass.

XXII

We journeyed now
With the ten demons. Ah, savage company—

But as the saying has it, one must go
With boozers in the tavern and saints in church.*

(11–14)

Io vidi già cavalier muover campo,
   e cominciare stormo e far lor mostra,
   e talvolta partir per loro scampo;
corridor vidi per la terra vostra,
   o Aretini, e vidi gir gualdane,
   fedir torneamenti e correr giostra;
quando con trombe, e quando con campane,
   con tamburi e con cenni di castella,
   e con cose nostrali e con istrane;
10 né già con sì diversa cennamella
   cavalier vidi muover né pedoni,
   né nave a segno di terra o di stella.
Noi andavam con li diece demoni.
   Ahi fiera compagnia! ma ne la chiesa
   coi santi, e in taverna coi ghiottoni.
Pur a la pegola era la mia 'ntesa,
   per veder de la bolgia ogne contegno
   e de la gente ch'entro v'era incesa.
Come i dalfini, quando fanno segno
20 a' marinar con l'arco de la schiena
   che s'argomentin di campar lor legno,
talor così, ad alleggiar la pena,
   mostrav' alcun de' peccatori 'l dosso
   e nascondea in men che non balena.
E come a l'orlo de l'acqua d'un fosso
   stanno i ranocchi pur col muso fuori,
   sì che celano i piedi e l'altro grosso,
sì stavan d'ogne parte i peccatori;
   ma come s'appressava Barbariccia,
30 così si ritraén sotto i bollori.
I' vidi, e anco il cor me n'accapriccia,
   uno aspettar così, com' elli 'ncontra
   ch'una rana rimane e l'altra spiccia;

I have seen horsemen moving camp before,
    And when they muster, and when an assault begins,
    And beating a retreat when they retire;

I have seen coursers, too, O Aretines,
    Over your lands, and raiders setting out,
    And openings of jousts and tourneys—with signs

By bell and trumpet and drum, and signals set
    On castles by native and foreign signalry:
    But I never saw so strange a flageolet

10 Send foot or horsemen forth, nor ship at sea
    Guided by land or star! We journeyed now
    With the ten demons. Ah, savage company—

But as the saying has it, one must go
    With boozers in the tavern and saints in church.
    Intent upon the pitch, I tried to know

All that I could of the nature of this pouch
    And those who burn in it. Like dolphins who warn
    Sailors to save their vessels, when they arch

Their backs above the water, so we could discern
20 From time to time a sinner show his back
    To alleviate his pain, and then return

To hiding quicker than a lightning stroke.
    And as at water's edge or in a ditch
    Frogs lie, concealing their feet and all their bulk

With snouts above the surface: at the approach
    Of Barbariccia, sinners who lay just so,
    Concealing themselves on every side, would twitch

And pull back under the boiling. I saw—and now
    My heart still shudders as I tell it—one stay,
30 Just as it happens that while one jumps below

e Graffiacan, che li era più di contra,
    li arrunciglò le 'mpegolate chiome
    e trassel sù, che mi parve una lontra.
I' sapea già di tutti quanti 'l nome,
    sì li notai quando fuorono eletti,
    e poi ch'e' si chiamaro, attesi come.
40   «O Rubicante, fa che tu li metti
    li unghioni a dosso, sì che tu lo scuoi!»,
    gridavan tutti insieme i maladetti.
E io: «Maestro mio, fa, se tu puoi,
    che tu sappi chi è lo sciagurato
    venuto a man de li avversari suoi».
Lo duca mio li s'accostò allato;
    domandollo ond' ei fosse, e quei rispuose:
    «I' fui del regno di Navarra nato.
Mia madre a servo d'un segnor mi puose,
50   che m'avea generato d'un ribaldo,
    distruggitor di sé e di sue cose.
Poi fui famiglia del buon re Tebaldo;
    quivi mi misi a far baratteria,
    di ch'io rendo ragione in questo caldo».
E Cirïatto, a cui di bocca uscia
    d'ogne parte una sanna come a porco,
    li fé sentir come l'una sdruscia.
Tra male gatte era venuto 'l sorco;
    ma Barbariccia il chiuse con le braccia
60   e disse: «State in là, mentr' io lo 'nforco».
E al maestro mio volse la faccia:
    «Domanda», disse, «ancor, se più disii
    saper da lui, prima ch'altri 'l disfaccia».
Lo duca dunque: «Or dì: de li altri rii
    conosci tu alcun che sia latino
    sotto la pece?». E quelli: «I' mi partii,

Another frog might linger where they lay:
  And Graffiacane, who was nearest, hooked
  Him by his pitch-thick hair, so it looked to me

As if he had caught an otter. (I could connect
  Each of them with his name, for I had noted
  Carefully who they were when they were picked,

And also what they called each other.) They shouted,
  "O Rubicante, grip him between your claws
  And flay him." "Master—this wretch who's so ill-fated

40 And fallen into the hands of enemies:
  I pray you, find out who he is," I said.
  Going to his side at once, he asked what place

He came from. "I was born," replied the shade,
  "In the kingdom of Navarre. My mother sent
  Me to become the servant of a lord,

For she had borne me to a rascal bent
  On destroying both himself and all he had.
  Being admitted to the establishment

Of good King Thibaut's household, I employed
50 Myself at barratry—which is the path
  I pay for in this boiling." So he said;

Then Ciriatto, the demon from whose mouth
  Two boar-like tusks protruded, made him feel
  How one of them could rip. The mouse in truth

Had come among some vicious cats; and still
  Barbariccia locked him in a tight embrace,
  Saying, "Stand back, while I enfork him well,"

But to my master: "Ask him what you please—
  If there is more you'd like to learn from him
60 Before he's butchered by another of us."

So my guide asked, "Among the sinners who swim
  Under the pitch, are any others you know
  Italian?" He said, "I parted with one who came

poco è, da un che fu di là vicino.
Così foss' io ancor con lui coperto,
ch'i' non temerei unghia né uncino!».
70 E Libicocco «Troppo avem sofferto»,
disse; e preseli 'l braccio col runciglio,
sì che, stracciando, ne portò un lacerto.
Draghignazzo anco i volle dar di piglio
giuso a le gambe; onde 'l decurio loro
si volse intorno intorno con mal piglio.
Quand' elli un poco rappaciati fuoro,
a lui, ch'ancor mirava sua ferita,
domandò 'l duca mio sanza dimoro:
«Chi fu colui da cui mala partita
80 di' che facesti per venire a proda?».
Ed ei rispuose: «Fu frate Gomita,
quel di Gallura, vasel d'ogne froda,
ch'ebbe i nemici di suo donno in mano,
e fé sì lor, che ciascun se ne loda.
Danar si tolse e lasciolli di piano,
sì com' e' dice; e ne li altri offici anche
barattier fu non picciol, ma sovrano.
Usa con esso donno Michel Zanche
di Logodoro; e a dir di Sardigna
90 le lingue lor non si sentono stanche.
Omè, vedete l'altro che digrigna;
i' direi anche, ma i' temo ch'ello
non s'apparecchi a grattarmi la tigna».
E 'l gran proposto, vòlto a Farfarello
che stralunava li occhi per fedire,
disse: «Fatti 'n costà, malvagio uccello!».
«Se voi volete vedere o udire»,
ricominciò lo spaürato appresso,
«Toschi o Lombardi, io ne farò venire;
100 ma stieno i Malebranche un poco in cesso,
sì ch'ei non teman de le lor vendette;
e io, seggendo in questo loco stesso,

From there, just now. Would I were still below
　Hidden with him, for then I'd need not dread
　Their hooks and talons." Then cried Libicocco,

"We have endured too much!" With that he clawed
　His grapple into the other's arm, and tearing
　Ripped out a muscle. Draghignazzo also made

70　As if he meant to give his legs a goring,
　　At which their captain wheeled against them all.
　　When they were somewhat quiet, without deferring

His questions my leader asked the sinner, who still
　Was staring at his wound: "Who was it you said
　You parted from when you did yourself such ill

By coming ashore?" "Fra Gomita," he replied,
　"He of Gallura, vessel of every deceit,
　Who kept the enemies that his master had

So cunningly in hand, they praised him for it.
80　He took their cash and sent them on their way
　　Smoothly, as he recounts. And he was great

In other enterprises, equally:
　No petty barrator but a lordly one.
　Don Michel Zanche of Logodoro and he

Keep company together; when they go on
　About Sardinia, their tongues don't tire.
　But O me—look at how that other demon

Is grinding his teeth! Though I would tell you more
　I fear he's getting ready to scratch my itch."
90　To Farfarello, whose eyes rolled eager for gore,

Their marshal turned and shouted his reproach:
　"Get back, vile bird!" The sinner: "If you would hear
　Tuscans or Lombards, there are some I can fetch—

But let the Malebranche stand back there
　So those who come will not fear their revenge,
　And I will make some seven souls appear

Canto XXII / 227

per un ch'io son, ne farò venir sette
quand' io suffolerò, com' è nostro uso
di fare allor che fori alcun si mette».
Cagnazzo a cotal motto levò 'l muso,
crollando 'l capo, e disse: «Odi malizia
ch'elli ha pensata per gittarsi giuso!».
Ond' ei, ch'avea lacciuoli a gran divizia,
110   rispuose: «Malizioso son io troppo.
quand' io procuro a' mia maggior trestizia».
Alichin non si tenne e, di rintoppo
a li altri, disse a lui: «Se tu ti cali,
io non ti verrò dietro di gualoppo,
ma batterò sovra la pece l'ali.
Lascisi 'l collo, e sia la ripa scudo,
a veder se tu sol più di noi vali».
O tu che leggi, udirai nuovo ludo:
ciascun da l'altra costa li occhi volse,
120   quel prima, ch'a ciò fare era più crudo.
Lo Navarrese ben suo tempo colse;
fermò le piante a terra, e in un punto
saltò e dal proposto lor si sciolse.
Di che ciascun di colpa fu compunto,
ma quei più che cagion fu del difetto;
però si mosse e gridò: «Tu se' giunto!».
Ma poco i valse: ché l'ali al sospetto
non potero avanzar; quelli andò sotto,
e quei drizzò volando suso il petto:
130   non altrimenti l'anitra di botto,
quando 'l falcon s'appressa, giù s'attuffa,
ed ei ritorna sù crucciato e rotto.

For the lone one that I am—and I won't change
  My place from where I sit, but summon them
  By whistling, as we do when we can emerge."

100 Cagnazzo raised his muzzle at this claim;
  Shaking his head from side to side, he said,
  "Just listen to this cunning trick—his aim

Is to jump back below." And he, who had
  A great supply of wiles at his command,
  Replied, "It's true that I am cunning indeed

At contriving greater sorrows for the band
  I dwell with." Then Alichino held himself in
  No longer, and opposed the others: "My friend,"

He said, "if you dare plunge back in again,
110 I'll not come merely galloping after you
  But beating my wings above the pitch. The screen

Formed by the bank will hide us when we go
  Down from this ridge: we'll see if you, alone,
  Are a match for all of us." O reader, hear now

Of a new sport: led by the very one
  Who first opposed it, all now turned their eyes
  To the other shore. Timing exactly when,

Feet firm against the ground, the Navarrese
  Suddenly leaped and instantly broke free
120 Out of their custody. Each demon, at this,

Felt stung by his misdoing—especially he
  Who caused the blunder. So crying out, "You're caught!"
  He flew away in pursuit, but futilely:

Wings could not gain on terror; down out of sight
  The sinner dove, and the demon swooped back up,
  Raising his breast—no different in his flight

Than when the wild duck makes a sudden escape
  By diving just as the falcon plummets close,
  Then veers back up, vexed at his thwarted grip.

Irato Calcabrina de la buffa,
   volando dietro li tenne, invaghito
   che quei campasse per aver la zuffa;
e come 'l barattier fu disparito,
   così volse li artigli al suo compagno,
   e fu con lui sopra 'l fosso ghermito.
Ma l'altro fu bene sparvier grifagno
140   ad artigliar ben lui, e amendue
   cadder nel mezzo del bogliente stagno.
Lo caldo sghermitor sùbito fue;
   ma però di levarsi era neente,
   sì avieno inviscate l'ali sue.
Barbariccia, con li altri suoi dolente,
   quattro ne fé volar da l'altra costa
   con tutt' i raffi, e assai prestamente
di qua, di là discesero a la posta;
   porser li uncini verso li 'mpaniati,
150   ch'eran già cotti dentro da la crosta.
E noi lasciammo lor così 'mpacciati.

130 Then Calcabrina, who was furious
       The trick had worked, went flying after the pair,
       Eager to see the sinner evade the chase

   So there could be a fight. When the barrator
       Had disappeared, the demon turned his claws
       Upon his comrade and grappled him in midair

   Above the fosse. But his opponent was
       A full-grown hawk equipped with claws to respond
       Truly and well; and as they fought, the brace

   Fell into the middle of the boiling pond.
140   The heat unclenched them at once; but though released
       They could not rise, because their wings were gummed

   And clotted. Barbariccia, like the rest
       Lamenting, hastily dispatched a squad
       Of four who flew across to the bank we faced,

   Each with a fork; hurrying from either side
       They descended to their posts with hooks extended
       To the mired pair, already baked inside

   Their crusts; and we two left them thus confounded.

XXIII

Their cloaks, cowls covering the eyes and face,
Resembled those of Cluny's monks in cut.

(56–57)

Taciti, soli, sanza compagnia
   n'andavam l'un dinanzi e l'altro dopo,
   come frati minor vanno per via.
Vòlt' era in su la favola d'Isopo
   lo mio pensier per la presente rissa,
   dov' el parlò de la rana e del topo;
ché più non si pareggia 'mo' e 'issa'
   che l'un con l'altro fa, se ben s'accoppia
   principio e fine con la mente fissa.
10 E come l'un pensier de l'altro scoppia,
   così nacque di quello un altro poi,
   che la prima paura mi fé doppia.
Io pensava così: 'Questi per noi
   sono scherniti con danno e con beffa
   sì fatta, ch'assai credo che lor nòi.
Se l'ira sovra 'l mal voler s'aggueffa,
   ei ne verranno dietro più crudeli
   che 'l cane a quella lievre ch'elli acceffa'.
Già mi sentia tutti arricciar li peli
20   de la paura e stava in dietro intento,
   quand' io dissi: «Maestro, se non celi
te e me tostamente, i' ho pavento
   d'i Malebranche. Noi li avem già dietro;
   io li 'magino sì, che già li sento».
E quei: «S'i' fossi di piombato vetro,
   l'imagine di fuor tua non trarrei
   più tosto a me, che quella dentro 'mpetro.
Pur mo venien i tuo' pensier tra ' miei,
   con simile atto e con simile faccia,
30   sì che d'intrambi un sol consiglio fei.
S'elli è che sì la destra costa giaccia,
   che noi possiam ne l'altra bolgia scendere,
   noi fuggirem l'imaginata caccia».

Silent, alone, sans escort, with one behind
    And one before, as Friars Minor use,
    We journeyed. The present fracas turned my mind

To Aesop's fable of the frog and mouse:
    Now and *this moment* are not more similar
    Than did the tale resemble the newer case,

If one is conscientious to compare
    Their ends and their beginnings. Then, as one thought
    Springs from the one before it, this now bore

10 Another which redoubled my terror: that—
    Having been fooled because of us, with wounds
    And mockery to make them the more irate,

With anger added to their malice—the fiends,
    More fiercely than a dog attacks a hare,
    Would soon come after us. I felt the ends

Of my hair bristling already from the fear.
    Intent on what was behind us on the road,
    "Master," I said, "unless you can obscure

Both you and me from sight, and soon, I dread
20   The Malebranche, already after us—
    And I imagine them so clearly, indeed

I hear them now." "Were I of lead-backed glass,
    I would not take your outward countenance in
    Quicker than I do your inward one in this,"

He said; "This moment, your thoughts entered mine—
    In aspect and in action so alike
    I have made both their counsels into one:

If the right bank is sloped so as to make
    A way to reach the next fosse, then we can
30   Escape the chase we both imagine." He spoke

Già non compié di tal consiglio rendere,
    ch'io li vidi venir con l'ali tese
    non molto lungi, per volerne prendere.
Lo duca mio di sùbito mi prese,
    come la madre ch'al romore è desta
    e vede presso a sé le fiamme accese,
40 che prende il figlio e fugge e non s'arresta,
    avendo più di lui che di sé cura,
    tanto che solo una camiscia vesta;
e giù dal collo de la ripa dura
    supin si diede a la pendente roccia,
    che l'un de' lati a l'altra bolgia tura.
Non corse mai sì tosto acqua per doccia
    a volger ruota di molin terragno,
    quand' ella più verso le pale approccia,
come 'l maestro mio per quel vivagno,
50 portandosene me sovra 'l suo petto,
    come suo figlio, non come compagno.
A pena fuoro i piè suoi giunti al letto
    del fondo giù, ch'e' furon in sul colle
    sovresso noi; ma non li era sospetto:
ché l'alta provedenza che lor volle
    porre ministri de la fossa quinta,
    poder di partirs' indi a tutti tolle.
Là giù trovammo una gente dipinta
    che giva intorno assai con lenti passi,
60 piangendo e nel sembiante stanca e vinta.
Elli avean cappe con cappucci bassi
    dinanzi a li occhi, fatte de la taglia
    che in Clugnì per li monaci fassi.
Di fuor dorate son, sì ch'elli abbaglia;
    ma dentro tutte piombo, e gravi tanto,
    che Federigo le mettea di paglia.

With barely time to tell me of his plan
    Before I saw them coming—wings spread wide,
    Eager to seize us, not far and closing in.

My leader took me up at once, and did
    As would a mother awakened by a noise
    Who sees the flames around her, and takes her child,

Concerned for him more than herself, and flies
    Not staying even to put on a shift:
    Supine he gave himself to the rocky place

40 Where the hard bank slopes downward to the cleft,
    Forming one side of the adjacent pouch.
    No water coursing a sluice was ever as swift

To turn a landmill's wheel on its approach
    Toward the vanes, as my master when he passed
    On down that bank that slanted to the ditch,

Hurtling along with me upon his breast
    Not like his mere companion, but like his child.
    Just as his feet hit bottom, on the crest

Above us they appeared—but now they held
50   Nothing to fear, for that high Providence
    That made them keepers of the fifth ditch willed

That they should have no power to leave its bounds.
    Down at the bottom, we discovered a set
    Of painted people, who slowly trod their rounds

Weeping, with looks of weariness and defeat.
    Their cloaks, cowls covering the eyes and face,
    Resembled those of Cluny's monks in cut.

These cloaks were gilded on the side that shows
    So that the eye was dazzled—but all of lead
60   On the inside: so heavy, compared to these

The capes inflicted by Frederick were made
    Of woven straw. O heavy mantle to bear
    Through eternity! As ever, we pursued

Oh in etterno faticoso manto!
    Noi ci volgemmo ancor pur a man manca
    con loro insieme, intenti al tristo pianto;
70 *ma per lo peso quella gente stanca*
    venìa sì pian, che noi eravam nuovi
    di compagnia ad ogne mover d'anca.
Per ch'io al duca mio: «Fa che tu trovi
    alcun ch'al fatto o al nome si conosca,
    e li occhi, sì andando, intorno movi».
E un che 'ntese la parola tosca,
    di retro a noi gridò: «Tenete i piedi,
    voi che correte sì per l'aura fosca!
Forse ch'avrai da me quel che tu chiedi».
80   *Onde 'l duca si volse e disse: «Aspetta,*
    e poi secondo il suo passo procedi».
Ristetti, e vidi due mostrar gran fretta
    de l'animo, col viso, d'esser meco;
    ma tardavali 'l carco e la via stretta.
Quando fuor giunti, assai con l'occhio bieco
    mi rimiraron sanza far parola;
    poi si volsero in sé, e dicean seco:
«Costui par vivo a l'atto de la gola;
    e s'e' son morti, per qual privilegio
90   *vanno scoperti de la grave stola?».*
Poi disser me: «O Tosco, ch'al collegio
    de l'ipocriti tristi se' venuto,
    dir chi tu se' non avere in dispregio».
E io a loro: «I' fui nato e cresciuto
    sovra 'l bel fiume d'Arno a la gran villa,
    e son col corpo ch'i' ho sempre avuto.
Ma voi chi siete, a cui tanto distilla
    quant' i' veggio dolor giù per le guance?
    e che pena è in voi che sì sfavilla?».

Our course by turning to the left, and bore
    Along with them, intent on how they moaned.
    But they came slowly, burdened as they were—

So that with every step we took we found
    Our company was new. I asked my guide,
    "Pray find some person here, by looking round

70 As we walk on, whom I know by name or deed."
    And one among them caught the Tuscan speech:
    "Stay your quick steps through this dark air," he cried

As we came past him. "Perhaps what you beseech
    You can obtain from me." At which my guide
    Turned back to me, with: "Wait: let him approach

And then proceed at his pace." So I stayed,
    And saw two coming who by their faces appeared
    In a great haste of mind to reach my side

Although their burden held them in retard,
80   As did the crowding. When they came up together
    They looked at me askance without a word

For some good while. Then, turning toward each other
    They said, "This one appears to be alive,
    Judging by how his throat moves; but if, rather,

These two are dead, what privilege can they have,
    To go unencumbered by the heavy stole?"
    And then to me, "O Tuscan, you who arrive

At the sad hypocrites' assembly: pray tell—
    Not scorning to so address us—who you are."
90   "At the great town," I said, "on the beautiful

Waters of Arno, I was born, and there
    I grew up, and the body I wear now
    I have always had—but who are you, who bear

Upon your cheeks these distillates of woe?
    What is your punishment that glitters so bright?"
    "The orange cloaks are lead," said one of the two,

E l'un rispuose a me: «Le cappe rance
son di piombo sì grosse, che li pesi
fan così cigolar le lor bilance.
Frati godenti fummo, e bolognesi;
io Catalano e questi Loderingo
nomati, e da tua terra insieme presi
come suole esser tolto un uom solingo,
per conservar sua pace; e fummo tali,
ch'ancor si pare intorno dal Gardingo».
Io cominciai: «O frati, i vostri mali . . .»;
ma più non dissi, ch'a l'occhio mi corse
un, crucifisso in terra con tre pali.
Quando mi vide, tutto si distorse,
soffiando ne la barba con sospiri;
e 'l frate Catalan, ch'a ciò s'accorse,
mi disse: «Quel confitto che tu miri,
consigliò i Farisei che convenia
porre un uom per lo popolo a' martìri.
Attraversato è, nudo, ne la via,
come tu vedi, ed è mestier ch'el senta
qualunque passa, come pesa, pria.
E a tal modo il socero si stenta
in questa fossa, e li altri dal concilio
che fu per li Giudei mala sementa».
Allor vid' io maravigliar Virgilio
sovra colui ch'era disteso in croce
tanto vilmente ne l'etterno essilio.
Poscia drizzò al frate cotal voce:
«Non vi dispiaccia, se vi lece, dirci
s'a la man destra giace alcuna foce
onde noi amendue possiamo uscirci,
sanza costrigner de li angeli neri
che vegnan d'esto fondo a dipartirci».

"So thick, that we their scales creak at the weight.
　　We both were Jovial Friars, and Bolognese:
　　As for names, I was Catalano, and that

100　Was Loderingo, and we were your city's choice—
　　The way they usually choose one man—
　　To keep the peace: and what we were still shows

In the Gardingo district." Then I began:
　　"O Friars, your evil—" but that was all I said,
　　For as I spoke my eye was caught by one

Upon the ground, where he was crucified
　　By three stakes. When he saw me there he squirmed
　　All over, and puffing in his beard, he sighed;

Fra Catalano, observing this, explained:
110　"The one impaled there you are looking at
　　Is he who counseled the Pharisees to bend

The expedient way, by letting one man be put
　　To torture for the people. You see him stretch
　　Naked across the path to feel the weight

Of everyone who passes; and in this ditch,
　　Trussed the same way, are racked his father-in-law
　　And others of that council which was such

A seed of evil for the Jews." I saw
　　Virgil, who had been marveling over the man
120　Doomed to be stretched out vilely crosswise so

In the eternal exile. He spoke words then,
　　Directed to the friar: "Be it allowed,
　　And if it pleases you, could you explain

What passage there may be on the right-hand side
　　By which we two can journey away from here,
　　Without requiring those black angels' aid

To come and take us from this valley floor?"
　　And he replied, "Nearer than you may hope
　　Is a rock ridge that starts from the circular

Rispuose adunque: «Più che tu non speri
    s'appressa un sasso che da la gran cerchia
    si move e varca tutt' i vallon feri,
salvo che 'n questo è rotto e nol coperchia;
    montar potreste su per la ruina,
    che giace in costa e nel fondo soperchia».
Lo duca stette un poco a testa china;
    poi disse: «Mal contava la bisogna
    colui che i peccator di qua uncina».
E 'l frate: «Io udi' già dire a Bologna
    del diavol vizi assai, tra ' quali udi'
    ch'elli è bugiardo e padre di menzogna».
Appresso il duca a gran passi sen gì,
    turbato un poco d'ira nel sembiante;
    ond' io da li 'ncarcati mi parti'
dietro a le poste de le care piante.

130 Great wall surrounding us, and spans the top
     Of all the savage valleys except for this—
     Where it is broken and fallen down the slope

Rather than arching over: and at that place,
     You can mount up by climbing the debris
     Of rock along the slopes of the crevasse

And piled up at the bottom." Silently
     My leader stood a moment bowing his head,
     Then, "He who hooks the sinners, back that way,

Supplied a bad account of this," he said.
140   The friar: "In Bologna the saying goes,
     As I have heard, that the Devil is endowed

With many vices—among them, that he lies
     And is the father of lies, I have also heard."
     And then my guide moved onward, setting the pace

With mighty strides, and with his features stirred
     To some disturbance by his anger yet;
     And leaving those burdened souls I too went forward,

Following in the tracks of his dear feet.

XXIV

That path of stones

Would not provide a road for those who wore
Lead mantles, for we—he weightless, I helped up—
Could barely make our way from spur to spur.

(30–33)

In quella parte del giovanetto anno
    che 'l sole i crin sotto l'Aquario tempra
    e già le notti al mezzo dì sen vanno,
quando la brina in su la terra assempra
    l'imagine di sua sorella bianca,
    ma poco dura a la sua penna tempra,
lo villanello a cui la roba manca,
    si leva, e guarda, e vede la campagna
    biancheggiar tutta; ond' ei si batte l'anca,
10   ritorna in casa, e qua e là si lagna,
    come 'l tapin che non sa che si faccia;
    poi riede, e la speranza ringavagna,
veggendo 'l mondo aver cangiata faccia
    in poco d'ora, e prende suo vincastro
    e fuor le pecorelle a pascer caccia.
Così mi fece sbigottir lo mastro
    quand' io li vidi sì turbar la fronte,
    e così tosto al mal giunse lo 'mpiastro;
ché, come noi venimmo al guasto ponte,
20   lo duca a me si volse con quel piglio
    dolce ch'io vidi prima a piè del monte.
Le braccia aperse, dopo alcun consiglio
    eletto seco riguardando prima
    ben la ruina, e diedemi di piglio.
E come quei ch'adopera ed estima,
    che sempre par che 'nnanzi si proveggia,
    così, levando me sù ver' la cima
d'un ronchione, avvisava un'altra scheggia
    dicendo: «Sovra quella poi t'aggrappa;
30   ma tenta pria s'è tal ch'ella ti reggia».

In that part of the young year when the sun
  Goes under Aquarius to rinse his beams,
  And the long nights already begin to wane

Toward half the day, and when the hoarfrost mimes
  The image of her white sister upon the ground—
  But only a while, because her pen, it seems,

Is not sharp long—a peasant who has found
  That he is running short of fodder might rise
  And go outside and see the fields have turned

10 To white, and slap his thigh, and back in the house
  Pace grumbling here and there like some poor wretch
  Who can't see what to do; and then he goes

Back out, and finds hope back within his reach,
  Seeing in how little time the world outside
  Has changed its face, and takes his crook to fetch

His sheep to pasture. I felt this way, dismayed
  By my master's stormy brow; and quickly as this,
  The hurt had found its plaster. For when we stood

Before the ruined bridge, my leader's face
20 Turned to me with a sweet expression, the same
  As I had first beheld at the mountain's base.

He opened his arms, after he took some time
  To consult himself and study the ruin well,
  And taking hold of me began the climb.

As one who works and reckons all the while
  Seems always to have provided in advance,
  So, lifting me up one great boulder's wall,

He kept his eye on another eminence,
  Saying, "Next, grapple that one—but make sure
30 That it will bear you, first." That path of stones

Non era via da vestito di cappa,
    ché noi a pena, ei lieve e io sospinto,
    potavam sù montar di chiappa in chiappa.
E se non fosse che da quel precinto
    più che da l'altro era la costa corta,
    non so di lui, ma io sarei ben vinto.
Ma perché Malebolge inver' la porta
    del bassissimo pozzo tutta pende,
    lo sito di ciascuna valle porta
40 che l'una costa surge e l'altra scende;
    noi pur venimmo al fine in su la punta
    onde l'ultima pietra si scoscende.
La lena m'era del polmon sì munta
    quand' io fui sù, ch'i' non potea più oltre,
    anzi m'assisi ne la prima giunta.
«Omai convien che tu così ti spoltre»,
    disse 'l maestro; «ché, seggendo in piuma,
    in fama non si vien, né sotto coltre;
sanza la qual chi sua vita consuma,
50 cotal vestigio in terra di sé lascia,
    qual fummo in aere e in acqua la schiuma.
E però leva sù; vinci l'ambascia
    con l'animo che vince ogne battaglia,
    se col suo grave corpo non s'accascia.
Più lunga scala convien che si saglia;
    non basta da costoro esser partito.
    Se tu mi 'ntendi, or fa sì che ti vaglia».
Leva'mi allor, mostrandomi fornito
    meglio di lena ch'i' non mi sentia,
60 e dissi: «Va, ch'i' son forte e ardito».

Would not provide a road for those who wore
 Lead mantles, for we—he weightless, I helped up—
 Could barely make our way from spur to spur.

Had it not been that on that bank the slope
 Was shorter than on the other, I do not know
 How he'd have fared, but I'd have had to stop

And would have been defeated; but it was true
 In each valley that the contour of the land
 Made one side higher and the other low,

40 Because of the way all Malebolge inclined
 Downward toward the mouth of the lowest pit.
 At length we reached the place at which we found

The last stone broken off, and there I sat
 As soon as I was up—so out of breath
 Were my spent lungs I felt that I could get

No farther than I was. "To cast off sloth
 Now well behooves you," said my master then:
 "For resting upon soft down, or underneath

The blanket's cloth, is not how fame is won—
50 Without which, one spends life to leave behind
 As vestige of himself on earth the sign

Smoke leaves on air, or foam on water. So stand
 And overcome your panting—with the soul,
 Which wins all battles if it does not despond

Under its heavy body's weight. And still
 A longer ladder remains for us to climb;
 To leave these shades behind does not fulfill

All that's required. If you understand me, come:
 Act now, to profit yourself." I got to my feet,
60 Showing more breath than I felt, and said to him,

"Go on, for I am strong and resolute."
 And so, ascending the ridge, we took our way:
 It was quite rugged, narrow and difficult,

Canto XXIV / 249

Su per lo scoglio prendemmo la via,
   ch'era ronchioso, stretto e malagevole,
   ed erto più assai che quel di pria.
Parlando andava per non parer fievole;
   onde una voce uscì de l'altro fosso,
   a parole formar disconvenevole.
Non so che disse, ancor che sovra 'l dosso
   fossi de l'arco già che varca quivi;
   ma chi parlava ad ire parea mosso.
70 Io era vòlto in giù, ma li occhi vivi
   non poteano ire al fondo per lo scuro;
   per ch'io: «Maestro, fa che tu arrivi
da l'altro cinghio e dismontiam lo muro;
   ché, com' i' odo quinci e non intendo,
   così giù veggio e neente affiguro».
«Altra risposta», disse, «non ti rendo
   se non lo far; ché la dimanda onesta
   si de' seguir con l'opera tacendo».
Noi discendemmo il ponte da la testa
80   dove s'aggiugne con l'ottava ripa,
   e poi mi fu la bolgia manifesta:
e vidivi entro terribile stipa
   di serpenti, e di sì diversa mena
   che la memoria il sangue ancor mi scipa.
Più non si vanti Libia con sua rena;
   ché se chelidri, iaculi e faree
   produce, e cencri con anfisibena,
né tante pestilenzie né sì ree
   mostrò già mai con tutta l'Etïopia
90   né con ciò che di sopra al Mar Rosso èe.
Tra questa cruda e tristissima copia
   corrëan genti nude e spaventate,
   sanza sperar pertugio o elitropia:
con serpi le man dietro avean legate;
   quelle ficcavan per le ren la coda
   e 'l capo, ed eran dinanzi aggroppate.

Far steeper than the last. To seem to be
    Not too fatigued, I was talking while I trudged,
    When a voice arose—one ill equipped to say

Actual words—from the new fosse we had reached.
    I don't know what it said, though I was now
    At the high point of the bridge which overarched

70 The ditch there, but whoever spoke from below
    Seemed to be moving. I turned quick eyes to peer
    Down into the dark, but the bottom didn't show—

Wherefore I said, "Master, pray lead from here
    To the next belt, and let us descend the wall:
    Just as I cannot decipher the things I hear,

So too I look but make out nothing at all
    From where we are." "I'll give no other response,"
    He said, "but do it, for fitting petitions call

For deeds, not words." Where the bridge's end adjoins
80 The eighth bank, we descended, and then that pouch
    Showed itself to me: I saw in its confines

Serpents—a frightening swarm, of weird kinds such
    As to remember now still chills my blood.
    Let Libya boast no more of her sands so rich

In reptiles, for though they spawn the chelydrid,
    Cenchres with amphisbaena, the jaculi
    And phareae, she never, though one include

All Ethiopia and the lands that lie
    On the Red Sea, has shown a pestilence
90 So numerous or of such malignancy.

Amid this horde, cruel, grim and dense,
    People were running, naked and terrified,
    Without a hope of hiding or a chance

At heliotrope for safety. Their hands were tied
    Behind their backs—with snakes, that thrust between
    Where the legs meet, entwining tail and head

Ed ecco a un ch'era da nostra proda,
    s'avventò un serpente che 'l trafisse
    là dove 'l collo a le spalle s'annoda.
100 Né O sì tosto mai né I si scrisse,
    com' el s'accese e arse, e cener tutto
    convenne che cascando divenisse;
e poi che fu a terra sì distrutto,
    la polver si raccolse per sé stessa
    e 'n quel medesmo ritornò di butto.
Così per li gran savi si confessa
    che la fenice more e poi rinasce,
    quando al cinquecentesimo anno appressa;
erba né biado in sua vita non pasce,
110 ma sol d'incenso lagrime e d'amomo,
    e nardo e mirra son l'ultime fasce.
E qual è quel che cade, e non sa como,
    per forza di demon ch'a terra il tira,
    o d'altra oppilazion che lega l'omo,
quando si leva, che 'ntorno si mira
    tutto smarrito de la grande angoscia
    ch'elli ha sofferta, e guardando sospira:
tal era 'l peccator levato poscia.
    Oh potenza di Dio, quant' è severa,
120 che cotai colpi per vendetta croscia!
Lo duca il domandò poi chi ello era;
    per ch'ei rispuose: «Io piovvi di Toscana,
    poco tempo è, in questa gola fiera.
Vita bestial mi piacque e non umana,
    sì come a mul ch'i' fui; son Vanni Fucci
    bestia, e Pistoia mi fu degna tana».
E ïo al duca: «Dilli che non mucci,
    e domanda che colpa qua giù 'l pinse;
    ch'io 'l vidi omo di sangue e di crucci».
130 E 'l peccator, che 'ntese, non s'infinse,
    ma drizzò verso me l'animo e 'l volto,
    e di trista vergogna si dipinse;

Into a knot in front. And look!—at one
    Near us a serpent darted, and transfixed
    Him at the point where neck and shoulders join.

100   No *o* or *i* could be made with strokes as fast
    As he took fire and burned and withered away,
    Sinking; and when his ashes came to rest

Ruined on the ground, the dust spontaneously
    Resumed its former shape. Just so expires
    The Phoenix in its flames, great sages agree,

To be born again every five hundred years;
    During its life, it feeds on neither grain
    Nor herb but amomum and incense's tears,

And at its end the sheet it's shrouded in
110   Is essence of nard and myrrh. As one who falls
    And knows not how—if a demon pulled him down,

Or another blockage human life entails—
    And when he rises stares about confused
    By the great anguish that he knows he feels,

And looking, sighs; so was that sinner dazed
    When he stood up again. Oh, power of God!
    How severe its vengeance is, to have imposed

Showers of such blows. My leader asked the shade
    To tell us who he was. "The time is brief
120   Since I rained down from Tuscany," he replied,

"Into this gullet. It was a bestial life,
    Not human, that pleased me best, mule that I was.
    I am Vanni Fucci, beast—and aptly enough,

Pistoia was my den." And, "Master, please
    Bid him not slip away, but ask what sin
    It was," I said, "that thrust him to this place,

For in his time I have known him as a man
    Of blood and rage." The sinner, who had heard,
    Without dissembling turned mind and face—which shone

poi disse: «Più mi duol che tu m'hai colto
ne la miseria dove tu mi vedi,
che quando fui de l'altra vita tolto.
Io non posso negar quel che tu chiedi;
in giù son messo tanto perch' io fui
ladro a la sagrestia d'i belli arredi,
e falsamente già fu apposto altrui.
140   Ma perché di tal vista tu non godi,
se mai sarai di fuor da' luoghi bui,
apri li orecchi al mio annunzio, e odi.
Pistoia in pria d'i Neri si dimagra;
poi Fiorenza rinova gente e modi.
Tragge Marte vapor di Val di Magra
ch'è di torbidi nuvoli involuto;
e con tempesta impetüosa e agra
sovra Campo Picen fia combattuto;
ond' ei repente spezzerà la nebbia,
150   sì ch'ogne Bianco ne sarà feruto.
E detto l'ho perché doler ti debbia!».

130 The color of shame—to me; then he declared,
    "That you have caught me here amid this grief
    Causes me suffering worse than I endured

When I was taken from the other life.
    I cannot refuse your question: I must be
    Thrust this far down because I was a thief

Who took adornments from the sacristy—
    For which another, falsely, was condemned.
    But, lest you delight too much in what you see

If ever you escape from this dark ground:
140   Open your ears to what I now pronounce,
    And listen. First, Pistoia strips her land

Of Blacks, then Florence changes her citizens
    And ways. From Val di Magra, Mars draws a great
    Vapor, and thick clouds muffle its turbulence

Till stormy, bitter, impetuous war breaks out
    On Campo Piceno—where suddenly, it breaks through
    And tears the mist and strikes at every White:

And I have told it to bring grief to you."

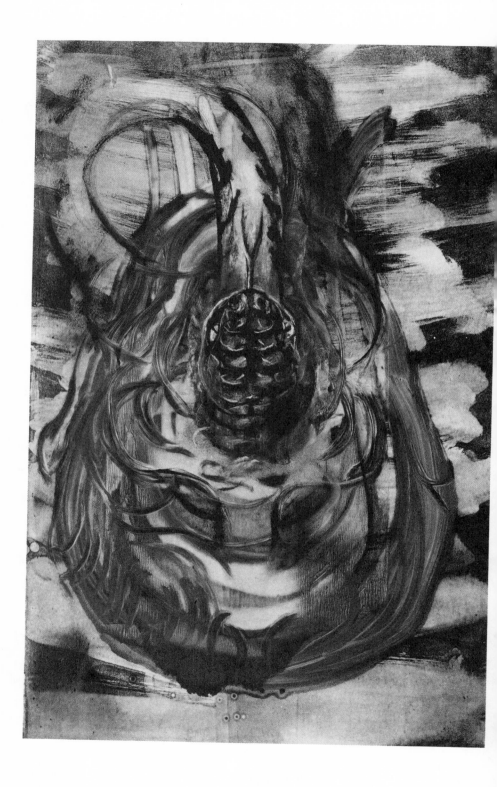

X X V

"Ah me, now look

At how you change, Agnello!—already you
Are neither two nor one."

(66–68)

Al fine de le sue parole il ladro
le mani alzò con amendue le fiche,
gridando: «Togli, Dio, ch'a te le squadro!».
Da indi in qua mi fuor le serpi amiche,
perch' una li s'avvolse allora al collo,
come dicesse 'Non vo' che più diche';
e un'altra a le braccia, e rilegollo,
ribadendo sé stessa sì dinanzi,
che non potea con esse dare un crollo.
10   Ahi Pistoia, Pistoia, ché non stanzi
d'incenerarti sì che più non duri,
poi che 'n mal fare il seme tuo avanzi?
Per tutt' i cerchi de lo 'nferno scuri
non vidi spirto in Dio tanto superbo,
non quel che cadde a Tebe giù da' muri.
El si fuggì che non parlò più verbo;
e io vidi un centauro pien di rabbia
venir chiamando: «Ov' è, ov' è l'acerbo?».
Maremma non cred' io che tante n'abbia,
20   quante bisce elli avea su per la groppa
infin ove comincia nostra labbia.
Sovra le spalle, dietro da la coppa,
con l'ali aperte li giacea un draco;
e quello affuoca qualunque s'intoppa.
Lo mio maestro disse: «Questi è Caco,
che, sotto 'l sasso di monte Aventino,
di sangue fece spesse volte laco.
Non va co' suoi fratei per un cammino,
per lo furto che frodolente fece
30   del grande armento ch'elli ebbe a vicino;

The thief held up his hands when he was through,
    And "God," he cried, making the fig with both—
    "Take these: I aim them squarely up at you!"

The serpents were my friends from that time forth,
    For then one coiled itself about his neck
    As if to say, "That's all then, from your mouth,"

And another went around his arms to snake
    Them tight and cinch itself in front, so tied
    They couldn't budge enough to gesture. Alack,

10 Pistoia, Pistoia!—Why haven't you decreed
    Your own incineration, so that you dwell
    On earth no more, since you surpass your seed

In evildoing? In all the circles of Hell
    I saw no spirit so arrogant to God,
    Not even him who fell from the Theban wall.

Speaking no more then, Vanni Fucci fled,
    And next I saw a centaur full of rage:
    "Where is he? Where is the bitter one?" he cried

As he charged up. I think more snakes than lodge
20   In Maremma's swamp were riding on his croup,
    Swarming along his back up to the edge

Of our human form. He bore behind his nape,
    Along the shoulders, a dragon with wings spread wide:
    If any blocked the path, it burned them up.

"This centaur's name is Cacus," my master said,
    "Who underneath the stones of Aventine
    Many a time has made a lake of blood.

He doesn't walk the same road as his clan
    Because by theft and fraud he tried to get
30   The splendid herd that lay near him—a sin

onde cessar le sue opere biece
sotto la mazza d'Ercule, che forse
gliene diè cento, e non sentì le diece».
Mentre che sì parlava, ed el trascorse,
e tre spiriti venner sotto noi,
de' quai né io né 'l duca mio s'accorse,
se non quando gridar: «Chi siete voi?»;
per che nostra novella si ristette,
e intendemmo pur ad essi poi.

40   Io non li conoscea; ma ei seguette,
come suol seguitar per alcun caso,
che l'un nomar un altro convenette,
dicendo: «Cianfa dove fia rimaso?»;
per ch'io, acciò che 'l duca stesse attento,
mi puosi 'l dito su dal mento al naso.
Se tu se' or, lettore, a creder lento
ciò ch'io dirò, non sarà maraviglia,
ché io che 'l vidi, a pena il mi consento.
Com' io tenea levate in lor le ciglia,

50   e un serpente con sei piè si lancia
dinanzi a l'uno, e tutto a lui s'appiglia.
Co' piè di mezzo li avvinse la pancia
e con li anterïor le braccia prese;
poi li addentò e l'una e l'altra guancia;
li diretani a le cosce distese,
e miseli la coda tra 'mbedue
e dietro per le ren sù la ritese.
Ellera abbarbicata mai non fue
ad alber sì, come l'orribil fiera

60   per l'altrui membra avviticchiò le sue.
Poi s'appiccar, come di calda cera
fossero stati, e mischiar lor colore,
né l'un né l'altro già parea quel ch'era:
come procede innanzi da l'ardore,
per lo papiro suso, un color bruno
che non è nero ancora e 'l bianco more.

That ended his crooked habits: he died for it.
   When Hercules's club rained onto his head
   Some hundred blows, he lived to feel ten hit."

While he was saying this, the centaur sped
   Beyond us, and three new spirits appeared below;
   They went unnoticed by me or by my guide

Until they shouted to us, "Who are you?"
   At which we ceased our talk and turned to them.
   I did not know them, but as people do

40 When chance disposes, one had some cause to name
   Another—"Where have we left Cianfa?" he said.
   To be sure my leader heard, I signaled him

To stay alert, with a finger that I laid
   From chin to nose. Reader, if you are slow
   To credit what I tell you next, it should

Be little wonder, for I who saw it know
   That I myself can hardly acknowledge it:
   While I was staring at the sinners below

A serpent darted forward that had six feet,
50 And facing one of the three it fastened on him
   All over—with the middle feet it got

A grip upon the belly, with each fore-limb
   It clasped an arm; its fangs gripped both his cheeks;
   It spread its hind feet out to do the same

To both his thighs, extending its tail to flex
   Between them upward through to the loins behind.
   No ivy growing in a tree's bark sticks

As firmly as the horrid beast entwined
   Its limbs around the other. Then, as if made
60 Out of hot wax, they clung and made a bond

And mixed their colors; and neither could be construed
   As what it was at first—so, as the track
   Of flame moves over paper, there is a shade

Canto XXV / 261

Li altri due 'l riguardavano, e ciascuno
gridava: «Omè, Agnel, come ti muti!
Vedi che già non se' né due né uno».

70 Già eran li due capi un divenuti,
quando n'apparver due figure miste
in una faccia, ov' eran due perduti.

Fersi le braccia due di quattro liste;
le cosce con le gambe e 'l ventre e 'l casso
divenner membra che non fuor mai viste.

Ogne primaio aspetto ivi era casso:
due e nessun l'imagine perversa
parea; e tal sen gio con lento passo.

Come 'l ramarro sotto la gran fersa
80 dei dì canicular, cangiando sepe,
folgore par se la via attraversa,

sì pareva, venendo verso l'epe
de li altri due, un serpentello acceso,
livido e nero come gran di pepe;

e quella parte onde prima è preso
nostro alimento, a l'un di lor trafisse;
poi cadde giuso innanzi lui disteso.

Lo trafitto 'l mirò, ma nulla disse;
anzi, co' piè fermati, sbadigliava
90 pur come sonno o febbre l'assalisse.

Elli 'l serpente e quei lui riguardava;
l'un per la piaga e l'altro per la bocca
fummavan forte, e 'l fummo si scontrava.

Taccia Lucano omai là dov' e' tocca
del misero Sabello e di Nasidio,
e attenda a udir quel ch'or si scocca.

Taccia di Cadmo e d'Aretusa Ovidio,
ché se quello in serpente e quella in fonte
converte poetando, io non lo 'nvidio;

That moves before it that is not yet black,
  And the white dies away. The other two
  Were looking on, and cried, "Ah me, now look

At how you change, Agnello!—already you
  Are neither two nor one." Now the two heads
  Had become one; we watched the two shapes grow

70 Into one face, where both were lost. The sides
  Grew two arms, fused from lengths that had been four;
  Thighs, legs, chest, belly merged; and in their steads

Grew members that were never seen before.
  All of the former features were blotted out.
  A perverse shape, with both not what they were,

Yet neither—such, its pace deliberate,
  It moved away. The way a lizard can dash
  Under the dog day's scourge, darting out

Between the hedges so that it seems a flash
80 Of lightning if it spurts across the road,
  So did a fiery little serpent rush

Toward the bellies of the two who stayed;
  Peppercorn black and livid, it struck out,
  Transfixing one in the place where we are fed

When life begins—then fell before his feet,
  Outstretched. The pierced one gazed at it and stood
  Not speaking, only yawning as if a fit

Of sleep or fever had taken him. He eyed
  The serpent, the serpent him. From this one's wound
90 And that one's mouth smoke violently flowed,

And their smoke met. Let Lucan now attend
  In silence, who has told the wretched fates
  Of Nasidius and Sabellus—till he has learned

What I will let fly next. And Ovid, who writes
  Of Cadmus and Arethusa, let him be still—
  For though he in his poet-craft transmutes

100

ché due nature mai a fronte a fronte
    non trasmutò sì ch'amendue le forme
    a cambiar lor matera fosser pronte.
Insieme si rispuosero a tai norme,
    che 'l serpente la coda in forca fesse,
    e 'l feruto ristrinse insieme l'orme.
Le gambe con le cosce seco stesse
    s'appiccar sì, che 'n poco la giuntura
    non facea segno alcun che si paresse.
Togliea la coda fessa la figura
110 che si perdeva là, e la sua pelle
    si facea molle, e quella di là dura.
Io vidi intrar le braccia per l'ascelle,
    e i due piè de la fiera, ch'eran corti,
    tanto allungar quanto accorciavan quelle.
Poscia li piè di rietro, insieme attorti,
    diventaron lo membro che l'uom cela,
    e 'l misero del suo n'avea due porti.
Mentre che 'l fummo l'uno e l'altro vela
    di color novo, e genera 'l pel suso
120 per l'una parte e da l'altra il dipela,
l'un si levò e l'altro cadde giuso,
    non torcendo però le lucerne empie,
    sotto le quai ciascun cambiava muso.
Quel ch'era dritto, il trasse ver' le tempie,
    e di troppa matera ch'in là venne
    uscir li orecchi de le gote scempie;
ciò che non corse in dietro e si ritenne
    di quel soverchio, fé naso a la faccia
    e le labbra ingrossò quanto convenne.
130 Quel che giacëa, il muso innanzi caccia,
    e li orecchi ritira per la testa
    come face le corna la lumaccia:
e la lingua, ch'avëa unita e presta
    prima a parlar, si fende, e la forcuta
    ne l'altro si richiude; e 'l fummo resta.

One to a serpent, and makes the other spill
    Transformed into a fountain, I envy him not:
    He never transformed two individual

100 Front-to-front natures so both forms as they met
    Were ready to exchange their substance. The twain
    Reacted mutually: the reptile split

Its tail to make a fork; the wounded one
    Conjoined his feet. The legs and thighs were pressed
    So tight no mark of juncture could be seen;

The split tail took the shape the other lost,
    Its skin grew softer, and the other's hard.
    I saw the arms draw inward to be encased

Inside the armpits; the animal's feet appeared
110   To lengthen as the other's arms grew less.
    The hind paws, twisting together like a cord,

Became the member man conceals. From his,
    The wretch had grown two feet. While the smoke veils
    Each one with colors that are new, and grows

Hair here and strips it there, the one shape falls
    And one comes upright. But neither turned aside
    The unholy lights that stared above the muzzles

They each were changing: the one who newly stood
    Drew his in toward his temples, and from the spare
120   Matter from that, ears issued from the head,

Behind smooth cheeks; what didn't course to an ear
    But was retained became the face's nose,
    And fleshed the lips to the thickness they should bear.

He that lay prone propelled his nose and face
    Forward, and shrank his ears back into the head
    As a snail does its horns. The tongue that was

Whole and prepared for speech was split instead—
    And in the other the forked tongue formed one piece:
    And the smoke ceased. The soul that had been made

Canto XXV / *265*

L'anima ch'era fiera divenuta,
   suffolando si fugge per la valle,
   e l'altro dietro a lui parlando sputa.
Poscia li volse le novelle spalle,
140   e disse a l'altro: «I' vo' che Buoso corra,
   com' ho fatt' io, carpon per questo calle».
Così vid' io la settima zavorra
   mutare e trasmutare; e qui mi scusi
   la novità se fior la penna abborra.
E avvegna che li occhi miei confusi
   fossero alquanto e l'animo smagato,
   non poter quei fuggirsi tanto chiusi,
ch'i' non scorgessi ben Puccio Sciancato;
   ed era quel che sol, di tre compagni
150   che venner prima, non era mutato;
l'altr' era quel che tu, Gaville, piagni.

130 A beast fled down the valley with a hiss;
     The other, speaking now, spat after it,
     Turned his new shoulders on it to address

The third, and said: "I'll have Buoso trot
     On all fours down this road, as I have done!"
     And so I saw that seventh deadweight transmute

And mutate—and may its strangeness excuse my pen,
     If it has tangled things. And though my eyes
     Were somewhat in confusion at the scene,

My mind somewhat bewildered, yet none of these
140   Could flee to hide himself so secretly
     That I could not distinguish well the face

Of Puccio Sciancato, who of the three
     Companions that we first took notice of,
     Alone was not transformed; the other was he

Whose death, Gaville, you have good cause to grieve.

XXVI

"Within the flames are spirits; each one here
Enfolds himself in what burns him."

(50–51)

Godi, Fiorenza, poi che se' sì grande
   che per mare e per terra batti l'ali,
   e per lo 'nferno tuo nome si spande!
Tra li ladron trovai cinque cotali
   tuoi cittadini onde mi ven vergogna,
   e tu in grande orranza non ne sali.
Ma se presso al mattin del ver si sogna,
   tu sentirai, di qua da picciol tempo,
   di quel che Prato, non ch'altri, t'agogna.
10 E se già fosse, non saria per tempo.
   Così foss' ei, da che pur esser dee!
   ché più mi graverà, com' più m'attempo.
Noi ci partimmo, e su per le scalee
   che n'avean fatto i borni a scender pria,
   rimontò 'l duca mio e trasse mee;
e proseguendo la solinga via,
   tra le schegge e tra ' rocchi de lo scoglio
   lo piè sanza la man non si spedia.
Allor mi dolsi, e ora mi ridoglio
20 quando drizzo la mente a ciò ch'io vidi,
   e più lo 'ngegno affreno ch'i' non soglio,
perché non corra che virtù nol guidi;
   sì che, se stella bona o miglior cosa
   m'ha dato 'l ben, ch'io stessi nol m'invidi.
Quante 'l villan ch'al poggio si riposa,
   nel tempo che colui che 'l mondo schiara
   la faccia sua a noi tien meno ascosa,

Rejoice, O Florence, since you are so great,
   Beating your wings on land and on the sea,
   That in Hell too your name is spread about!

I found among those there for their thievery
   Five of your citizens, which carries shame
   For me—and you gain no high honor thereby.

But if we dream the truth near morning time,
   Then you will feel, before much time has gone,
   What Prato and others crave for you—and come

10 Already, it would not have come too soon.
   And truly, let it, since it must come to pass:
   For it will all the heavier weigh me down,

The older I become. We left the place,
   And on the stairway that the jutting stone
   A little while before had offered us

On our descent, my guide climbed up again
   And drew me up to pursue our lonely course.
   Without the hand the foot could not go on,

Climbing that jagged ridge's rocks and spurs.
20   I sorrowed then, and when I turn my mind
   To what I saw next, sorrow again—and force

My art to make its genius more restrained
   Than is my usual bent, lest it should run
   Where virtue doesn't: so that if any kind

Star or some better thing has made it mine
   I won't myself negate the gift in me.
   As many as the fireflies a peasant has seen

(Resting on a hill that time of year when he
   Who lights the world least hides his face from us,
30   And at the hour when the fly gives way

come la mosca cede a la zanzara,
vede lucciole giù per la vallea,
30 forse colà dov' e' vendemmia e ara:
di tante fiamme tutta risplendea
l'ottava bolgia, sì com' io m'accorsi
tosto che fui là 've 'l fondo parea.
E qual colui che si vengiò con li orsi
vide 'l carro d'Elia al dipartire,
quando i cavalli al cielo erti levorsi,
che nol potea sì con li occhi seguire,
ch'el vedesse altro che la fiamma sola,
sì come nuvoletta, in sù salire:
40 tal si move ciascuna per la gola
del fosso, ché nessuna mostra 'l furto,
e ogne fiamma un peccatore invola.
Io stava sovra 'l ponte a veder surto,
sì che s'io non avessi un ronchion preso,
caduto sarei giù sanz' esser urto.
E 'l duca, che mi vide tanto atteso,
disse: «Dentro dai fuochi son li spirti;
catun si fascia di quel ch'elli è inceso».
«Maestro mio», rispuos' io, «per udirti
50 son io più certo; ma già m'era avviso
che così fosse, e già voleva dirti:
chi è 'n quel foco che vien sì diviso
di sopra, che par surger de la pira
dov' Eteòcle col fratel fu miso?».
Rispuose a me: «Là dentro si martira
Ulisse e Dïomede, e così insieme
a la vendetta vanno come a l'ira;
e dentro da la lor fiamma si geme
l'agguato del caval che fé la porta
60 onde uscì de' Romani il gentil seme.

To the mosquito) all down the valley's face,
  Where perhaps he gathers grapes and tills the ground:
  With flames that numerous was Hell's eighth fosse

Glittering, as I saw when I attained
  A place from which its floor could be made out.
  And as the one avenged by bears divined

That what he saw was Elijah's chariot
  Carried by rearing horses to Heaven's domain—
  For with his eyes he couldn't follow it

40 Except by looking at the flame alone,
  Like a small cloud ascending: so each flame moves
  Along the ditch's gullet with not one

Showing its plunder, though every flame contrives
  To steal away a sinner. I had climbed up
  To balance where the bridge's high point gives

A better view, and if I didn't grip
  A rock I would have fallen from where I stood
  Without a push. Seeing how from the top

I gazed intently down, my master said,
50 "Within the flames are spirits; each one here
  Enfolds himself in what burns him." I replied,

"My Master, to hear you say it makes me sure,
  But I already thought it; already, too,
  I wanted to ask you who is in that fire

Which at its top is so split into two
  It seems to surge from the pyre Eteocles
  Shared with his brother?" He answered, "In it go

Tormented Ulysses and Diomedes
  Enduring vengeance together, as they did wrath;
60 And in their flame they grieve for their device,

The horse that made the doorway through which went forth
  The Romans' noble seed. Within their fire
  Now they lament the guile that even in death

Piangevisi entro l'arte per che, morta,
 Deïdamìa ancor si duol d'Achille,
 e del Palladio pena vi si porta».
«S'ei posson dentro da quelle faville
 parlar», diss' io, «maestro, assai ten priego
 e ripriego, che 'l priego vaglia mille,
che non mi facci de l'attender niego
 fin che la fiamma cornuta qua vegna;
 vedi che del disio ver' lei mi piego!».
70 Ed elli a me: «La tua preghiera è degna
 di molta loda, e io però l'accetto;
 ma fa che la tua lingua si sostegna.
Lascia parlare a me, ch'i' ho concetto
 ciò che tu vuoi; ch'ei sarebbero schivi,
 perch' e' fuor greci, forse del tuo detto».
Poi che la fiamma fu venuta quivi
 dove parve al mio duca tempo e loco,
 in questa forma lui parlare audivi:
«O voi che siete due dentro ad un foco,
80 s'io meritai di voi mentre ch'io vissi,
 s'io meritai di voi assai o poco
quando nel mondo li alti versi scrissi,
 non vi movete; ma l'un di voi dica
 dove, per lui, perduto a morir gissi».
Lo maggior corno de la fiamma antica
 cominciò a crollarsi mormorando,
 pur come quella cui vento affatica;
indi la cima qua e là menando,
 come fosse la lingua che parlasse,
90 gittò voce di fuori e disse: «Quando
mi diparti' da Circe, che sottrasse
 me più d'un anno là presso a Gaeta,
 prima che sì Enëa la nomasse,
né dolcezza di figlio, né la pieta
 del vecchio padre, né 'l debito amore
 lo qual dovea Penelopè far lieta,
vincer potero dentro a me l'ardore
 ch'i' ebbi a divenir del mondo esperto
 e de li vizi umani e del valore;

Makes Deidamia mourn Achilles, and there
　　They pay the price for the Palladium."
　　"Master," I said, "I earnestly implore,

If they can speak within those sparks of flame—
　　And pray my prayer be worth a thousand pleas—
　　Do not forbid my waiting here for them

70　Until their horned flame makes its way to us;
　　You see how yearningly it makes me lean."
　　And he to me: "Your prayer is worthy of praise,

And therefore I accept it. But restrain
　　Your tongue, leave speech to me—Greeks that they were,
　　They might treat words of yours with some disdain."

My master waited as the flame drew near
　　For the right place and moment to arrive,
　　Then spoke: "O you, who are two within one fire:

If I deserved of you while I was alive—
80　If I deserved anything great or small
　　From you when I wrote verse, then do not move;

But rather grant that one of you will tell
　　Whither, when lost, he went away to die."
　　The greater horn of flame began to flail

And murmur like fire the wind beats, and to ply
　　Its tip which, as it vibrated here and there
　　Like a tongue in speech, flung out a voice to say:

"When Circe had detained me more than a year
　　There near Gaeta, before it had that name
90　Aeneas gave it, and I parted from her,

Not fondness for my son, nor any claim
　　Of reverence for my father, nor love I owed
　　Penelope, to please her, could overcome

My longing for experience of the world,
　　Of human vices and virtue. But I sailed out
　　On the deep open seas, accompanied

Canto XXVI / 275

100   ma misi me per l'alto mare aperto
     sol con un legno e con quella compagna
     picciola da la qual non fui diserto.
   L'un lito e l'altro vidi infin la Spagna,
     fin nel Morrocco, e l'isola d'i Sardi,
     e l'altre che quel mare intorno bagna.
   Io e ' compagni eravam vecchi e tardi
     quando venimmo a quella foce stretta
     dov' Ercule segnò li suoi riguardi
   acciò che l'uom più oltre non si metta;
110   da la man destra mi lasciai Sibilia,
     da l'altra già m'avea lasciata Setta.
   "O frati", dissi, "che per cento milia
     perigli siete giunti a l'occidente,
     a questa tanto picciola vigilia
   d'i nostri sensi ch'è del rimanente
     non vogliate negar l'esperïenza,
     di retro al sol, del mondo sanza gente.
   Considerate la vostra semenza:
     fatti non foste a viver come bruti,
120   ma per seguir virtute e canoscenza".
   Li miei compagni fec' io sì aguti,
     con questa orazion picciola, al cammino,
     che a pena poscia li avrei ritenuti;
   e volta nostra poppa nel mattino,
     de' remi facemmo ali al folle volo,
     sempre acquistando dal lato mancino.
   Tutte le stelle già de l'altro polo
     vedea la notte, e 'l nostro tanto basso,
     che non surgëa fuor del marin suolo.
130   Cinque volte racceso e tante casso
     lo lume era di sotto da la luna,
     poi che 'ntrati eravam ne l'alto passo,
   quando n'apparve una montagna, bruna
     per la distanza, e parvemi alta tanto
     quanto veduta non avëa alcuna.

By that small company that still had not
    Deserted me, in a single ship. One coast
    I saw, and then another, and I got

100 As far as Spain, Morocco, Sardinia, a host
    Of other islands that the sea bathes round.
    My men and I were old and slow when we passed

The narrow outlet where Hercules let stand
    His markers beyond which men were not to sail.
    On my left hand I had left Ceuta behind,

And on the other sailed beyond Seville.
    'O brothers who have reached the west,' I began,
    'Through a hundred thousand perils, surviving all:

So little is the vigil we see remain
110 Still for our senses, that you should not choose
    To deny it the experience—behind the sun

Leading us onward—of the world which has
    No people in it. Consider well your seed:
    You were not born to live as a mere brute does,

But for the pursuit of knowledge and the good.'
    Then all of my companions grew so keen
    To journey, spurred by this little speech I'd made,

I would have found them difficult to restrain.
    Turning our stern toward the morning light,
120 We made wings of our oars, in an insane

Flight, always gaining on the left. The night
    Showed all the stars, now, of the other pole—
    Our own star fallen so low, no sign of it

Rose from the sea. The moon's low face glowed full
    Five times since we set course across the deep,
    And as many times was quenched invisible,

When dim in the distance we saw a mountaintop:
    It seemed the highest I had ever seen.
    We celebrated—but soon began to weep,

Canto XXVI / 277

Noi ci allegrammo, e tosto tornò in pianto;
   ché de la nova terra un turbo nacque
   e percosse del legno il primo canto.
Tre volte il fé girar con tutte l'acque;
140   *a la quarta levar la poppa in suso*
   e la prora ire in giù, com' altrui piacque,
infin che 'l mar fu sovra noi richiuso».

130   For from the newfound land a storm had grown,
      Rising to strike the forepart of the ship.
      It whirled the vessel round, and round again

With all the waters three times, lifting up
      The stern the fourth—as pleased an Other—to press
      The prow beneath the surface, and did not stop

Until the sea had closed up over us."

XXVII

"I was a man of arms, and after that
Became a corded friar, hopeful to do

Penance by wearing the rope . . ."

(65–67)

Già era dritta in sù la fiamma e queta
  per non dir più, e già da noi sen gia
  con la licenza del dolce poeta,
quand' un'altra, che dietro a lei venìa,
  ne fece volger li occhi a la sua cima
  per un confuso suon che fuor n'uscia.
Come 'l bue cicilian che mugghiò prima
  col pianto di colui, e ciò fu dritto,
  che l'avea temperato con sua lima,
10 mugghiava con la voce de l'afflitto,
  sì che, con tutto che fosse di rame,
  pur el pareva dal dolor trafitto;
così, per non aver via né forame
  dal principio nel foco, in suo linguaggio
  si convertïan le parole grame.
Ma poscia ch'ebber colto lor vïaggio
  su per la punta, dandole quel guizzo
  che dato avea la lingua in lor passaggio,
udimmo dire: «O tu a cu' io drizzo
20 la voce e che parlavi mo lombardo,
  dicendo "Istra ten va, più non t'adizzo",
perch' io sia giunto forse alquanto tardo,
  non t'incresca restare a parlar meco;
  vedi che non incresce a me, e ardo!
Se tu pur mo in questo mondo cieco
  caduto se' di quella dolce terra
  latina ond' io mia colpa tutta reco,
dimmi se Romagnuoli han pace o guerra;
  ch'io fui d'i monti là intra Orbino
30 e 'l giogo di che Tever si diserra».

The flame already was quiet and erect again,
   Done speaking, and, as the gentle poet allowed,
   Leaving us, when behind it another one

Was drawing near, the confused sound it made
   Drawing our eyes toward its flickering tip.
   As the Sicilian bull (which bellowed loud

For the first time when he who gave it shape
   With his file's art was forced to give it his voice,
   Justly) would use a victim's cries, sealed up

10 Inside its body, to bellow—so that, though brass,
   It seemed transfixed with pain when it was heated:
   So, having at first no passage or egress

From fire, the melancholy words were transmuted
   Into fire's language. But after the words had found
   Their passage through the tip, and it vibrated

As the tongue had in trying to form their sound,
   We heard it say, "O you toward whom I guide
   My voice, and who a moment ago intoned

In Lombard, 'Now continue on your road,
20   I do not ask you more'—though I may be
   Late in my coming here, don't be annoyed

To stop and speak; you see that I am free
   Of annoyance, though I burn. If you just fell
   Into this viewless world from Italy,

Sweet land above, from which I carry all
   My guilt, then tell me: is it peace or war
   That occupies the Romagnoles?—I hail

From the hill country between Urbino and where,
   High up the ridge, the Tiber has its source."
30   I was still crouched and intently giving ear

Io era in giuso ancora attento e chino,
  quando il mio duca mi tentò di costa,
  dicendo: «Parla tu; questi è latino».
E io, ch'avea già pronta la risposta,
  sanza indugio a parlare incominciai:
  «O anima che se' là giù nascosta,
Romagna tua non è, e non fu mai,
  sanza guerra ne' cuor de' suoi tiranni;
  ma 'n palese nessuna or vi lasciai.
40 Ravenna sta come stata è molt' anni:
  l'aguglia da Polenta la si cova,
  sì che Cervia ricuopre co' suoi vanni.
La terra che fé già la lunga prova
  e di Franceschi sanguinoso mucchio,
  sotto le branche verdi si ritrova.
E 'l mastin vecchio e 'l nuovo da Verrucchio,
  che fecer di Montagna il mal governo,
  là dove soglion fan d'i denti succhio.
Le città di Lamone e di Santerno
50 conduce il lïoncel dal nido bianco,
  che muta parte da la state al verno.
E quella cu' il Savio bagna il fianco,
  così com' ella sie' tra 'l piano e 'l monte,
  tra tirannia si vive e stato franco.
Ora chi se', ti priego che ne conte;
  non esser duro più ch'altri sia stato,
  se 'l nome tuo nel mondo tegna fronte».
Poscia che 'l foco alquanto ebbe rugghiato
  al modo suo, l'aguta punta mosse
60 di qua, di là, e poi diè cotal fiato:
«S'i' credesse che mia risposta fosse
  a persona che mai tornasse al mondo,
  questa fiamma staria sanza più scosse;
ma però che già mai di questo fondo
  non tornò vivo alcun, s'i' odo il vero,
  sanza tema d'infamia ti rispondo.

When my guide nudged me, saying, "You may discourse
  With him: he is Italian." Already prepared
  To answer, I said: "That Romagna of yours,

O soul concealed below, is not yet cleared
  And never was—in her tyrants' hearts—of war:
  Though when I left, no war had been declared.

Ravenna still remains as many a year,
  Polenta's eagle brooding above the town
  So its wings cover Cervia. The land that bore

40 The long siege, once, and struck the Frenchmen down
  Into a bloody heap, finds itself now
  Held underneath the Green Paws once again.

Both the old mastiff and new of Verrucchio,
  Who treated Montagna in an evil way,
  Sink their teeth in, the way they always do.

Along the Santerno and the Lamone lie
  Cities the Lionet of the White Lair rules,
  Who changes sides and shifts his loyalty

From summer to winter. And the town that feels
50 The Savio bathe its flank, just as it lies
  Between a plain and mountains, also dwells

Somewhere between tyranny's and freedom's ways.
  And now I pray you—tell us who you are.
  Don't be more grudging than another was

In answering you, so may your name endure,
  Proudly in the world above." After the fire
  Roared in its way awhile, it began to stir

Its sharp tip rapidly, first here, then there,
  Then formed this breath: "If I believed I gave
60 My answer to one who'd ever go once more

Back to the world, this tongue of flame would have
  No motion. But since, if what I hear is true,
  None ever returned from this abyss alive,

Io fui uom d'arme, e poi fui cordigliero,
  credendomi, sì cinto, fare ammenda;
  e certo il creder mio venìa intero,
70 se non fosse il gran prete, a cui mal prenda!,
  che mi rimise ne le prime colpe;
  e come e quare, voglio che m'intenda.
Mentre ch'io forma fui d'ossa e di polpe
  che la madre mi diè, l'opere mie
  non furon leonine, ma di volpe.
Li accorgimenti e le coperte vie
  io seppi tutte, e sì menai lor arte,
  ch'al fine de la terra il suono uscie.
Quando mi vidi giunto in quella parte
80 di mia etade ove ciascun dovrebbe
  calar le vele e raccoglier le sarte,
ciò che pria mi piacëa, allor m'increbbe,
  e pentuto e confesso mi rendei;
  ahi miser lasso! e giovato sarebbe.
Lo principe d'i novi Farisei,
  avendo guerra presso a Laterano,
  e non con Saracin né con Giudei,
ché ciascun suo nimico era cristiano,
  e nessun era stato a vincer Acri
90 né mercatante in terra di Soldano,
né sommo officio né ordini sacri
  guardò in sé, né in me quel capestro
  che solea fare i suoi cinti più macri.
Ma come Costantin chiese Silvestro
  d'entro Siratti a guerir de la lebbre,
  così mi chiese questi per maestro

Not fearing infamy I will answer you.
  I was a man of arms, and after that
  Became a corded friar, hopeful to do

Penance by wearing the rope; indeed that thought
  Might well have been fulfilled, but the High Priest—
  May evil befall him!—led me to commit

70 Again the sins that I had practiced at first:
  And how and why, now listen and I'll disclose.
  My actions, when my form was still encased

In the flesh and bones my mother gave me, were those
  Of the fox, not the lion. I was expert
  In all the stratagems and covert ways,

And practiced them with so much cunning art
  The sound extended to the earth's far end.
  But when I saw that I had reached that part

Of life when we should let our sails descend
80 And coil the ropes—then what had pleased me before
  Now grieved me: penitent and confessed, I joined

An order and—woe to say!—my life as friar
  Would have availed me. The Prince of new Pharisees
  Nearby the Lateran was making war,

And not against the Saracens or Jews,
  His enemies all being Christians: and none
  Had been at Acre's conquest, nor one of those

Who went as merchants to the Sultan's domain;
  And he respected neither the supreme
90 Office and holy orders that were his own,

Nor in me the friar's cord which at one time
  Made those who wore it leaner. As Constantine
  Sought out Sylvester in Soracte, his aim

To have him cure his leprosy—this man
  Came seeking me as one who meant to find
  A doctor to cure the fever he was in,

a guerir de la sua superba febbre;
domandommi consiglio, e io tacetti
perché le sue parole parver ebbre.

100 E' poi ridisse: "Tuo cuor non sospetti;
finor t'assolvo, e tu m'insegna fare
sì come Penestrino in terra getti.

Lo ciel poss' io serrare e diserrare,
come tu sai; però son due le chiavi
che 'l mio antecessor non ebbe care".

Allor mi pinser li argomenti gravi
là 've 'l tacer mi fu avviso 'l peggio,
e dissi: "Padre, da che tu mi lavi

di quel peccato ov'io mo cader deggio,
110 lunga promessa con l'attender corto
ti farà trïunfar ne l'alto seggio".

Francesco venne poi, com' io fu' morto,
per me; ma un d'i neri cherubini
li disse: "Non portar; non mi far torto.

Venir se ne dee giù tra ' miei meschini
perché diede 'l consiglio frodolente,
dal quale in qua stato li sono a' crini;

ch'assolver non si può chi non si pente,
né pentere e volere insieme puossi
120 per la contradizion che nol consente".

Oh me dolente! come mi riscossi
quando mi prese dicendomi: "Forse
tu non pensavi ch'io löico fossi!".

A Minòs mi portò; e quelli attorse
otto volte la coda al dosso duro;
e poi che per gran rabbia la si morse,

disse: "Questi è d'i rei del foco furo";
per ch'io là dove vedi son perduto,
e sì vestito, andando, mi rancuro».

Of pride. He asked my counsel, and I remained
  Silent, because his words seemed drunk to me.
  And then he spoke again: 'Now understand,

100 Your heart should not respond mistrustfully,
  For I absolve you in advance, henceforth:
  Instruct me, so that I can find a way

To level Palestrina to the earth.
  I have the power to lock and unlock Heaven,
  As you know; for the keys are two, whose worth

Seemed not dear to my predecessor.' Then, driven
  To where the gravity of his argument
  Made silence seem worse counsel, I said: 'Given,

Father, that you are washing me of the taint
110 Of this sin into which I now must fall—
  Large promises with fulfillments that are scant

Will bring your high throne triumph over all.'
  And Francis came for me the moment I died,
  But one of these black cherubim of Hell

Appeared; and, 'Do not carry him off,' it said,
  'Do not deprive me: he must be carried down
  Among my servants, because he counseled fraud,

And I have hovered near his hair since then,
  Until this moment—for no one has absolution
120 Without repenting; nor can one will a sin

And repent at once, because the contradiction
  Precludes it.' How I shuddered—O wretched me!
  'Perhaps you did not think I was a logician,'

He said, and took me, and carried me away
  To Minos, who coiled his tail eight times around
  His scaly back, and gnawed it angrily

And then declared, 'This wicked one is bound
  For the fire of thievery.' So I am lost
  Where you see me wander, in this garment wound,

130   *Quand' elli ebbe 'l suo dir così compiuto,*
       la fiamma dolorando si partio,
       torcendo e dibattendo 'l corno aguto.
   Noi passamm' oltre, e io e 'l duca mio,
       su per lo scoglio infino in su l'altr' arco
       che cuopre 'l fosso in che si paga il fio
   a quei che scommettendo acquistan carco.

130 Bitter to myself." And as his discourse ceased
        The grieving flame departed, its horn's sharp point
        Tossing about and twisting as it passed.

     We journeyed on, my leader and I, and went
        To the next arch of the ridge: and looking under,
        We saw the fosse where they pay the due amount

     Who earned their burden by splitting things asunder.

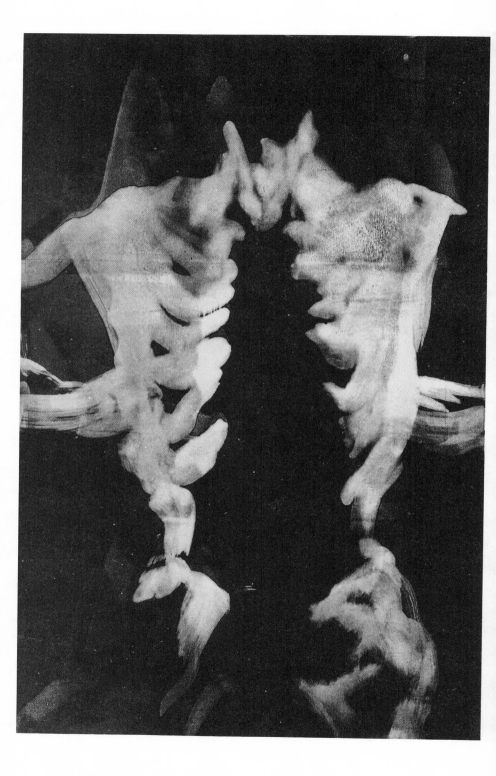

XXVIII

No barrel staved-in
And missing its end-piece ever gaped as wide
As the man I saw split open from his chin

Down to the farting-place . . .

(22–25)

Chi poria mai pur con parole sciolte
   dicer del sangue e de le piaghe a pieno
   ch'i' ora vidi, per narrar più volte?
Ogne lingua per certo verria meno
   per lo nostro sermone e per la mente
   c'hanno a tanto comprender poco seno.
S'el s'aunasse ancor tutta la gente
   che già, in su la fortunata terra
   di Puglia, fu del suo sangue dolente
10 per li Troiani e per la lunga guerra
   che de l'anella fé sì alte spoglie,
   come Livïo scrive, che non erra,
con quella che sentio di colpi doglie
   per contastare a Ruberto Guiscardo;
   e l'altra il cui ossame ancor s'accoglie
a Ceperan, là dove fu bugiardo
   ciascun Pugliese, e là da Tagliacozzo,
   dove sanz' arme vinse il vecchio Alardo;
e qual forato suo membro e qual mozzo
20 mostrasse, d'aequar sarebbe nulla
   il modo de la nona bolgia sozzo.
Già veggia, per mezzul perdere o lulla,
   com' io vidi un, così non si pertugia,
   rotto dal mento infin dove si trulla.
Tra le gambe pendevan le minugia;
   la corata pareva e 'l tristo sacco
   che merda fa di quel che si trangugia.
Mentre che tutto in lui veder m'attacco,
   guardommi e con le man s'aperse il petto,
30 dicendo: «Or vedi com' io mi dilacco!

Who could find words, even in free-running prose,
  For the blood and wounds I saw, in all their horror—
  Telling it over as often as you choose,

It's certain no human tongue could take the measure
  Of those enormities. Our speech and mind,
  Straining to comprehend them, flail, and falter.

If all the Apulians who long ago mourned
  Their lives cut off by Trojans could live once more,
  Assembled to grieve again with all those stained

10 By their own blood in the long Carthaginian war—
  Rings pillaged from their corpses poured by the bushel,
  As Livy writes, who never was known to err—

And they who took their mortal blows in battle
  With Robert Guiscard, and those whose bones were heaped
  At Ceperano, killed in the Puglian betrayal,

And the soldiers massacred in the stratagem shaped
  By old Alardo, who conquered without a weapon
  Near Tagliacozzo when their army was trapped—

And some were showing wounds still hot and open,
20 Others the gashes where severed limbs had been:
  It would be nothing to equal the mutilation

I saw in that Ninth Chasm. No barrel staved-in
  And missing its end-piece ever gaped as wide
  As the man I saw split open from his chin

Down to the farting-place, and from the splayed
  Trunk the spilled entrails dangled between his thighs.
  I saw his organs, and the sack that makes the bread

We swallow turn to shit. Seeing my eyes
  Fastened upon him, he pulled open his chest
30 With both hands, saying, "Look how Mohammed claws

vedi come storpiato è Mäometto!
　　Dinanzi a me sen va piangendo Alì,
　　fesso nel volto dal mento al ciuffetto.
E tutti li altri che tu vedi qui,
　　seminator di scandalo e di scisma
　　fuor vivi, e però son fessi così.
Un diavolo è qua dietro che n'accisma
　　sì crudelmente, al taglio de la spada
　　rimettendo ciascun di questa risma,
40　quand' avem volta la dolente strada;
　　però che le ferite son richiuse
　　prima ch'altri dinanzi li rivada.
Ma tu chi se' che 'n su lo scoglio muse,
　　forse per indugiar d'ire a la pena
　　ch'è giudicata in su le tue accuse?».
«Né morte 'l giunse ancor, né colpa 'l mena»,
　　rispuose 'l mio maestro, «a tormentarlo;
　　ma per dar lui esperïenza piena,
a me, che morto son, convien menarlo
50　per lo 'nferno qua giù di giro in giro;
　　e quest' è ver così com' io ti parlo».
Più fuor di cento che, quando l'udiro,
　　s'arrestaron nel fosso a riguardarmi
　　per maraviglia, oblïando il martiro.
«Or dì a fra Dolcin dunque che s'armi,
　　tu che forse vedra' il sole in breve,
　　s'ello non vuol qui tosto seguitarmi,
sì di vivanda, che stretta di neve
　　non rechi la vittoria al Noarese,
60　ch'altrimenti acquistar non saria leve».
Poi che l'un piè per girsene sospese,
　　Mäometto mi disse esta parola;
　　indi a partirsi in terra lo distese.
Un altro, che forata avea la gola
　　e tronco 'l naso infin sotto le ciglia,
　　e non avea mai ch'una orecchia sola,
ristato a riguardar per maraviglia
　　con li altri, innanzi a li altri aprì la canna,
　　ch'era di fuor d'ogne parte vermiglia,

And mangles himself, torn open down the breast!
   Look how I tear myself! And Alì goes
   Weeping before me—like me, a schismatic, and cleft:

Split open from the chin along his face
   Up to the forelock. All you see here, when alive,
   Taught scandal and schism, so they are cleavered like this.

A devil waits with a sword back there to carve
   Each of us open afresh each time we've gone
   Our circuit round this road, where while we grieve

40 Our wounds close up before we pass him again—
   But who are you that stand here, perhaps to delay
   Torments pronounced on your own false words to men?"

"Neither has death yet reached him, nor does he stay
   For punishment of guilt," my master replied,
   "But for experience. And for that purpose I,

Who am dead, lead him through Hell as rightful guide,
   From circle to circle. Of this, you can be as sure
   As that I speak to you here at his side."

More than a hundred shades were gathered there
50 Who hearing my master's words had halted, and came
   Along the trench toward me in order to stare,

Forgetting their torment in wonder for a time.
   "Tell Fra Dolcino, you who may see the sun,
   If he wants not to follow soon to the same

Punishment, he had better store up grain
   Against a winter siege and the snows' duress,
   Or the Novarese will easily bring him down"—

After he had lifted his foot to resume the pace,
   Mohammed spoke these words, and having spoken
60 He stepped away again on his painful course.

Another there, whose face was cruelly broken,
   The throat pierced through, the nose cut off at the brow,
   One ear remaining, stopped and gazed at me, stricken

70 e disse: «O tu cui colpa non condanna
       e cu' io vidi in su terra latina,
       se troppa simiglianza non m'inganna,
    rimembriti di Pier da Medicina,
       se mai torni a veder lo dolce piano
       che da Vercelli a Marcabò dichina.
    E fa sapere a' due miglior da Fano,
       a messer Guido e anco ad Angiolello,
       che, se l'antiveder qui non è vano,
    gittati saran fuor di lor vasello
80   e mazzerati presso a la Cattolica
       per tradimento d'un tiranno fello.
    Tra l'isola di Cipri e di Maiolica
       non vide mai sì gran fallo Nettuno,
       non da pirate, non da gente argolica.
    Quel traditor che vede pur con l'uno,
       e tien la terra che tale qui meco
       vorrebbe di vedere esser digiuno,
    farà venirli a parlamento seco;
       poi farà sì, ch'al vento di Focara
90   non sarà lor mestier voto né preco».
    E io a lui: «Dimostrami e dichiara,
       se vuo' ch'i' porti sù di te novella,
       chi è colui da la veduta amara».
    Allor puose la mano a la mascella
       d'un suo compagno e la bocca li aperse,
       gridando: «Questi è desso, e non favella.
    Questi, scacciato, il dubitar sommerse
       in Cesare, affermando che 'l fornito
       sempre con danno l'attender sofferse».
100 Oh quanto mi pareva sbigottito
       con la lingua tagliata ne la strozza
       Curïo, ch'a dir fu così ardito!
    E un ch'avea l'una e l'altra man mozza,
       levando i moncherin per l'aura fosca,
       sì che 'l sangue facea la faccia sozza,

With recognition as well as wonder. "Ah, you,"
  His bleeding throat spoke, "you here, yet not eternally
  Doomed here by guilt—unless I'm deceived, I knew

Your face when I still walked above in Italy.
  If you return to the sweet plain I knew well
  That slopes toward Marcabò from Vercelli,

70 Remember Pier da Medicina. And tell
  Ser Guido and Angiolello, the two best men
  Of Fano: if we have foresight here in Hell

Then by a tyrant's treachery they will drown
  Off La Cattolica—bound and thrown in the sea
  From their ships. Neptune has never seen, between

Cyprus and Majorca, whether committed by
  Pirates or Argives, such a crime. The betrayer
  Who sees from one eye only (he holds a city

Found bitter by another who's with me here)
80 Will lure them to set sail for truce-talks: then,
  When he has dealt with them, they'll need no prayer

For safe winds near Focara—not ever again."
  Then I to him: "If you'd have me be the bearer
  Of news from you to those above, explain—

What man do you mean, who found a city bitter?"
  Then he grasped one shade near him by the jaw,
  And opened the mouth, and said, "This is the creature,

He does not speak, who once, in exile, knew
  Words to persuade Caesar at the Rubicon—
90 Affirming, to help him thrust his doubt below,

'Delaying when he's ready hurts a man.' "
  I saw how helpless Curio's tongue was cut
  To a stub in his throat, whose speech had been so keen.

One with both hands lopped off came forward to shout,
  Stumps raised in the murk to spatter his cheeks with blood,
  "Also remember Mosca! I too gave out

gridò: «Ricordera'ti anche del Mosca,
   che disse, lasso!, "Capo ha cosa fatta",
   che fu mal seme per la gente tosca».
E io li aggiunsi: «E morte di tua schiatta»;
110   per ch'elli, accumulando duol con duolo,
   sen gio come persona trista e matta.
Ma io rimasi a riguardar lo stuolo,
   e vidi cosa ch'io avrei paura,
   sanza più prova, di contarla solo;
se non che coscïenza m'assicura,
   la buona compagnia che l'uom francheggia
   sotto l'asbergo del sentirsi pura.
Io vidi certo, e ancor par ch'io 'l veggia,
   un busto sanza capo andar sì come
120   andavan li altri de la trista greggia;
e 'l capo tronco tenea per le chiome,
   pesol con mano a guisa di lanterna:
   e quel mirava noi e dicea: «Oh me!».
Di sé facea a sé stesso lucerna,
   ed eran due in uno e uno in due;
   com' esser può, quei sa che sì governa.
Quando diritto al piè del ponte fue,
   levò 'l braccio alto con tutta la testa
   per appressarne le parole sue,
130   che fuoro: «Or vedi la pena molesta,
   tu che, spirando, vai veggendo i morti:
   vedi s'alcuna è grande come questa.
E perché tu di me novella porti,
   sappi ch'i' son Bertram dal Bornio, quelli
   che diedi al re giovane i ma' conforti.
Io feci il padre e 'l figlio in sé ribelli;
   Achitofèl non fé più d'Absalone
   e di Davìd coi malvagi punzelli.
Perch' io parti' così giunte persone,
140   partito porto il mio cerebro, lasso!,
   dal suo principio ch'è in questo troncone.
Così s'osserva in me lo contrapasso».

A slogan urging bloodshed, when I said
  'Once done it's done with': words which were seeds of pain
  For the Tuscan people." Then, when he heard me add,

"—and death to your family line," utterly undone
  By sorrow heaped upon his sorrow, the soul
  Went away like one whom grief has made insane.

I stayed to see more, one sight so incredible
  As I should fear to describe, except that conscience,
  Being pure in this, encourages me to tell:

I saw—and writing it now, my brain still envisions—
  A headless trunk that walked, in sad promenade
  Shuffling the dolorous track with its companions,

And the trunk was carrying the severed head,
  Gripping its hair like a lantern, letting it swing,
  And the head looked up at us: "Oh me!" it cried.

He was himself and his lamp as he strode along,
  Two in one, and one in two—and how it can be,
  Only He knows, who so ordains the thing.

Reaching the bridge, the trunk held the head up high
  So we could hear his words, which were "Look well,
  You who come breathing to view the dead, and say

If there is punishment harder than mine in Hell.
  Carry the word, and know me: Bertran de Born,
  Who made the father and the son rebel

The one against the other, by the evil turn
  I did the young king, counseling him to ill.
  David and Absalom had nothing worse to learn

From the wickedness contrived by Achitophel.
  Because I parted their union, I carry my brain
  Parted from this, its pitiful stem: Mark well

This retribution that you see is mine."

XXIX

That mass of people wounded so curiously
  Had made my eyes so drunk they had a passion
  To stay and weep. But Virgil said to me,

"What are you staring at? Why let your vision
  Linger there down among the disconsolate
  And mutilated shades?"

(1–6)

La molta gente e le diverse piaghe
   avean le luci mie sì inebrïate,
   che de lo stare a piangere eran vaghe.
Ma Virgilio mi disse: «Che pur guate?
   perché la vista tua pur si soffolge
   là giù tra l'ombre triste smozzicate?
Tu non hai fatto sì a l'altre bolge;
   pensa, se tu annoverar le credi,
   che miglia ventidue la valle volge.
10 E già la luna è sotto i nostri piedi;
   lo tempo è poco omai che n'è concesso,
   e altro è da veder che tu non vedi».
«Se tu avessi», rispuos' io appresso,
   «atteso a la cagion per ch'io guardava,
   forse m'avresti ancor lo star dimesso».
Parte sen giva, e io retro li andava,
   lo duca, già faccendo la risposta,
   e soggiugnendo: «Dentro a quella cava
dov' io tenea or li occhi sì a posta,
20 credo ch'un spirto del mio sangue pianga
   la colpa che là giù cotanto costa».
Allor disse 'l maestro: «Non si franga
   lo tuo pensier da qui innanzi sovr' ello.
   Attendi ad altro, ed ei là si rimanga;
ch'io vidi lui a piè del ponticello
   mostrarti e minacciar forte col dito,
   e udi' 'l nominar Geri del Bello.
Tu eri allor sì del tutto impedito
   sovra colui che già tenne Altaforte,
30 che non guardasti in là, sì fu partito».

CANTO XXIX

That mass of people wounded so curiously
   Had made my eyes so drunk they had a passion
   To stay and weep. But Virgil said to me,

"What are you staring at? Why let your vision
   Linger there down among the disconsolate
   And mutilated shades? You found no reason

To delay like this at any other pit.
   Consider, if counting them is what you plan:
   This valley extends along a circular route

10 For twenty-two miles. And already the moon
   Is under our feet: the time we are allowed
   Has now grown short, and more is to be seen

Than you see here." "If you had given heed
   To what my reason is for looking, perhaps
   You would have granted a longer stay," I said.

Meanwhile my guide went on, and in his steps
   I followed while I answered—but told him, too,
   "Inside that hollow, where for a little lapse

Of time I gazed so steadily just now,
20   I think a spirit of my own blood laments
   The guilt that brings so great a cost below."

The master answered, "Let your intelligence
   Distract itself with thoughts of him no more.
   Attend to other things, while he remains

Down where he is, below the bridge—for there
   I saw him with his finger point you out
   And fiercely threaten you. And I could hear

Them call him Geri del Bello. So complete
   Was your preoccupation with the one
30   Who once held Altaforte, you never set

«O duca mio, la vïolenta morte
    che non li è vendicata ancor», diss' io,
    «per alcun che de l'onta sia consorte,
fece lui disdegnoso; ond' el sen gio
    sanza parlarmi, sì com' ïo estimo:
    e in ciò m'ha el fatto a sé più pio».
Così parlammo infino al loco primo
    che de lo scoglio l'altra valle mostra,
    se più lume vi fosse, tutto ad imo.
40 Quando noi fummo sor l'ultima chiostra
    di Malebolge, sì che i suoi conversi
    potean parere a la veduta nostra,
lamenti saettaron me diversi,
    che di pietà ferrati avean li strali;
    ond' io li orecchi con le man copersi.
Qual dolor fora, se de li spedali
    di Valdichiana tra 'l luglio e 'l settembre
    e di Maremma e di Sardigna i mali
fossero in una fossa tutti 'nsembre,
50   tal era quivi, e tal puzzo n'usciva
    qual suol venir de le marcite membre.
Noi discendemmo in su l'ultima riva
    del lungo scoglio, pur da man sinistra;
    e allor fu la mia vista più viva
giù ver' lo fondo, là 've la ministra
    de l'alto Sire infallibil giustizia
    punisce i falsador che qui registra.
Non credo ch'a veder maggior tristizia
    fosse in Egina il popol tutto infermo,
60   quando fu l'aere sì pien di malizia,

Your eyes in his direction till he was gone."
And "O my guide," I said, "his violent death,
For which as yet no vengeance has been done

By any of those he shares dishonor with,
Is what has made him full of indignation—
And that is why he continued on his path

Without addressing me, and with this action
He makes my pity for him greater yet."
So we continued in our conversation,

40 Walking the ridge until we reached the spot
Where the next valley could first be seen below—
Down to the bottom, had there been more light.

Up above Malebolge's last cloister now
Where we could see its lay-brothers under us,
Their strange laments beset me, each an arrow

Whose shaft was barbed with pity—and at this,
I lifted up my hands and blocked my ears.
The suffering was such, if one could place

All of the sick who endure disease's course
50 In Val di Chiana's hospital from July
All through September, and all the sufferers

In Maremma and Sardinia, to lie
All in one ditch together, so was this place;
From it a stench, like that which usually

Is given off by festering limbs, arose.
Keeping as ever to the left, on down
We came, to the ridge's final bank. The fosse

Grew clearer to my sight, in which the one
Who serves as minister of the Lord on high,
60 Unerring Justice, lets her punishments rain

Upon the shades whose sin is to falsify;
She has recorded them upon her scroll.
I think it could not have been sadder to see

che li animali, infino al picciol vermo,
    cascaron tutti, e poi le genti antiche,
    secondo che i poeti hanno per fermo,
si ristorar di seme di formiche;
    ch'era a veder per quella oscura valle
    languir li spirti per diverse biche.
Qual sovra 'l ventre e qual sovra le spalle
    l'un de l'altro giacea, e qual carpone
    si trasmutava per lo tristo calle.
70 Passo passo andavam sanza sermone,
    guardando e ascoltando li ammalati,
    che non potean levar le lor persone.
Io vidi due sedere a sé poggiati,
    com' a scaldar si poggia tegghia a tegghia,
    dal capo al piè di schianze macolati;
e non vidi già mai menare stregghia
    a ragazzo aspettato dal segnorso,
    né a colui che mal volontier vegghia,
come ciascun menava spesso il morso
80 de l'unghie sopra sé per la gran rabbia
    del pizzicor, che non ha più soccorso;
e sì traevan giù l'unghie la scabbia,
    come coltel di scardova le scaglie
    o d'altro pesce che più larghe l'abbia.
«O tu che con le dita ti dismaglie»,
    cominciò 'l duca mio a l'un di loro,
    «e che fai d'esse talvolta tanaglie,
dinne s'alcun Latino è tra costoro
    che son quinc' entro, se l'unghia ti basti
90 etternalmente a cotesto lavoro».

Aegina's whole population fallen ill
   When such corruption crowded through the air
   That, down to the small worms, every animal

Succumbed (and afterward, the poets aver
   As certain, the ancient populace was restored
   Out of the seed of ants) than to see there,

70 All through that murky valley, how a horde
   Of shades lay languishing in scattered heaps:
   One lay upon his belly, another poured

Across his neighbor's shoulders, or perhaps
   Moved on all fours along the dismal track.
   In silence, walking with deliberate steps,

We went on, watching and listening to the sick,
   Who could not raise their bodies. I could see
   Two who were sitting propped up back to back,

As pan is leaned against pan to warm them dry,
80   Each of them spotted with scabs from head to foot.
   And I have never seen a stableboy

Who knows that he is making his master wait,
   Or one unhappy to be still awake,
   Work with a currycomb at such a rate

As each of these was laboring to rake
   His nails all over himself—scratching and digging
   For the great fury of the itch they tried to slake,

Which has no other relief: their nails were snagging
   Scabs from the skin as a knifeblade might remove
90   Scales from a carp, or as if the knife were dragging

Still larger scales some other fish might have.
   "O you who with your fingers scrape the mail
   From your own flesh, and sometimes make them serve

As pincers: say if any of these who dwell
   Below here with you come from Italy,
   So may your nails suffice you in this toil

«Latin siam noi, che tu vedi sì guasti
    qui ambedue», rispuose l'un piangendo;
    «ma tu chi se' che di noi dimandasti?».
E 'l duca disse: «I' son un che discendo
    con questo vivo giù di balzo in balzo,
    e di mostrar lo 'nferno a lui intendo».
Allor si ruppe lo comun rincalzo;
    e tremando ciascuno a me si volse
    con altri che l'udiron di rimbalzo.
100 Lo buon maestro a me tutto s'accolse,
    dicendo: «Dì a lor ciò che tu vuoli»;
    e io incominciai, poscia ch'ei volse:
«Se la vostra memoria non s'imboli
    nel primo mondo da l'umane menti,
    ma s'ella viva sotto molti soli,
ditemi chi voi siete e di che genti;
    la vostra sconcia e fastidiosa pena
    di palesarvi a me non vi spaventi».
«Io fui d'Arezzo, e Albero da Siena».
110 rispuose l'un, «mi fé mettere al foco;
    ma quel per ch'io mori' qui non mi mena.
Vero è ch'i' dissi lui, parlando a gioco:
    "I' mi saprei levar per l'aere a volo";
    e quei, ch'avea vaghezza e senno poco,
volle ch'i' li mostrassi l'arte; e solo
    perch' io nol feci Dedalo, mi fece
    ardere a tal che l'avea per figliuolo.
Ma ne l'ultima bolgia de le diece
    me per l'alchìmia che nel mondo usai
120 dannò Minòs, a cui fallar non lece».

That you perform throughout eternity—"
   My leader said, addressing one of the two.
   "Both of us are Italians, whom you see

100 Disfigured here," he answered, weeping. "But who
   Are you, who ask us?" My guide said, "I am one
   Who accompanies this living man; we go

Downward from level to level, and I mean
   To show him Hell." Their mutual support
   Was broken at his words; they turned to lean

Closer to me, both trembling and alert,
   With others who overheard what he had said.
   Drawing near me, my good master said, "Now start:

Speak to them as you choose." So I complied,
110 Beginning thus: "So that your memory
   In men's minds in the former world won't fade

But live on under many suns, tell me
   Who you and your people are; your punished state,
   Loathsome and hideous although it be,

Should not discourage you from speaking out."
   "I was of Arezzo," one answered, "and died by fire
   At Albero of Siena's orders, and yet

That which I died for is not what brought me here.
   The truth is that I told him, speaking in jest,
120 That I knew how to lift myself through air,

In flight: he, curious, but not much blessed
   With wit, asked me to train him in that skill;
   I failed to make him Daedalus—which sufficed

For him to have me burned: the sentence fell
   On me from one who held him as a son.
   But alchemy, which I plied in the world so well,

Is why I was doomed to this last ditch of ten
   By Minos, who cannot err in his decrees."
   I asked the poet, "Has there ever been

Canto XXIX / *311*

E io dissi al poeta: «Or fu già mai
    gente sì vana come la sanese?
    Certo non la francesca sì d'assai!».
Onde l'altro lebbroso, che m'intese,
    rispuose al detto mio: «Tra'mene Stricca
    che seppe far le temperate spese,
e Niccolò che la costuma ricca
    del garofano prima discoverse
    ne l'orto dove tal seme s'appicca;
130 e tra'ne la brigata in che disperse
    Caccia d'Ascian la vigna e la gran fonda,
    e l'Abbagliato suo senno proferse.
Ma perché sappi chi sì ti seconda
    contra i Sanesi, aguzza ver' me l'occhio,
    sì che la faccia mia ben ti risponda:
sì vedrai ch'io son l'ombra di Capocchio,
    che falsai li metalli con l'alchìmia;
    e te dee ricordar, se ben t'adocchio,
com'io fui di natura buona scimia».

130 Another people as vain as the Sienese?
        Certainly not the French themselves, by far."
      The other leprous one, at hearing this,

      Responded, "Some, you'll grant exceptions for:
        Stricca, who knew how to spend in moderation,
        And Niccolò, who was progenitor

      Of the costly cult of cloves—a fine tradition
        For the rich garden where such seeds take root.
        And let that company also be an exception

      Where Caccia d'Asciano freely spent out
140   His vineyard and his forest, and where the one
        They nicknamed Muddlehead displayed his wit.

      But so you know who seconds you in this vein
        Against the Sienese, come sharpen your gaze
        In my direction, where you may well discern

      The answer given to you by my face:
        I am Capocchio's shade—the counterfeiter
        Of metals by alchemy; if I trust my eyes,

      You recall how good I was at aping nature."

X X X

"*That monstrousness
Is Gianni Schicchi; he runs rabid among*

The others here, and graces them like this."

(29–31)

Nel tempo che Iunone era crucciata
   per Semelè contra 'l sangue tebano,
   come mostrò una e altra fïata,
Atamante divenne tanto insano,
   che veggendo la moglie con due figli
   andar carcata da ciascuna mano,
gridò: «Tendiam le reti, sì ch'io pigli
   la leonessa e ' leoncini al varco»;
   e poi distese i dispietati artigli,
10 prendendo l'un ch'avea nome Learco,
   e rotollo e percosselo ad un sasso;
   e quella s'annegò con l'altro carco.
E quando la fortuna volse in basso
   l'altezza de' Troian che tutto ardiva,
   sì che 'nsieme col regno il re fu casso,
Ecuba trista, misera e cattiva,
   poscia che vide Polissena morta,
   e del suo Polidoro in su la riva
del mar si fu la dolorosa accorta,
20 forsennata latrò sì come cane;
   tanto il dolor le fé la mente torta.
Ma né di Tebe furie né troiane
   si vider mäi in alcun tanto crude,
   non punger bestie, nonché membra umane,
quant' io vidi in due ombre smorte e nude,
   che mordendo correvan di quel modo
   che 'l porco quando del porcil si schiude.
L'una giunse a Capocchio, e in sul nodo
   del collo l'assannò, sì che, tirando,
30 grattar li fece il ventre al fondo sodo.
E l'Aretin che rimase tremando,
   mi disse: «Quel folletto è Gianni Schicchi,
   e va rabbioso altrui così conciando».

Once, in the time when Juno was furious
  With the Theban blood because of Semele—
  As more than once she showed them—Athamas

Grew so insane that, seeing his wife walk by
  Carrying their children one on either hand,
  He cried: "Come, let us spread the nets and try

To take the lioness with the cubs she spawned,
  As they pass by!" And reaching out to strike
  With pitiless claws, he took the one they named

10 Learchus, and whirled him, and dashed him on a rock;
  She drowned herself and the other child she held.
  And when Fortune brought down the Trojans, who took

Risks proudly once, all-daring—their kingdom quelled
  And blotted out entirely with their king—
  Hecuba, wretched, a captive, after they killed

Polyxena with her there witnessing,
  Saw her Polydorus washed ashore: the weight
  Of sorrow drove her mad, her soul so wrung

She began barking like a dog. And yet,
20 No fury of Thebes or Troy was ever seen
  So cruel—not any rending of beasts, and not

Tearing of human limbs—as I saw shown
  By two pale, naked shades who now ran up
  Biting, the way a pig does loosed from the pen.

One charged Capocchio and bit his nape,
  And sank his tusks in deep, and dragged him along
  On the hard bottom, letting his belly scrape.

The spirit from Arezzo, shivering
  Where he was left, told me, "That monstrousness
30 Is Gianni Schicchi; he runs rabid among

Canto XXX / 317

«Oh» diss' io lui, «se l'altro non ti ficchi
   li denti a dosso, non ti sia fatica
   a dir chi è, pria che di qui si spicchi».
Ed elli a me: «Quell' è l'anima antica
   di Mirra scellerata, che divenne
   al padre, fuor del dritto amore, amica.
40 Questa a peccar con esso così venne,
   falsificando sé in altrui forma,
   come l'altro che là sen va, sostenne,
per guadagnar la donna de la torma,
   falsificare in sé Buoso Donati,
   testando e dando al testamento norma».
E poi che i due rabbiosi fuor passati
   sovra cu' io avea l'occhio tenuto,
   rivolsilo a guardar li altri mal nati.
Io vidi un, fatto a guisa di lëuto,
50 pur ch'elli avesse avuta l'anguinaia
   tronca da l'altro che l'uomo ha forcuto.
La grave idropesì, che sì dispaia
   le membra con l'omor che mal converte,
   che 'l viso non risponde a la ventraia,
faceva lui tener le labbra aperte
   come l'etico fa, che per la sete
   l'un verso 'l mento e l'altro in sù rinverte.
«O voi che sanz' alcuna pena siete,
   e non so io perché, nel mondo gramo»,
60 diss' elli a noi, «guardate e attendete
a la miseria del maestro Adamo;
   io ebbi, vivo, assai di quel ch'i' volli,
   e ora, lasso!, un gocciol d'acqua bramo.
Li ruscelletti che d'i verdi colli
   del Casentin discendon giuso in Arno,
   faccendo i lor canali freddi e molli,

The others here, and graces them like this."
"Oh," I responded, "so may that other one
Not fix its teeth on you, disclose to us

What shade it is—before it bolts again."
He answered, "That one is the ancient soul
Of Myrrha the infamous, whose love was drawn

Toward her father beyond what's honorable.
She engaged in sin with him by falsifying
Herself as someone else; and Schicchi as well,

40   Who runs off yonder, counterfeited: when trying
To acquire the finest lady of the herd,
He pretended he was Buoso Donati dying

And willed himself a legacy, each word
In proper form." When both of the raging pair
On whom I kept my eyes had disappeared,

I turned to see the ill-born others there:
One would be shaped exactly like a lute
Had he been cut off at the groin, from where

A man is forked. The heavy dropsical state,
50   Which makes the body's members so ill sorted
With undigested humors the face seems not

To answer to the swollen belly, had parted
His lips—the way the hectic being spurred
By thirst curls one lip up, the other distorted

Toward the chin. He said, "You who have fared
To this unhappy world, and yet arrive
Unpunished—I know not why—think, and regard

The misery of Master Adam. Alive,
I had in abundance all I wanted; now,
60   Alas! one drop of water is what I crave.

The rivulets that down to the Arno flow
From the green hills of Casentino, and make
Their channels cool and spongy as they go,

Canto XXX / 319

sempre mi stanno innanzi, e non indarno,
  ché l'immagine lor vie più m'asciuga
  che 'l male ond' io nel volto mi discarno.
70 La rigida giustizia che mi fruga
  tragge cagion del loco ov' io peccai
  a metter più li miei sospiri in fuga.
Ivi è Romena, là dov' io falsai
  la lega suggellata del Batista;
  per ch'io il corpo sù arso lasciai.
Ma s'io vedessi qui l'anima trista
  di Guido o d'Alessandro o di lor frate,
  per Fonte Branda non darei la vista.
Dentro c'è l'una già, se l'arrabbiate
80 ombre che vanno intorno dicon vero;
  ma che mi val, c'ho le membra legate?
S'io fossi pur di tanto ancor leggero
  ch'i' potessi in cent' anni andare un'oncia,
  io sarei messo già per lo sentiero,
cercando lui tra questa gente sconcia,
  con tutto ch'ella volge undici miglia,
  e men d'un mezzo di traverso non ci ha.
Io son per lor tra sì fatta famiglia;
  e' m'indussero a batter li fiorini
90 ch'avevan tre carati di mondiglia».
E io a lui: «Chi son li due tapini
  che fumman come man bagnate 'l verno,
  giacendo stretti a' tuoi destri confini?».
«Qui li trovai—e poi volta non dierno—»,
  rispuose, «quando piovvi in questo greppo,
  e non credo che dieno in sempiterno.

Are constantly before me—nor do they lack
    Effect: their image parches me far worse
    Than the face-wasting blight with which I'm sick.

The unbending Justice that wracks me thus makes use,
    Fittingly, of the same place where I sinned,
    To speed my sighs the quicker on their course:

70 There is Romena, where I falsely coined
    The currency that bears the Baptist's face,
    For which, on earth, I left my body burned—

But if I could behold, here in this place,
    The miserable soul of Guido, or that
    Of Alessandro, or set my eyes on his

Who is their brother, I would not trade the sight
    For Fonte Branda! One is already inside—
    If the raging shades who course the circle about

Have spoken truly. But since my limbs are tied,
80 What use is that to me? Were I still light
    Enough to move even one inch ahead

Every hundred years, I would have set out
    Upon the road already, trying to find
    Him in this mutilated people—despite

The circuit being eleven miles around
    And at least half a mile across its track.
    It's because of them that I am in this kind

Of family: they persuaded me to make
    Those florins that contained three carats of dross."
90 I asked him, "Who are that pair of wretches who smoke

As wet hands do in winter, lying close
    Next to your body on the right-hand side?"
    "I found them here—they have not changed their place—

When I first fell like rain to this steep grade,
    And I believe that neither will turn over
    For all eternity. This false one made

Canto XXX / 321

L'una è la falsa ch'accusò Gioseppo;
   l'altr' è 'l falso Sinon greco di Troia:
   per febbre aguta gittan tanto leppo».
100 E l'un di lor, che si recò a noia
   forse d'esser nomato sì oscuro,
   col pugno li percosse l'epa croia.
Quella sonò come fosse un tamburo;
   e mastro Adamo li percosse il volto
   col braccio suo, che non parve men duro,
dicendo a lui: «Ancor che mi sia tolto
   lo muover per le membra che son gravi,
   ho io il braccio a tal mestiere sciolto».
Ond' ei rispuose: «Quando tu andavi
110 al fuoco, non l'avei tu così presto;
   ma sì e più l'avei quando coniavi».
E l'idropico: «Tu di' ver di questo:
   ma tu non fosti sì ver testimonio
   là 've del ver fosti a Troia richesto».
«S'io dissi falso, e tu falsasti il conio»,
   disse Sinon; «e son qui per un fallo,
   e tu per più ch'alcun altro demonio!».
«Ricorditi, spergiuro, del cavallo»,
   rispuose quel ch'avëa infiata l'epa;
120 «e sieti reo che tutto il mondo sallo!».
«E te sia rea la sete onde ti crepa»,
   disse 'l Greco, «la lingua, e l'acqua marcia
   che 'l ventre innanzi a li occhi sì t'assiepa!».
Allora il monetier: «Così si squarcia
   la bocca tua per tuo mal come suole:
   ché, s'i' ho sete e omor mi rinfarcia,
tu hai l'arsura e 'l capo che ti duole,
   e per leccar lo specchio di Narcisso,
   non vorresti a 'nvitar molte parole».

Her accusation defaming Joseph; the other
    Is the false Sinon, Trojan Greek," he responded.
    "They reek so badly because of raging fever."

100   One of the pair—perhaps because offended
    By such dark naming—made a fist and struck
    Him on his rigid belly, which resounded

Just like a drum. And Master Adam paid back
    That blow by striking his neighbor in the face
    With an arm that was just as hard, and spoke:

"Though I am kept from moving by the mass
    Of my too-heavy limbs, you can be sure
    I have an arm kept free for such a case."

The other answered, "When you went to the fire
110   Your arm was not so ready—though indeed
    For counterfeiting, it was ready, and more."

"Here you speak truth," the dropsied one replied.
    "However, at Troy, when truth was their demand,
    Your witness was not so true." "I falsified

In speech: you made false coinage," Sinon returned,
    "And I am in this place for a single sin—
    And you, for more than any other fiend."

"You perjurer, remember the horse again,"
    The one who had the swollen paunch came back,
120   "And may the fact torment you: your role is known

By the whole world." "And torment," answered the Greek,
    "To you—from thirst's tongue-cracking agonies,
    And the foul waters that swell your belly to make

It rise up like a hedgerow blocking your eyes."
    And then the counterfeiter answered, "Thus
    Disease, as usual, spreads your gaping jaws;

For if I suffer thirst or feel distress
    Engorged with humors, you burn, your head aches hard—
    And you would lick Narcissus's looking glass

130   *Ad ascoltarli er' io del tutto fisso,*
     quando 'l maestro mi disse: «Or pur mira,
     che per poco che teco non mi risso!».
  Quand' io 'l senti' a me parlar con ira,
     volsimi verso lui con tal vergogna,
     ch'ancor per la memoria mi si gira.
  Qual è colui che suo dannaggio sogna,
     che sognando desidera sognare,
     sì che quel ch'è, come non fosse, agogna,
  tal mi fec' io, non possendo parlare,
140   *che disïava scusarmi, e scusava*
     me tuttavia, e nol mi credea fare.
  «Maggior difetto men vergogna lava»,
     disse 'l maestro, «che 'l tuo non è stato;
     però d'ogne trestizia ti disgrava.
  E fa ragion ch'io ti sia sempre allato,
     se più avvien che fortuna t'accoglia
     dove sien genti in simigliante piato:
  ché voler ciò udire è bassa voglia».

130 Without delaying for too many a word
        Of invitation, if you only could."
        I listened to them intently—then I heard

    My master: "Stare a little longer," he said,
        "And I will quarrel with you!" When I heard him
        Speaking to me in anger as he had,

    I turned to him with such a feeling of shame
        That it still circles through my memory.
        As one who dreams he is harmed may in the dream

140 Wish that it were a dream—and therefore he
        Longs for the thing that is, as if it were not:
        So I, unable to speak, was yearning to say

    Something to excuse myself—and by doing that
        I did excuse myself, at the same time
        As I was failing to do it in my thought.

    "A greater fault would be cleansed by lesser shame
        Than yours a moment ago," the master said.
        "So let your sadness be disburdened: come—

    Do not forget I am always at your side,
        Should fortune bring you again to where you hear
150   People who are arguing as those two did:

    Wanting to hear them is a low desire."

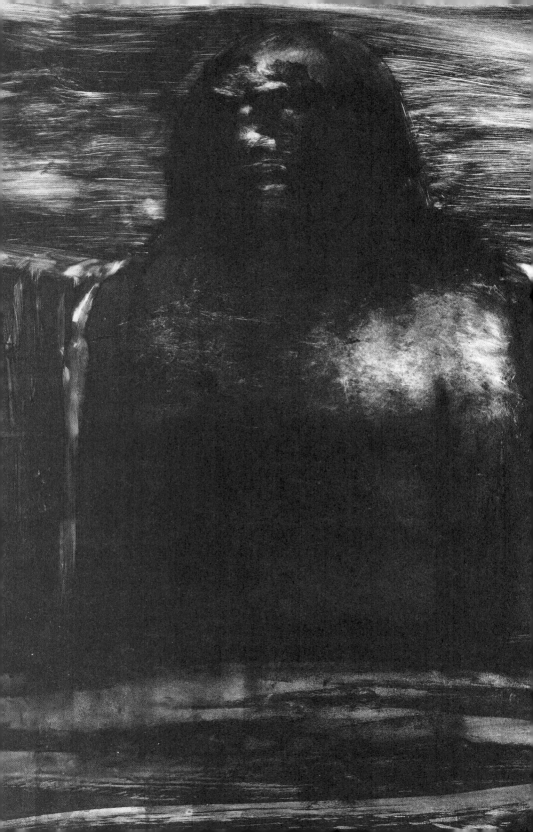

XXXI

As mist is vanishing,

Little by little vision starts picking out
    Shapes that were hidden in the misty air:
    Just so, as I began to penetrate

Into that thick and murky atmosphere,
    Fear gathered in me as my error fled—
    For, as on Montereggione's wall appear

Towers that crown its circle, here, arrayed
    All round the bank encompassing the pit
    With half their bulk like towers above it, stood

Horrible giants . . .

Una medesma lingua pria mi morse,
   sì che mi tinse l'una e l'altra guancia,
   e poi la medicina mi riporse;
così od' io che solea far la lancia
   d'Achille e del suo padre esser cagione
   prima di trista e poi di buona mancia.
Noi demmo il dosso al misero vallone
   su per la ripa che 'l cinge dintorno,
   attraversando sanza alcun sermone.
Quiv' era men che notte e men che giorno,
   sì che 'l viso m'andava innanzi poco;
   ma io senti' sonare un alto corno,
tanto ch'avrebbe ogne tuon fatto fioco,
   che, contra sé la sua via seguitando,
   dirizzò li occhi miei tutti ad un loco.
Dopo la dolorosa rotta, quando
   Carlo Magno perdé la santa gesta,
   non sonò sì terribilmente Orlando.
Poco portäi in là volta la testa,
   che me parve veder molte alte torri;
   ond' io: «Maestro, dì, che terra è questa?».
Ed elli a me: «Però che tu trascorri
   per le tenebre troppo da la lungi,
   avvien che poi nel maginare abborri.
Tu vedrai ben, se tu là ti congiungi,
   quanto 'l senso s'inganna di lontano;
   però alquanto più te stesso pungi».
Poi caramente mi prese per mano
   e disse: «Pria che noi siam più avanti,
   acciò che 'l fatto men ti paia strano,
sappi che non son torri, ma giganti,
   e son nel pozzo intorno da la ripa
   da l'umbilico in giuso tutti quanti».

One and the same tongue made me feel its sting,
   Tinting one cheek and the other, then supplied
   Balm: so I've heard Achilles' lance could bring

(The one his father gave him) first harm, then good.
   We turned our backs upon that valley of woes
   And climbed its girdling bank to the other side,

Crossing in silence. Here it was something less
   Than night and less than day, so that my vision
   Reached only a little way ahead of us;

10 But I could hear a horn blast—its concussion
   So loud it would make a thunderclap seem faint;
   And the sound guided my eyes in its direction

Back to one place, where all my attention went.
   After the dolorous rout, when Charlemagne
   Had lost his holy army and Roland sent

The signal from his horn, it must have been
   Less terrible a sound. Before my head
   Was turned that way for long, I saw a line

Of what seemed lofty towers. Then I said,
20   "Master, what city is this?" "Because you peer
   Into the dark from far off," he replied,

"Your imagination goes astray. Once there,
   You will see plainly how distance can deceive
   The senses—so spur yourself a little more."

And then he took me by the hand, with love,
   Saying, "Before we go much farther along,
   Learn now, in order that the fact may prove

Less strange: these are not towers but a ring
   Of giants—each one standing in the pit
30   Up to the navel." As mist is vanishing,

Come quando la nebbia si dissipa,
  lo sguardo a poco a poco raffigura
  ciò che cela 'l vapor che l'aere stipa,
così forando l'aura grossa e scura,
  più e più appressando ver' la sponda,
  fuggiemi errore e cresciemi paura;
40 però che, come su la cerchia tonda
  Montereggion di torri si corona,
  così la proda che 'l pozzo circonda
torreggiavan di mezza la persona
  li orribili giganti, cui minaccia
  Giove del cielo ancora quando tuona.
E io scorgeva già d'alcun la faccia,
  le spalle e 'l petto e del ventre gran parte,
  e per le coste giù ambo le braccia.
Natura certo, quando lasciò l'arte
50 di sì fatti animali, assai fé bene
  per tòrre tali essecutori a Marte.
E s'ella d'elefanti e di balene
  non si pente, chi guarda sottilmente,
  più giusta e più discreta la ne tene;
ché dove l'argomento de la mente
  s'aggiugne al mal volere e a la possa,
  nessun riparo vi può far la gente.
La faccia sua mi parea lunga e grossa
  come la pina di San Pietro a Roma,
60 e a sua proporzione eran l'altre ossa;
sì che la ripa, ch'era perizoma
  dal mezzo in giù, ne mostrava ben tanto
  di sovra, che di giugnere a la chioma
tre Frison s'averien dato mal vanto;
  però ch'i' ne vedea trenta gran palmi
  dal loco in giù dov' omo affibbia 'l manto.

Little by little vision starts picking out
    Shapes that were hidden in the misty air:
    Just so, as I began to penetrate

Into that thick and murky atmosphere,
    Fear gathered in me as my error fled—
    For, as on Montereggione's wall appear

Towers that crown its circle, here, arrayed
    All round the bank encompassing the pit
    With half their bulk like towers above it, stood

40 Horrible giants, whom Jove still rumbles at
    With menace when he thunders. I descried
    The face of one already, and the set

Of his great chest and shoulders, and a wide
    Stretch of his belly above the abyss's walls,
    And the arms along his sides. (Nature indeed,

When she abandoned making these animals,
    Did well to keep such instruments from Mars;
    Though she does not repent of making whales

Or elephants, a person who subtly inquires
50   Into her ways will find her both discreet
    And just, in her decision: if one confers

The power of the mind, along with that
    Of immense strength, upon an evil will
    Then people will have no defense from it.)

To me his face appeared as long and full
    As the bronze pinecone of St. Peter's at Rome,
    With all his other bones proportional,

So that the bank, which was an apron for him
    Down from his middle, showed above it such height
60   Three men of Friesland could not boast to come

Up to his hair. Extending down from the spot
    Where one would buckle a mantle I could see
    Thirty spans of him. The fierce mouth started to shout,

«Raphèl maì amècche zabì almi»,
    cominciò a gridar la fiera bocca,
    cui non si convenia più dolci salmi.
70 E 'l duca mio ver' lui: «Anima sciocca,
    tienti col corno, e con quel ti disfoga
    quand' ira o altra passïon ti tocca!
    Cércati al collo, e troverai la soga
    che 'l tien legato, o anima confusa,
    e vedi lui che 'l gran petto ti doga».
    Poi disse a me: «Elli stessi s'accusa;
    questi è Nembrotto per lo cui mal coto
    pur un linguaggio nel mondo non s'usa.
    Lasciànlo stare e non parliamo a vòto;
80 ché così è a lui ciascun linguaggio
    come 'l suo ad altrui, ch'a nullo è noto».
    Facemmo adunque più lungo vïaggio,
    vòlti a sinistra; e al trar d'un balestro
    trovammo l'altro assai più fero e maggio.
    A cigner lui qual che fosse 'l maestro,
    non so io dir, ma el tenea soccinto
    dinanzi l'altro e dietro il braccio destro
    d'una catena che 'l tenea avvinto
    dal collo in giù, sì che 'n su lo scoperto
90 si ravvolgëa infino al giro quinto.
    «Questo superbo volle esser esperto
    di sua potenza contra 'l sommo Giove»,
    disse 'l mio duca, «ond' elli ha cotal merto.
    Fïalte ha nome, e fece le gran prove
    quando i giganti fer paura a' dèi;
    le braccia ch'el menò, già mai non move».
    E io a lui: «S'esser puote, io vorrei
    che de lo smisurato Brïareo
    esperïenza avesser li occhi miei».

"Raphèl maì amècche zabì almi"—
    Sweeter psalms would not fit it—and then my guide
    Addressed him: "Soul, in your stupidity

Keep to your horn, and when you have the need
    Use that to vent your rage or other passion;
    Search at your neck the strap where it is tied,

70 And try to see it, O spirit in confusion,
    Aslant your own great chest." Having said that,
    He told me, "This is Nimrod: his accusation

He himself makes; for through his evil thought
    There is no common language the world can use:
    Leave him alone then, rather than speak for naught—

For every language is to him as his
    Is to all others: no one fathoms it."
    So, turning left, we quit that giant's place,

And at the distance of a crossbow's shot
80   Another, fiercer and greater, is what we found:
    What master could have fettered him like that

I do not know, but his right arm was chained
    Behind him and the other arm before,
    Clasped by a chain that also held him bound

From the neck down, so that it was wound as far
    As the fifth coil on the part of him that showed.
    "This proud one had a wish to test his power

Against supreme Jove: this is how he is paid,"
    My guide said. "Ephialtes is his name;
90   And when the giants made the gods afraid

Awesome endeavors were put forth by him.
    He cannot move these arms he strove with once."
    I said, "If it's possible for me to come

To where my eyes might have experience
    Of immense Briareus, I wish I could."
    "Antaeus, whom you'll see some distance hence,

Ond' ei rispuose: «Tu vedrai Anteo
   presso di qui che parla ed è disciolto,
   che ne porrà nel fondo d'ogne reo.
Quel che tu vuo' veder, più là è molto
   ed è legato e fatto come questo,
   salvo che più feroce par nel volto».
Non fu tremoto già tanto rubesto,
   che scotesse una torre così forte,
   come Fïalte a scuotersi fu presto.
Allor temett' io più che mai la morte,
110   e non v'era mestier più che la dotta,
   s'io non avessi viste le ritorte.
Noi procedemmo più avante allotta,
   e venimmo ad Anteo, che ben cinque alle,
   sanza la testa, uscia fuor de la grotta.
«O tu che ne la fortunata valle
   che fece Scipïon di gloria reda,
   quand' Anibàl co' suoi diede le spalle,
recasti già mille leon per preda,
   e che, se fossi stato a l'alta guerra
120   de' tuoi fratelli, ancor par che si creda
ch'avrebber vinto i figli de la terra:
   mettine giù, e non ten vegna schifo,
   doṿ Cocito la freddura serra.
Non ci fare ire a Tizio né a Tifo:
   questi può dar di quel che qui si brama;
   però ti china e non torcer lo grifo.
Ancor ti può nel mondo render fama,
   ch'el vive, e lunga vita ancor aspetta
   se 'nnanzi tempo grazia a sé nol chiama».
130 Così disse 'l maestro; e quelli in fretta
   le man distese, e prese 'l duca mio,
   ond' Ercule sentì già grande stretta.

Can speak, and is unchained as well," he said;
   "He will convey us to sin's profoundest abyss.
   The one you wish to see is farther ahead,

100 And he is bound and fashioned as this one is,
   Though somewhat more ferocious in his look."
   No tower was ever shaken by the throes

Of a great earthquake as Ephialtes shook
   Himself at hearing this. As never before
   I was afraid of dying, and wouldn't lack

A cause of death beyond that very fear,
   Had I not seen his fetters. Then we went on
   And reached Antaeus—who rose five ells or more,

Not reckoning his head, above the stone.
110 "O you, who—in that fateful valley that made
   Scipio inheritor of glory when

Hannibal along with all his followers fled
   Showing his back—once garnered as your prey
   A thousand lions: you through whom, it is said

By some, your brothers might have carried the day
   In their high war, if you had been there then
   Among the sons of earth in battle: pray,

Now set us down below—do not disdain
   To do so—where Cocytus is locked in cold.
120 Do not compel us to seek some other one

Like Typhon or Tityus. This man can yield
   The thing that's longed for here; therefore bend down
   And do not curl your lip. He can rebuild

Your fame on earth—he lives, and living on
   Longer is his expectation, if grace does not
   Summon him to itself untimely soon."

So spoke my master; and the giant stretched out
   In haste those hands whose grip clasped Hercules,
   And took my leader. Virgil, when he felt that,

Virgilio, quando prender si sentio,
   disse a me: «Fatti qua, sì ch'io ti prenda»;
   poi fece sì ch'un fascio era elli e io.
Qual pare a riguardar la Carisenda
   sotto 'l chinato, quando un nuvol vada
   sovr' essa sì, ched ella incontro penda:
tal parve Antëo a me che stava a bada
140   di vederlo chinare, e fu tal ora
   ch'i' avrei voluto ir per altra strada.
Ma lievemente al fondo che divora
   Lucifero con Giuda, ci sposò;
   né, sì chinato, lì fece dimora,
e come albero in nave si levò.

130 Said to me, "Now come here, that I may seize
     Good hold of you," and of himself and me
     He made one bundle. As seems to one who sees

The leaning tower at Garisenda, when he
     Is under the leaning side, and when a cloud
     Is passing over going the other way

From how the tower inclines, so in my dread
     Antaeus seemed to me as I watched him lean—
     That moment, I would have wished for another road!

But having stooped he set us gently upon
140   That bottom Lucifer is swallowed in
     Along with Judas; nor did he stay bent down,

But like a ship's mast raised himself again.

XXXII

. . . I turned, and saw before me and underfoot
  A lake that ice made less like water than glass;
  In Austria, never has the Danube set

So thick a veil above its current as this . . .

(22–25)

S'ïo avessi le rime aspre e chiocce,
    come si converrebbe al tristo buco
    sovra 'l qual pontan tutte l'altre rocce,
io premerei di mio concetto il suco
    più pienamente; ma perch' io non l'abbo,
    non sanza tema a dicer mi conduco;
ché non è impresa da pigliare a gabbo
    discriver fondo a tutto l'universo,
    né da lingua che chiami mamma o babbo.
10   Ma quelle donne aiutino il mio verso
    ch'aiutaro Anfïone a chiuder Tebe,
    sì che dal fatto il dir non sia diverso.
Oh sovra tutte mal creata plebe
    che stai nel loco onde parlare è duro,
    mei foste state qui pecore o zebe!
Come noi fummo giù nel pozzo scuro
    sotto i piè del gigante assai più bassi,
    e io mirava ancora a l'alto muro,
dicere udi'mi: «Guarda come passi:
20   va sì, che tu non calchi con le piante
    le teste de' fratei miseri lassi».
Per ch'io mi volsi, e vidimi davante
    e sotto i piedi un lago che per gelo
    avea di vetro e non d'acqua sembiante.
Non fece al corso suo sì grosso velo
    di verno la Danoia in Osterlicchi,
    né Tanaï là sotto 'l freddo cielo,
com' era quivi; che se Tambernicchi
    vi fosse sù caduto, o Pietrapana,
30   non avria pur da l'orlo fatto cricchi.
E come a gracidar si sta la rana
    col muso fuor de l'acqua, quando sogna
    di spigolar sovente la villana,

CANTO XXXII

If I had harsh and grating rhymes, to befit
    That melancholy hole which is the place
    All the other rocks converge and thrust their weight,

Then I could more completely press the juice
    From my conception. But since I lack such lines,
    I feel afraid as I come to speak of this:

It is not jokingly that one begins
    To describe the bottom of the universe—
    Not a task suited for a tongue that whines

10 *Mamma* and *Dadda*. May the muses help my verse
    As when they helped Amphion wall Thebes, so that
    Word not diverge from fact as it takes its course.

O horde, beyond all others ill-begot,
    Who dwell in that place so hard to speak about:
    Better for you to be born a sheep or goat!

When we were deep in the darkness of the pit
    Beneath the giant's feet, much farther down,
    And I still gazed back up the high wall of it:

"Watch how you step," I heard a voice intone,
20   "Be careful that you do not set your feet
    On the weary, wretched brothers' heads." Whereon

I turned, and saw before me and underfoot
    A lake that ice made less like water than glass;
    In Austria, never has the Danube set

So thick a veil above its current as this,
    Nor, under its cold sky, has the far-off Don:
    Had Mount Tambernic fallen to strike that ice,

Or Pietrapana, it would not even then
30   Creak, even at its edge. As the frog lies
    Snout above water to croak in the season when

livide, insin là dove appar vergogna
eran l'ombre dolenti ne la ghiaccia,
mettendo i denti in nota di cicogna.
Ognuna in giù tenea volta la faccia;
da bocca il freddo, e da li occhi il cor tristo
tra lor testimonianza si procaccia.
40 Quand' io m'ebbi dintorno alquanto visto,
volsimi a' piedi, e vidi due sì stretti,
che 'l pel del capo avieno insieme misto.
«Ditemi, voi che sì strignete i petti»,
diss' io, «chi siete?». E quei piegaro i colli;
e poi ch'ebber li visi a me eretti,
li occhi lor, ch'eran pria pur dentro molli,
gocciar su per le labbra, e 'l gelo strinse
le lagrime tra essi e riserrolli.
Con legno legno spranga mai non cinse
50 forte così; ond' ei come due becchi
cozzaro insieme, tanta ira li vinse.
E un ch'avea perduti ambo li orecchi
per la freddura, pur col viso in giùe,
disse: «Perché cotanto in noi ti specchi?
Se vuoi saper chi son cotesti due,
la valle onde Bisenzo si dichina
del padre loro Alberto e di lor fue.
D'un corpo usciro; e tutta la Caina
potrai cercare, e non troverai ombra
60 degna più d'esser fitta in gelatina:
non quelli a cui fu rotto il petto e l'ombra
con esso un colpo per la man d'Artù;
non Focaccia; non questi che m'ingombra
col capo sì, ch'i' non veggio oltre più,
e fu nomato Sassol Mascheroni;
se tosco se', ben sai omai chi fu.

The peasant woman often has reveries
   Of gleaning, spirits—livid to where the cheeks
   Turn color with shame—were locked inside the ice,

Teeth chattering the note a stork's beak makes.
   Each held his face turned down; they testified
   Cold by their mouths, and misery by the looks

Their eyes bore. After a time while I surveyed
   The scene around me, I glanced down at my feet,
   And saw two shades there packed in head to head

40 So tightly that their hair was interknit.
   "O you whose breasts are pressed together," I said,
   "Who are you?" They bent back their necks at that,

And having raised their faces to me, they shed
   Tears, welling now from eyes already moist
   To flow down over their lips, where the frost glued

Each to the other, ever more tightly fused:
   Iron clamps never held beam to beam so fast—
   And like two goats, each butted the one he faced

In a helpless rage. Another, who had lost
50 Both ears to frost, spoke with his face still down:
   "Why stare at us so long? If you insist

On knowing who these two are, the valley wherein
   Bisenzio's stream begins its long descent
   Once was their father Albert's and their own.

They issued from one body, and if you went
   All over Caina you could not find a shade
   Worthier to be frozen in punishment:

Not him whose breast and shadow the impaling blade
   In Arthur's hand pierced with one stroke; nor him
60 They called Focaccia; nor this other whose head

So blocks me I can see no farther: his name,
   Sassol Mascheroni, is one you recognize
   If you are Tuscan. And—so you need not claim

E perché non mi metti in più sermoni,
   sappi ch'i' fu' il Camiscion de' Pazzi;
   e aspetto Carlin che mi scagioni».
70 Poscia vid' io mille visi cagnazzi
   fatti per freddo; onde mi vien riprezzo,
   e verrà sempre, de' gelati guazzi.
E mentre ch'andavamo inver' lo mezzo
   al quale ogne gravezza si rauna,
   e io tremava ne l'etterno rezzo;
se voler fu o destino o fortuna,
   non so; ma, passeggiando tra le teste,
   forte percossi 'l piè nel viso ad una.
Piangendo mi sgridò: «Perché mi peste?
80   se tu non vieni a crescer la vendetta
   di Montaperti, perché mi moleste?».
E io: «Maestro mio, or qui m'aspetta,
   sì ch'io esca d'un dubbio per costui;
   poi mi farai, quantunque vorrai, fretta».
Lo duca stette, e io dissi a colui
   che bestemmiava duramente ancora:
   «Qual se' tu che così rampogni altrui?».
«Or tu chi se' che vai per l'Antenora,
   percotendo», rispuose, «altrui le gote,
90   sì che, se fossi vivo, troppo fora?».
«Vivo son io, e caro esser ti puote»,
   fu mia risposta, «se dimandi fama,
   ch'io metta il nome tuo tra l'altre note».
Ed elli a me: «Del contrario ho io brama.
   Lèvati quinci e non mi dar più lagna,
   ché mal sai lusingar per questa lama!».

Any more speech of me—my own name was
    Camiscion de' Pazzi and this is where I await
    Carlino's coming to make my sin seem less."

I saw a thousand faces after that,
    All purple as a dog's lips from the frost:
    I still shiver, and always will, at the sight

70 Of a frozen pond. All through the time we progressed
    Toward the core where all gravity convenes,
    I quaked in that eternal chill; and next—

I don't know whether by will or fate or chance—
    Walking among the heads I struck my foot
    Hard in the face of one, with violence

That set him weeping as he shouted out,
    "Why trample me? And if you have not come
    To add more vengeance for Montaperti's defeat,

Then why do you molest me?" I turned from him;
80   "Master," I said, "I pray you: wait for me here
    While I resolve a doubt concerning his name;

Then you shall hurry me on as you desire."
    My leader stopped, and I addressed the shade
    Who was still cursing as bitterly as before:

"And who are you who reviles another?" I said.
    "Nay, who are you," he answered, "who thus contrive
    To go through Antenora striking the head

And cheeks of others—which even were you alive
    Would be too much." "Alive is what I am,"
90   I told him, "and if fame is what you crave,

Then you might value having me note your name
    Among the others." He answered, "What I desire
    Is quite the opposite—get you gone, and come

To trouble me no more, inept as you are,
    Not knowing how to flatter at this great depth."
    Then I reached out and seized him by the hair

Allor lo presi per la cuticagna
    e dissi: «El converrà che tu ti nomi,
    o che capel qui sù non ti rimagna».
100 Ond' elli a me: «Perché tu mi dischiomi,
    né ti dirò ch'io sia, né mosterrolti
    se mille fiate in sul capo mi tomi».
Io avea già i capelli in mano avvolti,
    e tratti glien' avea più d'una ciocca,
    latrando lui con li occhi in giù raccolti,
quando un altro gridò: «Che hai tu, Bocca?
    non ti basta sonar con le mascelle,
    se tu non latri? qual diavol ti tocca?».
«Omai», diss' io, «non vo' che tu favelle,
110 malvagio traditor; ch'a la tua onta
    io porterò di te vere novelle».
«Va via», rispuose, «e ciò che tu vuoi conta;
    ma non tacer, se tu di qua entro eschi,
    di quel ch'ebbe or così la lingua pronta.
El piange qui l'argento de' Franceschi:
    "Io vidi", potrai dir, "quel da Duera
    là dove i peccatori stanno freschi".
Se fossi domandato altri chi v'era,
    tu hai dallato quel di Beccheria
120 di cui segò Fiorenza la gorgiera.
Gianni de' Soldanier credo che sia
    più là con Ganellone e Tebaldello,
    ch'aprì Faenza quando si dormia».
Noi eravam partiti già da ello,
    ch'io vidi due ghiacciati in una buca,
    sì che l'un capo a l'altro era cappello;
e come 'l pan per fame si manduca,
    così 'l sovran li denti a l'altro pose
    là 've 'l cervel s'aggiugne con la nuca:

And shook his scruff. "Now name yourself forthwith—
    Or not a hair will remain," I threatened him.
    He answered, "Though you pluck me bald in your wrath,

100 I will not tell you nor show you who I am,
    Not if you fall a thousand times on my pate."
    Already I had twisted round my palm

A length of hair, and pulled some clumps right out,
    And he was barking, with his eyes held down,
    When a new voice called: "Bocca, what is it—

What ails you? Are you so weary of the tune
    Your jaws create that now you are barking, too?
    What devil is at you?" "Now," said I, "I am done:

I have no further need to speak with you,
110 Accursed traitor, for now, to your disgrace,
    I will report about you what is true."

"Then go away," he answered, "tell what you choose—
    But don't be silent, if you do get out,
    About that one so quick just now to use

His tongue. Here he laments the silver he got
    From Frenchmen's hands. 'I saw him,' you can declare,
    'The man of Duera, down where the sinners are put

To cool.' And if they ask who else was there,
    The man of Beccheria is at your side,
120 Whose gullet was slit by Florence. Also here,

A little farther along your way, reside
    Gianni de' Soldanieri with Ganelon
    And Tebaldello who opened Faenza wide

While it was asleep." We had left him, moving on,
    When I saw two shades frozen in a single hole—
    Packed so close, one head hooded the other one;

The way the starving devour their bread, the soul
    Above had clenched the other with his teeth
    Where the brain meets the nape. And at the skull

Canto XXXII / 347

130 *non altrimenti Tidëo si rose*
    le tempie a Menalippo per disdegno,
    che quei faceva il teschio e l'altre cose.
  «O tu che mostri per sì bestial segno
    odio sovra colui che tu ti mangi,
    dimmi 'l perché», diss' io, «per tal convegno,
  che se tu a ragion di lui ti piangi,
    sappiendo chi voi siete e la sua pecca,
    nel mondo suso ancora io te ne cangi,
  se quella con ch'io parlo non si secca».

130 And other parts, as Tydeus berserk with wrath
       Gnawed at the head of Menalippus, he chewed.
       "You, showing such bestial hatred for him beneath,

Whom you devour: tell me your reason," I cried,
       "And, on condition that your grievance is right,
       Knowing both who you are and what wrong deed

This one committed against you, I may yet
       Repay you for whatever you may say,
       Up in the world above—by telling it,

If that with which I speak does not go dry."

XXXIII

Pausing in his savage meal, the sinner raised
  His mouth and wiped it clean along the hair
  Left on the head whose back he had laid waste.

La bocca sollevò dal fiero pasto
    quel peccator, forbendola a' capelli
    del capo ch'elli avea di retro guasto.
Poi cominciò: «Tu vuo' ch'io rinovelli
    disperato dolor che 'l cor mi preme
    già pur pensando, pria ch'io ne favelli.
Ma se le mie parole esser dien seme
    che frutti infamia al traditor ch'i' rodo,
    parlare e lagrimar vedrai insieme.
10   Io non so chi tu se' né per che modo
    venuto se' qua giù; ma fiorentino
    mi sembri veramente quand' io t'odo.
Tu dei saper ch'i' fui conte Ugolino,
    e questi è l'arcivescovo Ruggieri:
    or ti dirò perché i son tal vicino.
Che per l'effetto de' suo' mai pensieri,
    fidandomi di lui, io fossi preso
    e poscia morto, dir non è mestieri;
però quel che non puoi avere inteso,
20   cioè come la morte mia fu cruda,
    udirai, e saprai s'e' m'ha offeso.
Breve pertugio dentro da la Muda,
    la qual per me ha 'l titol de la fame,
    e che conviene ancor ch'altrui si chiuda,
m'avea mostrato per lo suo forame
    più lune già, quand' io feci 'l mal sonno
    che del futuro mi squarciò 'l velame.
Questi pareva a me maestro e donno,
    cacciando il lupo e ' lupicini al monte
30   per che i Pisan veder Lucca non ponno.
Con cagne magre, studïose e conte
    Gualandi con Sismondi e con Lanfranchi
    s'avea messi dinanzi da la fronte.

CANTO XXXIII

Pausing in his savage meal, the sinner raised
  His mouth and wiped it clean along the hair
  Left on the head whose back he had laid waste.

Then he began: "You ask me to endure
  Reliving a grief so desperate, the thought
  Torments my heart even as I prepare

To tell it. But if my words are seeds, with fruit
  Of infamy for this traitor that I gnaw,
  I will both speak and weep within your sight.

10 I don't know who you are that come here, or how,
  But you are surely Florentine to my ear.
  I was Count Ugolino, you must know:

This is Archbishop Ruggieri. You will hear
  Why I am such a neighbor to him as this:
  How, through my trust and his devices, I bore

First being taken, then killed, no need to trace;
  But things which you cannot have heard about—
  The manner of my death, how cruel it was—

I shall describe, and you can tell from that
20 If he has wronged me. A slit in the Tower Mew
  (Called Hunger's Tower after me, where yet

Others will be closed up) had let me view
  Several moons already, when my bad dream
  Came to me, piercing the future's veil right through:

This man appeared as lord of the hunt; he came
  Chasing a wolf and whelps, on that high slope
  That blocks the Pisans' view of Lucca. With him

His lean hounds ran, well trained and eager; his troop—
  Gualandi, Sismondi, Lanfranchi—had been sent
30 To ride in front of him. With no escape,

In picciol corso mi parieno stanchi
lo padre e ' figli, e con l'agute scane
mi parea lor veder fender li fianchi.
Quando fui desto innanzi la dimane,
pianger senti' fra 'l sonno i miei figliuoli
ch'eran con meco, e dimandar del pane.
40 Ben se' crudel, se tu già non ti duoli
pensando ciò che 'l mio cor s'annunziava;
e se non piangi, di che pianger suoli?
Già eran desti, e l'ora s'appressava
che 'l cibo ne solëa essere addotto,
e per suo sogno ciascun dubitava;
e io senti' chiavar l'uscio di sotto
a l'orribile torre' ond' io guardai
nel viso a' mie' figliuoi sanza far motto.
Io non piangëa, sì dentro impetrai:
50 piangevan elli; e Anselmuccio mio
disse: "Tu guardi sì, padre! che hai?".
Perciò non lagrimai né rispuos' io
tutto quel giorno né la notte appresso,
infin che l'altro sol nel mondo uscìo.
Come un poco di raggio si fu messo
nel doloroso carcere, e io scorsi
per quattro visi il mio aspetto stesso,
ambo le man per lo dolor mi morsi;
ed ei, pensando ch'io 'l fessi per voglia
60 di manicar, di sùbito levorsi
e disser: "Padre, assai ci fia men doglia
se tu mangi di noi: tu ne vestisti
queste misere carni, e tu le spoglia".
Queta'mi allor per non farli più tristi;
lo dì e l'altro stemmo tutti muti;
ahi dura terra, perché non t'apristi?

After a short run, father and sons seemed spent;
    I saw their flanks, that sharp fangs seemed to tear.
    I woke before dawn, hearing the complaint

Of my own children, who were with me there,
    Whimpering in their sleep and asking for bread.
    You grieve already, or truly cruel you are,

As you think of what my heart began to dread—
    And if not now, then when do you shed a tear?
    They were awake now, with the hour when food

40 Was usually brought us drawing near,
    And each one apprehensive from his dream.
    And then I heard them nailing shut the door

Into that fearful tower—a pounding that came
    From far below. Hearing that noise, I stared
    Into my children's faces, not speaking to them.

Inside me I was turned to stone, so hard
    I could not weep; the children wept. And my
    Little Anselmo, peering at me, inquired:

'Father, what ails you?' And still I did not cry,
50   Nor did I answer, all that day and night
    Until the next sun dawned. When one small ray

Found its way into our prison, and I made out
    In their four faces the image of my own,
    I bit my hands for grief; when they saw that,

They thought I did it from my hunger's pain,
    And suddenly rose. 'Father: our pain,' they said,
    'Will lessen if you eat us—you are the one

Who clothed us in this wretched flesh: we plead
    For you to be the one who strips it away.'
60   I calmed myself to grieve them less. We stayed

Silent through that and then the following day.
    O you hard earth, why didn't you open then?
    When we had reached the fourth day, Gaddo lay

Canto XXXIII / 355

Poscia che fummo al quarto dì venuti,
Gaddo mi si gittò disteso a' piedi,
dicendo: "Padre mio, ché non m'aiuti?".
70 Quivi morì; e come tu mi vedi,
vid' io cascar li tre ad uno ad uno
tra 'l quinto dì e 'l sesto; ond' io mi diedi,
già cieco, a brancolar sovra ciascuno,
e due dì li chiamai, poi che fur morti.
Poscia, più che 'l dolor, poté 'l digiuno».
Quand' ebbe detto ciò, con li occhi torti
riprese 'l teschio misero co' denti,
che furo a l'osso, come d'un can, forti.
Ahi Pisa, vituperio de le genti
80 del bel paese là dove 'l sì suona,
poi che i vicini a te punir son lenti,
muovasi la Capraia e la Gorgona,
e faccian siepe ad Arno in su la foce,
sì ch'elli annieghi in te ogne persona!
Che se 'l conte Ugolino aveva voce
d'aver tradita te de le castella,
non dovei tu i figliuoi porre a tal croce.
Innocenti facea l'età novella,
novella Tebe, Uguiccione e 'l Brigata
90 e li altri due che 'l canto suso appella.
Noi passammo oltre, là 've la gelata
ruvidamente un'altra gente fascia,
non volta in giù, ma tutta riversata.
Lo pianto stesso lì pianger non lascia,
e 'l duol che truova in su li occhi rintoppo,
si volge in entro a far crescer l'ambascia;
ché le lagrime prime fanno groppo,
e sì come visiere di cristallo,
rïempion sotto 'l ciglio tutto il coppo.
100 E avvegna che, sì come d'un callo,
per la freddura ciascun sentimento
cessato avesse del mio viso stallo,

Stretched at my feet where he had fallen down:
    'Father, why don't you help me?' he said, and died.
    And surely as you see me, so one by one

I watched the others fall till all were dead,
    Between the fifth day and the sixth. And I,
    Already going blind, groped over my brood—

70 Calling to them, though I had watched them die,
    For two long days. And then the hunger had more
    Power than even sorrow had over me."

When he had finished, with a sideways stare
    He gripped the skull again in his teeth, which ground
    Strong as a dog's against the bone he tore.

Ah, Pisa! You shame the peoples of the fair land
    Where *sì* is spoken: slow as your neighbors are
    To punish you, may Gorgona shift its ground,

And Capraia, till those islands make a bar
80   To dam the Arno, and drown your populace—
    Every soul in you! Though Ugolino bore

The fame of having betrayed your fortresses,
    Still it was wrong in you to so torment
    His helpless children. You Thebes of latter days,

Their youthful ages made them innocent!—
    Uguccione, Brigata, and the two
    My song has named already. On we went,

To where frost roughly swathes a people who,
    Instead of downward, turn their faces up.
90   There, weeping keeps them from weeping—for as they do,

Grief finds a barrier where the eyes would weep
    But forced back inward, adds to their agonies:
    A crystal visor of prior tears fills the cup

Below the eyebrow with a knot of ice.
    And though, as when a callus has grown numb,
    The cold had sucked all feeling from my face

già mi parea sentire alquanto vento;
    per ch'io: «Maestro mio, questo chi move?
    non è qua giù ogne vapore spento?».
Ond' elli a me: «Avaccio sarai dove
    di ciò ti farà l'occhio la risposta,
    veggendo la cagion che 'l fiato piove».
E un de' tristi de la fredda crosta
110   gridò a noi: «O anime crudeli
    tanto che data v'è l'ultima posta,
levatemi dal viso i duri veli,
    sì ch'io sfoghi 'l duol che 'l cor m'impregna,
    un poco, pria che 'l pianto si raggeli».
Per ch'io a lui: «Se vuo' ch'i' ti sovvegna,
    dimmi chi se', e s'io non ti disbrigo,
    al fondo de la ghiaccia ir mi convegna».
Rispuose adunque: «I' son frate Alberigo;
    i' son quel da le frutta del mal orto,
120   che qui riprendo dattero per figo».
«Oh», diss' io lui, «or se' tu ancor morto?».
    Ed elli a me: «Come 'l mio corpo stea
    nel mondo sù, nulla scïenza porto.
Cotal vantaggio ha questa Tolomea,
    che spesse volte l'anima ci cade
    innanzi ch'Atropòs mossa le dea.
E perché tu più volontier mi rade
    le 'nvetrïate lagrime dal volto,
    sappie che, tosto che l'anima trade
130   come fec' ïo, il corpo suo l'è tolto
    da un demonio, che poscia il governa
    mentre che 'l tempo suo tutto sia vòlto.
Ella ruina in sì fatta cisterna;
    e forse pare ancor lo corpo suso
    de l'ombra che di qua dietro mi verna.

I sensed a wind, and wondered from where it came:
"Master, who moves this? Is it not the case
All vapors are extinguished in this realm?"

100 "Soon," he responded, "you will reach a place
Where your own eyes—beholding what source this blast
Is poured by from above—will answer this."

And then one wretch encased in the frozen crust
Cried out to us, "O souls so cruel that here,
Of all the stations, you're assigned the last—

Lift the hard veils away from my face, I implore,
So that before the weeping freezes again
I can release a little of this despair

And misery that swell my heart." Whereon
110 I said, "If you would have me help you, disclose
To me who you are: if I don't help you then,

May I be sent to the bottom of the ice."
He answered, "I am Fra Alberigo, the man
Of fruit from the evil garden; in this place

I get my payment, date for fig." "Oh then,"
I said to him, "you are already dead?"
"I do not know what state my body is in,

Nor how it fares in the world above," he said.
"For Ptolomea's privilege is this:
120 Down to this place a soul is often conveyed

Before it is sent forth by Atropos.
So that you may more willingly scrape the cowl
Of tears made hard as glass that coats my face,

Know that as soon as a soul commits betrayal
The way I did, a devil displaces it
And governs inside the body until its toll

Of years elapses. Meanwhile, down to this vat
The soul falls headlong—so it could be true
That this shade, wintering here behind me, yet

Tu 'l dei saper, se tu vien pur mo giuso:
  elli è ser Branca Doria, e son più anni
  poscia passati ch'el fu sì racchiuso».
«Io credo», diss' io lui, «che tu m'inganni;
140 ché Branca Doria non morì unquanche,
  e mangia e bee e dorme e veste panni».
«Nel fosso sù», diss' el, «de' Malebranche,
  là dove bolle la tenace pece,
  non era ancora giunto Michel Zanche,
che questi lasciò il diavolo in sua vece
  nel corpo suo, ed un suo prossimano
  che 'l tradimento insieme con lui fece.
Ma distendi oggimai in qua la mano;
  aprimi li occhi». E io non gliel' apersi;
150 e cortesia fu lui esser villano.
Ahi Genovesi, uomini diversi
  d'ogne costume e pien d'ogne magagna,
  perché non siete voi del mondo spersi?
Ché col peggiore spirto di Romagna
  trovai di voi un tal, che per sua opra
  in anima in Cocito già si bagna,
e in corpo par vivo ancor di sopra.

130 Appears above on earth too: you must know,
     If you were sent down only a short time past.
     He is Ser Branca d'Oria; it's years ago

He first arrived here to be thus encased."
     "Now you deceive me, for I am one who knows
     That Branca d'Oria is not deceased:

He eats and drinks and sleeps and puts on clothes,"
     I told him. And he answered, "In the ditch
     Ruled by the Malebranche above, that seethes

And bubbles with the lake of clinging pitch,
140 The shade of Michel Zanche had not arrived
     When this, his killer, had a devil encroach

His body (as did his kinsman, when they contrived
     Together to perform their treachery)
     And take his place in it. Now, as I craved,

Reach out your hand and open my eyes for me."
     I did not open them—for to be rude
     To such a one as him was courtesy.

Ah Genoese!—to every accustomed good,
     Strangers; with every corruption, amply crowned:
150 Why hasn't the world expunged you as it should?

For with Romagna's worst spirit I have found
     One of you—already, for deeds he was guilty of,
     Bathed in Cocytus: in soul now underground

Who in body still appears alive, above.

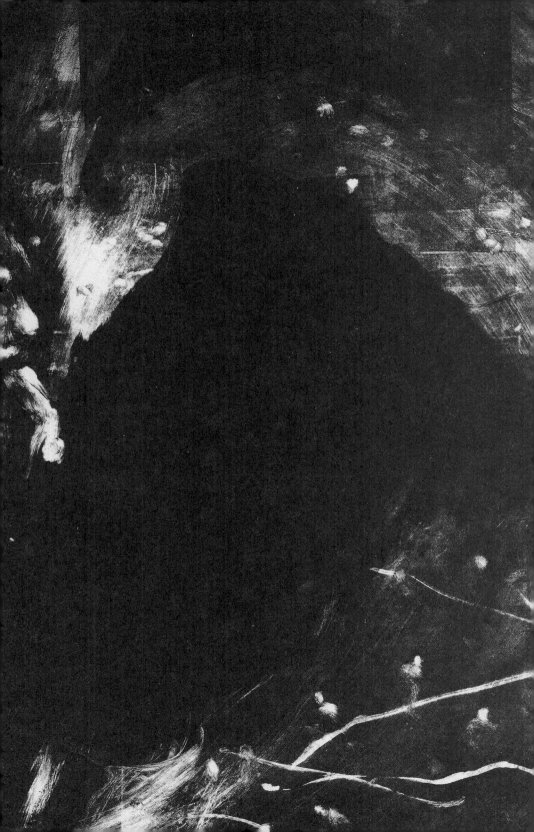

«Vexilla regis prodeunt inferni
  verso di noi; però dinanzi mira»,
  disse 'l maestro mio, «se tu 'l discerni».
Come quando una grossa nebbia spira,
  o quando l'emisperio nostro annotta,
  par di lungi un molin che 'l vento gira,
veder mi parve un tal dificio allotta;
  poi per lo vento mi ristrinsi retro
  al duca mio, ché non li era altra grotta.
10 *Già era, e con paura il metto in metro,*
  là dove l'ombre tutte eran coperte,
  e trasparien come festuca in vetro.
Altre sono a giacere; altre stanno erte,
  quella col capo e quella con le piante;
  altra, com' arco, il volto a' piè rinverte.
Quando noi fummo fatti tanto avante,
  ch'al mio maestro piacque di mostrarmi
  la creatura ch'ebbe il bel sembiante,
  d'innanzi mi si tolse e fé restarmi,
20 *«Ecco Dite», dicendo, «ed ecco il loco*
  ove convien che di fortezza t'armi».
Com' io divenni allor gelato e fioco,
  nol dimandar, lettor, ch'i' non lo scrivo,
  però ch'ogne parlar sarebbe poco.
Io non mori' e non rimasi vivo;
  pensa oggimai per te, s'hai fior d'ingegno,
  qual io divenni, d'uno e d'altro privo.

CANTO XXXIV

"And now, *Vexilla regis prodeunt*
   Inferni—therefore, look," my master said
   As we continued on the long descent,

"And see if you can make him out, ahead."
   As though, in the exhalation of heavy mist
   Or while night darkened our hemisphere, one spied

A mill—blades turning in the wind, half-lost
   Off in the distance—some structure of that kind
   I seemed to make out now. But at a gust

10 Of wind, there being no other shelter at hand,
   I drew behind my leader's back again.
   By now (and putting it in verse I find

Fear in myself still) I had journeyed down
   To where the shades were covered wholly by ice,
   Showing like straw in glass—some lying prone,

And some erect, some with the head toward us,
   And others with the bottoms of the feet;
   Another like a bow, bent feet to face.

When we had traveled forward to the spot
20   From which it pleased my master to have me see
   That creature whose beauty once had been so great,

He made me stop, and moved from in front of me.
   "Look: here is Dis," he said, "and here is the place
   Where you must arm yourself with the quality

Of fortitude." How chilled and faint I was
   On hearing that, you must not ask me, reader—
   I do not write it; words would not suffice:

I neither died, nor kept alive—consider
   With your own wits what I, alike denuded
30   Of death and life, became as I heard my leader.

Lo 'mperador del doloroso regno
  da mezzo 'l petto uscia fuor de la ghiaccia;
30   e più con un gigante io mi convegno,
che i giganti non fan con le sue braccia:
  vedi oggimai quant' esser dee quel tutto
  ch'a così fatta parte si confaccia.
S'el fu sì bel com' elli è ora brutto,
  e contra 'l suo fattore alzò le ciglia,
  ben dee da lui procedere ogne lutto.
Oh quanto parve a me gran maraviglia
  quand' io vidi tre facce a la sua testa!
  L'una dinanzi, e quella era vermiglia;
40   l'altr' eran due, che s'aggiugnieno a questa
  sovresso 'l mezzo di ciascuna spalla,
  e sé giugnieno al loco de la cresta:
e la destra parea tra bianca e gialla;
  la sinistra a vedere era tal, quali
  vegnon di là onde 'l Nilo s'avvalla.
Sotto ciascuna uscivan due grand' ali,
  quanto si convenia a tanto uccello:
  vele di mar non vid' io mai cotali.
Non avean penne, ma di vispistrello
50   era lor modo; e quelle svolazzava,
  sì che tre venti si movean da ello:
quindi Cocito tutto s'aggelava.
  Con sei occhi piangëa, e per tre menti
  gocciava 'l pianto e sanguinosa bava.
Da ogne bocca dirompea co' denti
  un peccatore, a guisa di maciulla,
  sì che tre ne facea così dolenti.
A quel dinanzi il mordere era nulla
  verso 'l graffiar, che talvolta la schiena
60   rimanea de la pelle tutta brulla.
«Quell'anima là sù c'ha maggior pena»,
  disse 'l maestro, «è Giuda Scarïotto,
  che 'l capo ha dentro e fuor le gambe mena.

The emperor of the realm of grief protruded
  From mid-breast up above the surrounding ice.
  A giant's height, and mine, would have provided

Closer comparison than would the size
  Of his arm and a giant. Envision the whole
  That is proportionate to parts like these.

If he was truly once as beautiful
  As he is ugly now, and raised his brows
  Against his Maker—then all sorrow may well

40 Come out of him. How great a marvel it was
  For me to see three faces on his head:
  In front there was a red one; joined to this,

Each over the midpoint of a shoulder, he had
  Two others—all three joining at the crown.
  That on the right appeared to be a shade

Of whitish yellow; the third had such a mien
  As those who come from where the Nile descends.
  Two wings spread forth from under each face's chin,

Strong, and befitting such a bird, immense—
50 I have never seen at sea so broad a sail—
  Unfeathered, batlike, and issuing three winds

That went forth as he beat them, to freeze the whole
  Realm of Cocytus that surrounded him.
  He wept with all six eyes, and the tears fell

Over his three chins mingled with bloody foam.
  The teeth of each mouth held a sinner, kept
  As by a flax rake: thus he held three of them

In agony. For the one the front mouth gripped,
  The teeth were as nothing to the claws, which sliced
60 And tore the skin until his back was stripped.

"That soul," my master said, "who suffers most,
  Is Judas Iscariot; head locked inside,
  He flails his legs. Of the other two, who twist

De li altri due c'hanno il capo di sotto,
  quel che pende dal nero ceffo è Bruto:
  vedi come si storce, e non fa motto!;
e l'altro è Cassio, che par sì membruto.
  Ma la notte risurge, e oramai
  è da partir, ché tutto avem veduto».
70 Com' a lui piacque, il collo li avvinghiai;
  ed el prese di tempo e loco poste,
  e quando l'ali fuoro aperte assai,
appigliò sé a le vellute coste;
  di vello in vello giù discese poscia
  tra 'l folto pelo e le gelate croste.
Quando noi fummo là dove la coscia
  si volge, a punto in sul grosso de l'anche,
  lo duca, con fatica e con angoscia,
volse la testa ov' elli avea le zanche,
80 e aggrappossi al pel com' om che sale,
  sì che 'n inferno i' credea tornar anche.
«Attienti ben, ché per cotali scale»,
  disse 'l maestro, ansando com' uom lasso,
  «conviensi dipartir da tanto male».
Poi uscì fuor per lo fóro d'un sasso
  e puose me in su l'orlo a sedere;
  appresso porse a me l'accorto passo.
Io levai li occhi e credetti vedere
  Lucifero com' io l'avea lasciato,
90 e vidili le gambe in sù tenere;
e s'io divenni allora travagliato,
  la gente grossa il pensi, che non vede
  qual è quel punto ch'io avea passato.
«Lèvati sù», disse 'l maestro, «in piede:
  la via è lunga e 'l cammino è malvagio,
  e già il sole a mezza terza riede».
Non era camminata di palagio
  là 'v' eravam, ma natural burella
  ch'avea mal suolo e di lume disagio.

With their heads down, the black mouth holds the shade
  Of Brutus: writhing, but not a word will he scream;
  Cassius is the sinewy one on the other side.

But night is rising again, and it is time
  That we depart, for we have seen the whole."
  As he requested, I put my arms round him,

70 And waiting until the wings were opened full
  He took advantage of the time and place
  And grasped the shaggy flank, and gripping still,

From tuft to tuft descended through the mass
  Of matted hair and crusts of ice. And then,
  When we had reached the pivot of the thighs,

Just where the haunch is at its thickest, with strain
  And effort my master brought around his head
  To where he'd had his legs: and from there on

He grappled the hair as someone climbing would—
80 So I supposed we were heading back to Hell.
  "Cling tight, for it is stairs like these," he sighed

Like one who is exhausted, "which we must scale
  To part from so much evil." Then he came up
  Through a split stone, and placed me on its sill,

And climbed up toward me with his cautious step.
  I raised my eyes, expecting I would see
  Lucifer as I left him—and saw his shape

Inverted, with his legs held upward. May they
  Who are too dull to see what point I had passed
90 Judge whether it perplexed me. "Come—the way

Is long, the road remaining to be crossed
  Is hard: rise to your feet," the master said,
  "The sun is at mid-tierce." We had come to rest

In nothing like a palace hall; instead
  A kind of natural dungeon enveloped us,
  With barely any light, the floor ill made.

100   «*Prima ch'io de l'abisso mi divella,*
maestro mio», diss' io quando fui dritto,
«a trarmi d'erro un poco mi favella:
ov' è la ghiaccia? e questi com' è fitto
sì sottosopra? e come, in sì poc' ora,
da sera a mane ha fatto il sol tragitto?».
Ed elli a me: «Tu imagini ancora
d'esser di là dal centro, ov' io mi presi
al pel del vermo reo che 'l mondo fóra.
Di là fosti cotanto quant' io scesi;
110   *quand' io mi volsi, tu passasti 'l punto*
al qual si traggon d'ogne parte i pesi.
E se' or sotto l'emisperio giunto
ch'è contraposto a quel che la gran secca
coverchia, e sotto 'l cui colmo consunto
fu l'uom che nacque e visse sanza pecca;
tu haï i piedi in su picciola spera
che l'altra faccia fa de la Giudecca.
Qui è da man, quando di là è sera;
e questi, che ne fé scala col pelo,
120   *fitto è ancora sì come prim' era.*
Da questa parte cadde giù dal cielo;
e la terra, che pria di qua si sporse,
per paura di lui fé del mar velo,
e venne a l'emisperio nostro; e forse
per fuggir lui lasciò qui loco vòto
quella ch'appar di qua, e sù ricorse».

"Before I free myself from the abyss,
　　My master," I said when I was on my feet,
　　"Speak, and dispel my error: where is the ice?

100　And how can he be fixed head-down like that?
　　And in so short a time, how can it be
　　Possible for the sun to make its transit

From evening to morning?" He answered me,
　　"You imagine you are still on the other side,
　　Across the center of the earth, where I

Grappled the hair on the evil serpent's hide
　　Who pierces the world. And all through my descent,
　　You were on that side; when I turned my head

And legs about, you passed the central point
110　To which is drawn, from every side, all weight.
　　Now you are on the opposite continent

Beneath the opposite hemisphere to that
　　Which canopies the great dry land therein:
　　Under the zenith of that one is the site

Whereon the Man was slain who without sin
　　Was born and lived; your feet this minute press
　　Upon a little sphere whose rounded skin

Forms the Judecca's other, outward face.
　　Here it is morning when it is evening there;
120　The one whose hair was like a ladder for us

Is still positioned as he was before.
　　On this side he fell down from Heaven; the earth,
　　Which till then stood out here, impelled by fear

Veiled itself in the sea and issued forth
　　In our own hemisphere. And possibly,
　　What now appears on this side fled its berth

And rushing upward left a cavity:
　　This hollow where we stand." There is below,
　　As far from Beelzebub as one can be

Luogo è là giù da Belzebù remoto
tanto quanto la tomba si distende,
che non per vista, ma per suono è noto
d'un ruscelletto che quivi discende
per la buca d'un sasso, ch'elli ha roso,
col corso ch'elli avvolge, e poco pende.
Lo duca e io per quel cammino ascoso
intrammo a ritornar nel chiaro mondo;
e sanza cura aver d'alcun riposo,
salimmo sù, el primo e io secondo,
tanto ch'i' vidi de le cose belle
che porta 'l ciel, per un pertugio tondo.
E quindi uscimmo a riveder le stelle.

130

130   Within his tomb, a place one cannot know
        By sight, but by the sound a little runnel
        Makes as it wends the hollow rock its flow

      Has worn, descending through its winding channel:
        To get back up to the shining world from there
        My guide and I went into that hidden tunnel;

      And following its path, we took no care
        To rest, but climbed: he first, then I—so far,
        Through a round aperture I saw appear

      Some of the beautiful things that Heaven bears,
140   Where we came forth, and once more saw the stars.

Through a round aperture I saw appear

Some of the beautiful things that Heaven bears,
Where we came forth, and once more saw the stars.

(XXXIV, 138–40)

NOTES

BY NICOLE PINSKY

The notes that follow are intended for students and general readers. They were written to approximate some of the literary and historical information Dante's original audience might have had, and are certainly not an interpretive guide.

I rely on the authority of previous editors, translators, and commentators—first and foremost on the volume of Commentary *that accompanies the prose translation of the* Inferno *by Charles S. Singleton, but also on the work of C. H. Grandgent, Henry Wadsworth Longfellow, Allen Mandelbaum, Mark Musa, Dorothy L. Sayers, and John D. Sinclair.*

The notes to Canto XI include Michael Mazur's annotation for his map of Hell, which illustrates that canto.

For some cantos, a brief commentary by John Freccero or Robert Pinsky precedes the notes.

—N.P.

CANTO I

The elements of Canto I—vivid, yet tangled and dark—are significant not only for the sometimes enigmatic meanings of any one image or passage but collectively as well, for the emotional, moral, and physical world they establish for the *Inferno*. All of these elements—the woods, the lost path, the mountain, the valley, the leopard, the lion, the wolf with her unappeasable hunger, the Hound who will defeat her, even the guiding figure of Virgil himself—embody the qualities of challenge and mystery that will characterize Dante's quest.

This sense of enigma, like the feeling of peril, is an essential part of the poem's drama. The way figures like the Hound or the sunny mountain may not correspond to exact, identifiable allusions or to definite allegorical meanings is consistent with the action of the quest—and with the appeal that has made the *Commedia* an immediate, enduring success with readers. The path Virgil suggests, and to which Dante agrees, is one where meaning will come in irregular pools and flashes, with effort, in a setting of uncertainty until the journey is done.

The metaphysical shape of Dante's course is clear and general, as indicated by the internal summary given in Canto I of the three realms—Hell, Purgatory, and Paradise. But the reality of his course is often particular and local, involving for instance the politics and topography of "low Italy" and historical or mythological names.

In a similar way, the broad, relatively lucid terms of Christian theology and cosmology are balanced by the allusive terms of prophecy, clouded yet highly specific, such as the much-debated birth of the heroic Hound between "felt and felt" or "Feltro and Feltro." Canto I thus establishes the mixed, densely woven nature of the *Commedia* as a whole and of the *Inferno* in particular: a fabric of imagination where varying textures of thought or experience shift and slide and recombine unpredictably. (R.P.)

1. The Bible (Psalm 90:10) allots seventy years as the span of a human life, so MIDWAY ON OUR LIFE'S JOURNEY is the age of thirty-five. Dante was thirty-five in 1300, the year in which the action of the *Inferno* takes place. Other time references in the poem (see Canto XXI) lead most scholars to think of the dark night in Canto I as the night before Good Friday: April 7, 1300. Scholars do not know precisely when Dante began to write the *Inferno*, but it was certainly some years later than 1300, after Dante had been exiled from Florence. By writing about a specific, past date, Dante is able to include many prophetic passages which "predict" political and historical events that occurred between 1300 and the time of composition.

   The gap of years also affords a distinction important throughout the *Commedia*: there is a difference between Dante the remembered and imagined pilgrim, who sets out on a remarkable journey in 1300, and Dante the poet, who writes about the journey years later. The words I FOUND MYSELF hint at this distinction by making Dante both subject and object of the poem's first verb. The same words, with their play on finding and being lost, also initiate a current of wit and wordplay that runs through the poem, even in its darkest passages. The first person singular of I FOUND MYSELF emphasizes the personal, particular experience of Dante, while the words OUR LIFE suggest the general, shared human experience of finding oneself spiritually lost.

2. The DARK WOODS correspond to a place of sin and corruption in the pilgrim's own soul, but also among the political, historical, and ecclesiastical figures of his time. In his *Convivio* (IV, xxiv, 12), Dante speaks of the "erroneous forest of this life."

11. The HILL: the path upward to righteousness; possibly the "hill of the Lord" of Psalm 24:3.

14. THAT BRIGHT PLANET is the sun; its RAYS, divine grace. Medieval (Ptolemaic) cosmology makes the sun a planet that moves around the earth.

17. The HEART'S LAKE is a cavity in the heart described by fourteenth-century science as the location of various passions, particularly fear. It was from there that blood was believed to be distributed to the body.

24. Dante's LEFT FOOT, associated with earthly desires, hinders his progress. *Piè fermo* is literally the "firm foot"; this translation follows the interpretive tradition in which the left foot belongs to the will and drags behind the right foot, governed by the intellect.

25–45. Many interpretations have been suggested for the LEOPARD, the LION, and the SHE-WOLF, but the earliest and still the most widely accepted is that they stand for three types of sin: lust, pride, and avarice, respectively. See also Jeremiah 5:6: "Wherefore a lion out of the forest shall slay them, and a wolf of the evenings shall spoil them, a leopard shall watch over their cities." The leopard reappears in Canto XVI.

29–32. The sun is in Aries, as it was believed to have been at the time of the Creation: WITH THE STARS ATTENDING IT / AS WHEN DIVINE LOVE SET THOSE BEAUTIFUL / LIGHTS INTO MOTION.

53. SUB JULIO: During the reign of Julius Caesar. Virgil was born in 70 B.C., and Julius Caesar died in 44 B.C.

55.· The pagan gods worshipped by the ancient Romans were, according to medieval theology, not merely FALSE GODS: they were GODS WHO LIED, demons or spirits who deliberately deceived their followers.

55–57. ANCHISES' NOBLE SON is Aeneas. In the *Aeneid*, Virgil tells the story of how Aeneas fled the fallen city of Troy (SUPERB ILIUM) and eventually founded Rome.

61. VIRGIL is regarded in Dante's poem as the model poet, and as an embodiment of art and human reason, exemplifying the best that can be attained without the benefit of Christian revelation. His *Fourth Eclogue* was considered to contain a prophetic anticipation of the coming of Christ.

78–87. This is one of the many cryptic "prophecies" and political allegories Dante includes in his poem, and scholars have never agreed about its exact meaning. In particular, there is debate over the intended identity of the Hound. The mysterious phrase "*nazion . . . tra feltro e feltro*"—BORN BETWEEN FELTRO AND FELTRO—admits several possibilities. If we translate *feltro* literally, as "felt," the Hound could be a member of the clergy (friars' cloaks were made of felt), perhaps a politician or the Holy Roman Emperor (officeholders were elected by votes cast into felt-lined urns). Another popular theory is that the Hound is meant to represent Cangrande della Scala, a benefactor of Dante's during his exile (*Cane grande* means "great dog"). Cangrande was born in Verona, which lies between the cities of Feltre and Montefeltro; these cities could well be the "two felts."

82. LOW ITALY may be topographical, or it may be in moral contrast with SUPERB ILIUM in line 57 above. The adjectives *superbo* (proud or superb) and *umile* (low) suggest the high state before a fall and the humiliation preceding a revival.

82–84. NISUS, TURNUS, EURYALUS, and CAMILLA are all characters in the *Aeneid*. Virgil alternates the names of Aeneas' comrades (Nisus and Euryalus) with those of his enemies (Turnus and Camilla): all four were martyred to advance the founding of the Roman Empire.

88–98. In these lines, Virgil gives a brief outline of what is to come in the three parts of the *Commedia*. Partly because of this passage, Canto I itself is generally viewed as an introduction or prologue to the entire poem as well as a part of the *Inferno*. When this introduction is counted separately, each cantica—*Inferno, Purgatorio, Paradiso*—has thirty-three cantos, with Canto I making an even one hundred.

92–101. The phases of the journey ahead: first, Dante will visit ANCIENT TORMENTED SPIRITS in Hell (the *Inferno*). The SECOND DEATH they face is eternal damnation at the Last Judgment. Next he will travel to Purgatory (*Purgatorio*), where the SOULS . . . ARE CONTENT / TO DWELL IN FIRE because, having repented and accepted their punishments, they know their suffering is temporary. In the third part of his journey, Dante will visit the realm of the EMPEROR WHO GOVERNS FROM ON HIGH (the *Paradiso*), and because Virgil was a pagan and lived IN REBELLION TO HIS LAW, he is forbidden to enter that realm.

97. The ONE WORTHIER who must replace Virgil as Dante's guide is Beatrice, the object of Dante's lifelong love. The historical Beatrice was probably Beatrice

Portinari, who was Dante's neighbor when they were children, and who died in 1290 at the age of twenty-four. Dante celebrates her in his *Vita Nuova* as a living woman, and in the *Divine Comedy* as far more than just a fictional representation of that woman: Beatrice stands for blessedness and divine grace.

CANTO II

Both Aeneas and St. Paul descended into Hell, according to Dante, the first as a prelude to the founding of the Roman Empire, the second in order to bear witness to his faith. Although Dante protests his unworthiness, it is clear that his own descent is meant both as a spiritual experience and as a prelude to political prophecy. He is not Aeneas and he is not Paul because in a sense he is both. It is not a question of merit or of intelligence, as some of the souls in Hell will mistakenly assume, but rather of election, symbolized by a relay of grace that extends from Heaven to Virgil, through three blessed ladies.

The action of the canto consists of a series of dramatic vignettes, contained within one another like a series of Chinese boxes. Virgil tells the story of his encounter with Beatrice, who told him of her encounter with Lucy, who told her encounter with a gentle Lady in Paradise. The encounter between Virgil and Beatrice, as Virgil reports it, was structured according to the rules of ancient rhetoric. Beatrice began with the obligatory flattery (*captatio benevolentiae*), promised to praise him before her lord, and sent him on his way with a peroration. Her exchange with Lucy, however, was biblical and penitential.

It seems puzzling at first that Virgil should recognize Beatrice. The terms of his praise make it clear that in his eyes she is more than a historical personage. He says that she is the person through whom alone humanity transcends the limitations of time and mortality, represented by the sphere of the moon. This can only mean that Virgil takes her for Lady Philosophy, the allegorical figure celebrated by Boethius in his *Consolation of Philosophy*. The poetic significance of this encounter and of this identification is that they represent Dante's interpretation of the wisdom of antiquity as an anticipation of Christianity.

When Lucy looks down from Heaven, however, she speaks the language of Christian allegory. The pilgrim was driven back to the dark woods by the wolf, but Lucy hears his weeping on the banks of a river over which the sea cannot boast (II, 86–87). The only river of which that can be said is the river Jordan, the final barrier faced by the Jews in the desert after they had crossed the Red Sea. The stages of Exodus, the escape from Egypt to the Promised Land, were interpreted by Christians as a figure for the experience of conversion. In Lucy's theological language, the pilgrim requires supernatural help to cross over Jordan. (J.F.)

6–8. The invocation to the MUSES follows the tradition of epic poetry. Dante echoes passages in the *Aeneid*: see III, 147 ("Night deepened; sleep on earth held living things"); VIII, 26–27 ("Now it was night, and through the lands of earth / Deep slumber held all weary living things"); and IX, 224–26 ("Earth's other creatures now had given over / Care in sleep, forgetful of their toil, / But the high Trojan captains, chosen men, / Held council"). It is somewhat less conventional for Dante to invoke the GENIUS OF ART and MEMORY, attributes he hopes to call upon within himself. As the genius or guiding spirit of art must inform Dante the poet, memory informs Dante the pilgrim.

All quotations from the *Aeneid* are from Robert Fitzgerald's translation (New York: Random House, 1983).

12–21. SILVIUS'S FATHER is Aeneas, whose journey to the underworld Virgil describes in the *Aeneid*, Book VI. When Aeneas founded Rome, this passage suggests, he prepared the way for the establishment of the Papacy.

22. St. Paul, the CHOSEN VESSEL (Acts 9:15), tells of his own ascent to the third heaven in his Second Epistle to the Corinthians (12:2–4).

26–35. I AM NO AENEAS OR PAUL: once again Dante recalls the *Aeneid*. Before Aeneas enters Hades (*Aeneid*, VI, 122–23), he compares himself with the earlier heroes Theseus and Hercules, who descended there while they were still alive. Coming as they do so soon after the invocation to the Muses, genius, and memory, Dante's FEARS and NULLIFYING UNEASE might be interpreted as characterizing Dante the poet—who is about to undertake a writing project of tremendous scope and difficulty—as well as Dante the pilgrim, for whom the journey ahead is a more literal, but exactly parallel, epic project.

43–44. Virgil's spirit DWELLED / IN LIMBO, where Catholic doctrine situates the souls of unbaptized babies and virtuous pagans—those to whom it was not given to know Christ (nor could they await His coming to harrow Hell like the good Old Testament Jews: see Canto IV, 43–51).

75–81. The first LADY in this gracious, courtly scene is apparently the Virgin Mary. LUCY (or Lucia) is a martyred virgin of third-century Syracuse, the patron saint of illumination and sight. Some scholars have suggested that Dante credited Lucy with his recovery from an affliction of his eyes.

81. RACHEL is an Old Testament heroine. Jacob was allowed to marry her only after marrying her older sister, Leah (Gen. 29:16–30).

101. THREE BLESSED LADIES: That is, Mary, Lucy, and Beatrice.

CANTO III

1–7. The famous inscription, in the "voice" of the gate. Hell is presented as a CITY OF WOES, which corresponds exactly to the heavenly city that was mentioned in the first two cantos. POWER, WISDOM, and LOVE are traditionally associated with the Father, the Son, and the Holy Spirit, respectively. NO THINGS WERE / BEFORE ME NOT ETERNAL, the gate proclaims; that is, the only things created by God before the fall of Lucifer (and the consequent creation of Hell) were everlasting: the heavens, the angels, and the elements.

15. THE GOOD OF INTELLECT is truth; God is the supreme truth.

30–37. SOULS UNSURE: these are the pusillanimous "neutrals" who, in life, would not take a stand. They are punished here along with ANGELS OF THAT BASE

SORT / . . . NEITHER REBELLIOUS TO GOD NOR FAITHFUL TO HIM. The occasion of the angels' wavering was Lucifer's rebellion against God; these angels did not take either side.

45–48. The waverers, who would not align themselves in life with any cause, are condemned forever to chase a meaningless banner. This is the first example of the infernal system of retribution called *contrapasso* (see Canto XXVIII, 127 and note): the punishment is suited to the specific wrongdoing, often requiring that the damned souls reenact their crimes in some form that grotesquely reflects the essence of the sin.

50. There is some debate as to the identity of HIM WHO MADE THE GREAT REFUSAL, and Dante seems to be deliberately obscure about it himself (see lines 43–44, where Virgil urges Dante not to speak of these souls). The most popular theory is that the soul is that of Pope Celestine V, who abdicated in 1294, only five months into his papacy, when political pressure proved too much for him. He was succeeded by Boniface VIII, despised by Dante.

64. ACHERON is the first of four rivers Dante will encounter in Hell. The names and descriptions of the rivers are largely borrowed from classical tradition, and from Virgil in particular.

77. Dante's description of CHARON, ferryman to the dead souls, relies heavily upon Virgil's. Characters such as Charon from Greek and Roman mythology appear frequently in Dante's Hell, often as demons.

105–8. WHAT THAT MEANS, by extrapolation, is that Dante is not destined for Hell: when he dies he WILL BE BROUGHT TO SHORE BY ANOTHER WAY, as Charon points out in line 76, and not come to this crossing where SOULS WHO ARE GOOD / NEVER PASS. Dante is defining himself as a soul not to be damned. He will be even more explicit about his own fate later in the poem.

CANTO IV

Canto IV moves in a series of unexpected turns from light to darkness and from darkness to light, as Virgil leads Dante from fore-Hell down into the first circle of Hell itself. From the dark of sleep, a thunderclap wakens Dante so that he opens his eyes—to peer down into another darkness, in which he can see nothing: the "*cieco mondo*," or blind world. Into this "sightless zone" (line 9) Dante is led for the purpose of seeing—led by Virgil, the guide who explains that he himself is benighted, unbaptized, and an inhabitant of this dark Limbo. Yet into this place, harrowing Hell with eternal Light, the Redeemer came to retrieve the souls of the blessed of the Old Testament. The catalogues of proper names—first of biblical patriarchs, then of poets, of heroes, and of thinkers—invoke the categorizing, perceiving light of knowledge: a taxonomy of truth enumerated here in the realm of unseeing.

And in this place, around a bright fire that displaces "a bleak / hemisphere of darkness" (lines 57–58), Dante finds the poets of antiquity who have been the luminaries of his own intelligence. He walks with them through the wood of "thronging spirits" (line 55) to the green meadow of the heroic souls, where the poets view them from a "spacious, well-lit height" (line 101). From this vantage "*aperto, luminoso e alto,*" Dante looks still higher to see the "Master of those who know" (line 116), Aristotle, surrounded by the great thinkers, their names an abundant, almost ecstatic identifying list.

Thus, in Canto IV, the *Inferno* describes itself as a journey that gathers light from a descent into darkness, a pilgrimage of knowledge that penetrating deeper seemingly turns away from the light, which yet reappears—and yet again vanishes, as in the canto's final line. (R.P.)

4–5. The swooning Dante has been mysteriously transported across Acheron without boarding Charon's ferry, which is reserved for wicked souls. This canto takes place in Limbo, the first circle of Hell.

25–32. Traditionally, Limbo is inhabited by the souls of unbaptized babies and figures from the Old Testament who died before the time of Christ, and hence before Christianity. Dante also includes the souls of virtuous pagans such as Virgil, both historic and mythological. The souls in Limbo are punished only in that they may never know God or see His truth, and must LIVE IN LONGING.

35–51. Christian tradition has long held that in A.D. 33, after Christ's death and before His Resurrection, He went to Limbo to claim the souls of the Old Testament heroes and transport them to Heaven. Although this "Harrowing of Hell" is apocryphal in origin, it became official Church dogma in 1215. Virgil died in 19 B.C., and would still have been relatively NEW TO THIS CONDITION at the time of Christ's descent into Limbo. In lines 35–39, Dante wants to be reassured in his Christian faith in the Harrowing of Hell, but asks indirectly, leaving Virgil to discern his COVERT MEANING. Christ is never directly named in the *Inferno*.

44. OUR FIRST PARENT is Adam.

49–50. ISRAEL is another name for Jacob, who had to work for Rachel's father for seven years before he was permitted to marry her. His SIRE is his father, Isaac.

73. Readers who experience Dante's poetry in translation will perhaps find comfort in the knowledge that although in this passage he reveres Homer as the greatest poet of antiquity, Dante could not read Greek. His knowledge of Homer would have come from translations—and not complete ones—and from other writers' references to Homer's works.

75. Three Latin poets: HORACE (65–8 B.C.) is known for his *Epistles* (including the *Ars Poetica*) as well as his *Satires* and *Odes*. OVID (43 B.C.–A.D. 17) is the author of the *Metamorphoses*; Dante draws a great deal of information about classical mythology from Ovid and quotes him widely in the *Inferno*. LUCAN (A.D. 39–65), also an important source for Dante, wrote the *Pharsalia*, an epic poem chronicling Julius Caesar's war with Pompey.

76. The NAME they all share is that of Poet: see line 67.

90–95. The great souls in Limbo are set apart in this NOBLE CASTLE, whose allegorical meaning has not been agreed upon by scholars. The SEVEN . . .

WALLS with their SEVEN GATEWAYS may stand for the seven virtues, or the seven liberal arts, or both.

104. ELECTRA in this case is Dardanus's mother, not Orestes' sister. Dardanus is the legendary founder of Troy.

106–10. All these characters are associated with Troy, and so with Rome. AENEAS and HECTOR are great Trojan warriors from the *Iliad*; Julius CAESAR would have considered himself Aeneas' direct descendant, and his presence here among the Trojan heroes emphasizes the link between Troy and Rome. The virgin CAMILLA gave her life on the battlefield fighting against the Trojans, and in the *Aeneid* Virgil links her metaphorically with PENTHESILEA, queen of the Amazons, who fought to defend Troy and was killed by the Greek hero Achilles. KING LATINUS ruled the Latini, defeated by the Trojans in the *Aeneid*; his daughter LAVINIA became the conqueror Aeneas' wife.

111–12. More Romans: BRUTUS is Lucius Junius Brutus, as opposed to the more famous Marcus Junius Brutus who betrayed Caesar—that Brutus will appear in another part of Hell, Cocytus (Canto XXXIV). This one led the Romans in their revolt against TARQUIN the Proud (seventh and last of the legendary kings of Rome) in 510 B.C., and became one of the first magistrates of the new Roman Republic. LUCRETIA was a Roman lady who committed suicide after she was raped by King Tarquin. Her treatment prompted Brutus's revolt. JULIA, MARCIA, and CORNELIA are all exemplars of female Roman virtue.

113–14. SALADIN OF ARABIA sits apart from the group because he alone among them is neither ancient nor Roman. This twelfth-century Egyptian Sultan fought against the Crusaders, but was nevertheless regarded by Westerners as a noble, just, and generous prince. He is in Limbo because he led a virtuous life but was not a Christian.

115. Dante must look up slightly to see the next group of spirits: they are the philosophers and thinkers who led contemplative lives, and they occupy a somewhat higher position than the last group, who were associated with action rather than with thought.

116–28. Aristotle (384–322 B.C.) is the ACKNOWLEDGED MASTER OF THOSE WHO KNOW. As the intellectual source for Thomas Aquinas, Aristotle was considered the great master thinker. Thus, his PHILOSOPHIC FAMILY includes all sorts of thinkers, not all of them "philosophers" in the strictest modern sense. Along with philosophers (PLATO, SOCRATES, DEMOCRITUS, ZENO, EMPEDOCLES, ANAXAGORAS, THALES, HERACLITUS, DIOGENES) the list includes physicians (DIOSCORIDES, HIPPOCRATES, GALEN), mathematicians (EUCLID, PTOLEMY), mythological poets (ORPHEUS, LINUS), and moral thinkers (CICERO, SENECA) arranged in groups more or less according to their intellectual disciplines. Many are ancient Greeks or Romans, but a few are more modern: the Arab physician and commentator on Aristotle known as AVICENNA died in 1037; AVERROËS was a Spanish Arab who died in 1198, and also wrote influential commentaries on THE PHILOSOPHER, Aristotle.

CANTO V

Out of the whirlwind of carnal sinners buffeted about like starlings in winter, a separate flock emerges, flying in single file and wailing mournfully, like cranes "chanting." Their poetic lament and the way in which they follow one another distinguish them from the random horde. These are literary lovers, drawn from the great tradition of ancient epic and medieval romance: Helen of Troy, Dido, and other "knights and ladies of antiquity," all of whom died for love. In the name of love, Dante calls out to Francesca and Paolo. They descend like doves to the nest, and Francesca tells their story.

The first part of her story describes their love in the clichés of medieval literature: a unique and irresistible passion, kindled on sight, swept them to their death. The second part of her story seems to contradict this: in fact, she confesses, their love was neither spontaneous nor predestined. It was suggested by their reading of the romance of Lancelot. In Hell, Francesca seems to be disabused of her romantic illusions. What appeared to have been love at first sight was in fact love by the book. Book and author seduced the lovers, just as Lancelot and Guinevere were seduced into adultery by the traitor Gallehault.

The damned in Dido's train bear witness to the power of literature more than to the irresistibility of love. They were literary characters who sinned and yet claimed to be blameless because of love potions, betrayals, or overpowering love at first sight. In his early poetry, Dante had insisted upon the inevitability of such love for those with "gentle hearts." The second part of Francesca's story exposes the bad faith of such claims. Hers is a cautionary tale, warning the suggestible reader about the dangers of romance, but it is also a palinode, Dante's second thoughts on his own theory of love and the gentle heart.

The episode portrays Francesca as a deluded victim of medieval romance, like a thirteenth-century Madame Bovary, but it also creates one more heroine in love's canon. It is therefore just as seductive as the literature against which it warns. Francesca's name would have been out of place in this company, being that of a provincial adulteress mentioned only in the chronicles, swirling about with these literary legends, had Dante not transformed her into their equal, a rival of Helen or of Dido the queen. In spite of the moralizing intent of the story, its effect is to show Dante's mastery of the genre he condemns. (J.F.)

2. Each circle of Hell, which is shaped approximately like a funnel, GIRDLES A SMALLER SPACE than the one above it.

3. MINOS is a mythological king and judge. Virgil casts him in the *Aeneid* as a judge of the underworld, and it is Dante who transforms him into a demonic creature.

35–36. The souls punished here in the whirlwind are those of the lustful. Like all the souls consigned to the first five circles of Hell (Cantos I–VIII) their sin—in a concept derived from Aristotle—arises from incontinence, or lack of restraint, which is intellectual as much as physical. Dante seems concerned with THEIR REASON MASTERED BY DESIRE, as is embodied by their situation buffeted helplessly by the wind, rather than simply with their sexual behavior itself. Reason, in the Augustinian moral system, is not mere logic-chopping but the quality of mind capable of perceiving truth. Ideally, reason's perceptions guide and anchor desire, which in itself can be as wild and aimless as the whirlwind.

50–51. The ancient Assyrian queen SEMIRAMIS became legendary for sexual excess; one legend says that she legalized incest, to justify her own behavior.

52–54. SHE WHO DIED: Dido is the Carthaginian queen who kills herself for love of Aeneas in Virgil's epic. The widow of the murdered SYCHAEUS, she BROKE HER VOW / TO [his] ASHES by becoming Aeneas' lover.

55. CLEOPATRA, queen of Egypt, was the lover of both Julius Caesar and Mark Antony. HELEN caused the rift that led to the Trojan War when she eloped with PARIS (line 58).

57. The idea that ACHILLES died for the love of the Trojan Polyxena was popular in the Middle Ages, but does not come from Homer.

58. TRISTAN is a hero from medieval French romances, the lover of Iseult, the wife of his uncle, King Mark of Cornwall.

65. THOSE TWO are Paolo and Francesca, historical contemporaries of Dante. Francesca was the wife of Gianciotto Malatesta of Rimini, but she fell in love with his brother, Paolo. Gianciotto murdered the lovers when they were discovered. The murder caused enormous scandal, and although Dante does not use Paolo's name at all, or Francesca's until line 103, there can be no doubt as to the identity of these lovers. The encounter that follows, in which Francesca tells Dante their sad tale, is one of the most celebrated passages in the *Commedia*.

71. ANOTHER: Again the direct mention of God is avoided in Hell.

87. The CITY is Ravenna, on Italy's Adriatic (eastern) coast, Francesca's home.

96. CAINA, in the ninth circle of Hell, contains the spirits of those who betrayed their kin. Francesca assumes that when Gianciotto—who was still living in 1300—dies, he will be sent there for murdering his wife and brother.

113. LANCELOT is a worthy knight in the Arthurian romances. He betrays King Arthur, becoming the lover of Arthur's wife, Guinevere.

122. GALEOTTO, or, in French, Gallehault, acted as messenger between Lancelot and Guinevere. The French version of his name has become a synonym for "pander" or "go-between."

CANTO VI

12. THREE-HEADED CERBERUS guards the gate to the underworld in classical mythology, and appears in that role in Book VI of the *Aeneid*. Dante portrays him as a horrible demon, though in classical accounts he is not much more than a three-headed guard dog.

23–29. In the *Aeneid* (VI, 554), Cerberus falls quiet when he is thrown a honey cake. Dante substitutes GOBBETS OF EARTH—which the gluttonous demon receives with enthusiasm.

46–47. As a common noun, CIACCO means "hog," and it is not clear whether

Dante meant it as a real name—it can also be short for Giacomo—or a nasty nickname. Scholars have not identified a historical "Ciacco," but there is a gluttonous courtier by that name in Boccaccio's *Decameron*. Boccaccio may have based his Ciacco on Dante's, or there may have been an established tradition drawn upon by both authors.

55. THE DIVIDED CITY is Florence. It was "divided" because of two warring political factions: the aristocratic Black Guelphs, led by the Donati family, and Dante's own party, the White Guelphs, whose main family were the Cerchi. The Guelphs began as one party, but after they defeated the Ghibellines internal strife began to surface, with the Black Guelphs receiving the protection of Pope Boniface VIII. This was the schism that eventually led to Dante's exile. In April of 1300 (that is, at the time when the *Inferno* takes place), the growing tension had not yet led to bloodshed.

58–66. The souls in Dante's hell are able to foresee the future. Ciacco's prophecy is accurate: the things he "foretells" had all come to pass by the time the exiled Dante wrote his poem, and some were only weeks away from the fictional date of April 1300. It was on May 1, 1300, that the White Guelphs (THE RUSTIC BLOC, so called because the Cerchi were country-born) drove the Blacks out of Florence. Later—WITHIN THREE YEARS—the Black Guelphs returned and, with the help of Pope Boniface VIII (ONE WHO WHILE WE SPEAK / IS TEMPORIZING), took the city back, exiling Dante along with hundreds of White Guelphs.

66–69. The identities of the TWO MEN . . . TRULY JUST are not known. Many scholars believe that Dante counted himself as one of the two, while others maintain that the reference is not specific. The pronouncement is rather biblical in tone, and it may be meant to recall Sodom and Gomorrah, where there were not ten good men (Gen. 18:32).

71–72. Dante names five dead Florentine politicians. FARINATA, MOSCA, TEGGHIAIO, and JACOPO RUSTICUCCI will appear in later Cantos (X, XXVIII, XVI, XVI respectively), but this is the only mention of ARRIGO.

79–80. Ciacco will not be the last soul in Hell to ask this favor of Dante.

87. To the wicked souls, Christ is THE HOSTILE POWER.

97–101. Dante's SCIENCE would be the Aristotelian doctrine that the perfection of the individual lies in the union of body and soul. Thus, after the Last Judgment, when the souls of the dead are reunited with their bodies, THEY CAN EXPECT TO COME CLOSER [to perfection] THEN THAN NOW. Since THE MORE / A CREATURE IS PERFECT, THE MORE IT PERCEIVES . . . PAIN, the suffering of the wicked will only increase.

106. PLUTUS is the god of wealth in classical mythology, and so it is no surprise to find him at the entrance to the fourth circle, where the souls punished are those who hoarded or overspent their riches. The Plutus whom Dante describes also seems to incorporate some characteristics of Pluto, god of the underworld: scholars do not agree on whether Dante had in mind one god or the other, or both.

CANTO VII

Set among the shades who squandered their substance and those who kept it point-
lessly to themselves, Canto VII begins with the clucking babble-language Dante has
invented for Plutus, the god of wealth. Elsewhere in Hell, down to the depth of
Cocytus, shades speak in comprehensible language: here, these materialists of the
fourth circle are all but inarticulate, just as—again unlike the souls in other circles
—they are indistinguishable from one another, all as alike as so many coins or
banknotes of the same value. Functionally stupid in their greed or in their dissipation,
they execute a dance of mindless contraries.

Virgil tells Dante about a deity who seems implicitly opposed to the incompre-
hensible, bloated Plutus: the goddess Fortune, celebrated by Virgil because unlike
Plutus she fosters the necessary circulation of goods among family lines and nations.
In contrast to the renewing variations of Fortune, wealth uncommunicated rots the
soul.

In a curious link, the poets proceed in this same canto to the fifth circle, where
the wrathful tear at one another in the mud, while under the muck below them the
sullen—the depressives—gurgle their despairing, unintelligible hymn of regret and
misgiving. The unintelligibility and conflict recall the opposites earlier in the canto,
suggesting parallels: as the collisions between hoarders and spendthrifts embody
fruitless energy directed at the material world, a fruitless, stagnant energy charac-
terizes what might be thought of as the emotional stinginess of the sullen and the
emotional wastefulness of the wrathful.

Canto VII, which begins with the guttural, subhuman voice of the god of wealth,
ends with the strangulated lament of those who begrudged their vital spirits in life.
Hoarding and wasting, raging and festering, all seem part of a single, ruinous abscess,
framed by mangled efforts at speech. (R.P.)

1. This utterance—apparently an invocation, and perhaps a warning or a threat
   —is spoken in words invented by Dante, and not in any real language. Virgil
   seems to understand it, however. Like all skillfully written nonsense (for ex-
   ample, Lewis Carroll's poem "Jabberwocky"), Dante's invented words suggest
   possible meanings: PAPE resembles the Latin exclamation of amazement *papae*
   as well as the words for "Pope" and "father"; ALEPPE, which can be used as
   an expression of grief, has also been associated with aleph, the first letter of
   the Hebrew alphabet, which can mean "first one." In short, Dante has suc-
   ceeded in putting evocative gibberish into outraged Plutus's mouth.
10–11. The Archangel MICHAEL punished Satan and the rebellious angels ABOVE,
   in Heaven (Rev. 12:7–9).
20. The whirlpool CHARYBDIS is one of the twin dangers of the Strait of Messina.
   Homer describes it and the treacherous rock Scylla in the *Odyssey*, and Dante
   would have known about it through Virgil's retelling in the *Aeneid*.
68. GUIDE: guides or "intelligences" that govern the motion of the heavenly spheres
   in Dante's ordering of the universe. These astronomical forces bear some re-
   semblance to angels, and some also to pagan gods: Fortune is a bit of both, it
   would seem, though she is given her place in the Christian order. Indeed, in

his *Convivio* (II, iv, 2–6), Dante says that "angels" and "gods and goddesses" are both simply names for the "intelligences."

87–88. It is just past midnight. When Virgil SET OUT, it was sunset, and the stars were rising. Now they have begun to set.

95. STYX is one of the five rivers that surround Hades in Greek and Roman mythology. It appears in the *Aeneid* (VI, 134, 323).

108. ACEDIA is torpor, a mental or moral sluggishness.

CANTO VIII

3. The TWO POINTS OF FLAME are a signal characteristic of medieval warfare.

18. PHLEGYAS is another figure from ancient myths. When his daughter Coronis was raped by Apollo, Phlegyas flew into a rage and burned the god's temple at Delphi to the ground. Apollo killed Phlegyas, whose shade was punished in the pit of Tartarus. In Book VI of the *Aeneid* he appears as a tormented spirit: "Phlegyas in his misery teaches all souls / His lesson, thundering out amid the gloom: / 'Be warned and study justice, not to scorn / The immortal gods.' " (618–20). It is Dante's innovation to make him the boatman of the Styx, where the souls of the wrathful are immersed.

24–30. Unlike everyone else in Hell, including Virgil, Dante is still alive and has a real body with bulk and weight (Aeneas has a similar experience when he boards a boat on the Styx [*Aeneid*, VI, 413–14]). Presumably it is because Phlegyas's skiff MADE A DEEPER CUT / INTO THE WATER with Dante's weight aboard THAN IT WAS WONT TO DO that the soul (Filippo Argenti) who sits up in line 29 notices Dante's presence.

58. FILIPPO ARGENTI was a Black Guelph, Dante's contemporary and political enemy. ARGENTI is a nickname—Filippo belonged to a family called Cavicciuli—which comes from the word *argento*, "silver." Filippo is said to have shod his horse with the precious metal. Boccaccio and others refer to his savage temper.

65. The name DIS can refer both to Hell's city and to its master, known also (in the classical tradition) as Pluto. In Dante's Hell these are other names for Lucifer.

67. The MOSQUES on the outskirts of Dis suggest the presence of Muslims—that is, to the medieval Christian mind, infidels.

78–79. THOSE WHOM HEAVEN HAD SPAT / LIKE RAIN are the fallen angels who followed Lucifer and rebelled against God.

118–21. Virgil recalls the legend which says that when Jesus came to Limbo (see Canto IV, 40–51), the demons resisted Him, and He broke open the gate. That was the outer, LESS SECRET GATE where Dante READ THE DEADLY INSCRIPTION in Canto III.

CANTO IX

16. THE FIRST CIRCLE is Limbo, where Virgil's spirit belongs.

19–29. Scholars believe that Dante invented this story of Virgil's previous descent to lower Hell. The witch ERICHTHO would have been familiar to Dante from Lucan's *Pharsalia*, where she is a sorceress able to conjure the souls of the dead.

35–39. The FURIES, also called the ERINYES or Eumenides, appear frequently in classical literature as bringers of wrath, retribution, and ceaseless torment. Dante's description does not stray far from those of Virgil, Statius, and Ovid.

40–41. Most commentators take the QUEEN / OF ETERNAL SORROWS to be Proserpina, also called Persephone or—as in the *Aeneid*—Hecate. She is the wife of Pluto, king of the underworld, and although she is referred to twice in the *Inferno*, she does not make an actual appearance.

46–47. MEDUSA, one of the three Gorgon sisters, had snakes growing from her head instead of hair. She was so horrible to look at that whoever saw her face was turned to stone.

48. The Greek hero THESEUS, according to legend, descended to Hell and tried to abduct its queen, Proserpina. He was caught and imprisoned in the underworld until he was freed by Hercules.

55–56. THE LESSON THAT UNDERLIES / THE VEIL OF THESE STRANGE VERSES I HAVE WRITTEN is a lesson just as enigmatic as the passage says it is. The words "these strange verses I have written" seem to refer back to the preceding tercet, where Virgil puts his hands over Dante's eyes protectively, not trusting Dante's own ability to keep from looking at what would be fatal to see. That action suggests a lesson to do with authority, with the value of not seeing, and with the limits of what the uninformed reader (or unperfected soul?) should undertake to look at unaided.

Following such an interpretation, it is possible to read the passage both as a justification of allegory compared to more direct ways of treating the subject of evil, and as a warning against excessive or overeager interpretation: it is not always best to see everything plainly and at once. It may be better to have the poet, or whatever authority Virgil represents, cover one's eyes.

71–76. No satisfactory theory has been offered for a specific identity of the ONE who comes FROM HEAVEN to open the gate. Dante may simply have intended him to be an anonymous angel.

80. The LITTLE WAND is a typical symbol of angels' power; it is sometimes used to contrast with the useless display of force and massive strength associated with devils.

81–89. The divine emissary rebukes the fallen angels—now devils—and reminds them of their past defeats. He recalls the way the rebels were CAST OUT / FROM HEAVEN for their crimes, and the treatment of CERBERUS, who had his THROAT AND CHIN . . . STRIPPED OF FUR when Hercules chained him and dragged him out of Hell. The detail about Cerberus's fur being stripped away is Dante's invention, though the story about Hercules comes from Virgil (*Aeneid*, VI, 391–97).

101–2. ARLES, in southern France, and POLA (now Pula), in what is now Croatia, are both sites of ancient Roman graveyards.

120. This is one of only two occasions in the *Inferno* when Dante and Virgil turn TO THE RIGHT. The aberration seems to be intentional, especially in light of

the fact that Dante always turns right, never left, in the *Purgatorio*. Various explanations have been offered for this break in the pattern, but none is convincing enough to be generally accepted by scholars. For more about turning left and right in the *Inferno*, see John Freccero's essay "Pilgrim in a Gyre," in *Dante: The Poetics of Conversion*, ed. Rachel Jacoff (Cambridge: Harvard University Press, 1986).

CANTO X

Arranged in sepulchers on the outskirts of the city of Dis are the heretics or, as Dante refers to them, the "Epicureans," who believed that the soul dies with the body. One of them, Farinata degli Uberti, towers over the rest, while Cavalcante de' Cavalcanti cowers beside him. Dante's ambivalent treatment of the Ghibelline Farinata reflects his own torn political loyalties: the poet was a Guelph, but he belonged to a faction of that party that was opposed to the papacy and nostalgic for the emperor. His ambivalence toward the second man is more personal, reflecting his problematic relationship to Guido, a fellow poet and the old man's son.

The drama of the episode is based upon a dizzying irony: the pilgrim does not know that the damned do not know the present and the damned are unaware of his ignorance. In Canto VI, Ciacco seemed to know the past and to predict the future, from which Dante mistakenly infers that the damned are omniscient. So Farinata's boast about the triumph of his party, long after their definitive defeat, seems absurdly empty, while Cavalcante de' Cavalcanti's anxiety about the whereabouts of his son seems inexplicable. The reply to Farinata stuns the Ghibelline captain, while the explanation to Cavalcante provokes a cry of pain.

The bewildering exchanges derive from divergent premises and quickly reach logical impasse. The confusion is meant to illustrate the effects of heresy, which, unlike all other sins, was thought to be a sin of the reason rather than the will. Knowledge of the present is the shared premise upon which understanding depends, yet the present itself cannot be defined or described. It is the interface of past and future. According to Augustine, it "occupies no space." The damned lack this knowledge; their temporality is a negative image of our own, a central nothingness expanding with time until it engulfs both past and future.

The drama of misunderstanding and of time is played out at the very center of the canto in syntax, where the past absolute tense in Italian takes upon itself a metaphysical meaning—Cavalcante fears that the use of a past tense means the end of his son's life, rather than the end of an action, as the speaker intends. Guido was once Dante's first friend; here, his refusal to undertake an infernal voyage seems to call his salvation into question. We know that at the time of the voyage, he had only a few months to live. The father's pain is expressed in words that echo Guido's "*Donna me prega*," his difficult and disabused love poem. (J.F.)

9. JEHOSHAPHAT, or Kidron, is a valley near Jerusalem. In Jewish and Islamic traditions, as well as Christian, it is regarded as the site where the Last Judgment is to take place (Joel 3:2, 12). After the Judgment, when the souls of the

heretics in Hell have been reunited with their bodies, their graves will be sealed forever.

11. The Greek philosopher EPICURUS (341–270 B.C.) did not believe in the immortality of the soul and taught that "pleasure"—that is, the absence of pain —was the greatest good. To the medieval Christian mind, this represented the ultimate heresy.

13–15. Dante's QUESTION was asked in line 7 about the souls of the heretics: MIGHT THEY BE SEEN? Dante would have known that many Florentines— Ghibellines especially—subscribed to Epicurean ideas; his SECRET WISH is to see for himself whether they (and, some commentators say, Farinata in particular) are here. In this passage, as elsewhere, Virgil appears able to read Dante's thoughts.

29. FARINATA degli Uberti was a Ghibelline leader of Florence who died in 1264, the year before Dante was born. His story would have been well known to Dante, and he is one of the MEN OF GOOD REASON Dante asks Ciacco about in Canto VI, 70–75. Farinata was instrumental in the expulsion of the Guelphs from Florence in 1248, but by 1258 the Guelphs had returned and cast out the Ghibellines in turn. In 1260, when the Ghibellines had defeated the Guelphs in battle at Montaperti, Farinata alone strenuously opposed the suggestion that his victorious party should destroy Florence (see lines 83–86). Farinata was posthumously condemned as a heretic and excommunicated in 1283. He was probably a "heretic" mostly in that he belonged to a political party that sought to limit the power of the Church.

44–48. Farinata's Ghibellines drove out the Guelphs, the party of Dante's family, TWICE: in 1248 and again in 1260. The Guelphs RETURNED TO CLAIM THEIR PLACE both times, however, and in 1300 (when the poem takes place) they were still in power.

48–66. The spirit who interrupts at this point is that of Cavalcante de' Cavalcanti, a Guelph with a reputation as an Epicurean. His son Guido was a poet and a close friend of Dante's. Cavalcante is entombed with Farinata although the two were from opposing political parties; their association may be based on the fact that Guido was married to a daughter of Farinata in an attempt to reconcile the factions.

55. Cavalcante expects to see his SON, Guido, with Dante, since the two poets were such good friends.

57–59. This is one of the most debated passages in the *Commedia*. This translation chooses to present the one who IS WAITING YONDER as the same as the one WHO GUIDES ME THROUGH HERE: that is, Virgil. ONE YOUR GUIDO PERHAPS HAD SCORNED has been interpreted by commentators as meaning God, or Beatrice, or—requiring a different translation—Virgil himself.

The nature of the disagreement about the passage may be illustrated compactly by composing different possible English versions. One alternate translation of the lines might interpret the one who waits "yonder" (understood as meaning "yonder in Paradise," rather than a few yards away) not as the one who guides, but as the one scorned: "My own strength has not brought me, but that of one / Who guides me here, toward one awaiting yonder / One whom perhaps your Guido had scorned." And a third version might choose to present Virgil as all three: the guide, and the one who waits, and the one who is scorned: "My own strength has not brought me, but that of one / Who guides me here, and is awaiting yonder; / Perhaps your Guido had scorn for him."

Underlying the conflicting viewpoints is the fact that the meaning of Guido's "scorn" (sometimes translated as "disdain") is a matter of speculation, based on little or no evidence. Disdain for guidance by God, by Beatrice, or by Virgil could suggest Cavalcante's agnosticism, or his skepticism about transcendent love, or his literary attitude toward epic or toward human reason. In any case, such scorn or disdain (Italian *disdegno*) can be taken as a contrast with Dante's willingness to be guided.

72. Farinata refers to THAT ART / OF RETURN from exile, mentioned by Dante in lines 47 and 48 just before Cavalcante's interruption.

74–76. THE LADY . . . WHO RULES THIS PLACE is Pluto's queen, Hecate, also identified with Proserpina and as the goddess of the moon. Her FACE . . . HAS KINDLED FEWER THAN FIFTY TIMES—that is, it will be fewer than fifty months—before Dante himself will KNOW HOW HEAVY THAT ART [of returning from exile] WEIGHS. In fact, it was almost exactly fifty months after April 1300 that a major diplomatic effort to return Dante and the other exiled White Guelphs to Florence met with failure.

77–79. Though some of the Ghibellines were granted amnesty, the Florentine people never pardoned the Uberti or permitted their return.

80. The ARBIA is a stream near the site of the battle at Montaperti, where Farinata led the Ghibellines to victory over the Guelphs in 1260.

103–4. In fact, Guido was gravely ill in April of 1300, and he died in August of that year.

112. The emperor FREDERICK II headed the Holy Roman Empire from 1215 to 1250. He was widely reported to be an Epicurean heretic.

113. The CARDINAL Ottavio degli Ubaldini, Bishop of Bologna, was so notorious that Dante is able to identify him by his title alone. He was an ardent Ghibelline and is supposed to have said that he had "lost [his] soul a thousand times" for his party.

122. HER RADIANCE is the glory of Beatrice.

CANTO XI

A note on the illustration (pages 106–7): Maps or pictorial plans of the *Inferno* appear with the text as early as the mid-fourteenth century. To this day, some kind of diagram or visual representation has been included in most editions, usually appearing in the introductory material or with scholarly notes at the end of the volume.

Dante has envisioned Hell as a descending series of circles with elaborate divisions and categories, many of which blend classical models of the underworld with early Christian eschatology. But Dante's plan is more specific than any antecedent; it even includes measurements. Dante as the pilgrim, and we as readers, cannot know the shape of Hell until told of it by Virgil in Canto XI. It is here, therefore, that I present both an aerial view and a map or "overlay" of the sort we have become used to from weather satellites and military reconnaissance, where many details are obscured by the cover of trees, the smoke of fires, or mist rising from fields of ice.

At the opening of Canto XI, Virgil uses the delay the poets need to get used to the stench from the abyss as an occasion for explaining the physical organization of Hell. They are already nearing Hell's second level (see "x" in the plan); Virgil's reference to "three lesser circles" (line 15) denotes the three subdivisions of the seventh circle, devoted to the sins of violence.

Dante and Virgil have entered through the first gate at the river Acheron at the lower right side of the image. They will descend to Malebolge near the upper center and arrive at the deepest pit, near the upper right corner. (M.M.)

7–8. ANASTASIUS II was Pope from 496 to 498. During the Middle Ages, he was widely believed to have been a heretic, taught by the deacon PHOTINUS to believe that Christ was conceived in the usual human manner, rather than by divine visitation.

12. This MATTER will turn out to be an explanation: in this canto, Virgil describes in detail the way Hell is laid out, and how the various types of sin are classified. The reader may find it helpful to refer to the illustration on pages 106–7 and to the chart on pages xxvi–xxvii.

14–65. Virgil explains the arrangement of the part of Hell that still lies ahead of (and below) the travelers. Three circles remain out of nine in all; Virgil describes them as LESSER (line 15) because they are smaller than the first six circles, being farther down in the "funnel" of Hell. When Virgil refers to the first (line 28), second (line 57), and third (LEAST, line 63) of these circles, he means the seventh, eighth, and ninth circles of Hell as a whole.

28–34. The seventh circle (first of the three to come, in Virgil's explanation) is divided into THREE RINGS; these are subdivisions, and not the same thing as circles. The seventh circle's three rings hold the souls of violent sinners, in three groups: those violent TO GOD, / TO ONE'S SELF, OR ONE'S NEIGHBOR, listed in order from the most to the least grave.

51. SODOM (Gen. 18–19) is a biblical city that Christian tradition associates with sodomy, or sex between men—considered a grave and unnatural sin in the Middle Ages. The French town of CAHORS was famous for usury, and its name almost synonymous with the practice.

53–54. This distinction, between simple FRAUD and treacherous FRAUD, determines the difference between the eighth and ninth circles of Hell. Fraud in general is the worst kind of sin, punished the most severely because, as Virgil points out in lines 24 and 25, FRAUD IS FOUND / IN HUMANKIND AS ITS PECULIAR VICE: among earthly creatures, only humans have the gift of reason, and only they can use it to defraud.

58–59. The crime of SIMONIACS is to sell church offices; of BARRATORS, to sell civic offices.

64. DIS in this case is Satan, not the city.

65–75. Dante wants to know why the souls they have already encountered are not punished inside the walls of the RED CITY (Dis). Virgil obliges in the lines that follow.

78–86. Virgil refers to Aristotle's *Nicomachean* ETHICS, in which the philosopher discusses the comparative gravity of the various types of sin. Aristotle's THREE DISPOSITIONS correspond to (and are the main source for) Dante's three main categories of sin, with MALICE equivalent to fraud and INSANE BRUTALITY to violence. The shades punished ABOVE, OUTSIDE, are all guilty of the lesser sins that Dante, like Aristotle, calls sins of INCONTINENCE; that is, they failed to restrain, or gave in to, various passions such as lust, greed, and anger. The incontinent sins are less grave than the others, perhaps because they are crimes of weakness rather than positive will. In general, the worse a sin is, the farther down in Hell its perpetrator is punished.

91. Dante refers to line 51, the PLACE where Virgil mentions Cahors.

97–101. The PHYSICS are another work of Aristotle's.

100–1. Nature is God's child, and art emulates nature—so art is like God's GRANDCHILD.

102–7. GENESIS 3:19 contains the injunction "In the sweat of thy face shalt thou eat bread," which Virgil interprets to mean that a person must earn a living by nature or by art. Usurers do neither, using money to make money; this offense to art and nature is an offense to God.

109–11. The arrangement of constellations in relation to CAURUS, the northwest wind, indicates that it is about four o'clock in the morning.

CANTO XII

3–7. It is generally presumed that the LANDSLIDE Dante refers to is one which occurred south of Trent hundreds of years before Dante was born, and which created a rock formation known as the Slavini di Marco.

10–11. The INFAMY OF CRETE was a monster known as the Minotaur, son of King Minos's wife, Pasiphaë, by a white bull. Seized by an unnatural longing for the bull, Pasiphaë had the architect Daedalus construct a wooden cow inside which she could conceal herself. In this disguise Pasiphaë satisfied her lust for the bull, and so the Minotaur was CONCEIVED WITHIN / THE FALSE COW'S SHELL. In some versions of the myth, the Minotaur is a man with a bull's head, and in others, a bull with the head of a man: most commentators believe that Dante had the latter in mind.

14–16. THE DUKE OF ATHENS is the hero Theseus, who slew the Minotaur and escaped the labyrinth where Minos housed his wife's grotesque offspring. Theseus was helped by Minos's daughter Ariadne, the monster's half sister.

25. Dante's is a NEW WEIGHT for these stones; they are unaccustomed to the presence of living flesh, as Chiron will shrewdly notice (see lines 72–74 of this canto, and the Translator's Note, page xxii).

29–30. THAT OTHER TIME Virgil visited lower Hell was when he was lured by the witch Erichtho, as he explains in Canto IX, lines 19–29.

31–33. The reference is to Christ's Harrowing of Hell after His death and before His Resurrection: see Canto IV, lines 35–51 and notes.

34–36. The tradition that says a great earthquake occurred at the moment of Christ's death comes from Matthew 27:51: "and the earth did quake, and the rocks rent."

35–37. Empedocles, among other PHILOSOPHERS, was supposed to have taught that the universe is controlled by the struggle between the forces of hatred and LOVE. When hatred reigns, the world is brought to order, but when love returns to supremacy, CHAOS ensues.

41. The RIVER OF BLOOD is called Phlegethon; it will be named in Canto XIV.

49. The CENTAURS are a race of archers, half human and half horse, who appear frequently in classical myths. They are often, though not always, associated with rape, violence, and mad rages. Like the Minotaur, they are physically half beasts—literal embodiments of the "insane brutality" (see note to Canto XI, lines 78–86) punished in the seventh circle.

57. CHIRON, a learned and unusually even-tempered Centaur, was tutor to the great Greek hero Achilles (see also line 64) and others.

60–62. NESSUS, according to Ovid (*Metamorphoses*, IX), was slain by Hercules for attempting to rape FAIR DEIANIRA, Hercules' wife. The dying Centaur had time to plan his VENGEANCE: he soaked a robe in his own poisoned blood and gave it to Deianira, saying that whoever wore the robe would instantly adore her. Deianira gave the robe to her husband, who went mad from the poisoned blood and destroyed himself.

65. PHOLUS is a relatively minor character in classical mythology; however, the name appears frequently as that of a Centaur.

76–77. The Centaurs are usually depicted as having the hindquarters and legs of a horse, and the upper body of a man, with the TWO NATURES JOINED at the abdomen.

82–83. Beatrice left off SINGING ALLELUIA in Paradise to seek Virgil and ask him to be Dante's guide.

100. This may be the spirit of the Macedonian ALEXANDER the Great, or of a Thessalian tyrant of the same name and approximate era, around 350 B.C. The latter hypothesis is preferred by recent scholars who point out that Dante's mentor Brunetto Latini pairs the Thessalian Alexander with Dionysius much as Dante links the two names in this tercet.

101. DIONYSIUS is not the god in this case: Dante means Dionysius the Elder (c. 430–367 B.C.), Tyrant of Syracuse (405–367 B.C.).

102–4. AZZOLINO and OBIZZO were both notorious tyrants from northern Italy who lived at around the same time as Dante. Azzolino was a Ghibelline, and Obizzo a Guelph. Obizzo was supposedly smothered by his son Azzo, who succeeded him. Some have taken Dante's term STEPSON (Italian *figliastro*) to indicate the unnaturalness of the act, or to cast doubt on Azzo's true paternity.

109–12. In 1271, Guy de Montfort murdered his first cousin, Prince Henry of Cornwall, WITHIN THE BOSOM OF GOD—that is, in the church of San Silvestro at Viterbo. It is Guy's shade that now appears immersed up to the neck in

Phlegethon. Legend holds that Henry's heart was placed inside a statue or box by the side of the river THAMES.

122–23. ATTILA, King of the Huns (434–453), PYRRHUS, Achilles' son, who killed King Priam of Troy, and SEXTUS, Pompey the Great's pirate son, were all famous for their cruelty.

125. Both RINIER PAZZO and RINIER DA CORNETO were highway robbers of Dante's time.

CANTO XIII

Canto XIII begins with a series of negatives. The images in the opening lines are of what is not: "The leaves not green, earth-hued; / The boughs not smooth, knotted and crooked-forked; / No fruit, but poisoned thorns." And this list of negatives is itself introduced by telling where Nessus had not yet reached (*Non era ancor di là Nesso arrivato*, so that the first word in Italian is *Non*). The list is followed by a figure that tells what sort of thicket wild beasts do *not* infest. And in this movement of the poem, Dante and Virgil penetrate to the region of Hell for those souls who violently negated their own being.

The image in Hell of the barren sin of despair is a dense abundance, a forest of anti-life with earth-colored foliage and contorted limbs: a wealth of lifelike non-matter, in other words, that in its luxurious vigor is both more and less alive than the life we know on earth. Despair is soul-lessness, and the shades who after Judgment will display their lifeless earthly bodies from the limbs of these trees appear less like living people than souls elsewhere in the *Inferno*.

The suicide abdicates from reality—maims the soul by wounding the body. In this circle appear souls whose dealings with others have been just, not cruel, in life above: and their having been just, which wins them sympathy, emphasizes the magnitude of the sin of destroying the soul. In the final lines, an apparent digression about Florence twists back to this truth, like a scorpion's tail: Florence abandoned Mars as patron, and took John the Baptist instead, for which the city has always suffered bad fortune in war, though the remnant statue of Mars at the Arno still ensures the city's survival, rebuilding itself after defeat. That sentiment—pagan in itself—turns into a Christian parable of endurance, courage, and patience in the last line, where the doomed shade's total, self-destructive despair is contrasted with the courage of those who rebuild over the ashes. In the Augustinian scheme, despair is a terrible sin, denying as it does both man and God. (R.P.)

6. The river CECINA and the town of CORNETO form the approximate boundaries of a Tuscan region called the Maremma, which in Dante's time was the wildest, densest part of Italy.

9–11. The HARPIES are yet another group of mythological monsters inhabiting the seventh circle who are part human and part beast. They have the bodies of great birds, with women's faces and enormous talons. In the *Aeneid* (III, 210–57), Virgil tells of how the Harpies appeared to the Trojans in the STRO-

PHADES (a group of islands) and drove them away, soiling the Trojans' food and predicting their COMING WOE and starvation.

17. The travelers are in the SECOND RING of the seventh circle; it is where those who were violent against themselves are punished. The HORRIBLE SAND mentioned in line 18 is the third ring.

44. The bleeding branch and the soul imprisoned inside it are indeed things Dante has WITNESSED . . . IN [Virgil's] VERSES: Aeneas encounters the soul of the Trojan Polydorus in similar circumstances (*Aeneid*, III, 22–48).

55–58. The shade is that of Pier della Vigna, a highly favored and trusted adviser in the court of the emperor FREDERICK II. He was eventually accused of treason, blinded, and cast out; despairing, he committed suicide.

61. By CAESAR'S RETINUE, Pier della Vigna means Frederick's court; in line 64 he will refer to Frederick as AUGUSTUS. The conceit is typical of the minister's courtly style of speaking.

62. The COMMON FATAL VICE is ENVY, named in line 73.

72. Pier della Vigna wants his name cleared in the world of the living. This is one of several places in the *Inferno* where the damned ask Dante to preserve their memories above.

108–22. The TWO who run through the wood are not suicides, but willful spendthrifts. Dante distinguishes them from the incontinent spenders punished in the fourth circle (Canto VII) because their sin is one of will rather than of weakness: the incontinent failed to control their spending, but these sinners committed violence against themselves by the deliberate, conscious destruction of their assets. THE ONE IN FRONT is Arcolano (LANO) da Squarcia, who died in 1288 in the "JOUSTING" of battle at Toppo. One story says that Arcolano permitted himself to be killed rather than face life as a pauper; this could explain his exclamation in lines 111 and 112. The other spendthrift is the Paduan nobleman JACOPO DA SANTO ANDREA (line 125), who died in 1239 after squandering a fortune by outrageous prodigality.

134–42. The soul is that of an anonymous Florentine suicide. He retells how his (and Dante's) CITY abandoned MARS, the pagan god of war, for John THE BAPTIST when the citizens converted to Christianity. The legend says that Mars punishes Florence with constant war and fighting—and that a piece of his SEMBLANCE, or statue, still preserved in the city (as indeed it was in Dante's time) is what permits it to be rebuilt each time it is laid waste. ATTILA the Hun burned Florence in A.D. 450.

CANTO XIV

9–10. The WOEFUL WOOD of the suicides is the ring above and around this third ring of the seventh circle; above and around the wood runs the SORROWFUL MOAT of Phlegethon.

13. CATO of Utica led the defeated Pompey's troops through the sands of the Libyan desert in 47 B.C.

16–20. Punished in this ring are the souls of those violent to God, either directly or through violence to nature or art. The SUPINE souls are blasphemers, those who SAT are the usurers, and the sodomites move RESTLESSLY ABOUT.

24–35. The rain of fire recalls the destruction of Sodom in Genesis 19:24: "Then the Lord rained upon Sodom . . . brimstone and fire."

26–29. This anecdote about the rain of fire during Alexander's invasion of India was popular in the Middle Ages, but it does not appear to be connected to any real adventure of Alexander's.

36. Even Virgil—who in an allegorical interpretation may represent human reason—was not able to overpower the STUBBORN FIENDS who barred the gate to Dis against the two poets (Canto VIII).

38–59. The GREAT ONE is CAPANEUS . . . ONE OF SEVEN KINGS / WHO BESIEGED THEBES. He boasted blasphemously that he could not be defeated, even by the great god JOVE (Jupiter)—so Jove struck him dead with a thunderbolt.

46–48. Assisted by the three Cyclopes, the god VULCAN forged thunderbolts at MONGIBELLO, which is Mount Etna. Legend says Jove used the thunderbolts to beat back the Titans who tried to climb Mount Olympus in the BATTLE OF PHLEGRA.

64–65. BULICAME, a sulfurous hot spring near Viterbo, had been well known since Roman times. The local PROSTITUTES used its water for their baths.

78–85. Jove's mother, RHEA, hid him from his father, Saturn (who sought to devour him), on Mount IDA, the highest peak on the island of CRETE.

86–98. Dante combines images from several external sources and from his own imagination in the heavily allegorical description of the OLD MAN of Crete. Much of the physical detail comes from Nebuchadnezzar's dream in Daniel 2:31–35, where the decreasingly valuable metals are revealed to represent a succession of kingdoms. To this Dante adds Ovid's idea (*Metamorphoses*, I) of the decline of civilization through a series of ages, each identified with a metal (GOLD, SILVER, BRASS, IRON) and each less noble than the one before it. The tears, and the way they form the infernal rivers, are Dante's own inventions. DAMIETTA is in Egypt.

111–18. Dante did not recognize PHLEGETHON, nor did Virgil call it by name, when he encountered it in the first ring of the seventh circle (Canto XII). He asks also about LETHE, the river of forgetfulness in classical mythology. Forgetfulness is not granted to the souls in Hell, so Dante will see Lethe OUT OF THIS ABYSS, in Purgatory.

CANTO XV

The discrepancy between the pilgrim's respect for Brunetto Latini and the poet's pitiless judgment is an example of infernal irony. It reinforces the fiction of the journey by pretending that Dante had no choice but to reveal the names of those he discovered among the sodomites. In fact, however, the portrait of Brunetto is an accusation of sodomy leveled against someone whom the pilgrim once respected and loved. As cruel as it is, retrospective disillusionment such as this with an authority figure has been part of the confessional theme ever since Augustine's rejection of Faustus, a Wizard of Oz of the fifth century.

The condemnation of Brunetto is unspoken, but implicit in the sterile landscape and in the phrase "Your image—dear, fatherly, benevolent," an inappropriate honorific for someone classified as a sodomite, but perhaps reminiscent of Plato's paradoxical description of Socrates as a "spiritual" father. The search for the true father was a theme in ancient epic and was part of Augustine's quest in the *Confessions*. In Canto XV of the *Paradiso*, when the pilgrim meets his ancestor Cacciaguida, it becomes clear in retrospect that Brunetto was a deceptive surrogate and that, for Christians, none but God should truly be called "Father.

To accuse Brunetto of "sodomy" is probably to accuse him of pedophilia, a refusal to acknowledge one's mortality or to accept the limitations that nature imposes upon the lover by reason of age. There is savage irony, then, in praising Brunetto for having taught the pilgrim how "man makes himself eternal," for this is the intellectual equivalent of the same temporal evasion: both the humanist and the sodomite pretend they can escape death. The last image of Brunetto, in which he is compared to a winning runner, epitomizes the pathos of the humanist who so lags behind his own generation that he seems to lead the next.

Brunetto's prophecy will be properly glossed in Paradise by Cacciaguida, in spite of Dante's mention of a "lady" who will explain. So, in Virgil's *Aeneid*, Aeneas is told to expect prophecy from the Sibyl, but in fact receives it from his father, Anchises. The prophecy, like all of the prophecies in Hell, is oracular, meaning that its truth is beyond the comprehension of the prophet and can be fully understood only retrospectively. So when Brunetto promises Dante future glory, he may be thinking of earthly fame, but we shall see in the last part of the *Commedia* that glory for Dante means Paradise, with Beatrice. (J.F.)

4–10. Dante compares the banks separating the bloody water from the burning plain to an earthly BULWARK. The PADUANS' walls must divert the flow of the BRENTA so that the city will not be flooded when CARENTANA—the Alpine region known today as Carinthia—FEELS THE HEAT and the snow melts. Some commentators have suggested that the geographic references are not merely coincidental: they seem to refer to cities with reputations for sodomy.

14. The SOULS described in this canto and the next one are the souls of sodomites: men who had sex with other men. The medieval Church condemned such practices, and homosexuality was generally considered unnatural in Dante's Europe. Virgil explains in Canto XI that the third ring of the second circle holds blasphemers (violent to God), sodomites (violent to God's child, nature), and usurers (violent to God's grandchild, art)—but the act of sodomy is not referred to directly in the cantos where its perpetrators actually appear.

20. The shade takes Dante BY THE HEM because the margin where the poets walk is elevated above the fiery plain: the spirit reaches up to touch Dante's garment.

28. BRUNETTO LATINI (c. 1212–1294) was a prominent Florentine Guelph. He was probably not Dante's teacher in the strict sense of the word, but may well have been a mentor. Latini was a writer as well as a politician; his best-known works are an encyclopedia written in French called *Li Livres dou Tresor*, and an Italian didactic poem known as the *Tesoretto*. The latter describes a moral

journey and may have served Dante as one model for the *Commedia*. There is no external evidence to suggest that Latini was a homosexual; Dante may or may not have invented that characterization. In any case, a strange tension is created between Dante the poet, who places his old master in the depths of Hell, accusing him of what was considered a dreadful crime, and Dante the pilgrim, the sympathetic character who proclaims that COULD I HAVE EVERY-THING FOR WHICH I LONG, / YOU WOULD NOT STILL ENDURE THIS BANISHMENT (lines 75–76).

47. Dante refers to Virgil simply as HE: the two poets never name each other while they are in Hell.

55–74. Brunetto Latini's prophecy draws on the legend which says that Florence was founded by Romans after they conquered the city of FIESOLE in the nearby hills of Tuscany. According to this tradition, Florence cannot be unified because its citizenry springs from two very different groups of forebears: UNGRATEFUL, MALIGNANT FOLK WHO DESCEND / FROM THOSE BROUGHT DOWN FROM FIESOLE, and the nobler, more civilized descendants of the Romans. The stereotype of the Florentines as BLIND (line 62) was widespread in the Middle Ages; its origin is uncertain. Latini (and through him, Dante the poet) places Dante among the SACRED SEED . . . OF ROMANS.

81–82. THE WAY MAN MAKES HIMSELF ETERNAL, which Dante claims Latini taught him, is by achieving fame and recognition that will last after his death. Latini says so in his *Tresor* (II, cxx, i).

85–87. Dante hopes that Beatrice, the LADY of line 87, will fully explain both Brunetto Latini's prophecy and ANOTHER TEXT, the words of Farinata's prophecy in Canto X.

106. PRISCIAN of Caesarea was a sixth-century Latin grammarian.

107. FRANCESCO D'ACCORSO was a Ghibelline lawyer of Brunetto Latini's generation who taught at Oxford and Bologna.

109–12. THE SERVANT OF SERVANTS is the Pope, in this case Dante's enemy Boniface VIII. The ONE he banished to Vicenza, where the river BACCHIGLIONE flows, is Andrea de' Mozzi, bishop of Florence from 1287 to 1295. The Pope transferred de' Mozzi to Vicenza because his reputation as a sodomite had become an embarrassment; shortly thereafter de' Mozzi died, his body DISTENDED IN ITS NERVE / AND MUSCLE—presumably from acts of sodomy.

116. TESORO is the Italian name for Latini's French work, the *Livres dou Tresor*.

118–21. Foot RACES were held outside VERONA every year on the first Sunday in Lent, starting in 1207. The races were run naked, according to Boccaccio, and featured prizes for the runners: for the winner, a bolt of green cloth, and for the loser, a rooster.

CANTO XVI

1. The NOISE is from the cataract that will appear in line 88.

7. Once again the CITY in question is Florence.

17. THE THREE . . . LINKED THEIR BODIES IN A WHEEL in order to keep

moving while conversing with Dante. The burning rain prevents the sodomites from standing still even for a moment.

18–20. Most commentators agree that the CHAMPIONS Dante describes are ancient Greek wrestlers, though some have suggested that the comparison is to medieval combatants.

30–38. The three Florentines are eminent politicians of the generation just before Dante's. All three were Guelphs. THE GOOD GUALDRADA was a lovely and virtuous ancestor of Florence's Conti Guidi, the family of GUIDO GUERRA. Guerra and the magistrate TEGGHIAIO ALDOBRANDI opposed the decision to attack Siena in 1260; the expedition took place anyway and resulted in the defeat of the Florentines at Montaperti and the return of the Ghibellines to Florence. In Canto VI, lines 71–74, Dante asked Ciacco about the fate of Tegghiaio and that of his partner in the wheel, JACOPO RUSTICUCCI. Rusticucci was a Guelph from a somewhat less important family than those of his companions. He implies in lines 37–38 that his FIERCE WIFE drove him to sodomy.

45. Dante explains his facial expression: Jacopo mistook his pity for contempt in lines 22–27.

60. GUGLIELMO BORSIERE's surname means "pursemaker." A Florentine of that profession, he appears as a character in Boccaccio's *Decameron* (I, 8).

66. WITH FACE UPLIFTED, Dante speaks in the direction of Florence itself.

83–91. This CATARACT is the runoff of Phlegethon as it pours down to the eighth circle. Dante compares it to the fall of the Acquacheta in the Apennines.

91–95. Scholars are quite divided as to the meaning of the KNOTTED . . . CORD which Dante takes from around his waist, and which Virgil uses to signal Geryon. THE LEOPARD WITH THE PAINTED FLANK appears first in Canto I (see lines 25–45, and note): one of three beasts which attack Dante, it is a symbol of lust and sexual temptation. Some commentators suggest that the cord is the mark of the Franciscan order, which Dante is sometimes said to have joined and then abandoned in his youth. More generally, it may stand for earthly defenses against cupidity, which Dante no longer needs now that he has seen the torments suffered by the lustful in Hell.

106–8. This tercet about fantasies that are true and truths that cannot be believed sets the stage for the appearance of Geryon, the emblem of fraud.

110. Dante calls the poem his *Commedia* for the first time.

CANTO XVII

1. The BEAST Geryon, with his deceptively human face and monstrous body, is the embodiment of the fraud punished in the circles below. In Greek mythology, Geryon is a giant with three heads and three bodies; Hercules slays him as one of his Labors. A medieval legend has Geryon offering hospitality to wayfarers, then murdering his guests. Dante invented a new, more grotesque form for Geryon in the *Inferno*, perhaps inspired by the locusts described in Revelation 9:7–10: ". . . and their faces were as the faces of men . . . And they had tails like unto scorpions, and there were stings in their tails."

16. In his *Metamorphoses* (VI, 5–145), Ovid tells the story of ARACHNE, a weaver so talented and so bold that she challenged the goddess Minerva to a competition. Minerva turned her into a spider for her presumptuousness.

18. The BEAVER was said to dangle its tail in the water to catch fish. Like the TARTAR and the TURK in line 14, and like the spider (Arachne) with its intricate web, the beaver presents an image of deception, lies, and fraud.

27. For the second and final time in Hell, Virgil and Dante move to the RIGHT (see Canto IX, line 120 and note).

31. The PEOPLE SITTING on the sand are the third group of sinners punished in the third ring of the seventh circle. Dante first caught sight of them in Canto XIV, line 19. They are the usurers, or moneylenders, and they are violent to God in that their usury is an offense to His grandchild, art: see Canto XI, lines 100–7 and notes.

50. The COLORS and DEVICE[s] on the usurers' purses, their only identifying features, are debased versions of family emblems or coats of arms.

52–64. The YELLOW background with the LION IN AZURE was the mark of the Gianfigliazzi family of Florence; they were Black Guelphs. The white GOOSE probably stands for a Ghibelline clan, the Ubbriachi. The Scrovegni family of Padua was represented by the SOW PORTRAYED IN AZURE, and many scholars identify the usurer who addresses Dante as Rinaldo Scrovegni, whose son Enrico commissioned the Scrovegni Chapel where Giotto painted his famous frescoes. Not all commentators agree about the identity of Scrovegni's NEIGHBOR VITALIANO, but most believe that Dante meant Vitaliano del Dente, known to have been a Paduan moneylender. This Vitaliano was still living in 1300. THE SOVEREIGN KNIGHT WHOSE SACK WILL SHOW / THREE GOATS is Giovanni Buiamonte, a Ghibelline of Florence.

96–98. PHAËTHON convinced his father, the sun god Apollo (or Helios), to let him take the reins of the sun's chariot for one day. The youth lost control of the horses, SPURNED / THE REINS, SO THAT THE SKY AS ONE STILL SEES [in the Milky Way] / WAS SCORCHED. Zeus was forced to kill Phaëthon with a thunderbolt to prevent him from burning up the earth. Ovid tells the story in the *Metamorphoses* (II, 1–328).

99–101. Ovid also tells the story (*Metamorphoses*, VIII) of ICARUS, who with his FATHER, Daedalus, flew from the Labyrinth of Crete on wings constructed by Daedalus of feathers held together with WAX. Icarus, unmindful of his father's warning, flew too close to the sun, whereupon the wax melted and Icarus fell into the sea and drowned.

119. A trained falcon STAYS ON THE WING until it catches its prey, sees the falconer recall it with a LURE, or becomes exhausted.

CANTO XVIII

1. MALEBOLGE is a name Dante invented; its literal translation would be "evil pouches." The Malebolge comprise the eighth circle, where sins of simple fraud are punished.

27–32. Pope Boniface VIII proclaimed the year 1300 the Church's first JUBILEE, granting absolution to those who came to confess and worship in Rome at certain churches and for specified lengths of time. Pilgrims flocked to Rome, creating the enormous crowds and the traffic that Dante compares to the flow of the two groups of sinners in this pouch.

43–44. This soul's efforts TO HIDE HIMSELF differ sharply from the actions of those who are punished above, and who begged Dante to speak of them and preserve their memories among the living.

48–55. VENEDICO CACCIANEMICO was a Bolognese Guelph who died in 1302 or 1303, though Dante seems to have believed that he had already died by 1300. He and the other souls marching in his direction are pimps or panders; Venedico was said to have sold his own sister GHISOLABELLA to the MARCHESE d'Este.

58–60. SAVENA and RENO are rivers that form the boundaries of Bologna; SIPA is a variant of sì ("yes") used in the dialect of that region. Venedico's point is that there are more Bolognese in the first pouch of Malebolge than in Bologna itself.

72–73. The ILL-BEGOTTEN SOULS in THIS OTHER GREAT ASSEMBLAGE are those of the seducers. Like the panders who share the pouch with them, they are fraudulent in that they deceived and took advantage of the innocent for their own pleasure or gain.

80–88. The hero of Greek myth JASON is most famous as the leader of the Argonauts on the quest for the golden fleece of the ram of COLCHIS. When the Argonauts landed on LEMNOS, Jason seduced and then abandoned HYPSIPYLE, who was herself something of a trickster: when the Lemnian WOMEN KILLED EVERY MALE, Hypsipyle secretly saved her father. Later, Jason also abandoned his wife MEDEA, who had helped him win the golden fleece.

114. ALESSIO INTERMINEI's family was prominent in Lucca; little is known about him, or about why Dante presents him as representative of the flatterers punished here in the second pouch.

124–26. The courtesan THAÏS is a character in Terence's play *Eunuchus*, which scholars say Dante probably knew only through Cicero's commentary (*De Amicitia*, XXVI, 98–99). Her flattering response to HER PARAMOUR comes either from Dante's imagination or from his misreading of Cicero, who attributes the remark to another of Terence's characters.

CANTO XIX

1–6. SIMON MAGUS (Simon the sorcerer) tried to buy spiritual powers from the apostles Peter and John (Acts 8:9–24). The souls in THE THIRD POUCH are all guilty of the sin of simony, which derives its name from Simon Magus: they used the Church and its offices fraudulently, for money and power.

11–24. The JUSTICE Dante sees in this pouch is another example of *contrapasso*:

those who abused the Church and its trappings are punished in openings like the ones in the baptismal fonts at Florence's SAN GIOVANNI, where Dante himself was baptized. Many commentators believe that Dante brings up the incident (lines 17–19) of the broken baptismal in order to clear his own name: he may have been accused of impiety for attacking the sacred object (see Foreword, pages xiv–xv).

30. The far, or inside, BANK of each pouch is SLOPING . . . MORE GRADUALLY because the entire Malebolge slopes toward the pit at the center.

45. VILE ASSASSIN[s] and hired killers were buried face down and suffocated.

48–53. The sinner mistakes Dante for Pope BONIFACE VIII, who was elected Pope in 1294. Boniface lived for another three years past 1300, which explains the soul's assertion that THE WRITING LIED: Boniface's death, apparently, had been foretold for 1303. Thus when Dante appears in 1300 and is taken for Boniface, he seems to be SEVERAL YEARS early. The real Boniface was Dante's political enemy, and partially responsible for the poet's exile. Dante condemns him for simony, and indeed many of his contemporaries report that Boniface used his office for financial and political gain. THE BEAUTIFUL LADY is the Church—the metaphor was common in Dante's time—and it is possible that Boniface did TAKE [her] . . . BY DECEIT; he was said to have engineered the abdication of Pope Celestine and his own election (see also Canto III, line 50 and note).

63–67. The sinner is Pope Nicholas III, who WAS VESTED WITH THE GREAT / MANTLE OF POWER—the Papacy—from 1277 to 1280. His family, the Orsini, had a SHE-BEAR as its emblem. He was accused of various types of simony and intrigue, and was guilty at the very least of nepotism—his desire TO AD-VANCE / THE CUBS.

71. THAT OTHER ONE is Boniface.

73–82. The LAWLESS SHEPHERD is a third corrupt Pope, Clement V, who died in 1314—he may or may not still have been alive when Dante wrote these lines. Nicholas's assertion that Boniface will not wait for Clement as long as Nicholas has waited for Boniface suggests that Dante did already know the date of Clement's death—but he may also simply have guessed well. Clement, a Frenchman, owed his election to the influence of THE KING OF FRANCE, Philip the Fair, and remained under Philip's control once he was Pope. He moved the seat of the Papacy from Rome to Avignon, France—he may never have been to Italy. Dante compares him to JASON, who bribed HIS MONARCH to make him high priest of the Jews, and then tried to enforce Greek customs and religion once he was in office (II MACCABEES 4:7–8).

85–88. Jesus asks PETER to FOLLOW Him in Matthew 4:19, and promises him the KEYS to the Kingdom of Heaven in Matthew 16:18–19.

88–91. MATTHIAS was chosen by lot to replace the traitorous apostle Judas Iscariot: Acts 1:24–26.

93–94. Nicholas may have taken a payoff in return for his support for the conspiracy against CHARLES of Anjou, King of Sicily and Naples. Charles had declined to marry Nicholas's niece.

99–104. Dante refers to the words of St. John in Revelation 17:1–4. The whore

John describes was traditionally taken to stand for pagan Rome; Dante seems to associate her with the corrupt Roman Church. In Dante's description, her SEVEN HEADS represent the seven sacraments of the Church, her TEN HORNS stand for the Ten Commandments, and her SPOUSE is the Pope.

108–11. The Emperor CONSTANTINE was supposed to have ceded power over the western part of his domain to the Church in the fourth century when he moved the seat of his government to Byzantium. THE FIRST RICH FATHER, to whom the gift was said to have been made, was Pope Sylvester I. Many years after Dante's death, the document describing the supposed "Donation of Constantine" was proved to be an eighth-century forgery.

CANTO XX

13–15. The souls condemned here practiced occult arts to see the future; as punishment for this impiety their heads are twisted around so they must look BACKWARDS.

34. AMPHIARAUS, one of the seven kings who fought against the Greek city of Thebes, foresaw his own death in battle and tried to avert it by fleeing, but was swallowed by an earthquake while running away.

39–43. Ovid's *Metamorphoses* (III, 322–31) tells that TIRESIAS, the soothsayer of Thebes, was transformed to a woman when he struck a pair of copulating snakes with his staff. Seven years later he was changed back to a man by again striking at coupled snakes.

44. The Etruscan soothsayer ARUNS came from near Carrara, the source of white marble; in *Pharsalia* (I, 584–638) Lucan credits him with predicting the civil war and Caesar's victory.

51. MANTO, the daughter of Tiresias and a prophetess, was supposed to have come to Italy.

53–54. BACCHUS'S / CITY: Thebes, traditionally considered Bacchus's birthplace.

60–62. On a small island in Lake Garda the three dioceses of TRENTINO, BRESCIA, and VERONA meet. A chapel on that island fell within the jurisdictions of all three bishops.

81–82. After Alberto da CASALODI became lord of Mantua in 1272, he followed the advice of PINAMONTE dei Buonaccorsi to win over his opposition by banishing his supporters. When the nobles favoring Casalodi were in exile, Pinamonte seized power.

83–84. Despite the definitive tone of Virgil's charge to Dante about his CITY'S TRUE INCEPTION, neither the digression concerning the origin of Mantua nor Virgil's emphasis upon the matter—this is his longest speech in the *Inferno*—has been adequately explained by commentators. Some believe that Virgil's reputation in the Middle Ages as a magician and the practice of telling the future through random selections from his writing (*sortes Virgilianae*) make his disclaimer appropriate in this region of Hell, where diviners are punished. The speech can be viewed as part of the developing relationship between the two poets, non-Christian and Christian. It is interesting, and perhaps puzzling, that in the *Aeneid* (X, 198–200), the actual Virgil—contrary to Dante's Virgil

here—attributes the founding of Mantua not to Manto but to Ocnis, son of
Manto and the river god of the Tiber.

92–93. GREECE / WAS SHORT OF MALES because the men were away at the
Trojan War.

94–96. CALCHAS was the augur who chose the most auspicious moment for the
Greek ships to sail from AULIS for Troy. EURYPYLUS was another soothsayer
among the Greek expedition.

97. MICHAEL SCOT or Scott (c. 1175–1235) was a Scottish scholar, astrologer, and
occultist believed to have served as court astrologer to Frederick II at Palermo.

99. GUIDO BONATTI was a thirteenth-century astrologer, author of a treatise on
astronomy. ASDENTE—medieval Italian for "Toothless"—was the nickname
of Maestro Benvenuto, a shoemaker of Parma who was known as a prophet
and soothsayer.

105. CAIN-IN-THE-MOON: Italian folklore sees the spots on the moon as the shape
of Cain carrying thorns; in this legend, he was banished to the moon by God
after trying to excuse himself for murdering his brother Abel.

CANTO XXI

If there is a comic section of the *Inferno*, it is in Canto XXI and Canto XXII, where
the demons of the Malebranche (literally, the "Evil-Claws")—with their names the
equivalent of Nastydog, Bad-Tail, Hogface, Snarleyhead—torment barrators, the
sellers of public office: the crime for which Dante was banished from Florence on
the accusation of his political enemies. Athletic, winged, coarsely menacing, the
Malebranche, overseeing the torment of barrators in the lake of pitch, combine fear
and comedy in a way that may suggest satire directed at those enemies.

The action of XXI is concluded, and that of XXII is impelled, by a fart: the military
signal emitted by the demon Malacoda when he sends off his troop to escort Dante
and Virgil along the lake of pitch where sinners are boiled. This ludicrous, grotesque
element alternates with real horror: in XXII, the sinner from Navarre staring at his
arm where the demon Libicocco has just torn out the muscle. This blending of modes
can seem cinematic, and at moments—when the two winged devils fight in midair
over the burning lake, or when Dante walks the gauntlet of barely restrained, threat-
ening demons—Dante's dramatic visual imagination anticipates similar scenes of
comic tension in classic adventure films.

But on another level the relatively cool, detached feeling of adventure-farce movies
has little to do with the hot intensity of Dante's narrative: when Virgil tells Dante
not to fear these devils, the poem is reaching for a moral terrain where the grotesque
tormentors and the justly tormented sinners—both recalling Dante's personal con-
cerns, as well as universal sources of fear—can both be put behind him. The rage
and sorrow driving the *Inferno* use this adventure-farce as a way to spend themselves.
Because Dante's goal is transcendent, the Malebranche must be not only terrifying
but low, and ultimately not terrifying at all, but self-defeating: the grimacing, barely
substantial creatures of bad air. (R.P.)

4. Dante and Virgil approach the NEXT FISSURE—the fifth pouch—of
MALEBOLGE.

8. In Dante's time the VENETIAN ARSENAL was one of Europe's greatest and most impressive shipyards.

36. The demons of the fifth pouch are collectively called MALEBRANCHE. The name literally means "Evil-Claws." (For more on this, see the lead note to this canto.)

36–42. SANTA ZITA is the patron saint of the city of Lucca. Lucca was governed in the Middle Ages by a council of ten ELDERS, who were chosen from the general population and rotated through short terms of office. The city's reputation for BARRATRY—the selling of public office—does not originate with Dante; a number of contemporaneous accounts support the accusation that unusually many Luccan public officials were corrupt. The reference to BONTURO in line 40 is sarcastic: Bonturo Dati apparently was the worst barrator in Lucca and routinely bought and sold political power.

49. The SACRED FACE of Lucca is a wooden crucifix, supposedly completed miraculously while Nicodemus, who had begun the carving, slept. Kept in the cathedral at Lucca, it was considered a holy object. Here the demon also uses the phrase mockingly to refer to the sinner's rear end.

50. The river SERCHIO flows near Lucca.

64–65. Virgil may mean that he WAS IN SUCH A FRAY on his previous journey through Hell (see Canto IX, 19–29 and note)—or perhaps he is referring to the encounter with the demons at the gates of Dis in Canto VIII, forgetting that in that case the intercession of a heavenly messenger was required.

76. MALACODA's name means "Bad-Tail."

92–95. Some scholars say that Dante was actually among the Tuscan Guelphs who besieged the Pisan fort of CAPRONA in August 1289.

107–9. Malacoda is lying: in fact, all the bridges of the sixth pouch are broken, as will become clear.

110–12. THE ROAD HERE WAS RUINED in the earthquake that took place when Jesus died on the Cross: the travelers saw other damage from that earthquake in Canto V and Canto XII. Malacoda's comment reminds us of the time, which Dante tracks carefully throughout the *Inferno*. The pilgrim's dark night in the woods was the night of Thursday, April 7. He battled the three beasts and met Virgil in the course of Good Friday, April 8, and entered Hell that evening. At midnight (see Canto VII, 87–88 and note) he had reached the fourth circle, and at four o'clock, he was about to enter the seventh (Canto XI, 109–11 and note). Now it is seven in the morning on Holy Saturday, April 9, 1300, and Jesus died at noon—FIVE HOURS LATER THAN NOW—1266 years and one day ago, when He was in His thirty-fourth year.

116–22. The demons' names are Dante's inventions; some of them have been interpreted as plays on the actual names of Luccan families.

CANTO XXII

4. The ARETINES are the people of Arezzo. In 1289 the Aretine Ghibellines were defeated at Campaldino by the Florentine Guelphs; Dante may have been present and seen the Aretine cavalry.

17–19. Medieval sailors believed that DOLPHINS jumping were a sign of stormy weather on the way.

43–51. Very little is known about this sinner. His name, according to early commentators, is Ciampolo, but scholars have discovered nothing more about him. THIBAUT II was king of NAVARRE from 1253 to 1270.

76–83. The Sardinian friar GOMITA was a chancellor to the judge Nino Visconti of Pisa. He was a notorious barrator, and eventually was hanged for selling some prisoners of Nino's their freedom.

84. Not much is known for certain about DON MICHEL ZANCHE OF LOGODORO, but it seems he may have replaced Fra Gomita as chancellor in Pisa, and that he was even more corrupt than the friar. Michel Zanche was murdered in 1275 by Branca d'Oria, who appears in Canto XXXIII.

115–16. THE VERY ONE / WHO FIRST OPPOSED loosening their grasp on the sinner was Cagnazzo, in lines 102–3.

CANTO XXIII

2. The FRIARS MINOR are the Franciscans, who took vows of poverty and humility. Virgil and Dante here emulate the Franciscan custom of traveling in pairs, with the senior brother going before.

3–8. Among the ancient Greek didactic animal fables attributed to AESOP is the one in which a MOUSE wishing to cross a river asks the help of a FROG, who ties the mouse to himself by a string and starts across the river. In midstream, the frog tries to kill the mouse by diving, but while the mouse is struggling to save himself, a bird of prey flying by notices the commotion and in some versions snatches up both frog and mouse, and in some only the treacherous frog. The moral is the bad end that comes to one who tries to harm others.

If Dante had in mind the version where the mouse survives, a likely application of the fable is that, like the innocent mouse, Dante and Virgil complete their crossing while their evil escort comes to grief. This would represent a similarity between the two stories' ENDS AND THEIR BEGINNINGS: at the beginning, a request for passage; at the end, a downfall for the evil-minded conductor while the intended victim continues along. However, if the relevant version is one where both the frog and the mouse are carried away, the outcome is roughly parallel to the fact that both the Navarrese and his tormentor are in the boiling pitch.

22. LEAD-BACKED GLASS: that is, a mirror.

57. CLUNY'S MONKS are Benedictines, an order sometimes thought of as living especially well.

61. The cloaks INFLICTED BY FREDERICK were supposedly made of lead: Frederick II was said to have forced traitors into such garments, then put them into a cauldron that was heated until the lead grew hot and eventually boiled.

98. The JOVIAL FRIARS, the military and religious order of the Knights of the Blessed Virgin Mary, were known as "jovial" because, despite the order's noble

purposes (defending widows and orphans, furthering peace in Italy), its members had a reputation for luxury and the enjoyment of worldly pleasures.

99–103. CATALANO di Guido di Ostia, a Guelph, and LODERINGO degli Andalò, a Ghibelline, participated in the founding of the Jovial Friars. For a time in 1265 and 1267 they shared the office of *podestà* (roughly equivalent to mayor or chief magistrate) in Florence. The sharing of the position supposedly was designed TO KEEP THE PEACE between Guelphs and Ghibellines. However, during their time in office, in keeping with the plans of Pope Clement IV, there was considerable corruption and strife, leading to the expulsion of the Ghibellines from Florence and to the destruction of the houses of the Uberti, a Ghibelline family, in the district of Florence called the GARDINGO.

110–18. THE ONE IMPALED THERE is Caiphas, the high priest who in the council of the Pharisees argued that THE EXPEDIENT WAY would be to give up ONE MAN —namely, Jesus—for the good of the many (John 11:49–50). HIS FATHER-IN-LAW is Annas, who with OTHERS OF THAT COUNCIL of the Sanhedrin collaborated in the decision, thereby sowing A SEED OF EVIL FOR THE JEWS: the fruit of this seed would be the fall of Jerusalem and the dispersal of the Jews.

138. HE WHO HOOKS THE SINNERS is Malacoda, who gave false information about the broken bridge in Canto XXI, lines 107–9.

CANTO XXIV

1–2. THE SUN moves through AQUARIUS (the Water Carrier) from January 20 to February 18.

5. Hoarfrost's WHITE SISTER is the snow.

31–32. THOSE WHO WORE / LEAD MANTLES are the hypocrites of Canto XXIII.

84. The list of Libyan serpents, like some of the imagery that follows, is based on Lucan's *Pharsalia* (IX, 711–14, 719–21), in which the CHELYDRID leaves a trail of smoke, the AMPHISBAENA has two heads, one at each end, and the JACULI can fly like arrows. The PHAREAE plough grooves in the earth with their tails. The CENCHRES move always in a single straight line.

94. In mythological lore the mineral HELIOTROPE (bloodstone) was supposed to cure snakebite and to render its carrier invisible.

105–10. In this account of the PHOENIX (derived from Ovid's *Metamorphoses*, XV, 392–407), the bird lives for FIVE HUNDRED YEARS, then builds a nest which bursts into FLAMES in which the bird dies, to be reborn from the ashes.

110–15. The account of ONE WHO FALLS and who WHEN HE RISES STARES ABOUT CONFUSED appears to describe an epileptic seizure.

123–28. VANNI FUCCI, illegitimate son (or "MULE") of Fuccio de' Lazzari, was a combative partisan of the Black Party in PISTOIA, well known as A MAN / OF BLOOD AND RAGE. Dante points this out while asking, in effect, why Fucci is punished among the thieves in this eighth circle of Hell, rather than in the seventh, boiled in the blood of Phlegethon with the shades of the violent.

135–37. Historical accounts survive of Vanni Fucci's robbery in 1293, with an accomplice, of a church in Pistoia. An innocent man was on the point of being executed when the truth was revealed. Fucci escaped.

138–48. Vanni Fucci's prophecy has two parts, one quite explicit and the second more veiled and allegorical. First he forecasts in terse summary the political events of 1300 and 1301 that led to Dante's personal catastrophe, his exile from Florence. Fucci, as an ardent follower of the Black Guelphs, does not want Dante, who is a White Guelph, to DELIGHT TOO MUCH in Fucci's shame and punishment: I HAVE TOLD IT TO BRING GRIEF TO YOU.

The prophesied events, which Dante had witnessed and endured by the time he composed the *Commedia*, are as follows: in May 1301, the Pistoian White Party, aided by the Whites who were in power in Florence, expelled the Blacks, also destroying their houses and property. The following autumn, Charles of Valois arrived in Florence, supposedly to maintain peace between the two parties, and therefore was admitted into the city unopposed. Once in a position of power, he betrayed the Whites and sided with the Blacks, who led riots against the houses of the Whites. During the following year, in a series of official banishments, FLORENCE CHANGE[d] HER CITIZENS / AND WAYS by exiling the Whites, including Dante.

The more blurred and allegorical part of the prophecy, according to many commentators, refers to Moroello Malaspina, a Black Guelph general called forth by the war god Mars to defeat the Whites in battle, as lightning—associated with VAPOR in the science of the time—BREAKS THROUGH / AND TEARS THE MIST. With this mixture of the pointed and the enigmatic, the contentious shade of Vanni Fucci hopes to disturb Dante the pilgrim as much as possible.

CANTO XXV

The notion of Horror as we know it from fiction or the movies involves detailed, uncanny transformation of the human body, with erotic and moral overtones: the overwhelmed stare of the zombie; the flickering eyes of the aroused mummy; the elegant neck bite that changes the virginal heroine forever; Jekyll or the Werewolf helplessly becoming stronger, hairier, more animal; the hunger of George Romero's living dead, relentless and contagious. The body may be snatched or bitten, invaded or inverted or duplicated, obscenely revived or repellently distorted, but above all it changes. The human takes on qualities of the animal or of inert matter. In this sense of the word, Horror has one of its earliest manifestations in Canto XXV.

The body does change in Ovid and Lucan—as Dante acknowledges here in his audacious challenge to the two Latin poets. But it could be argued that in the *Metamorphoses*, mutation is presented as a fact rather than a moral process: it is magical and objective rather than psychological. Dante implies something like this when he says that Ovid "never transformed two individual / Front-to-front natures so both forms as they met / Were ready to exchange their substance" (XXV, 99–101). That is, Dante suggests that not only will his image of transformation present the external account of an emotional or erotic change, as when a man becomes a snake or a woman becomes a fountain: he will give an account of moral interpenetration, and of psychological complicity. The idea of *contrapasso*, in which the suffering in Hell extends or reproduces the sin, gives this mutual transformation a dimension absent from Dante's pre-Christian models, he seems to claim.

The passage (*Metamorphoses*, IV, 576–89) where Ovid's Cadmus changes into a serpent seems to support Dante's boast. The passage, which Dante not only alludes to but borrows from, generates wonder and pathos; but the horror of losing one's nature to another, and the sense of "readiness" or complicity, are not part of Ovid's art. Similarly, Lucan's description of Sabellus putrefying from the legs up (*Pharsalia*, IX, 79–97) is vivid and impressive, but it does not accomplish the blend of sexual transformation, quasi-scientific detail, and subjective moral corruption associated with Horror. Dante's difference from his classical predecessors seems to be related, as he implies, to Christian ideas of form, nature, and substance.

The living dead of the *Inferno*—denied eternal life, yet full of a vigorous other-life—anticipate the Romantic creation of Horror as a literary and cinematic form, the nineteenth-century vampires and monsters conceived by Mary Shelley, Robert Louis Stevenson, and others. Dante's descriptions—in XXV, the way the lizard's hind legs twist together to form a penis, while from the man's penis a pair of feet grow; or the way the man's pierced navel emits a stream of smoke; or the description of the reptile's snout receding to form a human face—bring dark colors to Ovidian immediacy.

But this fleshly imagery writhes from the crannies of an exacting architecture. These thieves who ignored the boundary of *thine* and *mine* in life now merge as shades, their shells of personal identity made horribly permeable. Amid this blending "as if made out of hot wax" (lines 59–60), the eye of the poet identifies and delineates, carefully distinguishing such details as the uncanny yawn of the victim gazing down at the reptile who has bitten him. And a tough scholastic vocabulary of precise abstractions resists all the merging and shape-shifting: "With both not what they were, / Yet neither"—a phrase, on the other hand, possibly borrowed from Ovid's account of Hermaphroditus (*Metamorphoses*, IV, 373–79).

Canto XXV opens with one character gesturing obscenely at God with both hands, then proceeds from a snake-ridden centaur through a series of spectacular trans-formation scenes, each with a sexual energy counterweighted by a nausea or con-fusion of the rational intelligence—the witnessing intelligence that partly carries the day and partly, in the blur of the canto's closing lines, acknowledges its bewilderment. (R.P.)

2. MAKING THE FIG is an obscene gesture, still used in Italy, made by poking the thumb through the second and third fingers of the clenched fist.

12. The SEED that Pistoia is said to SURPASS is its founding by the conspirator Catiline and survivors of the army he led in his rebellion against the Roman Republic.

15. It is Capaneus (see Canto XIV, 37–59) WHO FELL FROM THE THEBAN WALL.

20. The swampy wilderness of the MAREMMA, on the Tuscan coast, was infested by snakes.

25–33. The CACUS of classical myth was the son of Vulcan and Medusa, a half-human monster. Using a subterfuge to hide the crime, he stole the cattle of Hercules, who saw through the trick and killed him, giving him a HUNDRED BLOWS though Cacus died after living only long enough to FEEL TEN HIT.

41. CIANFA Donati, a Florentine of noble family, is mentioned in contemporary accounts as a cattle thief and as breaking into shops. He has been transformed into the SERPENT that DARTED FORWARD in line 49.

42. TO BE SURE MY LEADER HEARD, I SIGNALED HIM: these words might be taken to mark the pilgrim's increasing confidence as the poem progresses, in contrast to his initial timidity and dependence upon Virgil.

49. The SERPENT here is Cianfa Donati, mentioned in line 41.

67. AGNELLO de' Brunelleschi was another Florentine nobleman known as a thief.

81. Just as the first serpent (line 49) is the transformed shade of Cianfa Donati, this FIERY LITTLE SERPENT . . . PEPPERCORN BLACK AND LIVID, is the shade of Francesco de' Cavalcanti, as becomes apparent in lines 144–45. (See note to 144–45.)

81–82. The TWO WHO STAYED after the transformation of Agnello in lines 49–77 are two Florentines of whom little is known: PUCCIO SCIANCATO Galigai (see line 142) and BUOSO (see line 133), who is about to be transfixed at the navel by the FIERY LITTLE SERPENT.

84–85. THE PLACE WHERE WE ARE FED / WHEN LIFE BEGINS is the navel. The thief, who took goods by violating rightful boundaries, is violated in the place where we first take nourishment.

91–96. LUCAN (*Pharsalia*, IX, 763–76) describes how the body of the Roman soldier SABELLUS was grotesquely reduced to a puddle of corruption by the bite of a little Libyan snake. In subsequent lines (IX, 790–97) NASIDIUS, another soldier, dies bloated and burning from the bite of another variety of serpent.

OVID describes the transformation of CADMUS into a snake (*Metamorphoses*, IV, 576–89) as punishment for killing a dragon sacred to Mars. In another passage (*Metamorphoses*, V, 572–641), the nymph ARETHUSA is transformed into a fountain by Diana, to protect her from the river god Alpheus.

112. THE MEMBER MAN CONCEALS is his penis.

117. THE UNHOLY LIGHTS THAT STARED ABOVE THE MUZZLES are their eyes.

129–33. THE SOUL THAT HAD BEEN MADE / A BEAST is BUOSO, believed by some commentators to be the nephew of the Buoso Donati mentioned in Canto XXX, line 42.

135. DEADWEIGHT: the Italian word *zavorra* means ballast, worthless stuff used to weight down a ship to improve navigation. The meaning here appears to be scornful.

137–39. The idea that the poet has perhaps TANGLED THINGS in his account of the transformations of the thieves, and his use of the terms CONFUSION and BEWILDERED, suggest that some of the difficulty readers may experience in keeping straight the identity of these thieves could be appropriate to the spirit of this canto. This idea recalls the way the hoarders and spenders of Canto VII remain an anonymous mass.

142. PUCCIO SCIANCATO ("Sciancato" means "the lame one") is the only one of the five thieves—three who appear at the beginning of the canto and two who

run up in reptile form—who goes untransformed. Cianfa, in the form of the six-legged serpent, stings Agnello and merges with him in lines 49–76; Francesco de' Cavalcanti, in the form of the fiery little serpent, changes forms with Buoso after piercing him in the navel.

One early source refers to Puccio as a particularly graceful and courteous thief.

144–45. HE / WHOSE DEATH the town of GAVILLE . . . [would] HAVE GOOD CAUSE TO GRIEVE is Francesco de' Cavalcanti, who was killed by some citizens of that place. His kinsmen avenged him by killing nearly everyone in the town, which is what gives Gaville reason to grieve his death.

CANTO XXVI

All the characters who speak in the *Inferno* are near contemporaries of the poet except for Ulysses, who will be mentioned several times more in the course of the *Commedia*. The ideals Ulysses expresses are reminiscent of those espoused by an equally self-confident Dante in an unfinished philosophical work, the *Convivio*. The voyage of Ulysses was taken in antiquity as an allegory for the education of the soul, whose return home was taken as a sign of its deliverance. Although he did not know Homer's text, Dante certainly knew of its happy ending. By changing it, he suggests that no one could survive such a journey on one's own.

Geryon is the emblem of the pilgrim's journey, and Ulysses' voyage is its counterpart. The difference between the two voyages is that Ulysses undertakes his "insane flight" alone, while Virgil guides the pilgrim on the shoulders of the monster. This is much like the opposition in Canto I between the pilgrim's abortive attempt to climb the mountain on his own and the longer, guided journey on which Virgil leads him. It might be said that the successful journey of the pilgrim begins after he survives the metaphoric drowning (Canto I, 18–21) to which Ulysses fell victim. What separates their fate is the will of God (XXVI, 134).

Dante may have known that Aeneas' speech to his men in Virgil's poem was modeled on Odysseus' speech to his men in the *Odyssey*. Dante reconstructs an imagined Homeric archetype by echoing Aeneas ("O brothers . . .") but transforming Aeneas' serenity into Ulysses' thirst for the unknown. This extraordinary act of literary triangulation suggests that Ulysses' disaster foreshadowed Aeneas' success, upon which Rome was founded. The result is the portrait of a Ulysses whose individualism is the antithesis of Aeneas' filial and civic piety. His intellectual pride is not unlike that of the younger Dante, whom he perhaps represents.

Dante stands apart here as the two ancient figures speak in the high style of ancient tragedy. This is a matter not of language but of the rhetoric the ancients considered appropriate for the discussion of lofty themes. In the Gospels, Christ established a new Christian rhetoric by speaking of the loftiest matters in the humblest idiom. When Dante speaks of Virgil's poem as *tragedy* and his own as *comedy*, he means that his poem is written in the humble speech of sacred Scripture. He illustrates the point in the next canto when Guido da Montefeltro undercuts the rhetorical decorum by interrupting in his native dialect. (J.F.)

5. FIVE OF YOUR CITIZENS: see note to Canto XXV, line 142.

7. According to one belief, dreams that came NEAR MORNING were prophetic.

9. Some commentators conclude that the PRATO wishing Florence ill is the neighboring small town of that name, which will join others in rebelling against Florence's power. Others think the reference is to Cardinal Niccolò da Prato, sent by Pope Benedict XI in 1304 to pacify the Florentine factions; failing, he left the town delivering curses and excommunication upon it.

36–40. THE ONE AVENGED BY BEARS was the biblical prophet Elisha: after some boys mock him, two bears come out of the forest and tear the boys (II Kings 2:23–24). Elisha also sees ELIJAH'S CHARIOT / CARRIED BY REARING HORSES (II Kings 2:9–12).

56. ETEOCLES and Polynices, twin sons of Oedipus and Jocasta, struggled against each other to gain the rule of Thebes, causing the war of the Seven against Thebes. The brothers finally killed each other in single combat. Their bodies were placed on a single pyre, but because of their eternal enmity the flame split in two.

58–62. ULYSSES AND DIOMEDES were Greek leaders in the Trojan War, known for their cunning. Ulysses devised the decisive trick of the wooden horse that the Trojans brought within their city walls, unaware of the Greek warriors hiding inside it. The defeat of Troy sent forth Aeneas and his companions, THE ROMANS' NOBLE SEED.

63–65. Ulysses and Diomedes used their guile to persuade Achilles to leave DEIDAMIA and his child by her to join the Greek forces, though they knew his death was prophesied. The PALLADIUM was a statue of Athena, believed to protect the city, which they stole from Troy. Scholars believe that all of this material came to Dante not from Homer but through the second book of the *Aeneid*.

74–75. It seems possible that in writing the words "GREEKS . . . MIGHT TREAT WORDS OF YOURS WITH SOME DISDAIN," Dante is acknowledging that he did not know Greek. The formal, rhetorical quality of Virgil's next words to the Greek shades may suggest the qualities of that language, or a traditional idea of the Greeks as haughty.

84. THE GREATER HORN OF FLAME is the spirit of Ulysses.

88. CIRCE was the enchantress who changed men to swine. She detained Ulysses on his voyage home to Ithaca after the Trojan War.

89–90. GAETA was founded by Aeneas and named after his nurse (*Aeneid*, VII, 1–5).

93. PENELOPE was the faithful wife of Ulysses.

103–4. The MARKERS that HERCULES LET STAND—the Pillars of Hercules— formed when that hero split a single mountain in two, are the promontories that face one another across the Strait of Gibraltar, once believed to be the westernmost limit of the navigable world.

105–6. CEUTA is a town in North Africa; SEVILLE, in Spain: Ulysses sailed westward beyond Gibraltar.

121–22. By ALWAYS GAINING ON THE LEFT they sail south, seeing only the stars of THE OTHER POLE: that is, the southern hemisphere.

127. In the geography of the *Commedia* there are no landmasses in the southern hemisphere except for the mountain of Purgatory, which is the MOUNTAINTOP Ulysses saw DIM IN THE DISTANCE. See Canto XXXIV, lines 122–28 and note.

CANTO XXVII

Guido da Montefeltro and Ulysses seem to be guilty of the same unnamed sin, having to do with political cunning. There is irony in juxtaposing the legendary hero with a contemporary *condottiere*, as if to say that the difference between the two sinners were merely a question of style. Virgil's disdain ("you speak—this one's Italian") underscores the difference in rhetoric between Ulysses' tragic style and the dialect that Guido thinks he overhears when Virgil takes his leave of Ulysses. Nevertheless, that difference would appear to be of no moral significance, given the identical collocation of the sinners.

The political cunning exhibited by Guido is more familiar to us than it would have been to Guido's contemporaries because we have come to associate such cunning with politics in the modern world. We think of Machiavelli as the first to have revealed politics' dirty secrets to "those who do not know," but in fact, Guido's revelations from Hell are of the same order. He tells the pilgrim that he is willing to tell the truth about his advice to the Pope only because he believes it will never be made public in the world above. His confession became the epigraph for T. S. Eliot's "Love Song of J. Alfred Prufrock."

There are several points of resemblance between Guido's story and Machiavelli's *Prince*. First of all, both texts refer to the image of the politician as lion or fox. Both refer to the political counselor as physician, rather than as lawyer, so that any violence he suggests can be considered therapy for the body politic. Guido's strategic advice—"promise much, deliver little"—is reminiscent of the chilling aphorisms of *The Prince*, tactically useless, but morally revealing. Finally, Machiavelli uses Pope Julius II as an example of an intrepid prince, while Dante refers to Boniface as "the Prince of new Pharisees."

The framework of Hell creates an extraordinary anachronistic illusion for the modern reader. Dante's text seems to anticipate and then refute Machiavelli's. It is as if Guido were the spokesman for the Florentine secretary, putting his faith solely in "what works," just as Machiavelli professed to be interested only in "effective truth." Guido's condemnation undercuts the value of his advice and at the same time it seems an answer to Machiavelli. The motif of the journey gives us a place to stand from which the remarks of the damned may be judged, but there is no such place in *The Prince*. It is as if it had been written in Hell. (J.F.)

6–11. THE SICILIAN BULL was a torture device sculpted in metal by the craftsman Perillus for the use of Phalaris, the tyrant of Agrigentum in ancient Sicily. Victims were sealed in the hollow bull, which was heated. Perillus supposedly GAVE IT SHAPE in such a way that the cries of pain from inside would sound as if the bull were bellowing. Perillus was punished for his cruel ingenuity when he WAS FORCED TO GIVE IT HIS VOICE, the maker being put inside by Phalaris as the device's first victim.

19. LOMBARD would be the dialect of Latin—or Italian—spoken by Virgil as a Mantuan.

27. THE ROMAGNOLES: the inhabitants of Romagna, a region of northern Italy between the Apennines and the Adriatic, to the north and east of Florence.

27–28. I HAIL / FROM THE HILL COUNTRY: scholars can identify the speaker as Guido da Montefeltro, a renowned Ghibelline military leader sometimes known as THE FOX (line 74). He joined the Franciscan order in 1296, abandoning secular pursuits. But it was believed that in 1298 he told Pope Boniface VIII, THE PRINCE OF NEW PHARISEES (line 83), how the citadel of Palestrina could be taken; it is for giving this advice—obeying the devious Boniface but betraying both his vows and the Colonna family, who had taken shelter in Palestrina—that he is here among the false counselors.

37–39. POLENTA'S EAGLE, heraldic symbol of the Polenta family, symbolized their continuing rule over RAVENNA and the smaller city of CERVIA. Guido da Polenta the Elder was the father of Francesca da Rimini, who speaks in Canto V.

40–52. Dante lists several examples of the forces that keep Romagna from peace: during THE LONG SIEGE of the Ghibelline city of Forlì by French and Guelph troops, the defenders led by Guido da Montefeltro—the shade Dante the pilgrim is addressing, not identified by him at this point—STRUCK THE FRENCHMEN DOWN, defeating the attackers and inflicting heavy losses. In Dante's time, Forlì was held by the Ordelaffi family, whose heraldic emblem included a green lion, hence the GREEN PAWS. THE OLD MASTIFF AND NEW OF VERRUC- CHIO are Malatesta, who captured Rimini in 1295, and his son Malatestino. Situated near the SANTERNO and LAMONE rivers, respectively, the cities of Imola and Faenza were governed by Maghinardo Pagani da Susinana, whose heraldic emblem depicted a lion on a white field. On the SAVIO River is the city of Cesena, by law a free municipality, which was dominated by Galasso da Montefeltro, cousin of Guido.

66. Guido da Montefeltro BECAME A CORDED FRIAR by joining the Franciscan order in 1296.

68. The HIGH PRIEST is Pope Boniface VIII, blamed by Montefeltro for his down- fall.

83–89. THE PRINCE OF NEW PHARISEES is Montefeltro's scornful epithet for Boniface VIII, who made war NEARBY THE LATERAN (the papal palace), contending against his opponents the Colonna family, eventually delivered into Boniface's hands by Guido da Montefeltro's advice. Boniface is accused of pursuing personal battles instead of seemlier kinds of combat: crusading against SARACENS OR JEWS in the Holy Land, or against Christians who transgress by doing business in THE SULTAN'S DOMAIN or by betraying ACRE, the last Christian outpost in the Holy Land, conquered by the Saracens in 1291.

92–94. The Emperor CONSTANTINE, according to legend, was afflicted with lep- rosy as punishment for persecuting Christians. He sought out Pope SYLVESTER on Mount SORACTE, where he was converted, baptized, and instantly cured.

97–117. Boniface asks Montefeltro for a way to defeat the Colonna faction and LEVEL PALESTRINA TO THE EARTH; Montefeltro's advice is to deal falsely with the Colonnas by making promises of complete amnesty that he does not intend to keep. This policy succeeds, the Colonnas surrender, their fortress of Palestrina is destroyed, and Montefeltro's soul is consigned to the eighth circle of Hell.

105–6. The two KEYS are those of papal authority ("And I will give unto thee the keys of the kingdom of heaven: and whatsoever thou shalt bind on earth shall be bound in heaven: and whatsoever thou shalt loose on earth shall be loosed in heaven" [Matt. 16:19]), which was given up by Boniface VIII's PREDECESSOR, Celestine V, possibly referred to as "he who made the Great Refusal" in Canto III. (See Canto XIX, lines 85–88.)

113–15. St. Francis comes to claim the soul of Montefeltro, who is one of his order, for Heaven; however, the soul is rightfully taken by one of the BLACK CHERU-BIM OF HELL instead. By believing Boniface's spurious absolution without repenting, Montefeltro doomed himself to Hell.

CANTO XXVIII

7. APULIANS: though modern Apulia is the southeast heel of the peninsula, on the Adriatic coast, in the Middle Ages the name indicated all of southern Italy, the locale of the bloodshed listed in the following lines.

10–12. According to LIVY's *History*, the CARTHAGINIAN military leader Hannibal returned home with a heap of gold RINGS taken from the fingers of slain Romans, as proof of his victory over them.

14. ROBERT GUISCARD (c. 1015–1085) was a Norman warrior, Duke of Apulia and Calabria.

15. AT CEPERANO, where Apulian barons were pledged to defend the pass on behalf of Manfred, natural son of Frederick II, they instead let through the troops of Charles of Anjou, leading to the death of Manfred in 1266.

17–18. NEAR TAGLIACOZZO, Alardo de Valéry devised the strategy by which Charles of Anjou defeated Manfred's nephew in 1268.

30. Apparently, Dante and his contemporaries believed that MOHAMMED, the founder of Islam, was a renegade Cardinal, a belief that helps explain his presence here among the schismatics.

32. ALÌ was Mohammed's nephew, son-in-law, and devoted follower. His succession to the Caliphate led to a dispute that caused the schism of Islam into Sunnites and Shiites.

53. FRA DOLCINO Tornielli of Novara was a leader of the Apostolic Brothers, a reformist sect that opposed the temporal power of the clergy, advocating a return to the austerity of the original Apostles. The Apostolic Brothers were accused of heretical practices, including the communal sharing of property and of women. After taking refuge in the mountains, Fra Dolcino and his followers were besieged and starved out, then massacred; he and his alleged mistress, Margaret of Trent, were burned alive in 1307.

70. PIER DA MEDICINA (d. 1271?) is described as a sower of discord.

71–82. SER GUIDO AND ANGIOLELLO: around 1215, Malatestino, Lord of Rimini, the one-eyed TYRANT, invited two noblemen of FANO, Guido de Cassero and Angiolello di Carignano, to a conference at LA CATTOLICA. Malatestino's men attacked their boat and threw them overboard in the seas near the cliff of FOCARA. Drowned, they had no need to pray for fair winds off that treacherous promontory.

75–76. NEPTUNE is the god of the sea; CYPRUS and MAJORCA represent the east–west breadth of the Mediterranean Sea.

78–79. The CITY / FOUND BITTER BY ANOTHER WHO'S WITH ME HERE is Rimini, ruled by Malatestino. "Another who's with me here" refers to Caius Curio (lines 92–93 and note), who at the Rubicon, north of Rimini, gave Julius Caesar advice leading to civil war.

92–93. Caius CURIO was bribed by Caesar to betray Pompey and, according to Lucan, urged Caesar to cross the river Rubicon—thus entering into rebellion —when he hesitated. The Rubicon flows near Rimini, which is why the city would be a bitter sight for Curio. The line in Lucan's *Pharsalia* (I, 281) is "*semper nocuit differre paratis*": "delay always undoes those who are prepared."

94–100. MOSCA de' Lamberti renewed the Ghibelline feud with the Guelphs in 1215 by inciting the Amidei family to murder the Guelph Buondelmonte dei Buondelmonti for breaking his engagement to one of their daughters. Later, the Lamberti family was exiled from Florence. Mosca is one of the "men of good reason" Dante asks Ciacco about in Canto VI, 70–75.

119–27. BERTRAN DE BORN, lord of Hautefort near Périgueux, was a soldier and troubadour poet who died in 1215 as a Cistercian monk. King Henry II of England is supposed to have believed that Bertran inspired the rebellion of the king's oldest son Prince Henry, known as the YOUNG KING.

123–24. The biblical King David's counselor ACHITOPHEL inspired the rebellion of ABSALOM, David's son, against his father.

127. THIS RETRIBUTION—in Italian, *contrapasso*—indicates the principle whereby the punishment in Hell is suited to each kind of sin, often by extending or distilling or literally reenacting the sin itself. The Italian word derives from *contrapassum*, the medieval Latin word used by translators of Aristotle's *Nicomachean Ethics*, and by Thomas Aquinas and others in commenting upon Aristotle.

In keeping with *contrapasso*, fomenters of schism are cut apart. Other examples include gluttons chewed by Cerberus, spendthrifts scattered in the wood, the lustful buffeted about in a wind, and murderers boiled in blood.

CANTO XXIX

10–11. THE MOON is below the travelers' feet on the other side of the globe because it is day in the inhabited hemisphere of land: the sun is over their heads. It is now early afternoon.

28–38. GERI DEL BELLO degli Alighieri was Dante's father's first cousin. He had a reputation as a troublemaker who set people against one another for sport; that is why Dante expected to see him among the schismatics in the ninth pouch. Commentators disagree about the details of Geri's life and especially his death; however, it seems likely that he met HIS VIOLENT DEATH at the hands of a member of the Sacchetti family, with whom the Alighieri feuded until 1342. In 1300, Geri's death was still unavenged, but one of the Sacchetti was murdered by Geri's nephews in 1310 in an apparent act of retaliation. This type of family vengeance was permitted by law.

29–30. THE ONE / WHO ONCE HELD ALTAFORTE is Bertran de Born (see Canto XXVIII, lines 119–27); Altaforte was his castle.

49–52. In Dante's time, the valley along the Chiana River (VAL DI CHIANA) was plagued by malaria, as were the wild Tuscan MAREMMA and the island of SARDINIA. The disease was at its peak in the summertime.

64–69. AEGINA was a beautiful nymph loved by Jupiter, who carried her off to an island where she bore the god a son. This son, Aeacus, renamed the island after his mother; it is to the island that Dante refers in line 64. Jupiter's jealous wife, Juno, struck the island with a pestilence that killed all who lived there except Aeacus. The lonely survivor begged Jupiter to intervene, and the god turned all the ANTS on the island into people: thus THE ANCIENT POPULACE WAS RESTORED. Ovid tells the story in his *Metamorphoses* (VII, 523–660).

116–28. The speaker is not named, but early commentators agree that he is the alchemist Griffolino, about whom little is known beyond the story he relates in this canto. ALBERO OF SIENA, whom Griffolino duped, was the son (or perhaps only the favorite) of the Bishop of Siena—the ONE in line 125—who subsequently had Griffolino burned at the stake for heresy. It is for the practice of ALCHEMY, however, and not THAT WHICH [he] DIED FOR—heresy—that Griffolino is punished among the falsifiers in THIS LAST DITCH OF TEN in Malebolge. DAEDALUS (line 123) was the inventor who escaped Crete on wings of wax and feathers. (See Canto XVII, lines 99–101 and note.)

128. MINOS is the demon who assigns sinners to the appropriate circles of Hell by wrapping his tail around himself. See Canto V, lines 3–11 and note.

134–41. STRICCA, NICCOLÒ, CACCIA D'ASCIANO, and MUDDLEHEAD (Bartolommeo de' Folcacchieri) are the names of thirteenth-century Sienese squanderers. Along with Arcolano da Squarcia (punished in Canto XIII: see lines 108–22 and note), they belonged to the notorious Spendthrift Club, the COSTLY CULT OF CLOVES whose purpose was the profligate spending of fortunes.

146–47. CAPOCCHIO was probably Florentine, though in some reports he is Sienese. Famous for his skill as an alchemist and a mimic—a falsifier of both metals and gestures—he was burned alive in 1293.

CANTO XXX

1–11. Ovid tells (*Metamorphoses*, III, 259–309) of how Jupiter's wife, JUNO, was jealous of her husband's infatuation for the THEBAN beauty SEMELE. Juno destroyed Semele, and then took vengeance on other Thebans as well, including Semele's sister Ino, the WIFE of ATHAMAS. Juno caused Athamas to become mad, whereupon he mistook Ino and her sons for a LIONESS and two CUBS (*Metamorphoses*, IV, 512–30).

12–19. When Priam, the KING of Troy, had been defeated and killed, his wife, HECUBA, was made to witness the sacrifice of their daughter POLYXENA. Their son POLYDORUS was murdered by his uncle, Polymestor the King of Thrace; the corpse of Polydorus was set adrift. Hecuba, mad with grief, BEGAN BARKING LIKE A DOG and in that form, having taken violent revenge on Polymestor, threw herself into the sea. This story, too, comes from Ovid (*Metamorphoses*, XIII, 404–575).

28. THE SPIRIT FROM AREZZO is Griffolino: see Canto XXIX, lines 116–28 and note.

30. GIANNI SCHICCHI falsified his identity: see lines 39–44 and note.

36–39. The princess MYRRHA, driven by incestuous passion, disguised herself as another woman and seduced her father, the King of Cyprus.

39–44. Gianni SCHICCHI was a Florentine who died in 1280. Early sources say that he was a skillful mimic and used this talent to impersonate the dying BUOSO DONATI, a wealthy man whose nephew Simone colluded in the fraud. Posing as Donati, Schicchi dictated a false will naming Simone as the main beneficiary. Dante follows the version of the story in which Schicchi includes for himself the bequest of Donati's best mule, THE FINEST LADY OF THE HERD.

53. The HECTIC is one suffering from fever.

58–89. MASTER ADAM was encouraged by the Conti Guidi of ROMENA — GUIDO, ALESSANDRO, and their unnamed brother—to make counterfeit replicas of the gold coins of Florence. The false coins were stamped, like the real ones, with John THE BAPTIST'S FACE (line 71), but were made of twenty-one rather than twenty-four carats of gold, and THREE CARATS OF DROSS (line 89). When the fraud was discovered, the Florentines were outraged, and in 1281 they burned Master Adam alive to punish him. The best-known FONTE BRANDA (line 77) is a fountain in Siena, but Master Adam may be referring instead to a smaller spring of the same name near Romena. Of the brothers Master Adam so despises, only Guido was already dead in 1300, so he must be the ONE . . . ALREADY INSIDE (line 77).

96–97. In Genesis 39:7–20, Potiphar's wife is the FALSE ONE who accuses JOSEPH of trying to rape her after he refuses her advances.

98. SINON convinced the Trojans that he had abandoned the Greeks and wanted to defect to the other side. He came bearing the gift of the wooden horse that was to be Troy's downfall.

129. NARCISSUS'S LOOKING GLASS is water: Narcissus fell in love with his own reflection in a pond (the story is told in Ovid's *Metamorphoses*, III, 407–512).

CANTO XXXI

3–4. The legend that says ACHILLES' LANCE could heal the wounds it caused is told by Homer (*Iliad*, XVI, 143–44), Ovid (*Metamorphoses*, XIII, 172), and others.

14–17. The Old French epic *Le Chanson de Roland*, composed around 1200, tells of the defeat of the rear guard of the Frankish emperor CHARLEMAGNE (742–814) at Roncesvalles during the crusade against the Spanish Saracens. The doomed paladin ROLAND blew a signal on his battle HORN too late to save himself, but his uncle Charlemagne heard the blast eight miles away.

36. MONTEREGGIONE is a fortified castle near Siena.

40–41. JOVE is still angry with the giants he defeated with thunderbolts in the battle of Phlegra (see Canto XIV, lines 46–48 and note).

56. The enormous PINECONE is more than twelve feet high. It now stands in the gardens of the Vatican.

60. People from FRIESLAND were supposed to be unusually tall.

64. The giant's words are apparently meaningless. Though many scholars have attempted translations or interpretations, Dante has Virgil say of Nimrod's language that NO ONE FATHOMS IT (line 77).

72–74. Although the Bible does not say who ordered the construction of the Tower of Babel, it was traditional in the Middle Ages to ascribe the ill-fated project to King NIMROD of Babylon. God became angry at the builders' ambition—the tower was to reach all the way to Heaven—and He caused the confusion of languages among the workers to prevent them from finishing. The story is from Genesis 11; Nimrod is named separately, in Genesis 10:8–9. Nimrod is not described in Genesis as a giant, though Dante was not the first medieval author to make him one. The Bible does call him a hunter (Gen. 10:9), which may be why he appears here with a horn.

87–91. Homer tells of how the Titan EPHIALTES and his brother Otus died attacking the gods on Olympus. Both brothers appear in Virgil's version of Hell (*Aeneid*, VI, 582).

95. BRIAREUS—also known as Aegaeon—was another of the giants who attacked Olympus. Dante does not follow Virgil's description (*Aeneid*, X, 565–68), in which Briareus has fifty heads and a hundred arms.

96–97. Legend says the Libyan giant ANTAEUS was invincible as long as he was touching his mother, Earth, with some part of his body. The hero Hercules killed Antaeus in a wrestling match by lifting him off the ground and crushing him while holding him aloft. Antaeus may be UNCHAINED because he was not among the giants who attacked the gods.

110–14. The Roman general SCIPIO defeated HANNIBAL and his Carthaginian troops in the FATEFUL VALLEY of the Bagradas River near Zama in Tunisia in 202 B.C. In Lucan (*Pharsalia*, IV, 601–2), Antaeus is said to feed on lions.

119. Antaeus will set the travelers down in the ninth and last circle of Hell, by the frozen lake COCYTUS.

121. TYPHON and TITYUS are also giants, both unfriendly to the Olympian gods.

133. The LEANING TOWER of GARISENDA is in Bologna. The passing cloud makes the tower appear to be falling toward the viewer.

CANTO XXXII

2. The MELANCHOLY HOLE, the pit of Hell whose floor is the frozen lake Cocytus, houses the worst sinners in Dante's universe: those guilty of treacherous fraud.

10–11. The MUSES made the music of AMPHION's lyre so beautiful that it charmed the stones down from the hills and made them stack themselves up to form the walls of THEBES.

27–28. TAMBERNIC (Italian *Tambernicchi*) has not been specifically identified by scholars, but presumably it is a mountain like PIETRAPANA, in the Apuan Alps.

51–54. The spirits are Alessandro and Napoleone degli Alberti, who killed each other around 1285 in a fight over the inheritance from their father, ALBERT, Count of Mangona. The family had a castle on the BISENZIO River, not far from Florence.

56. CAINA is the outermost part of Cocytus; in it are punished those who betrayed members of their own families. The place is named for Cain, who murdered his brother Abel in the world's first such betrayal (Gen. 4:8) (see Canto V, line 96 and note).

58–59. King ARTHUR ran his treacherous nephew Mordred through with a blow so violent that daylight shone through the wound, according to the French romance *Lancelot du Lac*.

59–60. FOCACCIA was the nickname of Vanni de' Cancellieri of Pistoia. He murdered his cousin in 1293.

62. SASSOL MASCHERONI is known to have murdered a relative; accounts differ as to whether it was a brother, a nephew, a cousin, or an uncle.

65–66. CAMISCION DE' PAZZI murdered a kinsman named Ubertino; little else is known about him. His relative CARLINO de' Pazzi was to betray his party, the White Guelphs, in 1302 by letting their enemies into the castle he was holding for them. Camiscion (like many of the souls in Hell, he can foresee "future" crimes) expects that for his more heinous misdeed, Carlino will be punished in the second realm of Cocytus, and that the gravity of Carlino's sin will make Camiscion's own SEEM LESS.

78. MONTAPERTI is the Tuscan village where the Ghibellines soundly defeated the Florentine Guelphs in 1260 (see Canto X, lines 29–48 and notes; line 80 and note).

87. ANTENORA is the second part of Cocytus. Punished there are the souls of those who betrayed their country or their political party. It is named for the Trojan Antenor, who according to medieval tradition betrayed Troy to the Greeks.

105. BOCCA degli Abati, a Florentine Guelph, is sometimes held to blame for his party's defeat at the hands of the Ghibellines at Montaperti in 1260. In the heat of battle, it is said, the traitor cut off the hand of the Guelphs' standard-bearer, throwing his party's troops into confusion.

114–18. Buosa da DUERA, a Ghibelline, took a bribe from the Frenchman Charles of Anjou in return for the French troops' free passage through Lombardy and Parma to Naples in 1265. In so doing, Buosa betrayed King Manfred of Naples.

119–20. Tesauro de' BECCHERIA, Pope Alexander IV's legate in Tuscany, was beheaded in Florence in 1258 for plotting with the then-exiled Ghibellines to overthrow the Guelphs.

122. GIANNI DE' SOLDANIERI betrayed his Ghibelline party, going over to the side of the rebels during an uprising against the Ghibellines in 1266. GANELON is the treacherous adviser who purposely sends Charlemagne's rear guard to their deaths in the *Chanson de Roland* (see Canto XXXI, lines 14–17 and note).

123–24. In 1280, the Ghibelline TEBALDELLO of the Zambrasi family betrayed his party, opening the gates of the city of FAENZA to the invading Guelphs.

130–31. TYDEUS, one of the seven kings who laid siege to Thebes (see Canto XIV, lines 38–59 and note), was mortally wounded in that battle by MENALIPPUS. Before dying, he managed to kill Menalippus and, enraged, gnaw at his enemy's skull and brains.

CANTO XXXIII

The moral poles of Dante's universe are occupied by children. Their suffering is the theme of the cantos of Ugolino, just as their joy is the theme of Canto XXXII of the *Paradiso*. The guilt of Ugolino scarcely seems relevant compared to the pain of his death and his condemnation, yet he seems to be unaware of the Christological significance of the children's suffering and his own. As they die, they echo the words first of Job—"The Lord gave, and the Lord hath taken away"—and then of the Saviour on the Cross—"My God, why hast thou forsaken me?" Ugolino's response is simply to repress his own grief for fear of increasing theirs.

The children's apparently naïve offer of their flesh to their father echoes Jesus' offer to the disciples in John 6: "Whoso eateth my flesh . . . hath eternal life." The disciples are scandalized by the offer, as have been Christians ever since. In his commentary on the Gospel, Augustine points out that Jesus is offering his *living* flesh, which is to say, his Word. Those who do not understand this Eucharistic offer think of his flesh as though it were meat. So here, the children offer their father their redemptive sacrifice, much as Isaac naïvely offered himself to Abraham. Because Ugolino does not understand, there is no redemption.

In the Old Testament, Israel was founded when God intervened in Abraham's sacrifice and the covenant was established between fathers and sons. The covenant came to be symbolized by the circumcision. This is the opposite of the Theban story of Oedipus and his father, in which the survival of the son depends upon the death of the father. The story of Ugolino is filled with Abrahamic promise, but ends in Theban tragedy when Ugolino, like Saturn, devours his children's flesh in order to survive, however briefly. Dante refers to Pisa as a new Thebes. In human society, there is no middle ground between Communion and cannibalism.

Ugolino is a literalist who cannot see the symbolism in his dream or in his children's offer. Christ's offer in the Gospel was allegorical, offering the living Word. This is the spiritual sense of the children's words. But Ugolino reads only death in his dream and only cannibalism in their words. In fact, his dream prefigures the infernal punishment, as he gnaws the enemy who gnawed him, and his children's words have biblical resonance. Nevertheless he takes their offer at face value and, when he is reduced to animality, finally accepts it, biting the flesh of his children in hunger as he had once bitten his hand in grief. (J.F.)

12–72. UGOLINO della Gherardesca was a Pisan nobleman deeply involved in power struggles and political intrigue. He was exiled from Pisa in 1275, when the Ghibelline leadership of the city decided he had been conspiring with Guelphs. He had returned both to Pisa and to political power by 1284: the Guelphs helped him become reinstated, whereupon he betrayed that party and allied himself again with the Ghibellines. As chief magistrate for the city, he yielded three Ghibelline-controlled castles to the enemy, supposedly to protect Pisa—but the act was viewed by some as treacherous.

Later, in 1288, Ugolino conspired with ARCHBISHOP RUGGIERI and several prominent Ghibelline families (the GUALANDI, SISMONDI, and LANFRANCHI among them) to oust from Pisan politics Ugolino's grandson and rival, Nino Visconti (Nino fled to Florence and became a friend to Dante). The archbishop then betrayed Ugolino in turn, using the matter of the three castles as an excuse for imprisoning him with his two young sons and two grandsons in a tower and eventually starving them to death.

77. In Italian *sì* is the word for "yes." In another work, the *De vulgare eloquentia*, a treatise on language and style, Dante distinguishes languages by the way they say "yes."

78–80. The islands of GORGONA and CAPRAIA sit in the Mediterranean not far from the mouth of the river ARNO. In Dante's time, they were possessions of Pisa.

84. Ugolino compares Pisa to the Greek city of THEBES, where so much fury and bloodshed occurs in the ancient myths.

87–89. In these lines, Dante and Virgil cross into Ptolomea (named in line 119), the third region of Cocytus, where those who betrayed their guests are punished. It appears to be named for Ptolemy of Jericho, who murders his banquet guests in the First Book of Maccabees (16:15–17) in the Catholic Bible—although Ptolemy XII of Egypt, who murdered Pompey, has also been suggested as the source of the name.

113–15. FRA ALBERIGO of Faenza was a Jovial Friar (see Canto XXIII, note to line 98). He had a kinsman named Manfred and Manfred's son murdered during a banquet at his home; the signal to his assassins was the phrase "Bring the fruit."

119. For comments about PTOLOMEA, see the note to lines 87–89.

121. In classical myths, ATROPOS is the last of the three Fates: she cuts the thread of a mortal's life when the time comes for the body to die and the soul to be SENT FORTH into the afterlife.

132. BRANCA D'ORIA—aided by the anonymous KINSMAN mentioned in lines 142–43—murdered his father-in-law, Michel Zanche, who was a guest in his home, in either 1275 or 1290 (depending on which scholar is consulted). Michel Zanche is one of the barrators in the fifth pouch of Malebolge: see Canto XXII, line 84 and note.

134–35. Branca d'Oria lived until about 1325.

148–53. ROMAGNA'S WORST SPIRIT is Fra Alberigo. The GENOESE Dante FOUND with him is Branca d'Oria.

CANTO XXXIV

1–2. Virgil's words, Latin for "The banners of the king of Hell advance," are a twisted echo of the first line of a well-known sixth-century Latin hymn sung during Holy Week, which begins "The banners of the King advance."

13–14. This is Judecca, the final division of Cocytus and the innermost part of Hell. In Judecca (which will be named in line 118), the worst sinners of all— those who betrayed their benefactors—are punished. The region is named for Judas Iscariot (see line 62 and note).

21. The CREATURE is Satan, whom Dante also calls by the names Lucifer, Beelzebub, and Dis. He was an angel of enormous BEAUTY before he rebelled against God and was cast down from Heaven.

62. Jesus' apostle JUDAS ISCARIOT betrayed his Master: this is the worst sin.

65–66. In 44 B.C., Marcus Junius BRUTUS and Gaius CASSIUS Longus conspired to kill Julius Caesar. Their crime was seen in the Middle Ages as an offense not only to the murderers' great benefactor, but to the progress and history of the Roman Empire and the Church.

69–90. Dante and Virgil climb feet first down Lucifer's body as far as THE PIVOT OF THE THIGHS: this midpoint of Satan's anatomy is exactly at the center of the earth. From there, in order to advance, the travelers must move *up* Satan's legs, toward the surface of the hemisphere opposite the one they have just come through. At the center, Virgil turns his body around 180 degrees and climbs headfirst into the southern hemisphere. Dante, not realizing WHAT POINT [he] HAD PASSED, becomes disoriented.

90–93. THE SUN IS AT MID-TIERCE at about 7:30 a.m.—fully twelve hours earlier than in line 67, when Virgil told Dante night was coming. The time changed when the wayfarers switched hemispheres; here in the southern half of the globe it is still the morning of Holy Saturday, April 9, 1300. To say that THE WAY / IS LONG ahead is a bit of an understatement: Virgil and Dante must climb halfway through the earth—as far again as they have come already—to reach the surface of the southern hemisphere. The journey will take them about twenty-four hours in all—the same amount of time as the trip through Hell.

111–18. In Dante's vision of the world, the northern HEMISPHERE contains almost all of earth's GREAT DRY LAND, with Jerusalem—THE SITE / WHEREON THE MAN [Jesus] WAS SLAIN—at its exact center, UNDER THE ZENITH.

122–28. Dante invented the notion that Satan, falling, struck the southern hemisphere at a point directly opposite Jerusalem. All the land in that half of the world, he says, fled from the impact and ISSUED FORTH in the northern hemisphere: that is why the southern hemisphere is almost entirely water. The one body of land that NOW APPEARS ON THIS SIDE will turn out in the *Purgatorio* to be the island of Mount Purgatory, where Dante must begin the next great leg of his journey. It is located exactly in the center of the southern hemisphere, opposite Jerusalem in the northern hemisphere. The land which forms the island is that part of the inner earth which, displaced by the falling Lucifer, FLED ITS BERTH and rose to the surface. The hollow passage to the surface, at whose bottom the travelers now stand, is the CAVITY that the dislodged earth left behind.

131. This RUNNEL may have as its source the river Lethe, flowing down from Purgatory—but Dante does not say so.

140. Dante's *Purgatorio* and his *Paradiso*, like the *Inferno*, end with the word STARS.